Empire

Empire

What Ruling the World Did to the British

JEREMY PAXMAN

VIKING

an imprint of

PENGUIN BOOKS

VIKING

Published by the Penguin Group
Penguin Books Ltd, 80 Strand, London WC2R ORL, England
Penguin Group (USA) Inc., 375 Hudson Street, New York, New York 10014, USA
Penguin Group (Canada), 90 Eglinton Avenue East, Suite 700, Toronto, Ontario, Canada M4P 2Y3
(a division of Pearson Penguin Canada Inc.)
Penguin Ireland, 25 St Stephen's Green, Dublin 2, Ireland (a division of Penguin Books Ltd)
Penguin Group (Australia), 250 Camberwell Road, Camberwell, Victoria 3124, Australia
(a division of Pearson Australia Group Pty Ltd)
Penguin Books India Pvt Ltd, 11 Community Centre,
Panchsheel Park, New Delhi – 110 017, India
Penguin Group (NZ), 67 Apollo Drive, Rosedale, Auckland 0632, New Zealand
(a division of Pearson New Zealand Ltd)
Penguin Books (South Africa) (Pty) Ltd, 24 Sturdee Avenue,
Rosebank, Johannesburg 2196, South Africa

Penguin Books Ltd, Registered Offices: 80 Strand, London WC2R ORL, England

www.penguin.com

First published 2011

I

The chapter epigraph on page 270 is taken from *The Siege of Krishnapur* by J. G. Farrell, published by
W&N Fiction, a division of the Orion Publishing Group, London. Reproduced with permission

Endpaper illustration: *Colonel James Todd Travelling by Elephant through Rajasthan with
his Cavalry and Sepoys*, reproduced by kind permission of the Bridgeman Art Library

Set in Bembo 12/14.75pt
Typeset by Jouve (UK), Milton Keynes
Printed in Great Britain by Clays Ltd, St Ives plc

A CIP catalogue record for this book is available from the British Library

Hardback ISBN: 978-0-670-91957-4
Trade Paperback ISBN: 978-0-670-91958-1

www.greenpenguin.co.uk

List of Illustrations

For Elizabeth, Jessie, Jack and Vita, for whom the imperial project meant long periods of either mental or physical separation. Independence is at hand

The British Empire Throughout the World
1905

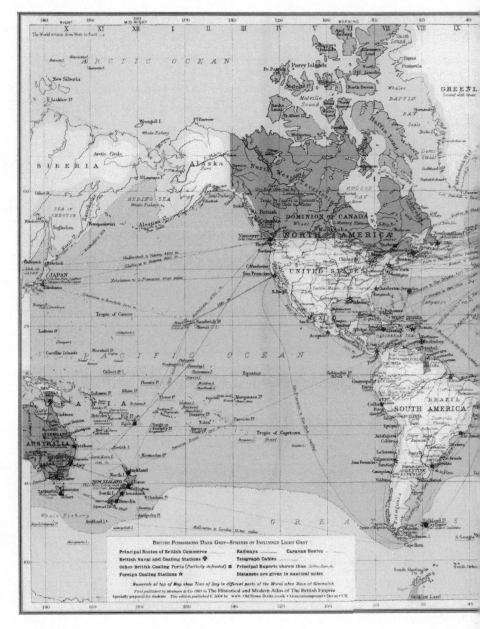

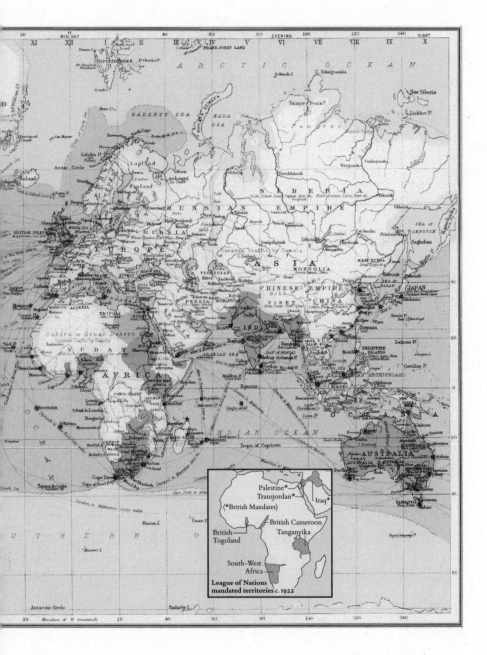

League of Nations
mandated territories c. 1922

Palestine*
Transjordan*
Iraq*

(*British Mandates)

British Cameroon
Tanganyika

British
Togoland

South-West
Africa

INTRODUCTION

'You're a Brit, aren't you?' It was an accusation. His face was twisted, angry and only about six inches away from mine. His breath was beery. I was backed against a wall outside a drinking club in west Belfast, and two of his friends stood on either side – there was no chance of running for it. This is how it begins, I thought, starting to panic. It ends with a beating in a lock-up garage or the back of a pub somewhere. Or worse.

It didn't, of course. Within less than a minute an older man had said something and the three youths laid off, sauntering away without a word: next time it really might be an undercover British soldier. I knew what a 'Brit' was, all right. But I had never been called one until I arrived in Northern Ireland to cover the war there in the 1970s.

Belfast was a dark place – and not just because its street lights had been knocked out in the many battle-zones across the city. It was a conflict murky with injustice, bigotry, exploitation, long memories and short fuses. The terminology reflected what you thought the violence was. The British preferred to call the everyday bombings, gunfights, murders, military funerals and armoured cars on the streets 'the Troubles'. It might look like a war, but it wasn't. To the IRA, the violence was definitely part of a war to force the British out of the last corner of their Irish colony. The 'loyalist' settler community, almost exclusively the descendants of Scots and others who had been brought to Ireland to make the place safe for England, fought for the right to remain British, despite not living in Britain. The epithet 'Brits' referred to the apparatus of imperialism, specifically the army, and by extension all of us who came to Ireland from England, Wales or Scotland, although it was really the English who were hated. I did not much like the term.

I had arrived in Ireland woefully ill-equipped to understand what was happening there. Anti-colonial wars belonged to another time in history. This is even more the case for many British people now: the average age in Britain is forty, which means that apart from a vague awareness of the war to reconquer the Falkland Islands or the cere-monial handing back of Hong Kong to the Chinese in 1997, most citizens have little sense of Britain as an imperial power.

Anyone who has grown up or grown old in Britain since the Second World War has done so in an atmosphere of irresistible decline, to the point where now Britain's imperial history is no more than the faint smell of mothballs in a long-unopened wardrobe. Its evidence is all around us, but who cares? It is the empty fourth plinth at the north-west corner of Trafalgar Square that interests us, not the three that are occupied by a king and a couple of imperial generals. Ask us what those generals did and we're lost. Even the most exotic empire-builders have sunk from our minds. Charles Gordon is a good example. His unhinged mission to Khartoum and subsequent beheading raised him to saint-like status in Victorian Britain. A statue, showing the great martyr befezzed and cross-legged on a camel was placed in the middle of the traffic at the main crossroads in

Khartoum, to remind the Sudanese who was boss. At independence in 1956 they took it down and sent it back to England, where it was re-erected at the school in Woking founded at Queen Victoria's behest as a memorial to the general. It stands there, grey and unexpected, to this day. They used to tell the story of a small boy taken after church each Sunday to admire the national hero. After several weeks' veneration, the child asked, 'Daddy, who is the man on Gordon's back?' But even the jokes have passed into history now.

And yet the sense of being British is clearly very different to being, say, Swedish or Mexican. No one would have a Mexican up against a wall in Ireland because of his nationality. Ever since the moment when I realized that there were people who saw me differently because of my country's history, I have wondered what that history has done to us as a nation. We think we know what the British Empire did to the world. But what did it do to us?

For the most part, we look back on our imperial history simply as the actions of men and women we cannot identify with, the product of motives we do not really understand. It is emotionally easier and politically more convenient to inquire no further. But it is not particularly helpful. If we accept – as any thoughtful Indian does – that the British Empire had a shaping influence on India, then where is the common sense in claiming that the same history has not had at least as important a role in Britain? Can we seriously pretend that a project which dominated the way that Britain regarded the world for so many hundreds of years has had no lasting influence on the colonizers, too? Without understanding how we looked at the rest of the world, we cannot really understand ourselves. It is nearly fifty years since the then US Secretary of State, Dean Acheson, minted the only remark for which he is remembered in Britain, that 'Great Britain has lost an empire and has not yet found a role.' The remark has since become tediously familiar, but the fact that the observation remains true all these years later reflects the continuing significance of the imperial experience. 'Finding a role' has (along with not going bankrupt) been the main task of every British government for the last sixty years. In a strange way, the one place which has yet properly to decolonize itself is Britain.

It is most obvious in international affairs, where the imperial habit remains a very hard one to break. When a British prime minister puffs out his chest and declares he 'will not tolerate' some African or Middle Eastern despot, he speaks not as a creature of a twenty-first-century political party in a dilapidated democracy but as the latest reincarnation of Castlereagh or Palmerston – somehow, British foreign policy has never shaken off a certain nineteenth-century swagger, and the implied suggestion that if anything happens to a British citizen, a Royal Navy gunboat will be dispatched to menace the impertinent perpetrators. It is not entirely their fault that British politicians bluster in this fashion – the frayed old frock coat comes with the job. The merest glance at regimental battle honours in the British army discloses a roll-call of colonial wars, from Abyssinia to Zululand, by way of everywhere from Canada to New Zealand. This long history of fighting in faraway places of which we know next to nothing has left the British army positively eager to be deployed across the world. When, for example, the Grenadier Guards were sent to Afghanistan in 2007, they arrived sporting battle honours from the Crimean War, the Opium Wars, a campaign against Islamist forces in Sudan in the 1890s, another to subdue the Boers in South Africa at the turn of the twentieth century, and a 'temporary' British intervention in Egypt which began in 1882 and lasted until the middle of the twentieth century. Once you've got that sort of pedigree you're keen to measure yourself against it. And perhaps, at another level, this history of involvement overseas also helps to explain why it is that British charities play such a disproportionately large role in international development and disaster relief.

When Edward Gibbon said, 'I have no way of judging of the future but by the past,' he acknowledged the determining influence that history has on the present. Can we, for example, understand the European Union without recognizing the French fear of the Germans and the Germans' fear of themselves? And in the United Kingdom it has proved very hard – if indeed anyone has really tried – to discard all that stuff about how Britannia rules the waves. It is the imperial heritage which gives the Foreign Office the supercilious vanity that it somehow understands the developing world better than countries which have not had the sola-topi experience. Despite being the biggest and most prosperous country in Europe, Germany does not command a permanent seat on the United Nations Security Council, because it lost the Second World War. Britain may have emerged from that conflict battered and broke, but it still possessed sufficient imperial presence to become one of the Permanent Five. And, had the United States not once been part of the British Empire, the much fetishized 'special relationship' would never have become such an obsession in the minds of British governments.

It goes much further. It was their empire which convinced the British that they were somehow special. Yet the disappearance of their empire has failed to persuade them that they are not so very different from much of the rest of Europe. Is it any wonder that Britain's relations with the continent are so tortured and its commitment to the 'ever closer union' sounds so hollow, when its relations with the rest of the world are managed by an institution housed in a great neo-classical building whose very design was intended to impress upon foreigners the unique splendour of British rule? The interior walls are covered in murals portraying 'Pax Britannica' as the reincarnation of the Roman Empire. (In the 1960s there were plans to pull the whole place down and replace it with something of glass, concrete and steel as a sign of Britain's new role in the world. The money ran out before the demolition contractors could move in, which was a rather better demonstration of the country's new status.) These heavy public buildings designed to make a statement about the solidity of British purpose can be found everywhere from Dundee to Dunedin: schools, parliaments, stock exchanges, police stations, railway termini, all executed in neo-classical or neo-Gothic style, regardless of whether or not either was appropriate for local conditions. Like the Foreign Office, they stand there still, slightly shabby on the outside, traceried with electric wires and plastered with plastic notices within, reminders of a vain and vanished glory, recalling the desert ruins of Shelley's sonnet 'Ozymandias' ('Look on my works, ye mighty, and despair!'). In the one-time colonies these buildings speak of the past. In Britain they are where the business of the present is transacted, and to suggest that we have somehow developed an ability to ignore the influence of our physical surroundings is to ask us to believe a great deal. As Winston Churchill remarked, 'We shape our buildings, and afterwards our buildings shape us.' We tiptoe into the future down marbled corridors ringing to the clip of Victorian heels.

And then there are Britain's constitutional arrangements, not least the country's continued possession of a monarchy. The anthropologist Arthur Hocart spent years attempting to understand the origins of kingship and concluded that all he could say with certainty was that when history began, there were gods and there were monarchs: the earliest-known religion was a belief in the divinity of kings. No rational person has believed that nonsense for centuries. But the fact that Britain is still ruled by a representative of this prehistoric institution is in large part the consequence of empire. Giving Victoria the bombastic title of empress in 1876 had been an empty, cost-free gesture by that great regal flatterer Benjamin Disraeli. But the monarchical tone of empire was useful in co-opting the support of other kings, from Bangalore to Zululand, enabling a form of colonization in which the new subject state might claim hardly to notice that it had been emasculated. One Basuto king is said to have told Victoria, 'My country is your blanket, O Queen, and my people the lice upon it.' Across the world, cities, provinces, lakes, mountains, gardens, parks, highways, stations, puddings and flowers were named after Victoria, and many of her people assumed that the Great White Queen was an integral part of the empire's success. She was not: she just got lucky. Her sons and grandsons, with their imperial tours, durbars, colonial statues, tributes and tiger-hunting were lucky, too. By the same token, you could say that Queen Elizabeth II was unlucky. Her role has been to preside over the disappearance of empire, as the number of British possessions has shrunk to a few curious dots in the seas and oceans of the world. But just as lands were claimed in the name of a British queen, so their independence required a royal witness, with Elizabeth or one of her family on hand to watch as the British flag was lowered and the flag of the new state raised. Look at any photograph of Commonwealth leaders since the early 1950s and the one face you can almost guarantee to find there is that of Elizabeth II, and it is largely due to her that the institution, such as it is, survives at all: like the empire, it smells of monarchy. Elizabeth may never have enjoyed her great-great-grandmother's title of empress of India, but the fact that other nations have taken her seriously has encouraged the British to do likewise.

And the empire did more than consolidate the position of the monarchy. It did much to make the political identity of Britain, too. Of the many elements which came together to create a 'British' identity – Henry VIII's break with Rome, say, or the adoption of a Scottish king when Elizabeth I died childless – the importance of England's growing basket of overseas possessions cannot be exaggerated. In the seventeenth century, as they watched the English begin to pile up overseas possessions, Scots had dreamed of a colony or so of their own and attempted to establish a settlement in Panama. They reckoned without the difficult terrain, the pestilential climate and the perfidious English. The scheme collapsed in 1700, and with it ambitions for a Scottish empire. Henceforth, the Scots would become some of the most effective builders of the joint enterprise of a *British* empire. In the first fifty years after the 1707 Act of Union, 30,000 Scots settled in America. Others would pour into Canada, Australia and New Zealand. By 1776 there were 220 Scots employed at the highest level of the administrations in Madras and Bengal: Sir Walter Scott would come to describe India as 'the corn chest for Scotland'. Explorers like Mungo Park cut through jungles. David Livingstone left Lanarkshire to become the most famous missionary in history. Scottish traders like William Jardine and James Matheson built a trading network across the Far East. One-third of colonial governors between 1850 and 1939 are said to have been Scots.

The army became the most visible means by which the distinctive characteristics of the subjugated Welsh, Scots and Irish were channelled into the British identity. By the early nineteenth century both Ireland and Scotland were sending disproportionately large numbers of soldiers to fight Britain's colonial wars. Irish formations like the 18th Regiment of Foot saw combat in North America, Egypt, China and South Africa, the Connaught Rangers in South America, India and in both wars against the Boers. The 1st Battalion of the 24th Foot, which became the South Wales Borderers, lost 540 of its men at

Isandlwana in the Zulu Wars. The Royal Welch Fusiliers, who had battled American revolutionaries at Bunker Hill, Yorktown and Lexington, remained inordinately proud of the archaic spelling of their name: Robert Graves, who served with them in the First World War, thought that it recalled the Wales of Henry Tudor and Owen Glendower. A similar integration of separateness happened in Scotland, where ordinary Scots were prohibited from wearing the tartan after the suppression of the 1745 rebellion, with the exception of the nation's regiments in the British army, all of which adopted them. The 'thin red line tipped with steel' that the *Times* correspondent William Russell saw repulsing Russian cavalry at Balaclava in 1854 was made up of kilted Highlanders of the 93rd Regiment. A genuinely new British political identity had been forged by the empire. Is it any wonder that, with the empire gone, increasing numbers ask what is the point of the Union?

And the empire changed not merely the political sentiments of the United Kingdom, but the very genetic make-up of its citizens. Since history began, Britain has been a nation of immigrants, whether Romans, Scandinavians, Irish, French, Jews, Italians or Dutch. But the empire drew migrants from across the planet. The world's oldest Chinatown is in Liverpool. Hundreds of thousands of Irish poured into English and Scottish cities in the middle years of the nineteenth century. By the end of the century there were about 50,000 Germans and perhaps 150,000 Russian Jews in the country. Immigrant families built banks such as Rothschilds, Barings and Warburgs, gave us high-street retailers like Marks and Spencer, Moss Bros, Burtons and Top Shop, and supermarkets like Tesco. The first British Indian MP was elected in 1892. In the second half of the twentieth century, vast numbers of migrants from one-time colonies in the Caribbean, Africa and the Indian subcontinent landed in Britain and changed the look and feel of many cities. These communities produced writers and artists who invigorated the native arts, sportsmen and women who raised standards of performance, and cooks who did the national cuisine a big favour.

The traffic in the other direction had been enormous, too. The distinctive character of the British Empire – unlike its Russian or Austro-Hungarian counterparts – was its immense geographical spread, from tiny atolls to entire continents. This was partly because its perpetrators lived on an island: it is striking that the age of imperialism begins only after Queen Mary had lost Calais, the last English possession in France, in 1558. Thereafter, the European concern of most British governments was merely to see that no individual power became strong enough to menace British possessions overseas. That the English had seawater in their veins tended to make overseas adventures more attractive than they might have seemed: when you are surrounded by sea, any journey anywhere involves travelling by water – the difference between visiting Norway and visiting New Zealand is merely one of degree.

There is no completely reliable estimate of how many people left Britain for a new life overseas during the years of empire, but most of them never returned, and by 1900 a majority of English-speakers were living outside Europe. The British diaspora created a network of family connections stretching from a grey, damp island in the North Atlantic to dusty sheep stations in Australia, rough-and-ready mining towns in Africa and snowy wildernesses in Canada. So while at any one time the imperial life was being lived only by a minority of the population, the colonial experience was familiar to many more. The awareness of 'abroad' lives on in the fact that more than three-quarters of the British population hold passports. In the United States – great immigrant nation that it is – the figure is less than a third.

When the British went to live in the lands they conquered they were confronted immediately with the question of what it was that made them distinct from the people among whom they lived. The number who asked the difficult question 'What's so special about us?' must have been small. Indeed, when you read the popular literature of the period its most offensive characteristic is the assumption of racial superiority over 'brutes' and 'savages'. As Cecil Rhodes put it, 'We are the finest race in the world and the more of the world we inhabit the better it is for the human race.' As the empire matured, a peculiar illogicality seized the British: we rule more of the world than any other nation, therefore we must be superior to any other nation. In fact, of course, it was technological advance and entrepreneurial flair which gave birth to the empire. But a belief in some moral pre-eminence offered reassurance to the anxious imperialist. For the majority of empire officials – district officers and magistrates, police-men, teachers, farmers and engineers – the role was perhaps justification itself. Yet it was a role in an alien land, and the customs and conventions of Hove or Huddersfield were absent. So the daily business of living in a British community – even a community of one or two, out in the bush – required the invention of a set of norms, of things which were done at certain times of the day, and things which were definitely not done at any time. These communities were obliged to define what being British meant. In the bungalows and clubs, the sundowners on the verandah and the suet puddings at the dinner table, they were acting out a version of what life was like at home. But it was a not-quite-perfect representation.

Creating and running this enormous enterprise required a certain type of individual, which gave Britain its idiosyncratic public-school system, designed to produce not intellectuals but 'sound chaps' – capable, dependable, resourceful. They were to be oblivious to discomfort and able to inspire respect, for through them was the reality of the British Empire to be made clear. Parents understood the job of the school. In *Tom Brown's School Days*, Squire Brown knew what he wanted from the education his son was to receive at Rugby. 'What is he sent to school for?' he asks. 'If only he'll turn out a brave, helpful, truth-telling Englishman, and a gentleman, and a Christian, that's all I want.' Add in a firm handshake and an ability to play cricket and you have the makings of a district officer. That such a key part of the British educational system was for generations geared not to mental achieve-ment but to something else – 'pluck' is perhaps the best word for it – seems at odds with the fact that Britain has nearly twice as many Nobel Laureates as France, five times the total of Italy, Russia or Japan. But these men and women of intellectual pre-eminence are a memorial not to the famous Victorian public schools, created expressly with the empire in mind, but to the country's grammar schools and to the huge intellectual contribution made by refugees and migrants. Let

Yorke Harberton, the hero of G. A. Henty's *With Roberts to Pretoria*, stand for all of the products of the imperial educational system:

> a typical public-school boy – straight and clean-limbed, free from all awkwardness, bright in expression, and possessed of a large amount of self-possession, or, as he himself would have called it, 'cheek' . . . a little particular about the set of his Eton jacket and trousers and the appearance of his boots; as hard as nails and almost tireless; a good specimen of the class by which Britain has been built up, her colonies formed and her battle-fields won . . .

Not all Henty's heroes came from such privileged backgrounds, for at most the public schools could educate only about 20,000 boys a year. But one of the lessons Henty and other imperial authors tried to teach was that the empire gave opportunities for anyone who had the guts to seize them with both hands. By the 1950s, total sales of Henty's novels were reckoned at about 25 million and they had become an important means of passing on the values of imperial education to anyone who could read.

The fate of many of the products of these schools is captured in one of Rudyard Kipling's most resonant poems about empire, 'Arithmetic on the Frontier' ('A great and glorious thing it is / To learn, for seven years or so, / The Lord knows what of that and this . . .'). It describes what happens when a young public-school subaltern is sent to the North-West Frontier.

> A scrimmage in a Border Station
> A canter down some dark defile
> Two thousand pounds of education
> Drops to a ten-rupee jezail.
> The Crammer's boast, the Squadron's pride,
> Shot like a rabbit in a ride!

The walls of churches across Britain are plastered with memorials to young men who died in inconsequential ambushes like this, or were carried off by fever in some obscure location the churchgoers at home could not place on a map of the world. The memorials to these imperialists created a sense that there really were corners of foreign fields that were forever England. The deaths of grander figures created a distinctive empire iconography, as familiar in its way as stained-glass representations of the Passion of Christ. Tableaux depicting the last moments of General Wolfe during the battle for Quebec, surrounded by his grieving officers and native Indian guide, of the mortally wounded Horatio Nelson lying in the bowels of HMS *Victory*, or of General Gordon serene on the steps of the palace in Khartoum, about to be speared to death, became familiar to countless numbers of citizens. The streets of our cities are peopled with statues and monuments to these generals, admirals and explorers who died to ensure that Britannia's bounds were set wider still and wider.

But the most vibrant legacy of empire evident every day is not its now deeply unfashionable poetry, music or paintings but the sports which were either invented or codified to keep its young men fit and occupied and somehow to pass on to the colonized, through cricket, soccer, rugby, tennis or golf, some of the imperial values. These sports were also supposed to inculcate personal courage and collective loyalty in the builders of empire. The supreme imperial game was cricket – as an 1868 guide to outdoor sport put it, 'We even think that square-leg to a hard hitter is no bad training for coolness at the cannon's mouth.' The belief is best expressed in Henry Newbolt's extraordinary poem 'Vitaï Lampada' (The Torch of Life), an account of a close-run battle in 1885 Sudan, which he saw through the prism of his days as a scholarship boy at Clifton College:

> There's a breathless hush in the Close to-night –
> Ten to make and the match to win –
> A bumping pitch and a blinding light,
> An hour to play, and the last man in.
> And it's not for the sake of a ribboned coat,
> Or the selfish hope of a season's fame,
> But his captain's hand on his shoulder smote –
> 'Play up! Play up! And play the game!'
>
> The sand of the desert is sodden red –
> Red with the wreck of a square that broke;
> The Gatling's jammed and the colonel dead,
> And the regiment blind with dust and smoke.

The river of death has brimmed its banks,
And England's far, and Honour a name,
But the voice of a schoolboy rallies the ranks –
'Play up! Play up! And play the game!'

It is absurd, of course – British victories against tribal peoples were so often the triumph of guns against spears. But it is the authentic language of empire. At the battle of the Alma in the Crimean War, Sir John Astley of the Scots Guards watched as a Russian cannonball cut through his company. He recalled in his memoirs that he had shouted to one of his men 'who was our best wicket-keeper' to catch it. The man replied, 'No sir! It had a bit too much pace on. I thought you was long stop, so I left it for you.' The cricket analogy was ever present. During the siege of Ladysmith in 1899 – two years after Newbolt had composed his famous lines – one Old Etonian wrote to his parents: 'I think we "played the game" in keeping the Boers busy with us here.'

A couple of generations have now grown up ridiculing that sort of attitude. Everyone knows that war is not a game, and no one is much interested in the idioms which made it possible for our ancestors to deal with danger and death. It has been a long time since the age and beliefs of empire seemed an attractive subject for creativity. From E. M. Forster and J. G. Farrell to Salman Rushdie and Zadie Smith, the stuff of fiction is the end of empire and its aftermath. In 1960, you might have gone to the cinema to see Kenneth More playing a polished British army captain smuggling a six-year-old Hindu prince out of danger in *North West Frontier*. By 1970 you were more likely to be watching *Carry On up the Khyber*, with Sid James as the military governor, Sir Sidney Ruff-Diamond, and Charles Hawtrey as the scandalously underpanted Private Widdle in the 3rd Foot and Mouth Regiment. In fiction, the hero of the hour was now Tom Brown's tormentor, the cad Harry Flashman. By the turn of the millennium, there was hardly an imperial hero who had not had a few buckets of mud thrown at him. The great explorers of Africa, such as Richard Burton, were racists. Captain Scott had condemned his men to icy deaths in Antarctica by vainglorious bungling. The sexuality of the hero of Khartoum, General Gordon, was suspect. Robert Baden-Powell, founder of the Boy Scouts, was cracked. The tone of movies had changed, too. David Lean's portrayal of a troubled egotist in *Lawrence of Arabia* (1962) was much less about grand imperial designs than about a romantic, misunderstood loner. The new heroes were the men and women who fought against the British brutes – the Mahatma in *Gandhi* (1982), the medieval Scottish rebel William Wallace in *Braveheart* (1995) or the modern Irish revolutionary in *Michael Collins* (1996).

By then, the British thoroughbred had become a rattle-ribbed old nag. The country had been exhausted and impoverished by two world wars, had withdrawn from its colonies and was demonstrably unsure quite where its future lay. The United States, the new global policeman, professed itself an enemy of imperialism and, in first undermining British attempts to manage the Palestine issue, and then seeing off the duplicity behind the plot to seize the Suez Canal in 1956, delivered mortal blows to the country's self-confidence. Colonies seemed to belong to another time in history.

And it had all passed so quickly. The fate of the crumbling Ottoman Empire worried European politicians for the best part of a century: the British Empire's illness was speedy and fatal and carried it off in a few decades. The British came out of both world wars on the winning side, and so never had the need to reimagine themselves as anything other than what they had once been, nor the need to think much about the legacy of their actions. All that was required was a readiness to accept themselves much as they had been beforehand, but in a diminished state. How much better it might have been to have had the chance to devise another destiny.

CHAPTER ONE

'To plunder, to slaughter, to steal – these things
they misname empire'
Tacitus, *c.* AD 98

There is not much to Port Royal these days, just a scrabble of streets, a couple of bare-shelved stores and an open sewer running down to the sea. It is certainly not royal, and – apart from the odd fishing boat pulled up on the black beach – not much of a port either. Half a dozen barefoot boys play cricket in the dirt, their wickets a plastic beer case and an up-ended table with two legs missing. There is a policeman, but nothing for him to do, for nothing much happens in Port Royal. A young man pushes a trolley through the rutted streets, a bowl of goat stew kept warm on some glowing charcoal. He has ambitions, he says: one day he plans to have his travelling restaurant mounted on full-sized bicycle wheels. Apart from a betting shack

where improbable numbers of dollars are staked on unlikely outcomes, the poverty-stricken fishing village of today bears little
relation to what went before. For once this collection of dilapidated
buildings at the south-eastern tip of Jamaica was one of the most
notorious places on earth. A couple of earthquakes, a terrible fire and
numerous hurricanes – each said to be God's judgement on the loose
morals of earlier residents – have removed most traces of its time as
'the wickedest city in the world'.

'This town is the Sodom of the New World,' wrote a seventeenth-
century clergyman who made the mistake of visiting the newly
established English colony, 'and since the majority of its population
consists of pirates, cutthroats, whores and some of the vilest persons in
the whole of the world, I felt my permanence there was of no use and I
could better preach the Word of God elsewhere among a better sort of
folk.' He departed on the same ship that had brought him, leaving the
place to its vagabonds, escaped jailbirds and prostitutes such as the
notorious 'No Conscience Nan', 'Salt-Beef Peg' and 'Buttock-de-Clink
Jenny'. The place floated on a sea of rum – by 1661 the town had stirred
itself to acquire a council, which, in the month of June alone, issued
over forty new licences for drinking dens. (There was no need of visiting clergy because the rum they served was so strong it was known as
'Kill Devil'.) A governor of Jamaica drily observed that 'The Spaniards
wondered much at the sickness of our people, until they knew of the
strength of their drinks, but then they wondered more that they were
not all dead.' Port Royal made the wild towns which grew up around
nineteenth-century gold strikes seem like quiet country villages, for one
simple reason. It was built not on digging gold out of the ground but on
stealing it. This tropical Klondike flourished on maritime gangsterism.
Jamaica lay 'in the Spaniard's bowels and in the heart of his trade'.

The parasitic process went like this. The Spanish robbed the Aztec
and Inca empires of Central and South America, and then transported the precious metals under armed guard to the Caribbean
coast, where they were loaded on to ships to be carried back to Spain.
The thugs of Port Royal simply put to sea, mugged the Spanish and
then scuttled back to Jamaica as fast as possible. The British were not
the first into this uncertain but often immensely profitable business,

for French pirates had begun falling upon Spanish convoys soon after they started to sail for Europe from the Americas. But the British were the most ruthless, and Sir Francis Drake's prayer 'I know many means to do her Majesty good service and to make us rich, for we must have gold before we see England,' can stand as a mission-statement for all of them. When Drake finally reached home – after plundering a mule train on the Panamanian isthmus loaded with gold and silver in 1573 – not only was he rich but he soon became an English national hero. There was something about the man's free-booting spirit that chimed with the mood of a sixteenth-century England, a nation beginning to feel that being an island gave both security and opportunity: when you have no troublesome land borders (the Welsh had been 'pacified' and the Scots were increasingly more envious than dangerous), all foreigners are exotic and it is easy to feel indifferent about what your citizens do to them. For anyone willing to face the risks involved, piracy was free enterprise, red in tooth and claw, open to anyone and offering the prospect of great wealth.

Its practitioners were a hugely varied bunch. In true pirate fashion, the origins of Edward Teach – 'Blackbeard' – are obscure. His end is not: in 1718 his severed head hung from the bowsprit of a ship sent from Carolina to tackle the menace of piracy. Another pirate, Stede Bonnet, was said to have been a gentleman plantation owner who took up robbery to escape his nagging wife. (Not that it was an entirely male world: two women pirates, Anne Bonny and Mary Read, were captured and escaped the gallows only when they revealed that they were pregnant, Anne Bonny ending her days as a respectable matriarch of eighty-four.) Howel Davis had been first mate on a slaving ship. Henry Mainwaring was the son of an MP and graduate of Brasenose College, Oxford: he was neither the first nor the last man to take up the trade after being employed by the Crown to *suppress* piracy, and he helped other 'respectable' citizens to embark on piratical careers by stage-managing bogus kidnappings, so that they could, if they chose, later return to normal life. William Kidd, hanged at execution dock in Wapping in 1701, was another who had decided that joining the pirates was a more lucrative career than the commission he had been given to hunt them down.

As the fates of some of these characters indicate, the British government was in two (or more) minds about those of its citizens who found the pickings of the Spanish Main – the Caribbean Sea alongside the mainland of Spanish America – irresistible. Medieval convention allowed those who had been robbed in foreign territory and been unable to get satisfaction in court to apply for permission to recoup any losses by force of arms. From this, it was only a small step to the invention of privateering, a system by which the Admiralty Court in London granted permission to private ships to attack the vessels of Britain's enemies. In exchange for a licence to steal, the government demanded a share of the proceeds. The pith-helmeted, district-officered empire which was wound up in the twentieth century had its origins in the chaotic free enterprise of places like Port Royal. For while Jamaica may have been on the fringes of the known world, it was integral to the London Treasury and a central part of the strategy for war against Spain. This pattern of using freelances or proxies was one the British would employ time and again as they built their empire. Sometimes territories were conquered at the order of governments, but much of the time the flag was planted by licensed companies or some freebooting capitalist given a nod or a wink in London.

One of the most spectacular of these adventurers was Henry Morgan, a Welshman thought to have arrived in Jamaica in the 1650s. Morgan obtained a licence to fight the Spanish at sea, but – like many similar figures in the centuries to come – recognized that a faraway government would be almost powerless to stop him doing as he pleased, and would be likely, moreover, to thank him for it afterwards. In July 1668 he led a group of pirates in an audacious attack on the fortified town of Portobello in present-day Panama, where the Spanish unloaded the mule trains which had carried their treasure down to the coast for onward shipment by armed convoy to Europe. Military cunning and piratical enthusiasm overwhelmed Spanish unpreparedness: Morgan seized the town and in the following four weeks denuded it of spoils worth more than Jamaica's agricultural exports for an entire year. He even forced the Spanish to pay him a ransom to leave Portobello. The individual pirate's share of the plunder from Portobello was five or six times the annual wage of a seventeenth-century seaman.

When news of the raid reached London, the Spanish Ambassador wrung his hands and moaned. The British gave their characteristic performance of sympathy, mild regret and practical indifference. What, they seemed to suggest, can we do? In truth, the British had discovered that contracting out the making of war – or money – was a policy which it was much easier to start than to finish.

When they would later come to justify their empire to the world (and to themselves), the political aspects of this robbery were presented as something rather more dignified. Early pirates talked of themselves as knights on some blue-water crusade against a corrupt, barbarous and lazy Spain. When someone had the impertinence to describe Henry Morgan in print as a buccaneer he sued the publishers for libel – and won. In 1664 the British had sent a new governor to Jamaica, bearing orders to improve relations with Spain and put a stop to privateering. Fortunately for Morgan, Sir Thomas Modyford's political convictions were more than a match for the promiscuity of 'No Conscience Nan'. He had brought with him hundreds of planters to whom he promised land on which they could grow sugar to feed the immense European appetite for the stuff. But clearing the dense jungle to create sugar plantations was a slow, laborious business – even when the work was done by slaves being imported from Africa. Within weeks of his arrival and his high-sounding proclamation to ban privateering, Modyford was writing home, explaining that he had changed his mind and would accomplish his mission step by step. In fact, the new Governor had decided there was simply too much money at stake in robbery. In 1667 he appointed Morgan admiral of the privateers and was already taking a cut of the proceeds himself.

Three years later came news that at long last the feuding between Britain and Spain was over. The Spanish had been plundering the New World since before the arrival of the British, but under the terms of the Treaty of Madrid they recognized Jamaica and other British possessions in the Caribbean. The pirates in Port Royal heard of the peace agreement when it was proclaimed with a drumbeat. But peace did not last long, and in August Modyford authorized Henry Morgan to put to sea, 'to do and perform all manner of exploits, which may tend to the preservation and quiet of this island', the sort of opaque instructions which in the centuries to come characterize so many imperial directions. Morgan's reputation meant that he had no trouble assembling the biggest gang of privateers ever brought together in the West Indies, who promptly interpreted the promotion of quiet in Jamaica as attacking Panama City, a military operation so ambitious that the Spanish had assumed it to be impossible. Had it not been for the remarkable endurance of the attackers, who sailed upriver and then marched through almost impenetrable jungle without food for four days, the Spanish would have been right about Panama City's security. But under Morgan's leadership the attackers fell upon 'the greatest mart for silver and gold in the whole world'. Although disappointed that the city was not holding more bullion, they still needed a train of 175 mules to carry their plunder down to the coast. Morgan arrived back in Port Royal in April 1671, to be greeted with the thanks of the colony and much business in the town's grogshops.

But the privateers were about to fall victim to changing fashions. The sack of Panama had been a brilliant feat of arms. But the mercantile class preferred predictable yields. Slaving, for example, was an especially lucrative and largely predictable trade. A new governor, Sir Thomas Lynch, was dispatched to Jamaica carrying orders to end privateering and to arrest Modyford and send him to England. To placate the Spanish, who were furious when they heard what had happened to Panama City, the order was extended to include the arrest of Morgan as well. The two men were shipped to England and locked up in the Tower of London. But Morgan's 'disgrace' did not last long. By 1674 he had been released and sent back to Jamaica, this time as lieutenant-governor. There, he set himself up in some style and invested in sugar production. More discreetly, he invested in the ships of other privateers, who for a while managed to go about their business under licences from the French. By 1682, under Morgan's patronage, Port Royal had become the most fortified town in English America. When he died, six years later, he had amassed a fortune which included three plantations, assorted servants and 122 slaves.

By then the privateers' days in the Caribbean were more or less done. Some travelled to North Africa, where they joined the Barbary pirates, whose raids the British did not suppress until the nineteenth century. A few struck out west, crossed the Panamanian isthmus, hijacked boats on the Pacific shore and set off on raids down the coast of South America. An archbishop of Quito remarked that had it not been for their absence of virtue, 'the buccaneers' daring in attack, their patience in enduring all sorts of toil and hardship, their perseverance despite the most terrible setbacks and their indomitable courage [might] arouse our admiration; we might call them heroes'. There spoke the vestiges of one empire to the harbingers of another. Wild, tough, enterprising, ruthless and often very much happier when away from the land they called home, the privateers had much in common with those who followed over the next few hundred years.

Sugar was the future. Experience of growing the crop in Barbados (the island had been captured by the British in 1627) had shown the phenomenal rewards to be had: at one point, in the middle of the seventeenth century, Barbadian sugar plantations promised speedy returns of up to 50 per cent on invested capital. And Europe's appetite was apparently insatiable: in the next 150 years, British sugar consumption grew by 2,500 per cent. Sugar made tea, coffee and drinking chocolate palatable, sweetened the porridge of working people and made possible the puddings for which the country was acquiring an international reputation. The demand was more than strong enough to ride out the occasional hiccup in production caused by hurricanes, droughts or plagues of locusts.

By the time of his death in 1710 – during a punch-up among the colony's politicians – Peter Beckford, for example, was reputed to own twenty estates, over a thousand slaves and £1,500,000 in further investments. He had arrived in Jamaica as a seaman, his son was Speaker of the Jamaican assembly, a grandson became lord mayor of London and an MP and a great-grandson the exquisitely sensitive collector and creator of the neo-Gothic mansion Fonthill Abbey in Wiltshire.

The planters were not immigrants – home was thousands of miles away. But their wealth allowed the so-called plantocracy to enjoy lives of cartoonish extravagance. As the appalled young wife of a newly arrived governor noted in her journal:

> I don't wonder now at the fever the people suffer from here – such eating and drinking I never saw! . . . I observed some of the party, to-day, eat of late breakfasts, as if they had never eaten before – a dish of tea, another of coffee, a bumper of claret, another large one of hock-negus; then Madeira, sangaree, hot and cold meat, stews and fries, hot and cold fish pickled and plain, peppers, ginger sweetmeats, acid fruit, sweet jellies – in short, it was all as astonishing as it was disgusting.

The sugar which made this self-indulgence possible was a merciless crop. Columbus had considered Jamaica the most beautiful island he had seen in the Indies. But before the fields could be planted the land needed to be cleared, dug and manured. At harvest time the cane had to be hacked down, stripped of its leaves, carried to the mill, crushed and cooked. In the early days of the plantations the labour was provided by prisoners, vagrants and indentured workers brought out from the British Isles, who toiled in the fields for a set number of years in exchange for a new life at the end. But white labourers needed to be constantly replaced. How much easier to make the back-breaking toil the task of people who could be kept at it for life, and anyway did not need to be paid. The men and women with black skins who had been seen by white adventurers along the coast of Africa would be much more resilient. Furthermore, some of the African kings were already in the habit of seizing captives and then selling them into slav-ery. In the 1560s Sir John Hawkins, one of the greatest of the seafarers to emerge from the English West Country, had pioneered a triangular trade, in which vessels sailed from England to Africa with a cargo of goods to be traded in Africa, picked up slaves for sale in the Spanish colonies of the Americas as a second consignment, and then returned home with a third cargo, offering a potential profit on every leg.

The British were not the first people into the slave business (some of Hawkins's slaves been captured from the Portuguese). But they came to dominate the trade. Indeed, one of the reasons that priva-teering began to trouble governments was the damage that investors claimed it did to trade in human beings when in retaliation the Spanish refused to buy the slaves the British had gone to the trouble of shipping across the Atlantic. Under the treaty which ended the War of the Spanish Succession in 1713, the British demanded – and got – the Spanish contract to import slaves to their territories in the Indies. Slaving now became huge business. In the 1740s, British ships transported 200,000 men, women and children, and Liverpool was well established as the country's leading slaving port. An estimated 85 per cent of the textiles manufactured in Britain were now being shipped to Africa on the first step of the triangular trade, and in 1772 'an African merchant' claimed to the government that the slave trade was 'the foundation of our commerce, the support of our colonies, the life of our navigation, and first cause of our national industry and riches'. In the 1780s the slavers carried the staggering total of three-quarters of a million people across the Atlantic, half of them in British ships. The estimated total number of human beings torn from their homes to be turned into beasts of burden thousands of miles away is reckoned at 11 million.

Every single one of those millions was a personal tragedy of broken families, to say nothing of the physical suffering of all those involved. Even those who might have managed to stay in contact were often separated at the slave marts into which they were driven on arrival in the West Indies. Few even retained the dignity of their own name and language. On the plantations, they were woken by a bell or conch shell at perhaps four in the morning and then worked from dawn to dusk. Overseers and drivers divided the slaves into three gangs – the first, comprising the strongest men and women, did the heaviest work of digging the soil, manuring, planting and then, at harvest time, cutting their way through the fully grown fields, carrying the cut cane or toiling in the sweltering factories where it was crushed, boiled, cooled into crystals and packed. The second gang, comprising teenagers, nursing mothers and old people, followed them through the fields, clearing the debris. A third gang, of very young and very old, fed the slaves and livestock, either watching their future life acted out before them or waiting for the point when feebleness made them of no further use to their owner. Disease and hardship demanded a constant supply of new slaves, either shipped in from Africa or bred on-site. All this to provide a luxury for the tea tables of Europe.

This system – opulence built on misery – could survive only by violence. Periodic rebellions proved that the spirit of resistance was not dead and the white population was greatly outnumbered by the slaves who made their way of life possible. Plantations could be very isolated from one another, each its own small tyranny, with orders enforced by the whip: the ingenious cruelty of some slave owners in devising ever more ghastly punishments was appalling. The most comprehensive account of white day-to-day plantation life comes from Thomas Thistlewood, who over thirty-nine years filled thousands of pages of diary with unreflective accounts of his doings each day. ('On the 7th December 1761 I paid Mr John Hutt 112 for two men and 200 for one boy and three girls. The new Negroes were soon branded with my mark TT on the right shoulder.') Thistlewood was neither a toff nor, it seems, especially badly behaved. In fact, he appears to have been less drunk less often than many of the grander estate owners. The son of a tenant farmer, he had arrived in Jamaica in April 1750 and within days had been offered a post as an overseer on one of the plantations. Unlike the slaves he supervised, Jamaica treated Thistlewood kindly and within a couple of decades this dull, brutal man had property of his own and had become a magistrate. His diaries make plain the extent to which the rape of slave women seems to have been commonplace. But what is most shocking is the malicious creativity involved in maintaining dominance. Within three months in 1756, for example, Thistlewood records that '[a slave named] Derby catched eating canes. Had him well flogged and pickled, then made Hector [another slave] shit in his mouth', that he 'rubbed Hazat with molasses and exposed him naked to the flies all day, and to the mosquitos all night', and that he 'flogged Punch well, and then washed and rubbed in salt pickle, lime juice and bird pepper; made Negro Joe piss in his eyes and mouth'.

The horrors of the Atlantic slave trade are now part of school history lessons, the cruelties the British inflicted on fellow human beings rightly taught as a cause of shame. The mechanics of the business, in which tribal chiefs collected captives from further and further into the interior of Africa for sale to the traders, the British creation of marshalling forts on the 'slave coast' between the Niger and Volta rivers, the disgusting conditions of the packed slaves on the 'Middle Passage' of the triangular trade and, at journey's end, the presentation of men, women and children like beasts in a market, should all be engraved on the national conscience. It is one of the most disgraceful episodes in British history. From the distance of the twenty-first century, the baffling, troublesome anxiety about it – as about some other aspects of the imperial experience – is how it was that our own forebears could have behaved like this. It illuminates the central mystery of so much of the empire: how could British people do to others what they would not have accepted being done to themselves? In the case of slavery there are only two possible explanations. Either the business was carried out in secrecy. Or those who conducted, invested in or facilitated the trade did not consider black people to be fellow human beings. The country was either ignorant or racist.

We can dismiss the first possibility. Writers from Jane Austen to Dr Johnson showed themselves plenty aware of the injustice which made the plantations viable. The wealth generated by the business was apparent everywhere. In Bristol it was said in 1685 that there was scarcely a shopkeeper in the city who did not have a stake in trade to the Americas – 'even the parsons talked of nothing but trade'. The entire British economy was transformed by slaving: traders needed credit to fund their voyages and insurance systems to protect their investment, which led to the rapid development of banking and financial services. When the Act of Union allowed Scotland to join in colonial trade, Glasgow boomed through the import of tobacco from Virginia and sugar from the West Indies, each the product of slave labour. Liverpool, though, was *the* slave city. At the height of the trade it was reckoned that over half the slaves carried by English ships had been stolen from Africa in Liverpool vessels. The city's Royal Institution 'for the promotion of Literature, Science and the Arts' was built as the home of a slaver. The Liverpool Exchange, later the Town Hall, was decorated with the carved heads of African elephants and slaves. Destitute children at the city's Bluecoat School owed their education to the forced labour of Africans. An actor who appeared drunk on a Liverpool stage – not for the first time – was hissed by the crowd. He steadied himself long enough to round on the audience with the words: 'I have not come here to be insulted by a set of wretches, every brick in whose infernal town is cemented with an African's blood.'

You would have had to be wilfully deaf and blind to remain ignorant of the profound change the slave trade was working in England during the seventeenth and eighteenth centuries. It was, in the words of one apostle, 'the mainspring of the machine which sets every wheel in motion', making possible the network of enterprises which brought tea and coffee to the sideboard, oils and wines to the lunch table, Chinese pottery and Persian silks to the drawing room. It created a wealthy commercial class with the means to shoulder aside the traditional landed aristocracy. Wealthy West Indian traders became a familiar sight about town and the subject of popular drama, their riches contaminating almost every area of national life, buying seats in parliament, building churches, funding schools and hospitals, educating orphans. The Society for the Propagation of the Gospel was the proud proprietor of its own plantation in Barbados, where for a time a red-hot iron was used to brand the word 'Society' on the chests of slaves. The Society tended not to preach sermons in the colonies based on the Exodus text about the promised land.* Slave traders effectively owned much of the British political class, who secured their interests in parliament. By the middle of the eighteenth century, families which would soon claim to be the very flower of the aristocracy were showing off the enormous wealth from their plantations by throwing up or elaborating vast country houses, like the Pennant family's mock-Norman castle at Penrhyn in North Wales, the Fitzherberts' Tissington Hall in Derbyshire or the Lascelles' great pile, Harewood House – 'St Petersburg Palace on a Yorkshire hill' –

---

* In February 2006, the Archbishop of Canterbury apologized for the 'shame and sinfulness of our predecessors', explaining that 'the body of Christ is not just a body that exists at any one time, it exists across history'. The previous year he had apologized for the sinfulness of missionaries in imposing *Hymns Ancient and Modern* on the people of Africa. The empire is very much alive in the Anglican Church. Indeed, the tensions between its different overseas sections may well be the death of it.

with magnificent gardens designed by Capability Brown and furniture specially made by Chippendale. The beautiful Codrington Library at that most unworldly of Oxford colleges, All Souls, was built with slaving money. The core of the British Museum's original collection of artefacts was amassed by Sir Hans Sloane, much of it with money from his marriage to the widow of a Jamaican planter. The National Gallery was established with the collection of Old Masters built up by John Julius Angerstein, much of whose money had been made by underwriting slave-ship insurance and ownership of plantations. All these exquisite sensibilities were nourished by barbarism. The British have *never* really had to confront the consequences of this trade because for them slavery happened thousands of miles away. The contrast is with the United States – where slaves lived, sweated and died within the national borders, where a civil war was fought over their freedom, and where discrimination against the descendants of slaves was a mainstream issue within living memory. Roughly 40 per cent of African Americans alive today have their ancestral roots in West Africa and remind contemporary Americans of the country's slaving past every day. But Britons with an Afro-Caribbean family background, who are also descendants of slaves, pass as a mere 'ethnic minority', while their white fellow citizens troop off to gawp at the splendour of Harewood House, and turn it into 'England's Large Visitor Attraction of the Year, 2009'.*

We are left with the unpleasant conclusion that, when the slave trade was at its height, mainstream British opinion simply did not consider that any wrong was being done. In 1672, King Charles II had granted the British Royal African Company the right to create a fleet for the 'selling, bartering and exchanging of, for or with any gold, silver, Negroes, slaves, goods, wares and manufactures' – a bill of fare which made the hierarchy quite explicit. A century later the belief that slaves were merely a commodity was still alive. In

---

* And compare the language of political leaders. Martin Luther King has a dream in 1963 that 'one day right there in Alabama, little black boys and black girls will be able to join hands with little white boys and white girls as sisters and brothers'. In 2006, Tony Blair mumbles about 'how we express our deep sorrow that it [slavery] could ever have happened and rejoice at the better times we live in today'.

November 1781 sickness broke out on the overcrowded decks of the Liverpool-registered slave ship the *Zong* during the Middle Passage. 'Normal' conditions on these ships were disgusting enough, the stench overwhelming. But when, predictably, dysentery or some other sickness broke out, conditions were horrific. On the *Zong* an epidemic began to spread among the Africans, and with each slave who died, the value of the cargo in the markets of Jamaica dropped. After seventy had perished, and with many more very sick, the captain – who had a financial stake in the voyage – came up with a way to protect his investment. In the sort of actuarial calculation possible only if all considerations of humanity were discounted, he realized that while deaths on board would become a charge on the shipowners, if the seriously ill were to drown at sea, jettisoned to 'save the ship', the problem was one for the insurance underwriters. He told the crew that water supplies were gravely low and that therefore the sick Africans, who would die anyway, should be thrown in the sea. The day after he reached this decision, fifty people were put over the side. The next day, another forty were forced overboard, followed on the third day by another twenty. All told, over 130 sick Africans were thrown into the sea. The story for the insurers was that they had had to be 'sacrificed' to preserve water supplies, which were dangerously low. Yet when the *Zong* reached Jamaica just before Christmas it had over 400 gallons of fresh water on board, more than enough to supply everyone – the result, the owners later claimed, of a sudden, unexpected downpour.

The lawsuit which followed was not a criminal prosecution for murder but a civil case in which the underwriters and shipowners argued about property. The Solicitor General, who represented the shipowners in court, asked, 'what is all this vast declaration that human people have been thrown overboard? . . . This is a case of chattels or goods. It is really so: it is the case of throwing over goods, for to this purpose, and the purpose of insurance, they are goods and property, whether right or wrong we have nothing to do with it.' The case eventually fizzled out in a familiar pattern of legal verbiage and lawyers' bills. But the attendant publicity sufficiently outraged a young man named Granville Sharp that he attempted – unsuccessfully as it turned out – to bring a private prosecution for murder against the slavers. Sharp, the godfather of the movement to remove the stain on Britain made by the slave trade, had in a previous case persuaded the Lord Chief Justice that a runaway slave who made it to Britain could not be forcibly returned to the colonies. 'Let Justice be done, though the Heavens may fall,' said the judge, in a ruling which went to the heart of the contradiction between 'freeborn Englishmen' and enslaved Africans. Sharp belonged to the Society for the Propagation of the Gospel (whose ownership of the Barbados plantation he was unaware of). And it is notable how much of the anti-slavery cause was made by religious believers, especially Nonconformists: nine of the twelve founding members of the London committee of the Society for the Abolition of the Slave Trade were Quakers. When, finally, the campaign achieved its goal it gave the British Empire a vital moral purpose.

Almost the only remark anyone now remembers of the great Victorian historian Sir John Seeley is his claim that 'We seem . . . to have conquered and peopled half the world in a fit of absence of mind.' Seeley delivered the lectures of which this half-truth was part at a time when the empire was in its late nineteenth-century pomp. That line about 'absence of mind' comforts the post-imperial generation almost as much as it comforted the Victorians, for it suggests that the British had never really wanted an empire at all, had had it somehow forced upon them. But while piracy may have been part of no great design, the 'absence of mind' line simply will not do. If there was nothing quite so precise as a single plan in the early stages, there was certainly an ambition, which showed itself in a series of schemes, haphazard, opportunistic and changeable as they may have been. By Seeley's time there had come talk of national destiny and a 'civilizing mission' to the world, but the empire grew at the hands of men who had multiple motives. Some would plant the flag because they had won battles, others in the name of science and discovery, still others because they were merely obeying orders. Often British power spread because it offered profit, sometimes it did so in the name of freedom, sometimes by mistake and at other times simply to stop someone else seizing land. The makers of empire were aristocrats, merchants, sailors, soldiers, missionaries, speculators, hard-cases, criminals. Some went to start a new life, others to escape an old one. The description 'Jack the Lad' would fit many of them.

One of the first people to use the term 'British Empire' seems to have been Queen Elizabeth I's astrologer, a clever and rather deluded Welshman called John Dee, in 1577. Dee advised the queen that she was entitled to claim large tracts of North America, because the place had been 'discovered' by a Prince Madog ab Owain of Gwynedd in 1170, some 300 years before Christopher Columbus clapped eyes on the place. Documentary proof to support this claim is no more readily available than is evidence to validate Dee's other convictions, such as his belief in the existence of a Philosopher's Stone which could turn base metals into gold, or his assertion that he could hold conversations with angels.

But it was a Devon man, Sir Humphrey Gilbert, who persuaded Elizabeth to let him cross the Atlantic to found the first English colony in North America. The characteristics of this founder of empire – visionary enthusiasm and slippery opportunism – occur time and again in the people who brought so much of the world under British rule. Gilbert's proposal was that he set out to find a route to China through a north-west passage, above the North American landmass. The motive was commercial – 'to possesse y welth of all the *East partes of the worlde*', and 'through the shortnesse of the voyage, we should be able to sell all maner of Merchandize, brought from thence, far better cheape, then either the *Portingal*, or *Spaniarde* doth, or may doe'. Gilbert laid out the goods with which he might return – gold, silver, silks, spices and precious stones. And it would not be a one-way traffic. God, he said, had reserved all the territory north of Florida for the English to 'plant a Christian habitation'. In a scheme which would later become a staple feature of British penal policy, he proposed to use the lands he discovered as a dumping ground for 'such needie people of our Countrie which now trouble the common welth, and through want here at home are inforced to commit outrageous offences, whereby they are dayly consumed with the Gallowes'. As well as the opportunity to offload individuals who would otherwise be a burden on the state, there was the additional pleasure of biffing the Spanish. In 1577 he proposed to the queen his scheme 'to annoy the King of Spayne' by attacking his fishing fleets off the coast of Newfoundland. The following year, Elizabeth gave him authority to seek out 'remote heathen and barbarous lands'.

There is about Humphrey Gilbert's proposal – as about many later pitches to potential sponsors of imperial expansion – a real whiff of excitement, the sort of drive which would before long lead men and women to attempt to cross Africa, climb mountains or push towards the Poles. Part of the impulse to explore was simply that it was there. In an age when the world has been mapped and plundered it requires something of an imaginative leap to appreciate the thrill suggested in this sort of project. Perhaps the closest modern equivalents are the exploration narratives of science fiction. Gilbert was certainly a hard enough nut for this voyage into the unknown, having shown utter ruthlessness during the campaign to put down a rising in England's first (and perhaps its last) major colony, Ireland. As a military governor he gave no quarter and accounts of the war there talk of supplicants being made to approach him through an avenue of severed heads. It was in the Irish colony, too, that Gilbert had learned the practice of 'planting' settler communities (the origins of the so-called loyalist community which still exists in that country, nearly a century after most of the island achieved independence).

In August 1583, Sir Humphrey Gilbert landed at St John's, Newfoundland and claimed for the Crown the harbour and all the land within a radius of 200 leagues. He immediately proclaimed three laws: that the religion was to be that of the Church of England; that those who menaced the Crown would be executed for treason; and that if anyone bad-mouthed the monarch they would lose their ears. The English coat of arms was cast in lead and attached to a wooden pillar, after which Gilbert set off again. Around midnight on 9 September, his ship ran into enormous seas. The last sighting of the man later to be called 'the father of English colonization' was of him standing on deck with a book in his hand. According to the sixteenth-century geographer Richard Hakluyt his final words, shouted across the tempest, were 'We are as near to heaven, by sea as by land.'

At this stage, if an empire was indeed being formed, it was a distinctively English one: the only function of the Scots and Irish was to provide some settlers. It took the arrival of a Scottish king to get the *British* Empire going. The invitation to the Stuart James VI to take the English throne had talked of 'one Imperial Crown'. (A Welsh member of parliament even proposed that James should take the title of emperor and his dominions be renamed 'Great Britain', thereby anticipating the Act of Union of 1707 by more than a hundred years.) The suggestion was not adopted, but by the time of the Act of Union the empire had become a fact: in 1600 there were no permanent English settlements in America; by 1700 there were seventeen different jurisdictions and the clear – and clearly understood – framework of an empire. If we had to find a one-word motive for these settlements, and for most of their successors across the world, it would have to be money. In 1610, for example, a group of thirty-nine men had sailed from Bristol to found a colony at Conception Bay, Newfoundland, under the sponsorship of some London and Bristol merchants who thought there were profits to be made from the spectacular yields of cod to be found in the local waters.* Another Newfoundland scheme, near by at Ferryland, was sponsored by James's Secretary of State, Sir George Calvert (later Lord Baltimore). Both failed to make a good enough return on investment, but left behind settlers. Newfoundland soon became England's first permanent colony in the New World, complete with a properly organized economy, a recognizable class structure and the beginnings of its own strange politics.†

There was a precedent for these settlements, for they followed a pattern set in what George Bernard Shaw called John Bull's Other Island. Ireland had been an anxiety to the English Crown for generations, and for a long time authority ran no further than 'the pale', or fence

---

* The explorer John Cabot, who had sailed to the New World on behalf of a group of Bristol merchants in 1497, had been dumbstruck by the quantities of fish, which seemed so abundant he wondered that his ship could move through them. The bounty lasted until the late twentieth century, when industrial fishing sucked the sea empty.

† 'I suppose everyone is someone else's Newfie,' as one exasperated Canadian put it.

and ditch, surrounding Dublin (and even then there were times when it was little more than a convenient fiction). The new Tudor state which emerged at the end of the Wars of the Roses was determined to assert its authority, and in 1541 Henry VIII had himself proclaimed king in Dublin, with the country formally annexed to England. The 'planting' of settlers had a political purpose: the Tudors put down resistance mercilessly (Humphrey Gilbert's processional avenue of severed heads being an example of their style), confiscating the land of those involved and giving it to settlers from England or Scotland. When, in September 1607, the Earls of Tyrconnell and Tyrone scrambled aboard a ship in Lough Swilly on the north coast of Ireland and fled the country ('the flight of the earls'), the English grabbed their chance, seized lands in the particularly troublesome northern province of Ulster and 'planted' them with English and Scottish settlers. Because England and Scotland had embraced the Reformation – unlike Ireland – these loyalists were marked out from their Catholic neighbours by their Protestant religion. The resulting sectarian tensions lasted into the twenty-first century.

The English continued creating plantations in Ireland for much of the sixteenth century; as would happen elsewhere in the empire, they offered those with high hopes and empty pockets the chance to acquire land, even if it came with the ever present possibility of rebellion or war. Although the scheme was less costly than maintaining heavily armed garrisons or fighting campaigns in Ireland, it was not cheap, and since James's government could not afford to fund the scheme itself, it forced the City of London to do so. Slightly against their better judgement, a dozen livery companies extracted what concessions could be had and began to ship in settlers. As with later imperial projects, funding for the scheme was raised by issuing a prospectus outlining delectable rewards. This approach seems to have been developed by the Tudor scholar Sir Thomas Smith, whose son was to lead an expedition to settle the Ards Peninsula in Ulster. Their manifesto invited adventurers – specifically the younger sons of the nobility or gentry – to join the project to acquire land and escape the overcrowding that beset them at home. ('England was never that can be heard of, fuller of people than it is today.') Did they really, the advertisement asked, fancy the alternative of trying to make do as clergymen in the current economic circumstances of 'excessive expence; both in diet and apparel'? By contrast, those who joined the project would be offered at least 300 acres of land, which would be more than enough to ensure a good living. 'I cannot see', said the proposal, 'how Fathers that haue many sonnes, or landed men that haue many younger brothers, can do better . . . than to prefer them, and set them forthe in this jorney with me.' Eight hundred young men answered the call.

The plantation of Ireland had an unmistakably strategic purpose. When Thomas Hacket dedicated a book to Elizabeth's man in Ireland, Sir Henry Sidney (who said he 'cursed, hated, and detested' the country), he made explicit comparison with the odious way the Spanish behaved in their colonies in the New World. But the real reference point – and it is one that is used again and again in the lifetime of the British Empire – was another empire altogether. Quite apart from the military benefits and the possible financial dividends for those involved, the English considered their settlements to be part of a civilizing mission to a culturally inferior people. The English purpose in Ireland, argued Sir Thomas Smith, was no different to that of the Romans when they first encountered the primitive ancient Britons. The Irish were culturally inferior to the English, and, he advised his son as he left for Ulster, the English should follow the models of Rome, Carthage and Venice.

The principles of colonization in Ireland were applied in North America, too. Many of the financial mechanisms – the creation of joint-stock companies, for example – were similar. Attitudes towards the indigenous peoples also echoed: like the Irish, native Americans were considered lazy, unsophisticated and feckless – adjectives which the British used of natives in plenty of later colonies. But these settlements in the Americas were quite unlike most of the later colonies in Africa or the South Seas. Elsewhere, while English might be the formal language of government, it existed alongside local languages, customs and hierarchies. In the plantations, the English language, English law and the Christian religion excluded others. And because so many of the American settlements were established in a time of philosophical ferment when Thomas Hobbes and John Locke wrestled with the relationship between the individual and the state, when the king was beheaded and John Milton glorified the republic (only for the monarchy then to be restored), these New World settlements had more than a whiff of the Utopian about them, which later found its most concise expression in the commitment in the Declaration of Independence to 'Life, liberty and the pursuit of happiness'. They offered sanctuary to the Nonconformist and were born with freedom in their very bloodstream. For a government in London, the long-term appeal of allowing or encouraging citizens to travel thousands of miles was the prospect of future dividends: Francis Bacon had said the 'planting of colonies is like the planting of woods'. In the short term it offered the opportunity to export surplus poor people, landless younger sons of the gentry, religious dissidents and other irritants.

One of the earliest promoters of colonial settlement, Captain John Smith (immortalized in the dreadful Disney cartoon *Pocahontas*), soon made a claim which recurs throughout British imperial history. Colonial settlement promised England the chance to save itself from the degeneracy which was the fate of every great society. Smith's fervent patriotism was undimmed by his colourful military background (he had fought for the Austrians against the Turks, killing three men in single combat before later being taken prisoner and sold into slavery). Joining the expedition to found a colony at Jamestown, in Chesapeake Bay, Virginia, in 1607 must initially have seemed just another adventure. Certainly, his fellow colonists did not find him a particularly congenial companion and he was soon in chains, accused of plotting mutiny. It was only when they opened the sealed box they had been given by the expedition's commercial sponsors that his travelling companions – largely 'gentlemen' – made the unfortunate discovery that the company had chosen the soldier-of-fortune as one of the governors of the settlement. Class sensitivities were outraged, and continued to damage the Virginia project. The 'gentlemen' might have been content to go in for a spot of dashing robbery of a Spaniard, but they were damned if they were going to undertake anything as menial as tilling the soil or running fishing boats. Successful colonies, Smith later observed with a shrug, really needed people who could practise a trade.

From his experiences in Virginia, and his later attempts to establish colonies further north on the American coast – the area he named 'New England' – Smith concluded that it was really no good using plantations merely as places to dispose of indigent toffs and riff-raff who would otherwise be in prison or begging on the streets: the ideal settlement should reflect a true cross-section of society. On the model of the colony at Jamestown, in which those who bought shares became entitled to a share of any profits, Smith hoped to raise money from investors in future settlement schemes. Though he (of course) made a point of emphasizing the missionary role of settlers – godly people who would be carrying the gospel to benighted parts of the world – what he really wanted was a selection of people with useful skills, who might be expected to know about such things as the cultivation of vines or the manufacture of glass. America, he warned, was not a place to be plundered for gold, silver or precious stones, but 'all you expect from thence must be by labour'. Sir Walter Raleigh (Humphrey Gilbert's half-brother) had sailed up the Orinoco, his mind filled with fantasies of cities piled with gold and silver. He returned to England in 1618, a broken man and shortly to face execution. John Smith's model for an American empire was entirely different: the example, he suggested, was not that of Spain and its plunder, but that of Holland, where a wealthy empire had been constructed on timber and the 'contemptible Trade of Fish'. The future of empire-building, he said, belonged not to swashbuckling buccaneers but to merchants in their counting houses.

There is one other characteristic perhaps worth noting about these early colonies. Although they were commercial positions, they were 'royal'. Throughout the empire's life foreign territories were claimed and administered in the name of the Crown: they were sometimes even spoken of as ornaments to royal necklaces or jewels in the crown. When the English revolution overthrew and executed the king in the middle of the seventeenth century, Oliver Cromwell turned out to be as interested in imperial possessions as any king or queen: it is striking that the freedom which was said to have engulfed England in the Commonwealth in 1649 did not represent an opportunity for the British 'dominions and territories' overseas to make their own destinies. They were simply declared now to belong to the 'people of England'. As it turned out, Cromwell colonized as enthusiastically as anyone – and even more brutally. His campaign to extinguish dissent in Ireland is remembered to this day for its savagery.* In 1654 he dispatched a fleet to the Caribbean with orders to seize Hispaniola, which might then be used 'for the transplanting as much of our peoples from New England, Virginia, the Barbados, the Summer Islands [Bermuda], or from Europe, as we see requisite'. (That attack failed, although other islands were taken.) At home, the increasingly vainglorious Cromwell was travelling the familiar route from revolutionary to tyrant, cheered on by sycophants like the poet Edmund Waller, whose 'Panegyric to my Lord Protector' referred to England as 'The seat of Empire'. The rumour went that parliament was considering offering him the title of emperor. The country was approaching the point where overseas possessions were a necessity of office.

---

* 'The Men Behind the Wire', the rousing 1970s republican protest song against the British government's policy of interning suspected IRA activists without trial, contained the verses:

> Not for them a judge and jury
> Nor indeed a trial at all
> But being Irish means you're guilty
> So we're guilty one and all
>
> Round the world the truth will echo
> Cromwell's men are here again
> England's name again is sullied
> In the eyes of honest men.

The internment policy was a direct inheritance from colonial experiences elsewhere in the world and was a political disaster in Ireland.

CHAPTER TWO

The grandest imperial tableau of the eighteenth century is Benjamin West's monumental *The Death of General Wolfe*. It purports to show the moment when the victor of the 1759 battle of Quebec breathed his last. In the foreground the young general's musket and hat lie on the ground. At his feet a loyal, half-naked native American kneels, chin on hand, a 'noble savage' contemplating a fallen god. To the general's right and left stand anxious red-coated officers, in front, in the tartan of the regiment he had raised to serve the British Crown, the clan chief of the Frasers; above the dying general's head a vast Union flag thrusts heavenwards. James Wolfe lies on his side, his eyes cast upwards at the clearing sky as the dark clouds of battle drift away. A waving messenger approaches, clutching the French flag. He brings news of the extinction of French claims on Canada.

It is pure propaganda, a political *pietà* created to sanctify the collection of overseas possessions which during the eighteenth century the British were increasingly justified in terming an empire. There was more. Handel's oratorios likened Britain to the biblical Israel, the captured flags of defeated enemies were laid up in St Paul's Cathedral and statues of exotic animals demonstrated the taming of the world. Benjamin West's painting is a fantasy, painted more than a decade after the battle: there were no Indians fighting with the British and half the officers depicted weren't even on the battlefield at the moment of Wolfe's death, the general having been struck by French rounds in the wrist, stomach and chest as he led a British charge. But none of that takes away from Wolfe's achievement in defeating a French army ensconced at the top of what its commander the Marquis de Montcalm believed to be unscalable heights. Wolfe's tactics in ferrying five thousand men across the St Lawrence River and then having them climb the cliffs in virtual silence ranks among the most brilliant in the history of all imperial wars. When the French poured out of their fort in Quebec on to the Plains of Abraham, they were cut down by British muskets.

The Seven Years War of 1756–63 has often been considered the first 'world war'. It certainly shares its European origins with the First and Second World Wars. But it might also be considered the point at which the British recognized the extent to which their destiny lay not in Europe but elsewhere. There was, anyway, little or no land to be had in Europe, and seizing it would incur lasting menace from some other continental power. But abroad was another matter. In the treaty which ended the War of the Spanish Succession, fifty years earlier, Britain had acquired Newfoundland, Nova Scotia and the Hudson's Bay territory in North America, along with Gibraltar and Minorca in the Mediterranean and St Kitts at the entrance to the Caribbean. Now the British had their eyes on other pieces of abroad. The talks to end the Seven Years War dragged on through the winter of 1762–3, with endless haggling over tiny islands and quick slashes

of the pen disposing of chunks of a continent or two. The British
negotiator in Paris was the stubby, self-important, gout-stricken Duke
of Bedford, whom public opinion at home judged to be in danger of
being altogether too soft on the French. Nonetheless, in the peace
agreement signed on 10 February 1763 he pushed the boundaries of
British rule further than most campaigns of conquest, and in so doing
profoundly changed the character of the growing empire.

The British had had colonies before the Treaty of Paris. But the
empire which followed was a very different enterprise. The colonies
in North America had been planted with British men and women
who grew crops for export to Britain and bought home-manufactured
goods in return. In language, law and customs they were Anglo-
Saxon. In the Caribbean white men owned and ran estates and made
the wealth to pass themselves off as toffs back home. In Asia, the British presence had been largely confined to trading, as the East India
Company ran cotton, silk and tea from ports at Calcutta, Madras,
Bombay and Canton. Now, the British became masters of much of
North America: under the terms of the treaty the French surrendered to them all their North American mainland territories east of
the Mississippi. Spain in turn gave up Florida. The limits of Britain's
dominion on that continent were very hard to determine, 'for to the
northward it would seem that we might extend our claims quite to
the pole itself', ran a popular account. 'To the westward our boundaries reach to nations unknown even to the native Indians of Canada.
If we might hazard a conjecture, it is nearly equal to the extent of all
Europe.' And, better than Europe, it was unpopulated by pesky
Europeans with armies and gunpowder.

It was now undeniable that Britain was the pre-eminent world
power. But it was the acquisition of territories elsewhere that would
enable the British to build what the world came to recognize as their
empire. Outside North America, the French ceded Senegal in Africa
and a further smattering of islands in the Caribbean. What really
changed things, however, was a battle which had occurred 7,000 miles
from Quebec. At Plassey in Bengal, in June 1757, Robert Clive had led
East India Company troops to a remarkable victory, and through
clever tactical planning, dishonesty and low cunning, had taken

control of an area bigger than Britain itself. In the Treaty of Paris the French essentially abandoned their ambitions in India. The British now had an entirely different sort of cornucopia lying before them, so that when in due course the American colonies seized the independence which had grown out of the Utopian ambitions of so many of their founders, India and the rest of the world offered the British an alternative focus of ambition. Unlike the English-speaking plantations of the Americas, these increasingly important new territories, with their local princes, profoundly different religious faiths, colourful cultural traditions and idiosyncratic legal systems, were an altogether more complicated proposition than what had gone before.

If the British were able to consider the world their oyster, it was one which had grown around a piece of French grit.

The Seven Years War had been a massively expensive enterprise for all concerned: the British national debt had virtually doubled. On top of that, the vast new territories offered up by the peace settlement promised further big bills for administration and protection. The obvious solution was to milk the colonial cow. The burden fell on the settlers in North America, for whom the London government proposed taxes on a range of commodities, including official papers, sugar, paint, lead, glass and, most famously, tea. This practice of making the cost of empire fall upon those who had been colonized was one that would later be applied elsewhere, sometimes with disgraceful consequences – oppressing people to pay for their oppression.* But in this case the plantation territories of New England contained plenty of settlers who came from families that had left the British Isles to escape overweaning government and religious discrimination: the military campaign of resistance they now began would deliver the colonies their independence from Britain. One of the most striking things about the war, whose trigger was the cry 'no taxation without representation', is the very British nature of the conflict, for that issue had

---

* In India, for example, the British monopolized salt and then devised a hugely profitable tax on it. Salt smuggling was prevented by a Customs Line in the form of a Great Hedge, which eventually ran for over 2,000 miles.

been a repeated theme in the nation's history, most notably in the English Civil War. Thomas Paine's *Common Sense*, the most influential revolutionary tract ever written, was published in Philadelphia as 'written by an Englishman'. This extraordinary state of affairs was made a great deal worse by the utter incompetence of the government in finding itself embarking on a war against its closest natural ally while having simultaneously failed to secure adequate counterbalancing allies elsewhere. The Earl of Sandwich, First Lord of the Admiralty, noted bleakly that 'If Russia declares against us, we shall then literally speaking be in actual war with the whole world.' His own actions spoke volumes: while the colonists in America were polishing the rolling sentences of the Declaration of Independence, he had been off on a three-week trout-fishing holiday.

The war was an unmitigated disaster. When news of the British surrender at Yorktown reached the Prime Minister, Lord North, he took it 'as he would have taken a ball in his breast', exclaiming, 'Oh god! It's all over,' and throwing his arms in the air. There was some bleak comfort in the retention of Canada and the West Indies, but when the former Foreign Secretary Lord Stormont saw that all thirteen of the rebel colonies had gone he despaired. 'There is not a ray of light left,' he sighed. 'All is darkness.' Culprits were sought. Charles James Fox (who had supported the revolutionaries, as he would later support the revolutionaries in France) blamed the king. Many others saw the loss of the colonies as the product of some moral decadence in the nation. The *Newcastle Chronicle* wailed that 'Everything human . . . has its period: nations, like mortal men, advance only to decline; dismembered empire and diminished glory mark a crisis in the constitution; and, if the volume of our frame [national story] be not closed, we have read the most brilliant pages of our history.' This piece of journalistic breast-beating turned out to be as wide of the mark as so many later, similar examples of the genre, for there was a century of increasing global dominance ahead. But it would be a very different sort of imperial enterprise. The war with the American colonists had been quite unlike previous conflicts, in which the enemy had generally been either a less technologically advanced people or a foreign-speaking, Roman Catholic power intent on destroying the nation's political and religious settlement. The colonists, by contrast, spoke the same language and enjoyed the same cultural traditions, and there was a sense in which all they sought were the rights their kin increasingly took for granted at home. Stoical souls in Britain refused to see it as a defeat in any real sense. 'Tho' we have not been conquerors,' said John Andrews, 'we yet remain unconquered.' But the plain fact was that the war *had* been lost, and lost catastrophically.

Lost, too, was an idea of what the empire was like. Henceforth the belief that it was something like an extended family would not be adequate. The second incarnation of empire was a much more diverse place and it would require a different style of government and a different sense of what it was for.

On the afternoon of 21 August 1770, a small party of sailors ran their boat ashore on the beach of a largely barren island off the north coast of what we now call Australia. From a distance, they had spotted a group of naked brown men on the shore, most of them carrying spears and one with a bow and arrow. But by the time they stepped ashore, the hunters had vanished. The *Endeavour*, the vessel from which the tender had set off, lay a short distance offshore, having bumped her way steadily up the east coast of the enormous landmass, producing the first outline maps of the great southern continent. There had been a terrifying near-catastrophe a few weeks earlier, when the man sounding the depths below the ship's keel had shouted 'Seventeen fathoms' and, before he could swing the lead again, the ship had suddenly grounded on part of what we now know as the Great Barrier Reef, tearing a hole in her bottom. The captain, James Cook, had managed to patch the boat up and was now planning a route home to Britain via the Dutch colonies in Indonesia and then around the Cape of Good Hope. Cook believed he had finally sighted a channel of clear water which bore off in the direction of the Dutch territories, but sought a higher vantage point than was available from his ship's mast. So he climbed to the top of a hill and spied out the sea. It seemed to offer the passage to the north-west that he was looking for. And then, just before re-embarking, Cook's men raised a pole, ran up a flag and claimed for their king the coastline of this vast new land 'together with all the bays, harbours, rivers and islands situate upon the said coast'. Three volleys of small-arms fire and three answering volleys from the ship rang across the wilderness. Then, keen to catch the tide, the sailors clambered into their boat and pulled for the mother-ship. In their little impromptu ceremony they had effectively added a continent to the British Empire. Not that they knew quite that, for Cook gave the place no name, and most of the rest of the landmass was still to be mapped. What is remarkable is how casually it all happened. Cook himself merely noted in his journal that he had already 'in the name of His Majesty taken possession of several places upon this coast'. Some of those who took part in the flag-planting didn't even bother to mention it in their records of the journey.

James Cook belongs to the cadre of modestly born, determined individuals who were to carve out imperial possessions across the world, a man you could tell to do a job and be confident that he would carry it out, even if it cost him his life – as in his case it eventually did.* He seems to have been immune even to the charms of the Polynesian women with whom so many of his crewmen contracted relationships (and to whom, all too often, they gave a dose of venereal disease). A tall figure with a small head, a farmer's complexion and a strong, beaky nose, he had been born in 1728 in a cold, two-room thatched cottage in north Yorkshire, the son of a farm labourer. By eighteen he was working on a North Sea coal-ship, and on joining the Royal Navy his exceptional navigation and charting skills earned him rapid promotion to the rank of master.

The voyages of exploration carried out under James Cook's command expressed the combination of motives which drove the new expansion of empire. Inevitably, competition with the historical enemy was part of it. When, in the 1760s, the Fellows of the Royal

---

* He was killed on a beach in Hawaii, or, as he preferred to call the place, the Sandwich Islands, after his patron the Earl of Sandwich. The Hawaiians scraped the flesh from Cook's body and burned it, distributing the bones among local chieftains. Cook's second in command eventually persuaded them to allow him to reunite the skeleton and bury it at sea.

Society heard that Paris was planning to dispatch expeditions to watch the transit of Venus across the sun (a predictable astronomical event vital for calculating the distance between the earth and the sun), they were troubled, demanding that Britain should do the same. The vessel which would carry British ambition was a one-time coal-ship, renamed the *Endeavour*. She was of no great size (a mere 106 feet long and under 30 feet wide) and was so crammed with scientific instruments that when she reached Rio de Janeiro the viceroy there found it impossible to believe that anyone would have embarked on such a dangerous expedition merely in the interests of science. Concluding that they must have some ulterior motive (he suspected spying or smuggling) he refused to allow the crew ashore. The 7,860 pounds of sauerkraut on board might have driven him to the alternative conclusion that the ship's captain was mad. That was certainly the conclusion the crew came to when Captain Cook attempted to force them to eat it.

Cook got his way by insisting that the officers eat the stuff, at which point the sailors demanded they be given the same privilege. It certainly saved some of their lives – as Cook intended – by protecting them from scurvy, the scourge of long-distance mariners.* This was an experiment with an immediate imperial application, for if British sailors could survive long journeys without becoming sick, the Royal Navy could defend territory anywhere. But the nutritional research was incidental. The main scientific purpose of the *Endeavour*'s voyage was encapsulated in Joseph Banks. Although much less well known than Captain Cook, in his way – both for what he did and for what he represented – Banks is every bit as significant a figure. In class, background and education he could hardly have stood in greater contrast. Where Cook had made his own way in the world, Banks was the son of an MP, had been educated at Eton and Oxford, was heir to a comfortable estate in Lincolnshire and was fifteen years younger than Cook. He stood over six feet tall, and oozed the confidence of

---

* The disease, whose effects included depression, lassitude, fever, diarrhoea, ulcers, acute pain in the joints, paralysing toothache and bulging eyes, was caused by a lack of vitamin C.

inherited wealth. But he shared Cook's commitment to exploring and claiming the world for the empire. (If he'd had his way Iceland would have been part of Britain.) In later life, festooned with the usual Establishment garlands of a baronetcy, public appointments and fashionable portraits, he became an enthusiastic proposer of the colonization of Australia; and it was he who supervised the shipping of plants to the new colony and he who contrived to smuggle high-quality merino sheep from Spain and thence, eventually, to Australia where they became the core of the national herd.

But his greatest contribution was in firing a popular belief in the intellectual and scientific purpose of empire. To say Banks was a devoted botanist fails quite to convey his obsession: there are plenty of stories of his being arrested for vagrancy after being discovered rolling around in hedgerows and ditches while out plant-hunting. As a student at Oxford he had paid out of his own pocket for the Cambridge professor of botany to deliver a series of lectures. He corresponded with the great Swedish 'prince of botanists' Carl Linnaeus, the father of taxonomy. More than eighty plants carry his name and he is given the credit for introducing species such as the eucalyptus and mimosa to Europe: as a result the domestic gardens of Britain bear the stamp of imperial exploration. Banks's unquenchable thirst to see, touch, weigh, measure and classify the natural world expressed the European Enlightenment's belief in science and rationality, and when talk began of an expedition to the South Seas he immediately proposed that he – and an entourage of assistants, two artists, four servants and two greyhounds – be included. The Royal Society endorsed the application of what they called 'A Gentleman of large fortune who is well versed in natural history'. The Admiralty was powerless to resist.

The two men were a formidable team. Cook was a great navigator and resolute captain, willing to enforce his beliefs in warding off scurvy by having those who refused his diet flogged: the expedition reached Tahiti without losing a single man to the disease. Apart from the 'pestiferous' flies which even ate the paint off botanical paintings as the artists worked, the island turned out to be a pleasant enough destination, populated by a gentle, sensual people whose women were unusually attractive. The Tahitians proved to have remarkable thieving skills, but the president of the Royal Society, the Earl of Morton, had advised the expedition to treat the native people they encountered kindly. In a note of guidance quite at variance with the usual depiction of brutal imperialists, he asked them 'To check the petulance of the Sailors, and restrain the wanton use of Fire Arms . . . shedding the blood of those people is a crime of the highest nature . . . They are the natural, and in the strictest sense of the word, the legal possessors of the several Regions they inhabit.' This was a comparatively easy request to heed, for the women wore few clothes and the main currency of barter seems to have been sex, which the islanders readily traded for hard-to-obtain commodities like iron: a British vessel visiting Tahiti not long before was said to have begun to fall apart as sailors levered the nails from the beams before they went ashore. On his return to England at the end of the voyage, Banks was caricatured as 'the Botanic macaroni'* who had been so seduced by the beauty of the women of this tropical paradise that he had returned to the *Endeavour* from one field trip stripped of almost all his clothes. As he explained things, it was the misfortune of the British to live in a changeable climate, where they were 'obligd to Plow, Sow, Harrow, Reap, Thrash, Grind, Knead and bake our daily bread', whereas in Tahiti, 'Love is the Chief Occupation . . . both the bodies and souls of the women are modeled into the utmost perfection for that soft science.'

(In time, this belief in what we might call the climatic theory of empire provided an apparently scientific justification for the expansion of Britain overseas: societies living in changeable, temperate weather of the kind that afflicted small islands off the coast of Europe were obliged to work hard to make the earth yield crops, which in turn created ambitions, markets, banks, law and decent government. Tropical

---

* A macaroni was a fop or dandy. As the *Oxford Magazine* had it while Banks was away at sea: 'There is indeed a kind of animal, neither male nor female, a thing of the neuter gender, lately started up amongst us. It is called a Macaroni. It talks without meaning, it smiles without pleasantry, it eats without appetite, it rides without exercise, it wenches without passion.' Apparently, the condition was caused by too much of a liking for pasta.

islands, where nature was more obliging, were obviously backward and needed to be brought to a higher level of development.)

Eventually, though, the expedition had to move on. Captain Cook had been issued with a secret set of orders from the Admiralty which he was to follow once the transit of Venus had been observed. These made clear a set of political and commercial objectives, too. From Tahiti he was to sail to explore the Great South Land believed to exist at the bottom of the world, to claim in the name of the king any new territories he came across, to make friends with any natives he encountered, and, at the end of his journey, to seal all logbooks and journals and hand them to the Admiralty. The crew were to be forbidden to talk of where they had been until given official permission to do so. This intelligence-gathering of distant parts would 'redound greatly to the Honour of this Nation as a Maritime Power, as well as to the Dignity of the Crown of Great Britain, and may tend greatly to the advancement of the Trade and Navigation thereof'. After three months in his Polynesian paradise, Cook departed to fulfil his orders. After a further three months, his ship reached the two islands of New Zealand, which he sailed around in a figure of eight, raising the flag on each and claiming them in the name of George III. Then, on 31 March 1770 he set his vessel westwards. Within a few weeks they had struck land again.

They had discovered the east coast of the world's only island continent. It would be another thirty years before Banks's protégé Matthew Flinders managed to circumnavigate what came to be called Australia, thereby demolishing the ancient myth of an enormous landmass covering the South Pole which had lain behind Cook's secret orders.* Joseph Banks's first impressions of the new continent were odd. He thought 'the countrey . . . resembled in my imagination the back of a lean Cow, covered in general with long hair'. But his ideas

---

* Flinders had been inspired to go to sea after reading *Robinson Crusoe*, which James Joyce famously took to be the great text of empire. Crusoe's transition from shipwrecked mariner to master of all he surveyed, complete with a subject people in the shape of his own black servant, had been accomplished by industry, technology, gunpowder, trade and religion. Flinders decided that 'Since neither birth nor fortune have favoured me . . . my actions shall speak to the world.'

about the place improved after Captain Cook put into a bay where the crew caught a lot of stingrays and Banks could go ashore, foraging for specimens. He returned with such an abundance of previously unrecorded leaves and flowers that Cook named the anchorage Botanist Harbour, which later became Botany Bay. Nine years later, when called before a parliamentary committee grappling with what was to be done about the bursting state of Britain's prisons, Banks advised that the continent's fertile soil, mild climate and absence of fierce wild animals made it ripe for use as a penal colony.

It was the American Declaration of Independence in 1776 which had brought the prisons issue to a head. The American colonies had long been a dumping ground for British criminals – selling offenders as labourers for the term of their sentence was a great deal cheaper than paying to accommodate them in prisons. When the colonies refused to accept any more convicts, the government simply locked them up on derelict ships moored in the Thames or off the English south coast. The hulks were clearly not a long-term solution, yet the drift of population into the growing cities and the rising cost of food ensured a steady stream of new inmates. When gangs of soldiers discharged from the army after the American war turned to crime, the need to find some alternative became urgent. There was talk of a penal colony in Africa★ – a new cargo for the first leg of the triangular trade. New Zealand was ruled out because the Maoris were said to be too fierce. Canada did not want riff-raff. Pilot-schemes for Honduras and Newfoundland failed. New South Wales, on the other hand, offered the advantage of being a very, very long way away and, as for the indigenous people, they were nomadic and would soon wander off somewhere else.

In January 1788, the first consignment of over five hundred male and nearly two hundred female felons arrived in Australia, aboard eleven vessels. The scenes that occurred when the previously segregated men and women came together after the best part of a year at

★ They would have been supervised by refugees from America who had stayed loyal to the Crown during the War of Independence and now needed another place to live.

sea may be imagined: on the first Sunday, the mission's commander, Captain Arthur Phillip, preached a sermon in which he heartily extolled the benefits of marriage. Many of the first white settlers took his advice. Over the following eighty years a further 161,000 convicts arrived in Australia.

Because he was born in the county, Captain Cook is generally included in most lists of famous Yorkshiremen. Yet his father was not English, and Cook might almost as easily stand for the new nation which was stamping itself upon the world. The British Empire was the creation of 'Britain'. But much of it was made by Scots.

A century earlier, as they watched the English accrue wealth and status from their overseas possessions, the Scots had begun to chafe at the unfairness of it all. The far edges of the Atlantic already nourished a New England. New France stretched from Canada towards the Gulf of Mexico. New Spain was governed by a viceroy in Mexico. Where was the New Scotland? Nova Scotia had not been a roaring success, King James only persuading socially ambitious Scotsmen that it was a worthwhile destination by the age-old expedient of promising honours – baronetcies in this case – for those who would export a few settlers there. Scotland – or the Edinburgh Establishment – yearned for more.

Cometh the hour, cometh William Paterson, who in 1696 persuaded the worthies of Scotland that he had just what they needed, in a plan for a 'New Caledonia' at Darien, on the thin strip of land between North and South America: from here, he claimed, the Scots would be able to trade with the Far East and so break the monopoly held by the English East India Company. Paterson had already hawked his settlement scheme around England, Holland and the Holy Roman Empire, and in each place they had seen him off. But, like a good salesman, after each reverse he refined his patter. Now he talked of the Panamanian isthmus as 'the door of the seas and the key of the universe'. 'Trade will increase trade,' he told them, 'and money will beget money, and the trading world shall need no more to want work for their hands, but will rather want hands for their work.' To a small, comparatively poor country living in the shadow of a much wealthier, mightier neighbour, this was beguiling talk: the Scots leaped at the idea and begged Paterson to take their money. According to some estimates, a fifth of the entire wealth of the country was invested in the Darien Scheme – others claim the figure was much higher. The first five ships set sail for the New World in the summer of 1698. But the unfortunate investors had reckoned without the fact that the climate in Darien was beyond filthy and soon the colonists began to die in alarming numbers. The local Indians turned out to be not much interested in buying their trinkets. The Spanish were under the impression that the whole area belonged to them, and eventually besieged the settlement of New Edinburgh. The English colonists in North America and the Caribbean refused to help supply the Scots because they did not want another fight with Spain.

Despite the dismal fate of the first settlers, a second fleet set out in late 1699, swept along on gusts of missionary fervour, acquisitiveness and national pride. This time the thousand additional settlers carried a cargo which included lots of little blue bonnets which they had been persuaded that local tribespeople might be desperate for. They were, unsurprisingly, unable to find a market for them in the jungle. The settlers' predicament was not made any more comfortable by three earnest ministers accompanying the expedition, who were soon wandering the jungle wailing to the settlers that 'We're all *doomed*.' The settlers' sins – or their vanity, unpreparedness or sheer bad luck – had found them out. The Darien Scheme was a disaster. Henceforth – apart from the occasional privateer – the Scots' only choice was to throw in their lot with the English.

The massive debt which now hung around the necks of so many eminent Scots was certainly one of the reasons for the 1707 Act of Union, which merged the governments of England and Scotland: apart from the relief of their debts, the commercial opportunities were enormous – as Robert Burns put it, the country had been 'bought and sold for English gold'. In return for surrendering their independence, the Scots gained generous representation in the Westminster parliament, while retaining their own legal and religious settlement. The attraction of Union for the English was the elimination of a potential colonial rival and the extinction of a commercial menace. Most of all, it seemed to promise an end to hundreds of years of suspicion, hostility and periodic war. Peaceful Union in turn created the possibility of a new international identity, which found common cause in a shared commitment to stable government, the monarchy, the military and Protestantism, all of which could find a focus in the empire. Many Scots seized with both hands the opportunities which now lay open to them. As early as 1731 a Scottish director of the East India Company was writing irritably to his brother asking him to stop recommending any more men for medical positions, 'for all the East India Company ships have either Scots Surgeons or Surgeon's mates, and till some of them die I can, nor will, look out for no more, for I am made the jest of mankind, plaguing all the Societys of England with Scots Surgeons'.

The suppression of the last Jacobite rising in 1745 clinched things. Now the imperial project became increasingly attractive also to Stuart families, who needed somehow to make up the wealth confiscated by a vindictive government in London. In Sir Walter Scott's words, India became Scotland's 'corn chest . . . where we poor gentry must send our youngest sons as we send our black cattle to the south'. For educated but indigent Scots, the empire was a blessing, and in the last quarter of the eighteenth century no one did more to promote their interests than the Edinburgh-born Tory minister and 'uncrowned king of Scotland' Henry Dundas. In Gillray's famous cartoon he stands, kilted, with one foot in London and the other in India, as fleets of merchant ships pass between his legs. Three of his brothers made the journey to the subcontinent, and two of them never returned. But India was much more than a family business: so great was Dundas's more general patronage that the wit Sydney Smith observed that 'as long as he is in office, the Scotch may beget younger sons with the most perfect impunity. He sends them by loads to the East Indies and all over the world.'

A pattern had been set. In the two centuries following the Union, Scotland provided governors, governors general, residents, district commissioners and agents. In the wildernesses of northern Canada the Hudson's Bay Company was represented by Orcadians. Kilted Highlanders were glorified for their roles in the Indian Mutiny and the Boer War. Tropical newspaper offices were presided over by men with soft Highland accents. Lowland doctors treated tropical sicknesses. Scots built enormous trading companies, created botanical gardens, commanded merchant vessels. There were Scottish farmers, shopkeepers, lawyers and teachers everywhere. 'We want more Scots. Give us Scots. Give us the whole population of Glasgow,' screamed the mayor of Sandhurst, South Australia. Glasgow itself was soon calling itself 'The Second City of the Empire', the Clyde was an imperial artery, and when a Glasgow company met the military's request for the world's first instant coffee (Camp Coffee – it had a large dose of chicory mixed in) its label showed a Sikh bearer waiting on a kilted Gordon Highlander. David Livingstone was a Scotsman and there were many, many more where he came from. Scottish engineers built roads and railways, bridges and barracks, everywhere.★ There were Highland Games in Alberta and Burns Nights in Singapore. 'Thank God we're all Scots here,' remarked Sir George Mackenzie, managing director of the Imperial British East Africa Company. Let the Edinburgh-born doctor Leander Starr Jameson, the reckless leader of the Boer War shambles that was the Jameson Raid, be the standard bearer for these empire-builders. He was the inspiration for Kipling's 'If'. A century on, it is still regularly voted the nation's favourite poem.

While Britain was making an empire, an empire was making Britain.

★ Montgomery Scott – the wonder-working 'Scotty' of the *Starship Enterprise* – stands for all of them. A small plaque inside the town museum in Linlithgow marks his supposed birthplace. The fact that Scotty will not be born for a couple of centuries is neither here nor there: there is a well-established pattern of Scotsmen going where no man has gone before.

CHAPTER THREE

'Tribute from the Red Barbarians'

By the late eighteenth century Britain was looking like a real world power. The American colonies might have been lost, but a sprightly arrogance had taken root – as the playwright Oliver Goldsmith had put it, the country 'is stronger, fighting by herself and for herself than if half Europe were her allies'. Britain had the strongest navy afloat and some of the world's most brilliant scientists.* The new

---

* A marriage consummated at home in the construction of the new Somerset House, the magnificent neo-classical building erected in the heart of London to allay an anxiety that the capital had too few grand edifices for Britain's swelling status. The close relationship between state and learning was reflected in its occupants: the navy had the west wing, various tax and supply offices had other parts, and their neighbours included the Royal Society, the Royal Academy and the Society of Antiquaries.

nation was fast mechanizing the manufacturing that could transform raw materials from abroad into finished products, and was well embarked upon the urbanization that would make it the first country in which the majority of citizens lived in towns and cities. Unlike many continental European countries, its politics were reasonably settled, while France was swept by revolution and then by tyranny, from which emerged a brilliant despot who styled himself 'emperor'. With the final defeat of Napoleon in 1815 Britain could turn its attention away from the continent again and look to the rest of the world. Within four years Stamford Raffles had founded Singapore, within ten years the British had invaded Burma, within twenty years there were colonies in Western Australia and the Falkland Islands, within thirty more colonies in Aden, New Zealand, Hong Kong and Natal. Continental European nations were racked by further revolutions, notably in 1848. By contrast, many of Wellington's generals went on to become colonial governors.

The possession of an empire was, though, never a uniquely British activity. Portugal and Spain had already taken territory in the Americas and Africa, and the Dutch had done so in southern Africa, South America and the Indies. The Ottoman Empire ran across north Africa, up through the Middle East and back across the Balkans, and at one point had laid siege to Vienna. The French still ruled land in the Caribbean, Africa, the Indian Ocean. At one time or another the Danes held colonies in the north Atlantic, Africa, the Caribbean and India. Sweden had possessions in Africa and the Caribbean and for a while ran a slave trade. The Russians held land in North America into the last third of the nineteenth century and still rule over resentful people scattered across nine time zones. 'Owning' colonies was considered a mark of significance, as the miserable Belgian presence in Africa testified: Belgium was created only in 1830, and yet by the turn of the twentieth century its king had his own slave state in the Congo. The newly unified nation of Italy also demanded its own 'empire', an ambition which reached its strutting apotheosis when the king had himself declared emperor of Abyssinia in 1936. Germany, another late entrant to the competition to enhance yourself by abasing others, established itself in Africa and the south Pacific.

The motives for seizing land were complex – sometimes commercial, sometimes military, to satisfy greed or scientific curiosity, to spread religion, to free and to oppress, to procure labour and to dump it, for strategic security and because governments had been bounced into it. But, as we have noted, the single most powerful incentive to travel and colonize was money.

In the middle years of the sixteenth century it had been commonly believed in Venice that if an Englishman could not get enough currants to eat at Christmas-time he would kill himself. This supposedly uncontrollable appetite for dried-up grape skins and other Italian delicacies offered a tidy living to anyone with the means to carry them from the Mediterranean to the North Sea. In 1583, a group of London merchants negotiated a formal arrangement to exclude competition and give themselves a monopoly in the business. The Venice Company became one of the first of the chartered companies that did so much to create the British Empire and to set a model for modern capitalism. In so doing, they disproved the subsequent Victorian claim that 'trade follows the flag' – the suggestion that, once red-coated British soldiers had subdued some foreign land, British merchants created a market. In fact, it was very often the other way around. Many of the architects of imperial progress sat not in parliament, the Admiralty or the War Office but in the nation's counting houses, and governments lived with the consequences of their decisions. The empire followed no organizing template: when the flag was planted it was often simply because some sharp-elbowed businessman had got there before anyone else. Untroubled by much political interference from home, those who were willing to take risks became not merely wealthy but immensely powerful. The illegitimate Highlander George Simpson, for example – the mid-nineteenth-century head of the Hudson's Bay Company who came to be known as 'the birchbark emperor' – was certainly the most powerful man in Canada and even travelled to St Petersburg to try to persuade the Russians to lease him Alaska.

Chartered companies were not unique to Britain – there were French, Dutch, Danish, Russian, Portuguese, German and Swedish equivalents – and nor was England the first country to develop them (that distinction is claimed by a Swedish mining company). But they indisputably laid many of the foundations of the British Empire, and in some places did much more. The first phase of Britain's foreign empire was driven by capitalism, spread by sea and largely confined to those places which could be controlled from the sea.* There were advantages for governments in leaving so much of the initiative with private enterprise. Chartered companies offered the Crown influence without the necessity of affluence. When Queen Elizabeth I sold exclusive rights to trade with 'the Great Turk' to a group of business-men she received an assured payment each year. Since the contract also required the 'Turkey Merchants' to promote English interests, she gained a rudimentary diplomatic service on the eastern shores of the Mediterranean as well. The charter of the Muscovy Company committed it to trade in 'Regions, Dominions, Islands and places unknown', and in trying to find a route to 'Cathay' by a north-east passage above the landmass of Europe the crew of one of its first fleets, made up of three little vessels, froze to death off Lapland.† The fur trappers and traders of the Hudson's Bay Company became the largest landowners in the world.‡ The Virginia Company 'owned' much of the Atlantic coast of North America and, since making a return on investment required the cultivation of cash crops, became licensed to 'plant' settlements there. On the other side of the ocean, the Royal African Company cultivated almost nothing, but enjoyed a monopoly on the west African slave trade for a period and for fifty

---

* The contrast is with empires like the Russian or Austro-Hungarian, or even, lat-terly, the absurd Italian Empire, which were essentially made by armies rather than navies.

† Macabre tales of how all the officers of the *Bona Esperanza* had been found as blocks of ice still seated around a table on board turned out to be the work of an imaginative reporter: they had actually been discovered lying on a beach. Aston-ishing stories of remote places became a staple of the imperial experience.

‡ Its territory of Rupert's Land comprised about 15 per cent of the entire acreage of North America, so when the Dominion of Canada was formed, the company was, by a long margin, the biggest private landowner. Nowadays its intrepid his-tory is reduced to a chain of department stores selling, among much else, its distinctive green, red, yellow and blue colours knitted into hats, scarves and teddy-bear jackets.

years supplied the Royal Mint with gold (thereby coining 'the guinea').

They were not called 'merchant venturers' for nothing: anyone who placed their faith in these companies took a risk that they might never see their money again. The distances were so vast and communications so slow that they might have to wait a year or more before they knew whether they had made any profit at all. But a risk divided is a risk reduced and the companies minimized the danger to investors by selling shares in their ventures, and then offering the security of limited liability. In their internal organization, the companies developed the single-minded focus on profit, the effective chain of command and the incentivizing of employees that are the marks of efficient capitalism. The most famous chartered company of all, the East India Company, ended up translating a British trading and diplomatic presence into an overseas government. But it was clear from the start that what motivated 'the grandest society of merchants in the universe' (it never really did modesty) was money rather than conquest: if it was necessary to fight, it would do so, but colonies were merely a means to an end. The Company was obliged to raise an army to defend its interests, and created dockyards in order to build ships, but its soldiers' job was to secure trade and the ships' purpose was to carry cargo home to Britain. And for those with the nerve to seize opportunity, the rewards could be lavish. Robert Clive arrived in India in 1744 as a clerk. He returned from Bengal to England nine years later with the means to buy a country estate. A further five-year stint in India turned him into one of the richest men in Britain. (The influx of such East India Company 'nabobs' who had amassed astronomical fortunes by trade, pillage and intimidation set off a characteristically British bout of class anxiety. 'What is England now?' worried Horace Walpole. 'A sink of Indian wealth, filled by nabobs . . . A country overrun by horse-races! A gaming, robbing, wrangling, railing nation without principle, genius, character or allies.')

On 26 September 1792 three ships left the sheltered anchorage between the coast of Hampshire and the Isle of Wight for a very long voyage. The vessels carried 700 men, including artists, botanists, diplomats, scientists and soldiers, accompanied by a gaggle of priests. It would be a year before they achieved the object of their journey, a meeting with the emperor of China, Qianlong, who turned out to be a surprisingly sprightly eighty-three-year-old.

The mission, under the leadership of Viscount Macartney, hoped to solve an increasingly pressing problem. The British merchant-venturers had done very nicely out of the chartered-company system. But there was a glaring difficulty with China, for whose products, such as silk and porcelain, Europe had developed a healthy appetite. Most especially, the British had discovered an apparently unquenchable thirst for tea – by the time of Macartney's mission, they were importing more than 15 million pounds of Chinese tea every year. Joseph Banks had also given Macartney – himself a keen botanist – detailed instructions on which oriental specimens to collect for the Royal Botanic Gardens at Kew. But what British products could the Chinese be persuaded to buy in return? The trade delegation planned to show the Chinese emperor what his country was missing. To help, they had brought along all sorts of trinkets and gizmos they thought might amuse the old man – a small planetarium, scientific instruments, examples of Birmingham metalware and pieces of Wedgwood pottery.

After a year of travelling, the British were looking rather shabby. They were so exhausted and flea-bitten that when the Chinese crowds saw them, they fell about laughing. As Lord Macartney's valet put it later, the delegation bore 'greater resemblance to the sight provided by the removal of paupers to their parishes in England than the expected dignity of the representative of a great and powerful monarch'. The visitors had also underestimated the country they were visiting, for Imperial China considered itself the centre of the world and superior to all other civilizations. The dignity of the viscount's party was not enhanced when Chinese officials took one look at their cargo and on the emperor's orders demanded that retinue and baggage be transferred to thirty-seven Chinese junks before being allowed to proceed upriver towards the city of Jehol – the emperor's summer retreat. For the avoidance of doubt a sign was nailed to one of the masts. It read 'Tribute from the Red Barbarians'.

Protocol was a tricky question. Naturally, when the delegation finally reached the emperor's palace, they tried to look their best. Lord Macartney overlaid a velvet suit of spotted purple with the bright-red mantle of a Knight of the Bath. His secretary, Sir George Staunton, dusted off the robes he had worn when given an honorary doctorate by Oxford University. Thus arrayed, they made their way towards the emperor, their dignity not much improved when they had to fight their way to their early-morning audience in the Garden of Ten Thousand Trees through wandering hordes of dogs, pigs and cows. At 7.00 a.m. the emperor arrived, borne on a chair by sixteen men dressed in gold, his ministers and advisers trotting behind. The leader of the visiting yahoos was admitted to The Presence, together with his secretary and page. How should they acknowledge the dignity of the ruler of the world? Visitors to the celestial throne were normally glad to fall to their knees and touch their foreheads to the ground in a kowtow. Macartney had explained to the Chinese officials beforehand that unfortunately he really wouldn't be able to manage this, since he only went down on one knee even in front of his own king, George III. Someone suggested a compromise – perhaps the portrait of King George III the barbarians had brought with them could be hung on the wall behind the throne so that he could convince himself that he was kowtowing to his own king? Still Macartney refused to go for anything more than a one-knee bow, and the Chinese did not care for his offer to kiss the emperor's hand. The next difficulty was that the only British person who spoke much Chinese was Lord Macartney's twelve-year-old page, a feat which impressed the emperor, but did not make for easy conversations – all exchanges were therefore conducted through two priests brought from Italy. As they spoke little or no English, negotiations were translated first into Latin and then into Chinese. This cumbersome arrangement did not inhibit what modern diplomats would call a free and frank exchange of views when the viscount laid out the objects he had brought with him. He offered the emperor a pair of watches and a letter from George III. The emperor responded with gifts of ceremonial sceptres and a rebuff. For it was soon clear that whatever the odd-looking visitors had brought, China did not need. As the emperor explained to the British king, in a letter of masterly disdain, the two countries were utterly different in their customs, 'and even were your envoy competent to acquire some rudiments of them, he could not transplant them to your barbarous land'. As for the finest products of British industry, 'Strange and costly objects do not interest me. As your ambassador can see for himself, we possess all things. I set no value on objects strange or ingenious and have no use for your country's manufactures.'

This was as comprehensive a failure as a trade mission could accomplish, even though when they returned to England the delegation did their best to belittle China: Macartney talked of it as a 'tyranny of a handful of tartars over more than three hundred million of Chinese', while his valet regaled the reading public with news that the Chinese ate the fleas they picked off their clothes and his comptroller reported that 'there is not a water closet, nor a decent place of retirement in all China'. It was he, too, who provided the most resonant epitaph on the trade mission: 'We entered Peking like paupers; we remained in it like prisoners; and we quitted it like vagrants.' Macartney's tedious and expensive journey had accomplished nothing. Yet the need to find something the Chinese might be prepared to buy became ever more pressing, as the British succumbed more and more to that most harmless of vices, drinking tea, whose fashionability is said to have been established by Charles II's wife, Catherine of Braganza, and which was soon being described as a 'necessity' of life. The trade was wonderful business for what an anonymous pamphlet called 'the lordly grocers of Leadenhall Street', where the East India Company had its imposing headquarters.* The Company, meanwhile, knew it certainly had one commodity it could sell to the Chinese in exchange.

---

* The headquarters was demolished, but contemporary accounts depict a splendid building, inside which a white marble statue showed Britannia 'seated on a globe by the sea-shore, receiving homage from three female figures, intended for Asia, Africa, and India. Asia offers spices with her right hand, and with her left leads a camel; India presents a large box of jewels, which she holds half open; and Africa rests her hand upon the head of a lion. The Thames, as a river-god, stands upon the shore, a labourer appears cording a large bale of merchandise, and ships are sailing in the distance' (Knight, ed., *London*, vol. V, pp. 61–2).

In the middle of the nineteenth century the Red Barbarians returned, and this time they came not with trinkets but with warships.

Because in a factory at Ghazipur the East India Company was refining massive quantities of opium.★ It was not a commodity either introduced or invented by the British, as Mughal emperors of India had been exporting the drug for years (and some had acquired something of a taste for it themselves). Like much else in the commercial development of the subcontinent, opium now became the subject of an East India Company monopoly. It was not that the Company was unaware of its disabling, addictive properties for its Governor General in Bengal, Warren Hastings, had declared that the drug was 'not a necessity of life but a pernicious article of luxury, which ought not to be permitted'. Unfortunately, the sentence did not end there, but continued with the clause 'but for the purpose of foreign commerce only'. Opium may have been pernicious, but it was also precious. The main export market was in China.

The British were not the first foreigners to run drugs into China – the Arabs had been there before them, and both Dutch and French trading companies had developed lucrative businesses in the seventeenth century. What was different about the British was the scale and ruthlessness of the trade. By the middle of the 1830s over 30,000 cases of opium – each about the size of a small chest of drawers – were being smuggled into China each year. To protect the good name of those involved, the British deployed the usual subterfuges of illicit trades. Rather than being sold directly, the drug was first passed on to middlemen, some of whom might in other circumstances have passed as elders of the kirk. The most prominent of these were a couple of Scotsmen, William Jardine, a former ship's surgeon, and James Matheson, the grandson of a Highland minister. The company the

★ The factory – the world's largest legal opium facility – still exists, exporting most of its production to western pharmaceutical companies. The management does not encourage visitors, but those who have managed to get inside talk of a serious monkey problem. Fortunately the creatures do not impede the production process very much because they're addicted to opium and spend most of the day lying around.

two men founded became one of the greatest imperial trading houses, whose gleaming Hong Kong headquarters testifies to its continuing commercial success, although you will search the history section of its website in vain for an account of the company's period as drug-runners.* At the time, neither of the two men professed the slightest ethical anxiety about what they were doing. Jardine declared that investing in opium was 'the safest and most gentlemanly speculation that I am aware of'. Matheson considered the trade 'morally equivalent' to the sale of brandy or champagne in Britain.

In 1836, however, the Chinese emperor issued an order that, unlike champagne, opium was no longer to be either imported or used in China. The traders were not especially worried, since they had had little difficulty in finding corrupt officials willing, for a price, to turn a blind eye. But this occasion proved to be different. In March 1839 a new, incorruptible official was appointed to enforce the emperor's will. Apart from destroying existing stocks of the drug, Lin Zexu tried to appeal to Queen Victoria's better nature by letter. In the name of humanity he begged her to halt a trade which was enslaving so many of his countrymen and warned her that if the British did not stop shipping opium from India, he would ensure it was destroyed on arrival in China. His letter never reached the queen, who anyway did not possess the powers which the Chinese emperor took for granted. Soon the official had laid siege to the warehouses, or 'factories', in which the foreigners stored their drugs in Canton. Once the dealers had surrendered their opium, he expelled them from China. Twenty thousand cases of opium were then crushed, shovelled into pits or dissolved in the sea.

Now the only way for the British traders to return to China was by force. Their problem was that not everyone shared their dewy-eyed enthusiasm for drug-dealing. Matheson was especially worried about the attitude of the Church and wrote to William Jardine suggesting

---

* The closest acknowledgement is a single sentence: 'Reflective of the times in which it traded, the Group has led the way in many businesses and has helped bring prosperity to the region,' which must have taken the corporate public-relations department a good few meetings to compose.

that they line up some congenial journalists to make their case in the newspapers. Opposition to the trade was not without its own powerful voices. The young MP William Gladstone (who was to see the consequences of drug dependency for himself when his troubled sister, Helen, became addicted) declared that 'a war more unjust in its origin, a war calculated in its progress to cover this country with a permanent disgrace, I do not know and I have not read of'. But the traders had friends in high places, while with serpentine casuistry Jardine argued that the problem of the drug business lay not with suppliers but with buyers, claiming that once the British had sold the product to the Chinese intermediaries who would ferry it ashore it ceased to be their responsibility. The Foreign Secretary, Lord Palmerston, was soon making a similar case in his speeches. While the British government did not for a moment dispute the right of the Chinese to determine what did or did not come into their country, it simply could not stand idle when they tried to stop British citizens earning an honest living.

By June 1840, British ships and troops were arriving off the coast of China. (The traders seized the opportunity to send their own vessels, too, laden with opium.) The Chinese fatally underestimated the technological superiority of the British forces. The governor of the province at the mouth of the Yangtze River sent the emperor the reassuring news that it would be deadly for the British to put soldiers ashore, since their legs were so stiff and their trousers so tight they could not get up if they fell over. His strategic advice also included the judgement that the British would be at a serious disadvantage because they had insufficient bows and arrows. In the event, the British naval force included a weapon never seen in combat before. The *Nemesis*, an iron-clad, steam-powered, paddle-driven gunboat of 184 feet, had been built in Liverpool and could make short work of the Chinese junks. It was commanded by a remarkably skilled captain and its draught was shallow enough to allow the invaders to navigate the rivers. Thousands more troops followed, and then more ships, including additional steam-driven gunboats. By the late summer of 1842, the British controlled the Yangtze, threatening Nanking and, beyond it, the imperial capital. The Chinese sued for peace.

The emperor's representative appealed to the British. 'Multitudes of our Chinese subjects consume it [opium], wasting their property and destroying their lives. How is it possible for us to refrain from forbidding our people to use it?' he asked the British negotiator, Sir Henry Pottinger. But Pottinger had written orders and would not be budged. He also presented a massive bill for compensation due to the traders. On 17 August 1842, the emperor consented to the Treaty of Nanking, allowing the British a permanent presence at ports from Canton to Shanghai, agreeing to pay reparations and ceding Hong Kong to Britain as a colony. China was now safe for British drug traders. Unsurprisingly, when news of the outcome of the First Opium War reached London, it did not meet with universal celebration. In an editorial, *The Times* suggested that it ought to be Britain paying some reparation to China for a war 'which could never have arisen had we not been guilty of this national crime'. Gladstone worried about the judgement God would pass on the nation. A change of government brought about a bizarre state of affairs when in January the following year Palmerston's successor as foreign secretary, Lord Aberdeen, instructed Pottinger that the drug smugglers were to get no official protection. Pottinger shrugged his shoulders, passed on the information to Jardine, Matheson and the others and looked the other way.

Chinese resentment at the unfair conditions imposed by the Treaty of Nanking festered for decades,* and fourteen years later erupted into war again, after which the British carried on selling opium for the rest of the century. Periodically British statesmen wondered whether China as a whole might be added to the empire. It was decided that nothing much would be gained by taking on the responsibility – Britain was really interested only in the money to be

* And continues to fester. Residents of Hong Kong enjoy greater freedom and prosperity than the vast majority of their mainland Chinese counterparts. But the official history of the place, and the displays at the Hong Kong Museum, bristle with resentment. A British trade delegation to China in November 2010 triggered a minor diplomatic spat when they wore red paper poppies in memory of British war dead, without realizing that poppies on British lapels were unlikely to inspire affection.

made by trading with the country, and running India was quite enough of a headache already. 'We have as much empire as the nation can carry,' as the lofty Liberal Sir W. Vernon Harcourt put it in 1892. By then, the two taipans, Jardine and Matheson, were long dead, having returned to Britain and acquired Highland estates, seats in parliament and, in Matheson's case, a baronetcy.*

As the anxieties expressed over the opium trade testify, the hard-faced capitalism which drove much imperial expansion was offset by an increasing sense that empire ought to be about some higher function. Many came genuinely to believe that the British could do good in the world. The conviction had been bolstered when the country at last tackled the injustice which lay behind much of its earlier wealth. For, fifty years earlier, the country had become the first European nation to abandon slavery. This bold act was to lay the foundations of the belief that building the British Empire had a higher moral purpose.

The enslavement of Africans had corrupted just about everything – almost the only section of British society which could be said to have entirely clean hands was the Society of Friends (the Quakers), whose experience of persecution made them more than willing to empathize with fellow human beings upon whom God's light shone as readily as it did on white men. For the rest of late eighteenth-century Britain, from the customers of the coffeehouses to the king's closest advisers, slavery was an ugly fact – conveniently distant. Among those who were obliged to think about the practice, a wilful blindness prevailed: as one member of parliament wrote, slavery was 'not an amiable trade', but 'neither was the trade of a butcher an amiable trade, and yet a mutton chop was, nevertheless, a very good thing'. To be sure, there must have been some who shared Dr Johnson's belief that no man is by nature the property of another. (He is said once to have raised his glass in Oxford and proposed

---

* James Matheson carried his shameless enthusiasm for the opium trade to the grave. When he died in the south of France in 1878 (aged eighty-two) his body was returned to the Highlands and interred in a huge grey-stone mausoleum at Lairg, on the banks of Loch Shin. Beneath eight Corinthian columns decorated with what look very like carved opium-poppy seed-heads, a memorial commemorates the 'high repute' of his trading house.

a toast 'to the next insurrection of negroes in the West Indies'.) But they were either mute or largely ignored.

That parliament was eventually jolted out of its complacency is testimony to the power of campaigns and campaigners to change the world, a reflection of an innate commitment to decency. The role of religion in this enormous transformation cannot be exaggerated. Thomas Clarkson had been intended for a career in the Church when, thinking about the slave trade, he decided that 'it was time some person should see these calamities to their end'. As the eighteenth century ended and the nineteenth began, his marathon journeys across the land took the anti-slaving message to uncountable thousands, and everywhere he went – even in cities where he expected to be rebuffed – he found support. Ordinary citizens might appear powerless to change the law, but they had realized that they could change their own behaviour. 'There was no town through which I passed in which there was not some individual who had left off the use of sugar,' he recorded. William Wilberforce's tireless efforts in parliament to have the trade made illegal were grounded in his evangelical beliefs, but the individuals trying to justify slavery were powerful and well heeled and it cannot have been easy. Even the royal family defended the slave trade, with the Duke of Clarence (who, in 1830, became King William IV) calling the abolitionists 'either fanatics or heretics'. Yet nothing drives action like a sense of mission, and the campaign against what the poet Robert Southey called 'the blood-sweetened beverage' took root across the land. In Birmingham pamphlets argued that those who used the products of slavery were 'as guilty of flagellation and murder as those actually employed in that abominable trade'. In Leicester, Elizabeth Heyrick, the widow of a young cavalry officer, organized a consumer boycott which within a year had persuaded a quarter of the town to lay off sugar. It was, as Victor Hugo might have put it later, an idea whose time had come, greater than the tread of mighty armies.

Oddly, anti-French hostility helped the abolitionists' moral argument. Their supporters in parliament claimed it stood in heroic contrast to the way things were done across the Channel. The 1807 decision to ban the transport of slaves in British ships provided proof of the ethical superiority of the country's population. 'The people of England are not going to consent that there should be carried out in their name, a system of blood, rapine, robbery and murder,' thundered Sir Samuel Romilly. On the other hand, he could not resist pointing out that the historic enemy was now being led by a Corsican tyrant. The French had also enslaved hundreds of thousands to work their Caribbean sugar plantations, and Romilly invited MPs to look into Napoleon's conscience as he lay in bed, to 'contemplate the anguish with which his solitude must be tortured by the recollection of the blood he has spilt, and the oppressions he has committed' in the course of his ruthless climb to supreme power in France. He went on to imagine the feelings which accompanied his friend Wilberforce to bed after the vote to ban the slave trade: 'how much more enviable his lot, in the consciousness of having preserved so many millions of his fellow-creatures, than that of the man, with whom I have compared him, on a Throne to which he has waded through slaughter and oppression'.

There was no material advantage to be gained by abolishing slavery, no territory to be conquered by the act, no gain either tactical or strategic. It was a decision taken for purely altruistic reasons, as noble as participation in the slave trade was contemptible. The Royal Navy was now ordered to begin anti-slavery patrols off the coast and up the rivers of tropical west Africa, a thankless task with few prospects of promotion and every chance of catching a nasty disease. In the first fifty years of these patrols, British citizens freed 150,000 men, women and children considered by others to be citizens of nowhere. And, apart from being a good thing in itself, it began to change the way many of the British saw their role in the world. Their unsuccessful attempt to retain the colonies in North America had cast them in the role of deniers of liberty. The abolition of slavery could attest to an idea of the British as champions of freedom. Hostility to slavery did not abate in the years which followed. When the Foreign Secretary put his signature to the Treaty of Paris in 1814, allowing the French to continue trading in slaves for a further five years, three-quarters of a million people put their own to a petition of protest.

The commercial impulse which drove traders to seek new markets

and to enforce their demand to trade at the point of a gun if necessary
was as powerful as ever. But the moral fervour which infused the campaign to abolish the slave trade bestowed another sense of purpose on
British imperialism. The country had demonstrated its willingness to
fight the good fight at home, and now it would do the same in the rest
of the world. The campaign against slavery would last well into the
closing decades of the nineteenth century, as the great public support
for David Livingstone's mission to root out Arab slave traders in
Africa demonstrated. The moral conundrum of empire – how could
we deny others the freedom we demanded for ourselves? – now had
an answer. It might seem paradoxical to associate colonizers with freedom, but in this case the two were deeply connected. Before long, the
British were apostles for a new gospel in which Christianity and commerce were said to be natural bedfellows.

CHAPTER FOUR

'I stand astonished at my own moderation'
Robert Clive, 1773

On the map, the second edition of the empire – the phase which the world considers 'the' British Empire – was a very different thing from what had gone before. In the middle of the seventeenth century the empire, such as it was, lay at the fringes of the Atlantic. Two hundred years later, it was scattered across the world, and the British Foreign Secretary, Lord Palmerston, could boast that 'a British subject, in whatever land he may be, shall feel confident that the watchful eye and the strong arm of England will protect him against injustice and wrong'. The Atlantic empire did not become a worldwide empire according to some great plan but by the opportunism of businessmen, the ambition of adventurers, the self-confidence of the military, a gathering sense of national purpose and a series of accidents. The place where this development of imperial purpose was most observable was in the grandest of all the imperial possessions, India.

Here, in the bustle of its massive population, the complexity of its cultures, the overwhelming nature of its heat, dust and smells, the strangeness of its holy men, was a world as different from a damp, ordered north Atlantic island as could be imagined. 'There is so much of everything!' was the authentically awestruck exclamation of one Englishwoman when she disembarked in Bombay.

> I had never seen so many people; a mixture of brown faces, and dirty white garments and spotless uniforms, and helmets, mixed up with oxen, mangy dogs, crows, and beggars, and driving through narrow streets between tall colour-washed houses, with vivid trees jammed between them, jingling victorias and bullock carts round you, and parrots shooting across the road over your head, black crows squawking. People. People. People. And your frock stuck to your shoulders.

Preventing other powers getting their hands on this bustling, unfathomable land determined the decisions of governments in the grandest buildings in London and cost the blood of young men in the sands of Afghanistan. It necessitated the raising of regiments, the acquisition of other colonies and the deployment of navies. In the heyday of imperial India men of unimaginable wealth with brown skins and Oxford drawls were manipulated by white-skinned functionaries on official salaries. The men who administered India considered themselves an elite and the most elite of all was the viceroy, who represented the Crown and acted like royalty himself. When India became independent in August 1947, the empire lost four out of five of its citizens and freedom beckoned for all the others: without India, the empire was no more than a sounding gong.

The British had arrived in the east for much the same reason as other Europeans: they saw a chance to make money. In 1616 Sir Thomas Roe had presented himself to the Mughal emperor to request trading rights. He stayed at the emperor's court for three years, ingratiating himself with presents including an English coach, swords, hats, mastiffs and liberal quantities of alcohol, which the notionally Muslim emperor enjoyed very much indeed. Roe did not anticipate the creation of a massive British colony: having looked at the way the existing Dutch and Portuguese trading missions operated, he concluded that it was a mistake to seek a land empire. 'Let this be received as a rule that if you will profit, seek it at sea, and in quiet trade,' he told the East India Company.

It is easy enough to imagine the seductive impression Mughal India must have made upon foreign visitors, for it was almost certainly the richest empire in the world at the time. Inside the vast Red Fort in Delhi (constructed a few years after Roe's departure) cool water in pools set into the floor reflected gold and silvered ceilings. The walls were decorated with delicate mosaics and fountains played in the gardens. At the fort's heart was a marble audience chamber where the emperor sat on a gem-encrusted peacock throne; above his head, picked out in gold on the ceiling, were the words 'If there be paradise on earth, it is this, it is this.' India was a place where anyone willing to take a few risks might make immense sums of money very quickly, as the experience of Thomas Pitt, the son of a West Country vicar, showed. He had first set himself up at Balasore in the Bay of Bengal as a dealer in sugar and horses in 1673, after jumping ship. His business career culminated in his purchase of a 410-carat diamond ('the unparalleled jewel of the world') which was smuggled to Europe and finally sold for many times its original price to become part of the French Crown Jewels. 'Diamond' Pitt had by then acquired the usual perquisites of wealth – English country estates and a seat in the House of Commons. His grandson and great-grandson both became prime minister. 'Get rich quick' might have been the recruiting slogan for the East India Company, which by the early eighteenth century had established four trading stations in forts at Surat, Madras, Bombay and Calcutta.

The man who did more than anyone else to transform the British presence in India into something distinctly imperial was Robert Clive. He had never looked likely to follow his father into the law – too headstrong, too unstable, too daredevil. Local legends in his home town of Market Drayton, Shropshire, talked of his climbing the local church tower and sitting there atop a gargoyle, of protection rackets in which his gang threatened to smash the windows of merchants who refused to pay up. There was certainly plenty of fighting. His family must have let out something of a sigh of relief when at the age of seventeen he took ship to become a clerk with the East India Company. The story of his rise from clerk to colonel, tearaway to tycoon, is the story of the British transition from trade to empire. When Robert Clive arrived at the Company's Fort St George in Madras in June 1744 to begin work as a 'writer', the British presence in India was still confined to a handful of forts on the coast, of which St George was the oldest, with high walls and barracks and spired church within. The French were established in a similar toehold, along the coast at Pondicherry. Clive was ill suited to life as a clerk and prone to depression: he tried to shoot himself and was saved only because his pistol failed to fire. Twice. Then, in September 1746, a French warship appeared off the coast and with minimum inconvenience captured St George. Clive escaped and by three days of night marching reached Fort St David,* the next British base, 50 miles away. Here Clive enlisted as a soldier. It was the making of him, his reputation secured when he led the defence of Arcot in 1751 against a vastly greater Indian and French force, including cavalry, infantry, elephants and artillery. He returned to England 'the Conqueror of the Indies' and a national hero. His magnificent suits of clothes (including the full costume of an Indian prince) made little dent in the £40,000 he had piled up from his management of the army's supplies – there was plenty left over to pay off his parents' mortgage, and to buy a London townhouse and a seat in parliament. Then, in 1755, the East India Company offered him the post of governor of Fort St David. It was too enticing to refuse.

Quite apart from the immense plunder to be had in India, there was an established system of taxes to be milked by the Company: it

---

* The fort and all surrounding land within the range of a shell (local villages are still occasionally referred to as 'cannonball villages') had been bought by the Company from the local Maratha king. It was renamed St David on the orders of the Governor, Elihu Yale – whose benefactions would later be memorialized in the name of the New England university. In fact, a more significant donor to that institution was Yale's friend Jeremiah Dummer, but fortunately for students they did not choose to name the place after him.

was the good fortune of the British traders to be at their boldest in India when the Mughal Empire, which had dominated much of the subcontinent since the early sixteenth century, was losing its grip.* In Bengal, the wealthiest part of India, the Company had, for example, achieved more or less complete control of the export of silk and sugar, cotton and jute, salt and saltpetre by the middle of the eighteenth century. But then in 1756 the old nawab died and was succeeded by his nephew and adopted son, Siraj ud-Daula, who decided that the foreign presence was impertinent, demanded gifts from the European trading companies and, when the British refused, attacked Calcutta. There now occurred an event which would overshadow British attitudes to India for a century or more.

As Siraj ud-Daula's massive forces advanced through the city, many of the British simply took to their heels, abandoning comrades, wives and children and fleeing to ships in the port. The Company's fort was left in the hands of those who could not or would not flee, under the command of John Zephaniah Holwell, a Dublin-born doctor, now employed as the East India Company's tax collector. On the afternoon of Sunday, 20 June, Holwell surrendered. The victorious nawab ordered that the English prisoners be confined in the garrison's dungeon. This turned out to be a cell about 20 feet square, into which, Holwell subsequently claimed, 146 people were marched at the point of swords. There were two small barred windows. In addition to the heat of so many bodies crammed together, it was early in the rainy season and the night especially hot and muggy. Those at the windows offered increasingly vast sums of money to the guards outside to release them, who said they could do nothing

---

* The Mughal Empire in India had been founded by Babur, born in what is now Uzbekistan and said to be descended from both Tamerlane and Genghis Khan. He invaded India in the early sixteenth century and within little more than a decade had created an empire which stretched across the north of the subcontinent, from Afghanistan to Bengal. He was reputedly enormously strong (capable of jogging along with a fully grown man on each shoulder) and to have swum across all the rivers he encountered during his invasion. He also drank prodigiously, enjoyed drugs and had a hobby of stacking up the severed heads of those who had displeased him.

without the nawab's authority, and he was busy with his post-battle debauch. The temperature inside the dungeon continued to rise. One of the prisoners tried to slake his thirst by sucking the perspiration from Holwell's shirtsleeves. The doctor attempted to drink his own urine. No one could breathe properly and the temperature climbed higher still. Some prisoners sank to the floor, others became delirious or fell into comas. As the imperial historian Thomas Babington Macaulay wrote:

> Nothing in history or fiction . . . approaches the horrors which were recounted by the few survivors of that night . . . the prisoners went mad with despair. They trampled each other down, fought for the places at the windows, fought for the pittance of water with which the cruel mercy of the murderers mocked their agonies, raved, prayed, blasphemed, implored the guards to fire among them. At length the tumult died away in low gaspings and moanings.

When dawn broke and the nawab had recovered from the night before, the door was opened. Macaulay described how 'twenty-three ghastly figures, such as their own mothers would not have known, staggered one by one out of the charnel-house. A pit was instantly dug. The dead bodies, a hundred and twenty-three in number, were flung into it promiscuously and covered up.' The Black Hole of Calcutta was a horror story to rival anything among the Gothic tales which swept Britain in the late eighteenth and early nineteenth centuries.

But Macaulay – one of that line of Highlanders who became pillars of empire (he had served on the Governor General's Council in India) – was writing over eighty years after the event. There are various inherent improbabilities in the story (how was it physically possible to force 146 Europeans into a space so small, and if it was so gargantuan a crime, why did the East India Company not include it in its list of demands for compensation later?). Macaulay had reason enough to exaggerate the drama and Holwell, his source, sufficient incentive to obscure the embarrassment of his surrender with a story of grotesque human rights abuse. Holwell paid for a memorial to be erected at the site, but it was demolished in 1821, on the orders of the then Governor General after becoming 'the lounging place for lower class loafers of all sorts who gossip squatting around and against it'. Exactly what happened and how many lives were lost will never be known, but the significance of the Black Hole of Calcutta lies much more in what it was held to represent as a terrible example of the fate which could await Europeans in this strange land – in 1901 the Viceroy, Lord Curzon, commissioned a replacement monument, believing that the event had laid the foundations for British India. It was now nearly a century and a half after the night in question, yet for the purposes of imperial propaganda the memorial recorded that '146 British inhabitants of Calcutta were confined on the night of 20th June 1756, and . . . only 23 came out alive.' As the Calcutta poet Rabindranath Tagore observed many years later, it 'proclaimed to the heavens that exaggeration is not a monopoly of any particular race or nation'.* But precise numbers were not the point. Clearly, far too many people were crammed into a horribly confined space. The symbolic warning tale of the Black Hole of Calcutta was still being taught in British schools in the 1960s.

Retribution (generally inevitable in British India) came in the form of an expedition sent up from Madras under the command of Robert Clive. It landed in Bengal in December 1756 as news arrived that hostilities had officially resumed between Britain and France, in what later became known as the Seven Years War. Clive retook Calcutta with little trouble and then decided he would finish off Siraj ud-Daula and his French backers for good. By February the intimidated nawab had agreed to pay reparations. But it was not enough. A coterie of Bengal bankers and merchants was willing to offer Clive big financial rewards for unseating the nawab and replacing him with someone more congenial. Clive's choice was Mir Jafar, the intensely ambitious

---

* By his own account, Holwell himself seems to have survived the ordeal remarkably well. Within an hour of being dragged out from under a pile of corpses he was able to hold a conversation with Siraj ud-Daula and then walked three miles. The next day, despite being covered in boils and wearing heavy fetters, he marched the same distance, under 'an intense hot sun'. No trace of the Black Hole now remains, and the memorial obelisk commissioned by Lord Curzon has been moved to the graveyard of St John's, the earliest surviving church in the city.

child of Arab immigrants who had risen to become one of Siraj ud-Daula's commanders. Treachery now outdid treachery: if the financial backers thought they were dealing with an English gentleman, they did not know their man, for unknown to them Clive drew up two different versions of the agreement and forged the signature of the British admiral who was supposed to guarantee its trustworthiness.

It was 23 June 1757, a year since the Black Hole of Calcutta, and the weather was sweltering when Clive's East India Company army closed on the nawab at Plassey. A mile away stood Siraj ud-Daula's vast forces, perhaps 50,000 strong, along with wives, concubines, servants, traders, children and associated hangers-on. Astrologers and other crackpots were on hand to advise on tactics. Many of the infantry had been press-ganged into service and would be readied for battle with doses of opium. Characteristically, commanders would then ride into combat on elephants, presenting lovely targets for sharpshooters, while the doped-up infantry rushed forward – as one not unsympathetic observer put it, 'both in their garb and impotent fury, resembling a mob of frantic women'. In support of this swirling mob, though, Siraj ud-Daula had forty pieces of heavy artillery, supervised by a team of French gunners.

Early in the morning, the nawab's guns began to shell the Company troops. Clive's plan was to wait out the bombardment and then, outnumbered twenty to one though they were, to counterattack late at night, relying on Mir Jafar to improve the odds by withdrawing his forces from the field. Suddenly, it began to pour with rain; with their gunpowder soaked, the nawab's cannon were immediately put out of action. When Mir Jafar kept his promise, wheeling his forces off downriver, away from the fighting, the battle was as good as decided. The Company forces broke cover and chased down the nawab's fleeing soldiers. Clive's dispatch to the Company informed them that 'five hundred [enemy] horses are killed and three elephants. Our loss is trifling, not above 20 Europeans killed and wounded.' Siraj ud-Daula, who had attempted to escape 'disguised in a mean dress . . . attended only by his favourite concubine . . . and eunuch', was caught and put to death later.

Clive's victory effectively doubled the size of British-controlled

India, turning him into perhaps the most powerful British citizen of all time, with 40 million people living under his authority – five times the population of his home country. He had also transformed a seaborne trading enterprise into a land empire. The government in London – months away by sea – had had no say in this massive acquisition. But, whether they desired it or not, they now had an empire in India.

And with it came enormous personal temptations for Clive. As Macaulay put it, 'In the field . . . his habits were remarkably simple . . . But when he was no longer at the head of an army, he laid aside this Spartan temperance for the ostentatious luxury of a Sybarite.' Like others who joined the Company, Clive was in India to make his fortune – the phrase 'buccaneering capitalists' might have been invented for them – but he was in a class of his own: inventive and bold on the battlefield, scheming and devious in business. He made political deals the way he made business deals, audaciously, promiscuously, arrogantly, and was always ready to redefine what they meant. Victory at Plassey had delivered him the cornucopia of Bengal, and Clive set an example by immediately filling his boots. Having installed Mir Jafar on the throne, he turned to the question of payment due from his puppet, the first instalment of which was sent downriver to the British fort in a convoy of seventy-five boats under naval escort, perhaps the biggest haul of booty in history. Clive used the spoils of India as a shortcut to the trappings of eminence in England – country estates, works of art, to say nothing of the seat in parliament, along with others for his father and a close friend. Soon came a peerage to mark his victory. To his disappointment, it was only an Irish one, so he changed the name of his estate in County Clare to Plassey.

But there was more to come. The survival of the nawabs depended upon their ability to enforce the payment of taxes, and the Company's army (much of it drawn from traditional mercenary or warrior sections of Indian society and officered by men recruited in Britain) was much the most powerful force in the land. The Indian princes' military inferiority increasingly rendered them hostage to the Company. Mir Jafar, for example, was soon utterly dependent upon British forces, and the Company could insist that he foot the bill not merely for his own security but for their investment and campaigns else-where.

Clive returned to India in 1765 and found the Company's army poised for a possible advance on Delhi, the seat of the Mughal emperor. He settled instead for a treaty with the emperor by which the Mughals recognized the British as tax collectors in Bengal, Orissa and Bihar in return for being left alone. The nawab had become now little more than an ornament. (Clive, characteristically, realized that the arrange-ment would make the Company even more attractive to investors, and used the development for some serious insider dealing.) When Clive arrived back in England again in July 1767, his personal fortune was estimated at £400,000, an enormous sum at the time. The govern-ment festooned him with more honours, of course, installing him in the Order of the Bath and making him a lord lieutenant, but the mood was changing. Apart from snobbish resentment of the nabobs (and Clive was the biggest nabob of all) there were mounting ethical anxi-eties: precisely how had this great wealth been acquired when there were stories of appalling famines among ordinary Indians in which, it was reported, 'the living were feeding on the dead'? The British upper classes could contain their distaste for new money as long as they were being cut in on any profits to be had, but when Company shares fell (long after Clive had liquidated much of his holding, of course) those who had borrowed to invest turned on him in fury. In the House of Commons, 'Gentleman Johnny' Burgoyne claimed that all land seized by British subjects belonged to the Crown, that Clive had certainly had no excuse for accepting massive personal payments and that the forging of Admiral Watson's signature was outrageous. India was the worst example of oppression in history. 'We have had in India revolu-tion upon revolution,' he declared, 'extortion upon extortion.' But Clive was insouciant. Called to explain himself he remarked that 'an opulent city lay at my mercy; its richest bankers bid against each other for my smiles; I walked through vaults which were thrown open to me alone, piled on either hand with gold and jewels . . . Mr Chairman,' he sighed, 'at this moment I stand astonished at my own moderation.'

In November 1774 Baron Clive of Plassey – now aged forty-nine – was playing cards with friends at his house in Berkeley Square when he left the table and did not return. His health had been bad for some time; what had seemed an especially unshakeable cold refused to go away and instead became so bad that he was able to relieve the discomfort only with the use of opium – a habit he had acquired in India. Perhaps the drug killed him – it seems to fit the spirit of post-imperial times to believe in some sort of just deserts, although rumours at the time said he left the room to stick a penknife into his throat. They buried him in the little redbrick church at Moreton Say in Shropshire, beneath a plaque inscribed with the words 'Primus in Indis'. Disgusted by England's readiness to genuflect before wealth and power, the radical Thomas Paine danced on his grave. 'Lord Clive is himself a treatise upon vanity, printed in a golden type. The most unlettered clown writes explanatory notes thereon, and reads them to his children.'

The parliamentary investigations into Clive's behaviour in India of course exonerated him. He had appealed to MPs' fellow-feeling with the words 'leave me my honour, take away my fortune'. They certainly left him the latter. His role in establishing British rule in India can hardly be exaggerated. Had he not taken ship, perhaps someone else of similar avarice and equally steady nerve – of one nationality or another – would have emerged in his place. But it was Clive who was there, Clive who gave the Company its commanding presence and Clive whose reputation lives with the shame of events like the famine his administrative system exacerbated.

The sheer scale of the East India Company's operations meant it was now impossible for the pretence to be maintained that it was a mere trading enterprise. In 1773 British parliamentary legislation decreed that a governor general for Bengal, to be advised by a Council, should be appointed by the British government. The first man to hold the post was Warren Hastings, an earnest, slightly shy and comparatively sophisticated son of an impoverished Cotswold clergyman. From an early age he yearned to recover the family estate at Daylesford, and everyone knew that if you wanted to make a lot of money quickly, the best thing to do was to join the East India Company. Clive was a trader turned warrior. Hastings was a trader turned bureaucrat.

Appointed to extinguish corruption and reform the administration of justice in Calcutta at the same time as sorting out the Company finances, he was in the wrong place at the wrong time. For on his watch the two most powerful forces of empire, trade and morality, collided. Hastings sailed for home in 1785, expecting the thanks of an appreciative nation. 'I have saved India, in spite of them all, from foreign conquest,' he wrote. '[I have] become the instrument of raising the British name.' He had reckoned without the deadly fusion of jealousy and probity.

One of the men appointed to serve on the Council concocted by the British government to advise Hastings had been Philip Francis. The two men came to loathe each other. After serving six years in India, during which time he made a small fortune at the card table, was dragged through the courts for seducing another man's wife and fought a duel with Hastings (which both men survived), Francis returned to England in 1781, where he bought himself a seat in parliament and began doing his utmost to destroy Hastings. His accusations – of venality, unnecessary violence and wholesale corruption – did not get far at first, for Francis was widely considered an India bore. But when he fed his information to the great parliamentary orator Edmund Burke he acquired the most powerful of allies. Burke's often contradictory opinions cannot be reduced to coherence other than by seeing them through the prism of his unique high-mindedness. In contrast to the chancers of the Company, whose interest was mere pillage, what was being done in his country's name and by his country's citizens mattered intensely to Burke. It was not that he felt there was anything uniquely evil about the young men who took ship to India: they were no 'worse than the boys whom we are whipping at school, or that we see trailing a pike, or bending over a desk at home'. The problem was that they rolled into India in wave after wave 'with appetites continually renewing for a food that is continually wasting'. The British relationship with India was thus entirely one of serial plundering and the visitors brought neither art nor education nor even kindness to the people. 'Were we to be driven out of India this day,' he wrote, 'nothing would remain, to tell that it had been possessed, during the inglorious period of our dominion, by anything better than the orangutan or the tiger.' Francis's evidence seemed to offer Burke the chance to confront the Company. Parliament and the nation were already in one of Britain's periodic fits of morality when, in February 1788, he rose to impeach Warren Hastings.

The ancient Westminster Hall, where Charles I had faced his accusers and been sentenced to death, was packed. The doors opened at 9.00 a.m., but crowds had been gathering since six o'clock, some of the would-be spectators having slept in coffeehouses to be sure of getting a seat. As the imperial historian Macaulay described it (although he had not been born at the time), 'there were gathered together, from all parts of a great, free, enlightened, and prosperous Empire, grace and female loveliness, wit and learning, the representatives of every science and of every art.' The queen sat in the royal box, in a light-brown satin dress, surrounded by a retinue of children and nobles. One hundred and seventy lords in gold and ermine processed into the chamber, followed by the Prince of Wales. Two hundred MPs had crammed inside, and in the gallery sat the president of the Royal Academy and society portraitist, Sir Joshua Reynolds, for whom Hastings had once posed as the high-minded orientalist, wearing an embroidered silk waistcoat and clutching a handful of documents in Persian. Near by in the gallery the theatrical superstar Sarah Siddons gazed down, as did Edward Gibbon, who had recently completed his monumental *History of the Decline and Fall of the Roman Empire*. What resonances would he hear today?

It was worth waiting for. Burke's opening speech was spread over four days, was packed with horrific detail and steamed with moral disdain. He was a man possessed, claiming to have 'brought before you the head, the chief, the captain-general in iniquity; one in whom all the frauds, all the peculations, all the violence, all the tyranny in India are embodied, disciplined and arrayed'.

He charged Warren Hastings with betraying the trust of parliament, dishonouring the character of Britain and subverting the rights of Indians, 'whose country he has laid waste and desolate'. He talked of 'oppressed princes, of undone women of the first rank, of desolated provinces, and wasted kingdoms'. The way the Company collected taxes was a disgrace. Burke claimed that enforcers employed by the local officials to whom Hastings had delegated tax collection behaved grotesquely. Fathers were flogged to extract money from them. Sometimes their children were beaten before their eyes. Virgins were brought into court where they were 'cruelly violated by the basest and wickedest of mankind'. There was more. 'The wives of the people of the country only differed in this; they had lost their honour, in the bottom of the most cruel dungeons . . . but they were dragged out, naked and exposed to the public view, and scourged before all the people . . . they put the nipples of the women into the sharp edges of split bamboos and tore them from their bodies.' He was, he said, ashamed to go on. Even Hastings admitted later that listening to it had made him feel 'the most culpable man on earth'. When Burke's colleague Richard Sheridan took up the demolition job, people were said to be paying 50 guineas a time for tickets. Sheridan wasn't a dramatist and impresario for nothing. After several days his speech culminated in the assertion that 'the condemnation we look for will be one of the most ample mercies accomplished for mankind since the creation of the world!' And then, with the words 'My lords, I have done,' he collapsed backwards into Burke's arms.

After this melodramatic start, the trial dragged on for seven years, constantly interrupted by other Westminster business of one kind or another, and the public grew increasingly bored with the spectacle, especially when, across the Channel, France erupted into revolution. Eventually the trial petered out. The twenty-nine peers who claimed to be competent to pass judgement did so, and acquitted Warren Hastings by generous margins. He retired to the country estate at Daylesford which his Indian gains had allowed him to recover and lived out the rest of his days as a Cotswold squire.

What had really been on trial, said Burke, was the honour of the entire nation. His own motives seem mixed – he resented the ghastly nabobs buying up seats in parliament, acquiring country piles and marrying the daughters of indigent gentry. But the impeachment of Hastings marked the point at which Britain became the first of the modern empires to mount a detailed interrogation of what was being done abroad in its name. It was part of a wider moral awakening in the dying years of the eighteenth century, of a piece with a growing revulsion at the cruelties of the slave trade. But unlike slavery, which was wrong in principle, what was on trial with Hastings was merely the practice of imperialism. The British were too in love with their empire to challenge its expansion, which continued apace – by 1823, just about all of India was under either direct or indirect British authority. The proposition that Burke laid out – that the colonizer had a moral duty to those he colonized – became the central ethical tenet of the British Empire. Of course, it was better than the opposite principle, which had underlain piracy and slavery. But there was something inherently nonsensical about it: would not the moral duty have been better exercised by not seizing the land in the first place? How could the ultimate purpose of colonization be freedom?

The touchstone issue for the new morality of empire became the question of religion. Charles Grant was another young Scot who had embarked for India intending to restore his family fortunes: he had been named after Bonnie Prince Charlie, a short time before his own father was cut down at Culloden. (The son did well enough in India to buy an estate on Skye and to take a seat in parliament when he returned.) But during the family's time in the subcontinent Grant's two young daughters had been carried off by smallpox. Tragedies like this were very common, but Grant considered their deaths to be divine punishment for his way of life. The experience turned him into an evangelical Christian, convinced not merely of the injustice of slavery but that it was the duty of the British Empire to turn India Christian. Without the influence of Christian missionaries, the land would be left to idolatry, immorality, dishonesty, depravity and general wickedness. His attempt to get a 'Pious Clause' inserted into the renewal of the Company's charter in 1793 failed. But he found a ready ally in William Wilberforce, then labouring to persuade parliament to legislate against the slave trade. Wilberforce saw a readiness to continue to allow 'our fellow subjects in India' to wallow 'under the grossest, the darkest and most degrading system of idolatrous superstition' as 'the foulest blot' on the moral character of the country.

The East India Company was unenthusiastic about having Christian missionaries tramping about the place telling its troops that their misguided religions would see them all destined for hell. This was not because it was especially concerned about freedom of religious belief, merely that it cared a great deal more about making money. As long as the local holy men raised no objections to what the Company traded, the Company would raise no objections to what they preached, so was perfectly happy to see them blessing the colours of sepoy regiments. Christian missionaries declaring the whole lot of them to be heathens was not likely to be conducive either to a peaceful country or to good trade. But Wilberforce and others had their blood up. The caste system ('a detestable expedient for keeping the lower orders of the community bowed down in an abject state of hopeless and irremediable vassalage', he called it in parliament) was a form of hereditary slavery. The weapon to destroy it was Christianity. 'Our religion is sublime, pure and beneficent,' he went on. 'Theirs is mean, licentious and cruel.' Against this tide of moral self-confidence the Company's restrictions on missionary activity would simply have to yield. The India Bill of 1813 obliged the East India Company to license missionaries to travel the country preaching Christianity and imperial destiny.

There was an immediate opportunity to do good with the practice of *sati*, a tradition in which widows threw themselves (or were thrown) on to the funeral pyres of their newly dead husbands. Here was a custom grotesque enough to appal even the fiercest advocate of cultural tolerance. Nonetheless, it still took until 1829 for the Governor General, Lord William Bentinck, to act. The Governor General held the splendidly paternalist belief that India was 'a great estate, of which I am the chief agent', and he ruled as a clumsy, unpopular autocrat. (There were even made-up rumours that he planned to knock down the Taj Mahal, so that he could recycle the marble.) But he was sufficiently affected by the new mood of empire that he reformed the education and judicial systems, replaced Persian with English as the official language, built roads and bridges and established a college to teach western medicine. On the memorial erected to honour Bentinck in Calcutta was inscribed the judgement of Macaulay, that he 'infused into oriental despotism the spirit of British freedom', an expression only really comprehensible in the context of British India. It was under Bentinck that *sati* was finally suppressed, his self-confidence finding an echo in General Sir Charles Napier, who was reported to have replied, when facing down a defender of the practice of tossing women on to funeral pyres, 'It is your custom to burn widows. Very well. We also have a custom: when men burn a woman alive, we tie a rope around their necks and hang them. Build your funeral pyre and beside it my carpenters will build a gallows. You may follow your national custom – then we shall follow ours.'

There is no evidence that *sati* was practised all across India. But its prevalence was not the point. Its suppression was a dramatic and emotional demonstration of the ethical purpose of empire. Soon, there was another dragon to slay, when one of Bentinck's subordinates, William Sleeman, began a campaign against the Thugs, a secret sect, he revealed, who worshipped the goddess Kali by falling on travellers and strangling them with a silken cord. After robbery, the bodies were buried in graves dug with a sacred pickaxe. This, too, became a practice Bentinck determined to stop: hereditary lord confronted hereditary murderer. Again, the precise scale of *thuggee* will never be known – no doubt many different groups of murderers, from muggers to discharged soldiers, also had their crimes attributed to the cult. Indeed, there are some who noisily claim that the whole cult thing was got up by the British to justify their 'civilizing mission'. What is unarguable is that when Sleeman was given charge of a force to eradicate highway murder he was remarkably successful. By deploying decent detective methods – including the assiduous collection of evidence, the cultivation of informants and the offer of rehabilitation to those who would turn queen's evidence, thousands of alleged murderers were brought to justice, to be hanged, imprisoned or transported. It was an achievement spoken of in the same breath as the abolition of slavery.

In 1857, the 10th of May fell on a Sunday. As the sun began to sink in the sky, British officers and their families at the military camp at Meerut, about 40 miles from Delhi, prepared for evening prayers at the garrison church. Boots and belts were being buffed when suddenly, soon after five in the afternoon, the place exploded in shouts, shots and screams. Indians, both civilians and sepoy soldiers of the

East India Company army, burst through the cantonment, setting fire to buildings and looting weapons from the armouries. A few officers found their horses and rode out to confront the furious mob as it rampaged around, only to be hacked down or chased away. The pregnant wife of an infantryman was disembowelled by a rebel butcher, a patient sick with smallpox was set alight. By night-time much of the military compound was ablaze, about fifty men, women and children were dead, and the rioters had set off on horses for Delhi, intent on spreading the mutiny against foreign rule across the country.

The following morning, the Mughul emperor was disturbed by the sound of shouts outside the Red Fort in Delhi. The current tenant hardly matched the grandeur of his surroundings. His palace had been designed as an earthly reflection of the delights after death promised in the Koran. But Bahadur Shah Zafar was a feeble, henpecked valetudinarian, under the impression that he possessed magical powers. Although his 'court' still issued bulletins each day, the emperor's dominions had shrunk to the point where they extended scarcely further than the rooms of his palace, around which the old man would shuffle, leaning on a stick and stroking his waist-length beard. The Company paid him courtesy and a large annual allowance in exchange for his staying inside the palace composing poetry and painting the occasional miniature, leaving it free to go about its business. The angry mutineers now planned to ask this eighty-two-year-old poet to be the figurehead for a campaign to throw the British out of India. Bahadur Shah Zafar's first reaction was to send the commander of his personal guard, a Colonel Douglas, to see what was up. The mutineers killed him. More and more rebels poured into the city. Shops were looted. More Europeans were hunted down and killed – neither gender nor age was any protection. The angry soldiers had no plan: the uprising was an incoherent expression of anger, and in the long term it was destined to fail. But in the meantime the revolt's enormous, merciless energy terrified the British. It was one of the biggest shocks the empire ever experienced, and it changed it for ever.

In the shorthand version of history, the trigger for what the British called the Indian Mutiny – and what patriotic Indians prefer to term the Indian Rebellion or the First War of Independence – was a decision to issue locally recruited troops with a new paper cartridge, the tip of which had to be bitten off before the powder could be poured down the barrel of the Enfield rifle issued to Company soldiers. To keep the powder dry, the cartridges had to be covered in a waterproof coating and the rumour flew around the soldiery that the impermeable substance chosen was pork and beef fat. If it was true, this was the worst possible choice, outraging both Muslims, to whom the pig was unclean, and Hindus, to whom the cow was sacred. The decision about which type of fat to use was never intended as a deliberate insult – in fact, the manufacturers at the arsenal at Dum Dum, near Calcutta, would have been perfectly happy to have the cartridges coated in some substance like beeswax, just as long as the covering kept the powder dry. The problem for the British was that the sepoys were inclined to take it as a deliberate snub, because they were already unhappy. All armies live with a background chorus of belly-aching, but the sepoys had genuine anxieties – about their pensions, about the limited chances of promotion, about service overseas – as well as feeling a growing unease at the increasingly high-handed behaviour of the Company. (Its latest device for extending territory was the invention of a 'Doctrine of Lapse', by which it claimed ownership of any principality being incompetently administered or where the ruler died without a natural heir.) Many Indians were additionally troubled by the series of reforms bringing railways, ports, telegraphs and new roads, while Christian missionaries were ever more obvious in towns and countryside. (The missionaries were not particularly effective, but they made quite a lot of noise about the evils of Hinduism and Islam.) Barrack-room stories went around about how the Company was trying to undermine the ancient religions of India by adding cow's blood to salt and by grinding pig and cow bones into the soldiers' flour. It was hard to still rumours like these when growing numbers of junior officers were choosing to spend their time drinking in the officers' mess instead of forming a bond with their men, and it looked increasingly as if, not content with removing their wealth, the British now also wanted to remove the Indians' way of life.

Someone remembered a Brahmin prophecy that British rule would last for only a hundred years after the battle of Plassey: the centenary fell in June 1857.

At the end of March that year, Mangal Pande, a young soldier with the 34th Native Infantry, had emerged on to the parade ground at Barrackpore from a session of cannabis-smoking and taken a wild shot at one of his European officers. In the tussle which followed, Pande turned his gun on himself. The unfortunate man failed to take his own life, was dragged before a court martial and publicly hanged. In what became an established pattern of behaviour when a unit showed signs of restiveness, his regiment was disbanded. A few weeks later, in the British base at Meerut, eighty-five troopers with the 3rd Light Cavalry were ordered to load their weapons with the new cartridge. When they refused, all were court-martialled, sentenced to ten years' hard labour and, in the middle of the parade ground, under the eyes of the rest of the garrison (and the guns of European soldiers) stripped of their uniforms and riveted into shackles and chains. Some of them wept with shame, one soldier crying out, 'I was a good sepoy. I would have gone anywhere for the service. But I could not forsake my religion.' In the commotion of the evening of 10 May, some of their comrades broke into the gaol and freed them. The uprising had begun.

The rebellion never enveloped the whole of India. But it spread with amazing speed and occurred in the hugely important area around the Grand Trunk Road, the old Mughal route from the Afghan border through the north of India to Bengal. This was the heart of British military might in the subcontinent. The rebels found a merciless leader in the Nana Sahib of Cawnpore. According to contemporary accounts, when he first heard about events 250 miles distant in Delhi, Nana Sahib told a British officer that he 'lamented the outbreak', and offered to provide protection for European wives and families. But Nana Sahib – a fleshy, middle-aged man – was the adopted son of the previous king, and therefore a victim of the Company's new Doctrine of Lapse which decreed that only natural-born sons could succeed to their fathers' lands. When the mutineers contacted him he decided to take their side. On 6 June he laid siege to the British encampment, which was now packed with refugees who had poured into Cawnpore as news of the uprising spread. For nearly three weeks the rebel forces pounded the British with cannon and sniper shots. The medical supplies were destroyed by fire. Unable to move, unable even to bury their dead, the British were soon also ravaged by thirst, hunger and disease. Survivors later talked of how some of the besieged were blinded by shellfire and shrapnel or broken by despair. Under the constant bombardment, some went mad. Women did their best to comfort the children, but both suffered at least as badly as the men. The British commander, General Sir Hugh Wheeler, smuggled a desperate call out to the British garrison at Lucknow – 'Surely we are not to die like rats in a cage?' But no help came. When his own son was decapitated by artillery fire ('Here a round shot came and killed young Wheeler,' someone later scrawled at the site; 'his brains and hair are scattered on the wall'), the general's spirit broke.

On the evening of 24 June, the shelling stopped. After a couple of hours the British sentries watched as a figure emerged from Nana Sahib's lines. It was a stumbling, barefoot woman, and as she came closer they identified her as Rose Greenway, one of Nana Sahib's prisoners. She was carrying a piece of paper. It was addressed to 'The Subjects of Her Most Gracious Majesty, Queen Victoria', and it offered safe passage by boat down the Ganges to Allahabad, well over 100 miles away. The officers argued hotly over whether the promise could be trusted and whether they should accept an offer of any kind. But the place was filled with sick and dying and General Wheeler had learned that they had a mere three days' supply of food left. So, on the morning of 27 June, summoning what was left of its dignity, a miserable procession made its way to the riverbank. All were gaunt and haggard, military uniforms tattered, many of them in their underclothes. Those who could walk helped to carry the sick and wounded. 'The old – battered and bruised –', recalled one of the very few survivors, 'babbled like children; others had a vacant stare in their eyes, as if they beheld visions of the future. Many a little child was raving mad.'

When they reached the water's edge they found a flotilla of boats waiting and those who could do so waded out to them, dragging the injured. In what seemed a surprisingly kind gesture, Major Edward Vibart of the 2nd Bengal Light Cavalry found that Indian soldiers he had previously commanded insisted upon carrying his bags. Then suddenly, instead of pushing off, the boat crews jumped overboard and from all around the rebels – including those who had just carried Major Vibart's bags – poured musket fire and grapeshot into the boats. The thatched roofs on some of the vessels caught fire, and those who leaped into the water and made it to the bank then had to evade the swords of mutineer cavalrymen in the shallows. Captured British soldiers were either shot or beheaded, their bodies tied into bundles of five or six and thrown in the river. A single boat escaped, chased downriver by rebels, and eventually two English officers and two Irish privates struggled ashore in territory belonging to a sympathetic rajah to tell the story of an almost unthinkable calamity.

But the worst was still to come at Cawnpore. Over one hundred women and children who had been previously captured and had not been part of the safe-passage offer were gathered together and forced into a nearby bibighar, the flat-roofed single-storey building built to house the native mistress of an English officer. Here, with very little food and in unspeakable conditions, the relatively healthy attempted to nurse the many sick and wounded, tormented by the July heat and jeered at by their gaolers. Finally, after almost two weeks of imprisonment, a group of mutineers approached the building, forced the muzzles of their muskets through the shutters and opened fire. This was too inefficient to act as a final solution, so, late in the afternoon of Wednesday, 15 July, five men, two of them butchers in their aprons, opened the doors of the building and went to work. One of them emerged twice from the building to get a new sword, because he had broken the blade. Within an hour, the screams had come to an end. Wives, daughters and more than a hundred children had been dismembered. The next morning, as a crowd of spectators looked on, a team of scavengers was sent into the building and, to their astonishment, discovered among the human remains a few women and children huddled against the wall, covered in the blood of the corpses among whom they had spent the night. Seeing the open door, two women ran outside and threw themselves down a well in the yard.

The scavengers then threw the limbs, torsos and heads of the dead after them. The children who had survived the night were either thrown alive into the well after them, or decapitated.

The well was 50 feet deep and 9 feet across, but the rebels were afraid that not all the corpses would fit down the shaft. So they chopped some up and used the pieces to fill the gaps.

The next scene in what the historian Sir Charles Crosthwaite later called 'the Epic of the Race' took place at Lucknow, capital of the province of Oudh, some 50 miles away. Nineteenth-century European visitors had been astonished by the opulence of the city, adorned as it was with columns and gilded domes, gardens and fountains. 'Not Rome, not Athens, not Constantinople: not any city I have ever seen appears to me so striking and so beautiful as this,' an awestruck foreign correspondent wrote of the place at the time; 'the more I gaze, the more its beauties grow on me.' This luxury long predated the arrival of the East India Company, but, unsurprisingly, its traders liked what they saw. At first they had treated the province as a buffer state against the Mughal Empire, to protect Bengal. But, as the Company's confidence grew, they began to assume control, through the usual arrangements of installing local residents (representatives) and engineering the succession of pliant nawabs. (One of these, a visitor reported, 'would surprise visitors by appearing dressed as a British admiral or as a clergyman of the Church of England'. The nawab's main object of affection was an English drayhorse, which he fed so extravagantly that the wretched animal could hardly move.) By the mid-1850s the province of Oudh – often called 'the granary of India' – provided the British with a steady income, a little of which was used to keep the nawabs sweet. The British community maintained retinues of servants, played cricket and croquet, worshipped their God, held horse-races, entertained each other to dinner, staged amateur theatricals and kept bands which had been taught European tunes.

When the revolt struck Lucknow, the party ended. The following extracts are taken from different days in the 1857 diary kept by an English clergyman's wife:

It is impossible to describe the horror of the last few days. Captain and Mrs Macdonald and their children were murdered, the poor babies snatched out of their parents' arms and cut to pieces before their eyes . . .

I walked round our fortifications last night with James; they are wonderfully strong, and the engineers say we can hold out against any number as long as provisions last . . .

Poor Miss Palmer's leg was shot off this afternoon . . .

Very heavy firing all day: ten Europeans wounded: five buried this evening . . .

Poor Mr Polehampton is seized with cholera. There is no hope of his recovery . . .

Mrs Hersham's and Mrs Kendal's babies died: they get diarrhoea, for which there seems no cure . . .

Part of the roof of the Residency fell in this morning and buried six men of the 32nd; only two were dug out alive . . .

The smell in the churchyard is so offensive that it has made J. quite ill; and when he came back he vomited about two hours incessantly . . .

Mr Graham committed suicide this morning; he was quite out of his mind . . .

Three prisoners were brought in, and were undergoing a summary trial by drum-head court-martial, when a round shot struck and killed the trio . . .

The hospital is so densely crowded that many have to lie outside in the open air, without bed or shelter – amputated arms and legs lying about in heaps all over the hospital and little can be done to alleviate the intense discomfort and pain of the poor sufferers . . .

Mrs D.'s baby was christened this afternoon. Charlie D. was one godfather; I stood proxy. There were twenty-five funerals this evening . . .

Poor C.D. was quite delirious when I went to him this morning. It will indeed be wonderful if he lives, for not a single case of amputation during the siege has recovered . . .

★

This horrific drama was being played out in and around the elegant red-stone buildings the British had had built for them at Lucknow.

The most imposing of these was the vast Residency, the seat of British power, and the scene of balls and investitures, billiard tournaments and concerts. Now it was punctured by cannonballs and reeked of sickness and decomposition. The improvised fortifications around the compound eventually extended to a circumference of about a mile. Inside, at the start of the siege, sheltered almost 800 British soldiers, about 50 drummers, 160 European civilians, 720 loyal Indian troops, a further 700 camp-followers and some 500 women and children. They were surrounded by the best part of 10,000 mutineers and supporters. One of the striking aspects of the diaries and recollections of the survivors is how the spirit of free enterprise which had animated the British in India still flourished in the appalling siege conditions, with some people almost starving, while others enjoyed dinners accompanied by sherry, champagne and claret. When someone died, their effects were auctioned off, with astonishing prices being commanded by food and soap.

As the siege dragged on for month after month, conditions inside the barricades grew worse and worse. Traders who had never wielded a gun took duty on the battered walls, one of them wearing a suit cut from the baize which had covered the Residency billiard table. At the sound of another assault, men struggled from the makeshift hospital to the battlements, the strain causing their wounds to reopen. Wives made bandages from their underclothes, nursed the wounded and prepared what food was available, which, the moment it was laid on a plate, was so covered in flies that no one could see what it was any longer. Children ran messages (the local school at La Martinière was subsequently awarded a British medal for the role played by its pupils). From outside the compound the mutineers taunted them with British bugle calls and turned British artillery on British citizens. Starving pack animals and horses went mad and then died, adding to the stench of severed limbs and overflowing latrines. Some especially horrific vignettes became particularly well known later, like the mother who sat sewing with her ten-year-old daughter and a baby at her side when a cannonball crashed through the wall and tore off the little girl's head. The shock was so great that the mother lost her milk and her baby died of starvation. Those not killed or maimed by the incoming fire were prey to cholera, smallpox, dysentery and scurvy: by the middle of July, Europeans were dying at the rate of ten each day (none of the records seems to have bothered with a tally of the number of loyal Indians who perished). The chaplain's wife recorded that her husband had had to conduct 500 funerals inside the embattled compound.

Just when it seemed things could get no worse, they did. A relief force fought its way through to the Residency and then became trapped inside; the main consequence was that there were now many more mouths to feed, and no more food than previously. (One of the rebels' taunts was to mount chickens and chapattis on poles and wave them at the defenders.) Finally, in November, a second relief column reached Lucknow. When the soldiers broke into the rebel strongholds, slaughter was savage and indiscriminate. Women and children died alongside the mutinous sepoys – anyone attempting to surrender was bayoneted. But the 'Cawnpore Dinner' – 6 inches of steel – was just the start of it. 'The scene was terrible,' said a Lieutenant Fairweather, 'but at the same time it gave me a feeling of gratified revenge.' Loyal soldiers now butchered any rebel they could find, beheading some and trying, literally, to tear others to pieces. A witness counted nearly 2,000 corpses dragged by elephants from the rebel positions to be thrown into mass graves.

The savagery of the British revenge afterwards is striking. Entire villages were burned down; mutineers were smeared in pig fat before execution, tied to the muzzles of cannon and blown to pieces. At the site of the Cawnpore massacre rebels were made to lick the dried blood from the floor of the bibighar. In particular, there was the treatment of women and children to be avenged. A brigadier serving in Punjab believed that the gallows were too good for the mutineers. 'Let us propose a Bill for the flaying alive, impalement, or burning of the murderers of the women and children at Delhi,' he said. 'The idea of simply hanging the perpetrators of such atrocities is maddening.' Such a reaction was only to be expected of a military man who had previously demonstrated his commitment to law and order by personally lopping the heads off criminals and piling them up on his desk. But the desire for vengeance affected everyone. Charles Spurgeon, the 'Prince of Preachers', thrilled an audience of 25,000 at the

Crystal Palace in London when he told them that it was time for a holy war on the Indians. The Mutiny became the stuff of epic poetry and bad art. Edward Armitage's hugely popular painting *Retribution* caught the mood – an enormous, well-muscled Britannia towering over the corpses of a mother and child, driving a sword into the chest of a tiger. *The Times* demanded that 'every tree and gable end should have its burden in the shape of a mutineer's carcass'. 'I wish I were Commander in Chief in India,' the normally quite civilized Charles Dickens wrote to Angela Burdett-Coutts. 'I should do my utmost to exterminate the Race upon whom the stain of the late cruelties rested . . . and raze it off the face of the Earth.'

Mercifully, wiser counsels prevailed. Although it earned him the contemptuous nickname 'Clemency' Canning, the Governor General, Viscount Canning, attempted to insist that punishment be confined merely to those Indians who had perpetrated specific acts. He even abolished the East India Company's Doctrine of Lapse, which had given Nana Sahib such incentive to join the rebels in Cawnpore. But although he presided over an administration which established the first Indian universities, developed a new penal code and devised and revised the taxation system, Canning was never quite the hand-wringing liberal that his nickname suggests. While he appreciated the need to nurture an elite sympathetic to the British, the peasants were another matter. 'Our endeavour to better, as we thought, the village occupants of Oudh has not been appreciated by them,' he said, and therefore they deserved 'little consideration from us'. But he was wise enough to recognize that confiscating their lands would merely pro-voke resentment. Canning concluded that if the peasants were going to retain their blind fealty to local chieftains, then the British might as well do whatever they could to make life better for the existing ruling class. From now on, the British would run much of India with and through the indigenous princes, a form of indirect rule that would become a model for elsewhere in the empire. Most significantly, the British realized that India was too important for its government to be left in the hands of a commercial company, however grand. From now on, India would fall under the Crown. This made Canning the first man to become viceroy of India. The old poetry-writing emperor,

Bahadur Shah Zafar, direct descendant of Genghis Khan, was taken under cavalry escort from Delhi on a bullock cart, and eventually exiled to a prison in Burma where he died. At four in the afternoon of 7 November 1862, Captain Nelson Davies watched as his body was lowered into an unmarked grave inside the prison compound. Captain Davies reported to London that, after a speedy interment, turf was laid on the grave and a bamboo fence erected at some distance, so that 'by the time the fence is worn out, the grass will again have properly covered the spot, and no vestige will remain to distinguish where the last of the Great Moghuls rests'.

CHAPTER FIVE

'We had scarcely breakfasted before he announced to me the startling fact that he had discovered the sources of the White Nile'
Richard Burton, 1860

In June 1774 a Scotsman arrived in London telling astonishing tales. His appearance was quite astonishing, too – 6 feet 4, with a shock of red hair and a very bad temper. His body bore the evidence of captivity and of long wandering in the mountains; he had parasitic worms in his leg, malaria and dysentery. He was also said to have survived an elephant charge. The desert had affected his breathing, so that his lungs were reported to 'heave like an organ-bellows'. Sometimes, when he was especially animated in conversation, his nose would begin to bleed.

He had been, he said, in a country called Abyssinia where he had braved lions and crocodiles, met holy men who 'had neither ate nor drank for twenty years' and witnessed remarkable things – banquets in which meat was carved from live cows tethered to a table, and raucous orgies in which there was 'no coyness, no delays, no need of appointments or retirement to gratify their wishes'. Most importantly, he had stood in a patch of swamp and raised half a coconut shell to propose three toasts, first to King George III, then to the girl he (wrongly) believed to be waiting for him at home, and finally to Catherine the Great, to celebrate something amazing. For James Bruce claimed to have become the first European to have travelled to the source of the most celebrated river in the world.

If this was true, Bruce had settled a question which had baffled learning since long before Ptolemy. (As it turned out, it was not true – he was nowhere near the source of the White Nile, and the place he was celebrating – which was not even the place where the Blue Nile began – had anyway been 'discovered' by a Portuguese priest many years previously.) Bruce was fêted in London and elected a fellow of the Royal Society, even though the Society's president considered him a 'brute'. But not everyone quite believed him. Dr Johnson, who had appointed himself an expert on Abyssinia, thought Bruce 'not a distinct relater' and soon came to doubt whether he had been to that country at all. Many of the public agreed. The author of the fantastical *Adventures of Baron Munchausen* dedicated one of his volumes to Bruce, saying they might be useful to him on his next journey. None of this mockery made Bruce – who retired back to Scotland – a particularly happy man. He had a right to be angry, for much of what he claimed to have seen was confirmed by later travellers. Most of all, while he might not have put the source of the Nile on the map, he had lodged the search for it in the public mind. James Bruce was a man ahead of his time. Within twenty-odd years of his arrival in London, the British began to develop an almost insatiable curiosity to know more about what lay beyond their little island. This appetite for knowledge of the world expressed the self-confidence of the Enlightenment. But it was more. In the person of the individual explorer on a dangerous mission, the empire united personal challenge, the destiny of mankind and the political purpose of the nation. To map was to conquer, and conquering led to ownership. The dogged struggles of their countrymen in desert and jungle gave the British a deep conviction about their national destiny and those who died while attempting to plant the flag achieved a sort of martyrdom.

Inscribed on brown wooden boards just inside the front doors of the imposing redbrick headquarters of the Royal Geographical Society in Kensington Gore, London, are the names of the winners of the Society's Gold Medal. The roll-call includes missionaries like David Livingstone, Arctic adventurers like James Clark Ross, big-game hunters like Frederick Courtney Selous, mystics like Francis Younghusband and archaeologists like Gertrude Bell, as well as Edward Eyre, who walked across much of Australia, Joseph Thomson, who once convinced menacing Masai warriors that he was superhuman by removing his false teeth and brewing up a fizzing froth of Eno's fruit salts, and Lady Franklin, who repeatedly sponsored expeditions to discover the remains of her husband who had perished trying to find the North-West Passage. The modern RGS likes to proclaim its credentials as a research institute. But it is an unmistakably imperial creation, its headquarters acquired by Lord Curzon, the former Viceroy of India, in the days when its membership included dukes, earls, baronets and knights, together with hundreds of naval and military officers. The men and women who won the endorsement of this bemedalled body sallied forth full of ambition and returned as newspaper heroes, best-selling authors, highly paid lecturers, hymned in the music halls and courted by portrait-painters. The commercially minded could make a fortune from advertising endorsements. (Henry Morton Stanley, for example, appeared in advertisements for Bovril, Keble's pies, Edgington tents and 'Victor Vaissier's CONGO SOAP'.)

By the middle of the nineteenth century, the most ambitious geographical challenge of the age was that which had animated James Bruce – the search for the source of the Nile. Early Victorian maps show a roughly accurate understanding of the coastline of Africa, with a little detail of the interior of the continent coloured in the north and south but most of the rest left as a vast expanse of white nothingness – there were rumours that much of what lay beyond the coast was only desert. Like the United States' ambition to land a man on the moon in the latter half of the twentieth century, the attraction of discovering the source of the most famous river in the world was irresistible to an empire in its pomp. There was the incidental benefit that planting the Union flag at the head of the Nile would prevent some other European power from doing so.

The two men chosen for the task were Richard Francis Burton and John Hanning Speke, a partnership which ended in sensational bitterness. It goes without saying that both were immensely brave. Each was also a tremendous egotist. There – save for the fact that they had both been officers in the Indian army – the similarities end. 'As the prime minister of an Eastern despot, he would have been splendid,' was Lord Salisbury's verdict on Burton, and there was certainly no one like him in British public life. He belonged to that breed of Englishmen who believe that 'Little islands are all large prisons' and in the course of his lifetime became intimately familiar with places from Peru to Syria, from west Africa to the Rocky Mountains. His father had plans for him to become a clergyman, which would have been a very bad idea indeed, and Burton dropped out of Oxford to join the Indian army, determined to 'be shot at for sixpence a day'. As well as his considerable mental talents – he developed a system which enabled him to learn a new language within a month, and mastered forty languages and dialects during his lifetime – Burton was hard as nails. Convinced that you could learn nothing of a culture without immersing yourself in it, he became a master of disguise, travelling through the bazaars of India, sitting in mosques, playing chess and lying around in opium dens, pretending to be a half-Persian, half-Arab merchant, having stained his face, arms, hands and feet and grown a beard and shoulder-length hair. So confident was Burton of his disguise that he claimed to have investigated male brothels in Karachi at the request of a senior officer.* In 1852 Burton proposed to the Royal

---

* Apart from some enigmatic observations about the use of the scrotum, no trace of this report has ever been found. During a visit to India in 1876, a woman asked Burton's devoted wife whether their marriage had been blessed with children, and was told, 'No, thank God; nothing to separate me from my Dick.'

Geographical Society that he make the hajj, or pilgrimage, to the Islamic holy cities of Mecca and Medina, from which infidels were banned. Discovery would have meant certain death, but Burton so successfully refined his disguise that he was able to pass himself off as an itinerant sufi. His account of the penetration of the forbidden Muslim holy cities made him something of a national hero: his descriptions of his adventures count among the best non-fiction of the nineteenth century. He would not, however, be mistaken for an intellectual on first sight – big-browed and strong-jawed, with a prodigious moustache and beard tumbling over each side of his upper lip and hanging from his chin like rusty chain-mail. He looked, thought one man who met him, 'like a prize-fighter', an impression not diminished by the scars on his face left by a lance which had pierced both cheeks. But it was the eyes which everyone remarked upon. In a typically extravagant phrase, the poet Swinburne described a 'look of unspeakable horror in those eyes which gave him at times an almost unearthly appearance . . . the brow of a god and the jaw of a devil'.

In 1856 this remarkable man applied for leave from the army to enable him to make an attempt on the true source of the Nile. He was granted two years' paid absence, with the endorsement of the Foreign Office and the RGS. His partner on the expedition was six years younger, tall, slim, fair-haired and blue-eyed, clean-living, fit and determined. John Hanning Speke came from a West Country family which could trace its roots back to the Saxons. He had the English country gentleman's interest in field sports and had decided to travel the Nile well before he met Burton, his main motive being to kill and preserve birds and animals for a museum he was developing at his father's house: there were, he said, very few species left in India, Tibet or the Himalayas which he had not shot already. He was also intensely ambitious and quite fastidious: he hardly drank, so Burton's pleasure in drink, drugs and pornography and his preoccupation with African genitalia left Speke a little cold. It was not the most auspicious of teamings, but Burton claimed that he owed Speke the opportunity to join him (despite the fact that 'he was not a linguist . . . nor a man of science, nor an accurate astronomical observer'), because they had travelled together in Somalia in 1855. That journey had ended with Speke captured and at the point of death, with his gaoler stabbing a spear into his shoulder and then through each thigh. Astonishingly, Speke still retained the strength to make a run for it, to be reunited with his surviving companions. Burton later made the odd claim that 'before we set out, [Speke] openly declared that, being tired of life, he had come to be killed in Africa'.

For the expedition to find the source of the Nile the two men decided that, instead of following the river upstream from Egypt, they would land on the east coast of Africa and strike inland. They arrived on the island of Zanzibar in December 1856. It was a foul, stinking place, racked by malaria, dysentery, venereal diseases, yellow fever and elephantiasis, some instances of which, Burton noted, caused the scrotum to swell so much that it hung down around men's knees. Zanzibar still had a flourishing slave trade, which the British Empire was committed to terminating. But that was not their concern: despite the support of the Royal Geographical Society and the sponsorship of the British Foreign Office, they would make their journey under the red flag of the sultan of Zanzibar. The two men did not travel especially light and the final column of porters and guards numbered 132, with a drummer and standard bearer at the front and the two white men bringing up the rear. The porters in the middle carried sacks of brightly coloured beads, bolts of cloth and rolls of brass wire, to pay the expedition's way among local tribes. The rest of the baggage included tents and bedding, rifles and pistols, sextants, compasses, sundial, rain-gauge, barometer, pedometers, thermometers, telescope, hammers, chisels and saws, stationery (down to sealing wax), two dozen penknives, four umbrellas, 2,000 fishing hooks, a case of brandy (to be supplemented by several more later), cigars and several canisters of snuff.

The porters travelled in a cacophony of shouting, whistling, singing and imitations of the shrieks and cries of birds – the noise was intended not merely to amuse them but to deter any potential attackers. The party fought its way through swamps and scrub, up mountains and across rivers: 10 miles a day was good going. Tribal chiefs demanded tribute to allow the expedition to pass, thorn-bushes tore at their clothes, insects bit them mercilessly. If a hare or antelope crossed their path, the porters dropped their loads to chase it, and if successful, tore it limb from limb and ate it raw. On other occasions they squabbled, became lethargic when smoking drugs, mutinous when not. The two explorers fell sick with fever, hallucinated, starved, became so weak they could not walk, while at other times an ulcerated tongue prevented Burton from giving any orders at all. His account of the journey, *The Lake Regions of Central Africa*, describes how tribal chiefs amuse themselves by chopping limbs off people who displease them, how an ancient witch-doctor tried – and failed – to cure his sickness and notes the different practices of tribes like the Wanyamwezi and the Wagogo, from clothing and sex to favoured methods of intoxication. Speke does not figure prominently in the narrative and when he does appear it is generally to be described as under the weather, weak, obtuse, or having done 'nothing at all'. Burton does, however, include Speke's own account of the incident in which a small black beetle crawled into his ear while he was asleep. When the beetle reached his eardrum Speke said it had the same sort of effect as a swarm of bees attacking a train of donkeys. Unable to remove the beetle by pouring melted butter into his ear canal, Speke decided to try to dig it out with the blade of his penknife. In silencing the beetle he also made himself deaf and the entire side of his head and neck swelled up in buboes – it was, he said, the most painful experience of his life. (When he blew his nose his ear made an audible whistle, and six months after the event bits of beetle were still dropping out of his ear.)

The two men landed on the east coast of mainland Africa from Zanzibar in June 1857. A year later, they had reached the Arab slave station at Tabora, in what is now western Tanzania, having already made the momentous discovery of the existence of Lake Tanganyika. Burton had hoped that the lake might turn out to be the source of the Nile, but it was not high enough above sea level for that, and anyway the river on which they had pinned their hopes turned out to flow in the wrong direction. 'I felt sick at heart,' Burton wrote. The camp at Tabora was comfortable, and especially congenial to Burton who enjoyed the company of Arabs – that they were in Africa as slavers did not trouble him unduly. Speke, however, was restless and anxious to see what truth there was in the tales the traders told of a much bigger lake three weeks' journey to the north. While Burton stayed in camp to recuperate and write up his notes, Speke set off again.

On 3 August 1858 John Hanning Speke stood on the shores of a massive body of water. He was instantly, instinctively – and unscientifically – convinced he had found what they were looking for. He stayed at the lake only three days and then rushed back to rejoin Burton, unable to contain his excitement. 'We had scarcely breakfasted,' recalled Burton, 'before he announced to me the startling fact that he had discovered the sources of the White Nile.' In the absence of any proof or even eyewitness testimony, Burton was unconvinced. But Speke would hear no doubts. And now came the oddest part of their epic journey. The two men simply decided not to discuss the matter further. 'After a few days it became evident to me that not a word could be uttered on the subject of the Lake, the Nile, and his trouvaille generally without offence,' said Burton. 'By tacit agreement it was, therefore, avoided.' In a letter to the Royal Geographical Society later, Speke gave his side of the breakdown. Burton, he said, 'used to snub me so unpleasantly when talking about anything that I often kept my own counsel. B is one of those men who never *can* be wrong, and will never acknowledge an error so that when only two are together talking becomes more of a bore than a pleasure.' Richard Burton's line was not that he was especially miffed at being absent when the object of their shattering journey had been achieved, but that Speke was essentially guessing when he claimed that the lake (now, inevitably, christened Lake Victoria) was the source of the Nile. They should stick to what they had properly investigated.

At the end of September 1858, the expedition set off on the journey back to the coast. By now, both men were sick and exhausted and had to be carried for much of the way. At Zanzibar, in March the following year, they took ship for Aden, where they would join another vessel for the onward journey home to England. But it was there that the two men who had shared such hardships parted. By Burton's account, they had agreed that they would go public with their discoveries only once both were back home. Instead, Speke set off for England on board HMS *Furious*, and when Burton reached England, twelve days behind him, he discovered that the younger man had already contacted the president of the Royal Geographical Society to pass on his theory about the source of the Nile. London was transfixed by the news that an Englishman had almost certainly settled the greatest challenge in exploration, and £2,500 was immediately raised to send him back to Africa to confirm his discovery. When the gaunt figure of Burton reached home, he discovered there was a great deal less popular interest in his more meticulous account of Lake Tanganyika, for the obvious reason that it was not the fabled source of the Nile.

Speke found his companion for his next expedition to be altogether more congenial. Captain James Augustus Grant was another officer in the Indian army, and had even taken part in the relief of the siege of Lucknow. But yet again, at the culmination of their journey, Speke contrived to keep the climax to himself. Grant had been immobilized for three months by an infected sore in his leg, during which time Speke had been a virtual prisoner of King Mutesa in Buganda. When Grant finally rejoined him, Speke argued that they should split the caravan, with Grant preparing the ground for their return, while he pressed on to investigate stories of massive waterfalls where Lake Victoria spilled its banks. Conscious that his injured leg would not allow him to match the furious pace which Speke now proposed – 20 miles each day – Grant claimed to be entirely happy with the arrangement. On 21 July 1862, Speke reached the Nile, where he told his men 'they ought to shave their heads and bathe in the holy river, the cradle of Moses'. They turned to march towards the source of the river.

And so, one week later, on 28 July, Speke cast his eyes upon the great enigma of geography, the falls where Lake Victoria pours into the River Nile. 'It was a sight that attracted one for hours,' Speke wrote, 'the roar of the waters, the thousands of passenger-fish leaping at the falls with all their might; the Wasoga and Waganda fishermen coming out in boats and taking post on all the rocks with rod and hook, hippopotami and crocodiles lying sleepily on the water.' He named the place Ripon Falls, after the first Marquess of Ripon, president of the Royal Geographical Society when the expedition was organized. Then, reunited with Grant, Speke set off downstream on the Nile. At Gondoroko in southern Sudan, on 13 February 1863 – nearly two years and five months after starting their journey – they met Samuel Baker and his future wife, Florence (he had bought her in a slave auction), who had come upriver to search for them. Samuel and Florence offered the two men a cup of tea, Baker noting that:

> Speke appeared the more worn of the two: he was excessively lean, but in reality he was in good tough condition; he had walked the whole way from Zanzibar, never having once ridden during that wearisome march. Grant was in honourable rags; his bare knees projecting through the remnants of trousers that were an exhibition of rough industry in tailor's work. He was looking tired and feverish, but both men had a fire in the eye, that showed the spirit that had led them through.

As soon as he was able to do so, Speke cabled London: 'The Nile is settled.'

But the Nile was not entirely 'settled'. Speke had neither circumnavigated the lake nor given the river a comprehensive survey. Burton, for one, still nursed a grievance and clung to the possibility that Lake Tanganyika might be the source. The missionary and explorer David Livingstone was also sceptical. To settle the matter once and for all, a meeting was arranged for September 1864 by the British Association for the Advancement of Science. It was to be held in Bath, where Burton and Speke would present their arguments to an audience of geographers and scientists. But there was to be one final chapter in this extraordinary story. As the audience gathered on the morning of what had come to be known as 'The Nile Duel', a note was passed around. When the contents of the note were read to Burton, he staggered and sank into a chair, with the words, 'By God, he's killed himself!'

Whether Speke took his own life or was the victim of an extraordinarily timed accident will never be known. The day before the debate the two men had been in the same room, but cut each other dead, with Speke said to have left the room exclaiming, 'I can't stand this any longer!' He had then gone off to his uncle's nearby estate to shoot partridges. At about 4 p.m., his companions saw the explorer standing on top of a low wall. They heard a shot and saw him fall. When they reached him they found an awful wound to his chest. It looked as though he had clambered over the wall and then tried to pull his loaded gun – which had no safety catch – up after him. By the time they managed to get a doctor to him, Speke was dead. An inquest returned a verdict of accidental death.

These epics of nineteenth-century exploration gave the expansion of empire a clear focus. They were fantastical tales of wild landscapes, weird animals, extreme hardship and utterly different cultures, and their heroes men whose steely fortitude seemed to express a national purpose. Many of the protagonists of these epics also had a talent for self-promotion. Newspaper editors recognized that there were few things their growing readership would enjoy more with their breakfast marmalade than news of battles against the odds and they soon began the modern habit of sponsoring expeditions and paying small fortunes for first-hand accounts written by the explorers themselves. (The practice extended to wars as well, with correspondents like G. W. Steevens regaling readers of the *Daily Mail* with accounts of the glorious thrill of imperial battles – 'the only complete holiday ever invented'*– in places like Sudan and South Africa.)

The readership of newspapers was growing fast and as a journalistic proposition the explorer was irresistible. He braved danger and endured extreme hardship in thrilling contrast to the ordered calm of the suburban terrace. He could, like David Livingstone, be driven by hatred of the slave trade, or like Joseph Thomson – dead at thirty-seven – he could be so enigmatic as to declare, 'I am not an empire-builder. I am not a missionary. I am not truly a scientist. I merely want to return to Africa to continue my wanderings.' The motivation was secondary to

* The holiday ended during the Boer War siege of Ladysmith, where Steevens died of typhoid, aged thirty-one.

the fact of their national identity. These were Britons who were taming the world.

Does any of this matter now, other than as a ripping yarn? The
waterfalls which tumbled out of Lake Victoria, through which Speke
intended to offer the Marquess of Ripon immortality by naming
them Ripon Falls, largely disappeared when a dam was built in the
1950s. If the name of Speke is known at all, it is more likely to be as a
deprived area of Liverpool, once home to the Bryant and May match
factory and the Triumph sports-car plant, both long-gone British
brands. Richard Burton has his splendid tomb in a Mortlake cemetery in the shape of an Arab tent, but mention the name and you are
likely to have to explain that you're not talking about the Welsh actor
twice married to the actress Elizabeth Taylor. The accounts these
explorers wrote of their journeys are underpinned by a now offensive tone of utterly superior certainty: the white man knows best.
But it is impossible to read them without being struck by their
delight in the exuberant strangeness of the people, animals and plants
they encountered. As for the act of discovery, the planting of a flag
changed no physical reality. Terra Incognita was only land unknown
to European cartographers, Newfoundland had merely been found
by people who just hadn't happened to know it existed. Not a single
characteristic of the lake which Speke had reached was altered by his
calling it Victoria, any more than naming the highest mountain on
earth Everest after a one-time surveyor general of India changed its
height by an inch.

But the proliferation of British place names on maps gave an illusion that the world was being remade. At some primitive level the
stories of discovery have nurtured a sense of British endeavour, of
the solitary individual against the world, eccentric, outnumbered,
bloody-minded and convinced he's right, a sick and shrunken nation's
determination to hold its place in the world. It is perhaps most keenly
demonstrated in the cases of those explorers who died executing
their missions – Mungo Park and his sole remaining British companion throwing themselves into the River Niger and drowning, Captain
Cook bludgeoned and stabbed to death on a beach in Hawaii, Sir
John Franklin and his men perishing in the snow and ice, or the last

glimpse of George Mallory and Andrew Irvine as they toiled towards
the summit of Everest. There was something about these deaths
which was taken to express the spirit of Britain. They seemed to be
tableaux of self-sacrifice in the pursuit not of commercial gain but of
human endeavour. It did not matter if the mission had failed – in
some ways that made the impression more potent. Perhaps the acme
came with the last message left by Captain Robert Falcon Scott,
exhausted, hungry, frost-bitten and snow-blind in his Antarctic tent
in 1912. 'For God's sake look after our people . . .' 'Our people' was
more than the valiant, frozen band on the Ross Ice Shelf.*

By the turn of the twentieth century it had become easy for the British to feel special. The 1851 Great Exhibition had not only celebrated
home-grown enterprise but had seemed to demonstrate the readiness
of other nations to bring their tribute offerings. When the exhibition's Crystal Palace closed its doors, it had made enough profit for
an expanse of Kensington to be turned over to the building of 'Alber-
topolis' on which stood the Victoria and Albert Museum, the Natural
History Museum, Imperial College, the Royal Albert Hall, the Science Museum and the Royal Colleges of Art and Music, demonstrating
individually and collectively the nation's eminence. When Victoria
was redesignated as empress of India in 1876, her subjects basked in a
little of the reflected glory. But if they wanted to feel they really
were masters of all creation, they just took themselves off for an
afternoon at the London Zoo. Here, as the century wore on, the
growing numbers of strange animals testified to Britain's increasing
domination of the world.

The Zoological Society of London – the first of its kind in the
world – was an imperial invention, founded by the creator of Singapore, Sir Stamford Raffles, in a marriage between the nineteenth-century

---

* As time ticked down to the centenary of Scott's death, attitudes changed. A 1979
double-biography of Scott and Amundsen by Roland Huntford portrayed the former as incompetent and deceitful. An inquiry in the late 1990s talked of Huntford's
'devastating evidence of bungling' (quoted in Spufford, *I May Be Some Time*, p. 4).
It was not that the facts had changed, merely that empire and empire-makers were
seen differently.

thirst for knowledge and the accumulation of British colonies. By the middle years of the century, 'nature study', from pressed flowers to shell and butterfly collecting, had become a fashionable, improving activity, and as the empire grew fatter, 'the zoo' developed as one of the most popular places of entertainment in London. Greater and greater grew the number of explorers, colonial officials, scientists and retired sea-captains among its members, more abundant and stranger the specimens shipped to Britain. The zoo was imperial exploration for everyone. Its *Handbook* suggested that the weekend visitor exercise his imagination. 'In his mind's eye he may track the pathless desert and sandy waste; he may climb amid the romantic solitudes, the towering peaks, the wilder crags of the Himalayan heights . . . or peer among the dark lagoons of the African rivers, enshrouded by forests whose rank green foliage excludes the rays of even a tropical sun.' The caging of wild and exotic animals in the middle of London brought the conquest of wild and exotic lands to the heart of safe and ordered Britain.* The world was stranger and more exotic than ever might have been imagined. But all of its creatures, whether magnificent and menacing or small and cuddly, could be brought before the people of London, caged and displayed for their entertainment, amid cropped lawns and gravel paths.

The greatest attraction among the animals on show was a celebrity hippopotamus named Obaysch which had been brought to the zoo with much pomp. He was named after the island on the White Nile where he had been captured as a baby in 1849 before being offered as an ingratiating gift to the British by the ruler of Egypt.

* In 1882, the defeated king of the Zulus, Cetshwayo, was brought to London and taken on tours which included the Houses of Parliament, the bustling docks, the glittering shops of Bond Street and, oddest of all, an outing to the zoo, where he could look upon animals which, however exotic to cockneys, were native to his home continent. The king's own position was not very different to that of the animals, with crowds gathering each day outside the house rented for him in Kensington and newspapers recording his every move. To avoid being mobbed, he had had to travel to the zoo inside a closed carriage. The king returned to Africa as comfortable in tailored frock coat as he had ever been in traditional near-nudity, and died on a Native Reserve, the human safari park of its day.

Obaysch was shipped down the Nile with a guard of Nubian soldiers, installed in the British Consul's garden, lured on to a Pacific and Orient steamer by his keeper and a couple of professional snake charmers and taken to Southampton. On the train journey from there to London, crowds at every station clamoured for a glimpse of the beast, but generally had to make do with the sight of his Egyptian keeper, Hamet, who, because he slept with Obaysch, was understandably keen to get an occasional breath of fresh air. Once installed in the zoo, Obaysch was a sensation. Thousands of people lined up at weekends to see what *Punch* dubbed 'HRH' – His Rolling Hulk. 'The long lines of carriages which are daily to be seen at the entrance of the society's garden are conclusive evidence that the hippopotamus . . . is the great icon of the day,' observed the *Illustrated London News* in 1850. Indeed he was. Attendances at the zoo soared – even Queen Victoria took her children. The following year, the magazine was still burbling with excitement about Obaysch – it was a millennium and a half since an animal like him had been seen in Europe, a comparison which explicitly compared the British with the Roman Empire – at the expense of the latter, considering that Pliny believed that hippos walked backwards to confuse anyone trying to track them. Obasych did not really do much at the zoo, just lying around on the edge of his pond, ministered to by Hamet and occasionally grunting. The zoo authorities soon acquired a female hippo from the Nile, with whom, after sixteen years of indifference, Obaysch eventually produced a calf. Charles Dickens wrote an article arguing for other zoo animals to be given parity of esteem. But in vain. Obaysch was the zoo's superstar, celebrated in souvenir models and, most unlikely of all, in the newly composed 'Hippopotamus Polka'.

CHAPTER SIX

'Let not England forget her precedence of
teaching nations how to live'
John Milton, 1645

LIVINGSTONE READING THE BIBLE.

It was the last thing he expected to see.

In 1896, a parched American explorer reached the banks of the
Tana River in northern Kenya. Arthur Donaldson Smith, a doctor
and big-game hunter, had begun his journey at Berbera in Somaliland: it had taken fifteen months in the wilderness to reach the river.
Now he estimated there were perhaps three or four more days of
hardship to endure. Only seven white men were believed to have
passed this way before and he wondered vaguely about the chances
of a group of Africans arriving in canoes. Suddenly, shimmering
through the heat haze, from around a bend upstream what should

appear but a canoe. More extraordinary was what it contained – a white man in a white suit, holding a pink umbrella above his head. The American fired two rifle-shots into the air and was answered by two shots from the canoe. As the boat approached, the American drew up his porters in a line behind him. The canoe neared the bank, and the man stepped ashore. The American felt that 'introductions by a third party are unnecessary in these remote regions'. The two men shook hands and the new arrival introduced himself. He was, he explained, the Reverend Robert Ormerod and he was looking for a site to build a new mission station. However unexpected this encounter was to the American, he really should not have been surprised. For missionaries might turn up anywhere. In fact, the remoter the terrain, the better. Making converts was hard work, but missionaries greatly increased their chances if no one had been prospecting for converts in the area before them. The need to find new souls to save took them to places which held no appeal for merchant-venturers, gold-prospectors or imperial strategists.

By the late nineteenth century, flag-planting was inseparable from cross-carrying. 'It is religion which has given the comparatively small United Kingdom its imperial power and responsibilities,' said the secretary of the Free Church of Scotland's mission arm. By the turn of the twentieth century there were an estimated 12,000 British missionaries scattered across the world – the provisional wing of empire and often a damn nuisance to colonial administrators, who objected to their supercilious presumption that they knew better than them what was best for the natives. 'Confound all these parsons,' exclaimed the Governor of Uganda, Sir Hesketh Bell. But the missionaries had to be lived with. 'They spread the use of the English language. They induct the natives into the best kind of civilisation,' wrote one official. 'In fact each mission station is an essay in colonisation.' Or as Lord Salisbury put it, 'First the missionary. Then the consul. Then the general.' Or, often enough, first the missionary, then the trader.

Their energy and fortitude were astonishing – some missionaries might walk a thousand miles or more in a year. Alfred Tucker, for example, had been serving as a curate in Durham when, in 1890, he offered his services to the Archbishop of Canterbury as a potential missionary. Had he paused to think he might have deduced that the Archbishop's decision to raise him immediately to the rank of bishop of Eastern Equatorial Africa (what became Kenya, Uganda and much of Tanganyika) hinted at how unattractive the posting was (the two previous bishops had died in harness). Instead, he left his wife and baby at home and set out for Africa, reaching Uganda in December that year, after a four-month trek from the coast on foot, in the company of a gun-runner. Dressed in tweeds, with a broad-brimmed hat and an enormous moustache, the new bishop set about trying to settle the consequences of the Africans' eager embrace of Christianity: Anglican and French Catholic missionaries and their communities were on the point of war. Peace accomplished, there was further work ahead, for Uganda was not at the time part of the empire. The Imperial British East Africa Company, which had been given the rights to exploit the territory, was making no money, so Tucker raised sufficient funds from evangelicals in Britain to make it worth their while staying for another year. Two years later the British government declared the territory a protectorate. In his youth, Bishop Tucker had been an enthusiastic walker, cricketer and footballer, which had blessed him with a sufficiently iron constitution to survive nearly twenty years of sleeping rough and tramping across the country with his Bible and paintbox (his memoirs are illustrated with his own paintings). At fifty-nine he could still ride six hours from one mission station to another, and then play – and win – three sets of tennis.*

When they returned from the bush to retirement in Harrogate or Eastbourne, these men and women (for this was an endeavour in which both sexes took part) produced memoirs which appeared under titles like *The Congo for Christ* (by the Reverend J. B. Myers) or *In Dwarf Land and Cannibal Country* (by the Reverend A. B. Lloyd). The stories they told, of danger and hardship, followed by reward

---

* And he was certainly not unique. At the age of fifty-one, Bishop John Hine of the Universities Mission to Central Africa – a stick-thin, feeble-looking figure with a huge beard and a preference for the company of cats to that of women – led a mission into Northern Rhodesia (now Zambia), a country over twice the size of England. He walked nearly 3,000 miles in two years.

and redemption, had the effect of evangelizing for empire, which, in some eyes, was making up 'by victories of the Cross overseas, for the losses of their Church at Home': the further religious scepticism advanced in Britain, the harder British missionaries laboured abroad. Mission work took the zeal which had driven the anti-slavery movement in Britain and gave it a new focus, convincing many at home that the expansion of the empire was God's work. In truth, missionaries were often resented in the colonies, or tolerated for as long as they were present and afterwards forgotten about. The most famous missionary of all, David Livingstone, made only one convert in his entire career, an African chief who later decided he had made a mistake and preferred polygamy to paradise.*

Who could doubt the rightness of the British Empire when it was expressed through such a man as David Livingstone? In person he could come across as dour and brusque, social awkwardness accentuated by an arm which had been mangled in an attack by a lion. He stood about 5 foot 8, with cropped hair and moustache setting off a well-tanned explorer's face. But he was blessed with an ability to convey his convictions in clear and passionate language. One Englishman who heard him on his 1857 speaking tour recalled how 'when excited, a varied expression of earnest and benevolent feeling, and remarkable enjoyment of the ludicrous . . . passes over [his face] . . . When he speaks to you, you think him at first to be a Frenchman; but as he tells you a Scotch anecdote in the Glaswegian dialect, you make up your mind that he must be, as his face indicates, a countryman from the north.' The story this Scotsman told was of an astonishing walk he had made, right across Africa, armed with not much more than a Bible, walking stick, magic lantern, sextant, compass and nautical almanac. It made him into a national hero, led to an invitation to call on Queen Victoria and saw him showered with honours. Soon Livingstone was planning a return to Africa, further to advance 'Christianity, Commerce and Civilization', a trinity which ensured a

---

* On the subject of polygamy, an unfortunate consequence of the missionaries' encouraging men to discard 'surplus' wives was the spread of syphilis, because abandoned wives were often driven to prostitution.

healthy public subscription and the endorsement of a government eager to discover the commercial possibilities of trade up the Zambezi into the heart of Africa. The new expedition left England in March 1858, intending to travel upriver in a series of increasingly shallow-draught boats to the point where they could establish the headquarters from which they would explore, evangelize and disrupt the Arab slavers taking their sorry traffic down to the coast.

In Africa, those around him felt the full force of his manic obsession. One by one he fell out with his companions. Fresh volunteers arrived with supplies three years after his expedition had left England, but they too lapsed into sickness or fell foul of Livingstone's mad determination. Even his most loyal assistant, the expedition doctor John Kirk, noted that 'Dr L is out of his mind . . . he is a most unsafe leader' and 'about as ungrateful and slippery a mortal as I ever came in contact with'. Kirk had reason to be worried, for, by insisting they shoot a set of rapids by canoe, Livingstone had nearly drowned him. Eventually, the British government had had enough and recalled Livingstone to England after six years. His homecoming this time was much less fêted than his return from the walk across Africa. But in 1866 he was off again. Now he planned not merely to spread the gospel and fight the slavers, but possibly also to find the headwaters of the Nile. This, Livingstone's last journey, ran into trouble almost from the point of his arrival in Africa. Progress was much slower than expected. Porters deserted. Scientific equipment was damaged. Diversions were necessary. The medicine chest was stolen. Wet weather necessitated further detours. Supplementary stores ordered up from the coast were not at the rendezvous point. As year succeeded year, Livingstone succumbed to one sickness after another – cholera, dysentery, pneumonia, ulcerated feet and haemorrhoids. He had pulled out many of his own teeth and appears to have been hallucinating much of the time. 'I am terribly knocked up,' he scrawled with the juice of a berry in the margins of one of his surviving books. As he suffered in solitude, a vast audience at home had begun to hunger for news of his fate, for by now missions to 'darkest Africa' were much more than low-key matters of mere evangelism. What had become of the lone, lost Scot, Mr Valiant-for-Truth abandoned in the jungle, was a gift of a story to the rapidly growing mass media. James Gordon Bennett of the *New York Herald* recognized the commercial potential of a world scoop and Henry Morton Stanley's marathon journey to discover Livingstone's fate was the result.

Stanley's celebrated greeting, when he eventually found Livingstone at Ujiji, in what is now western Tanzania – 'Dr Livingstone, I presume?' – guaranteed the immortality of both men. Afterwards, they travelled together for a while, and then Stanley left Livingstone to continue his search for the source of the Nile. One year later, Livingstone was still in Africa, but by now he was a very sick man able to travel only if carried in a litter by his porters. His death in 1873 – he was discovered, it was said, kneeling in prayer – provided Britain with another imperial *pietà*. It was seven years since he had left home. His heart was removed and buried in Africa, but the devotion of his loyal servants in embalming the body and returning it to England was made to seem almost divinely ordained. Livingstone lay in state at the Royal Geographical Society headquarters and his elaborate funeral in Westminster Abbey in April 1874 consecrated imperialism. The tenacity and charm of the man who lies beneath the black slab in the floor of the Abbey had been matched by a cranky pigheadedness. And yet he retained the capacity to inspire the country, even more in death than in life. He really hated slavery, even if he was ineffective in making converts. The *British Quarterly Review* commented that 'his death has bequeathed the work of African exploration and civilisation as a sacred legacy to this country'. The empire really was God's work.

Of course, the evangelical impulse was born out of a conviction that the missionaries' beliefs were superior: it could not be otherwise. It is also true that a special kind of casuistry rooted itself in the minds of the imperial clergy, that the empire was something which had been spread not by exploration, trade or force of arms, but by Providence. One especially overexcited clergyman proclaimed that 'the flag which is always unfurled over every land and every sea' was merely 'the Cross three times'. In 1902, the secretary of the Society for the Propagation of the Gospel, Henry Hutchinson Montgomery, declared that 'the clergy are officers in an imperial army', serving both England and Christ. Yet, even at the time they went about their work, British missionaries could be sneered at by members of the imperial establishment. It was not merely that they took the flag to places which had no immediately obvious benefit to the empire, but that they didn't act the part. Members of the Universities Mission to Central Africa – which had been established to respond to Livingstone's appeal to spread the word in Nyasaland – lived as near to the Africans as they could, celibate, eating native food, paid almost nothing and sleeping in mud huts. They died of malaria and blackwater fever in great numbers, but where others might have seen courage and conviction, they often earned only contempt. The first colonial proconsul in the area, Sir Harry Johnston (said to have been the inspiration for Edgar Wallace's imperialist potboiler *Sanders of the River*), thought it 'pathetic . . . to see highly educated men from Oxford and Cambridge hollow-eyed and fever-stricken, crouching in little huts which no native chief would deign to occupy'. But they were people who practised what they preached. When Bishop Hine, for example, discovered that the (white) church council at the new church of St Andrew's in the town of Livingstone (named after the explorer) planned to reserve it for white use, he simply refused to consecrate the place until they recognized the principle of racial equality. 'I am better among native races than pushing bigoted colonists,' said the Bishop.

The lasting memorial to these men and women is the array of schools they established. Without them, great swathes of the developing world would simply have had no education. Blantyre in Malawi (named after Livingstone's birthplace), for example, became a fiefdom of the Church of Scotland, and even today the Synod is associated with dozens of Malawian primary schools. The town's church of St Michael and All Angels, which claimed to be the first permanent Christian church between the Nile and the Zambezi, is an extraordinary piece of architecture, built to no preordained plan from over eighty different types of brick, all made by local people. At Nkoloti primary school, a much more modest collection of single-storey tin-roofed buildings on the outskirts of the town, the roll has grown so enormously that it now numbers almost 8,000 children, who have to be accommodated in two separate shifts.

By the twentieth century, the missionaries had justified the enmity of some of the empire-builders, for they preached freedom and the mission schools educated many of the heroes of the independence struggle. The man whose face adorns Malawian banknotes, for example, the Reverend John Chilembwe – still celebrated as the first Malawian freedom fighter – was an alumnus of the missions in Blantyre.*

In a sense, all empire-builders were missionaries. How else was a chap to justify to himself the suffering he experienced in his moments of loneliness, sickness and introspection than that it was all being endured in the name of some greater cause? The most eminent claim in the moral justification of empire was the fact that the British had made the trading and keeping of slaves illegal. Frederick Lugard, who was later to become the splendidly moustached governor general of Nigeria, had begun his African career in 1888 fighting Arab slave traders, saying, 'I can think of no juster cause in which a soldier may draw his sword.' Even those, like the young Winston Churchill, who considered that the British might as well continue to pile up colonies, if only because everyone else was at it, talked up the moral justice of the cause. In *The River War*, his account of how Kitchener's machine guns made short work of poorly armed Sudanese, Churchill justified the imperial mission in characteristically rolling sentences. 'To give peace to warring tribes, to administer justice where all was violence, to strike the chains from the slave, to draw the richness from the soil, to plant the earliest seeds of commerce and learning, to increase in whole peoples their capacities for pleasure and diminish their chances of pain – what more beautiful ideal or more valuable reward can inspire human effort?' In the eyes of people like that, the entire imperial purpose was a vocation to civilize the world, an enterprise in salvation.

It rested on a conviction not merely that different races had different characteristics, but that the qualities of the British were superior

---

* Chilembwe is the only Christian minister I have heard of who not only sanctioned killing a man (a local white estate manager, William Jervis Livingstone, in 1915) but then preached his Sunday sermon with his victim's head displayed on a pole beside him.

to all others. The belief is anathema in the twenty-first century, both because it is offensive and because it is scientific nonsense. Yet it is illuminating to see how willing even the most enlightened Victorians were to entertain the idea of some hierarchy of races. Mid-century Britain was transfixed, for example, by the return from the Arctic of the explorer John Rae in 1854. He had set out to discover what had become of the expedition led by Sir John Franklin which had attempted to establish whether a north-west passage to China might exist through the ice floes of northern Canada. Nine years had passed since Franklin – a decent, reliable, if overweight man of fifty-nine – and his carefully chosen crew had set sail. Common sense decreed that all 129 of them must be dead. But, chivvied along by Franklin's widow, expedition after expedition set forth to discover their fate. Rae returned to England with relics from Franklin's expedition which he had acquired from Inuits he had met in the Arctic. In a dispatch to the Admiralty he related how the Inuit had described bodies and graves, from which Dr Rae concluded beyond doubt that the expedition had all perished. The imagined spectacle of a hand-picked Royal Navy team freezing to death in pursuit of knowledge, commerce and the spread of civilization was a noble tableau in the great imperial tradition. But the day after his arrival in London, Rae's report for the Admiralty was published in *The Times* and, in a single subversive sentence, questioned the entire 'civilizing' purpose of the empire. 'From the mutilated state of many of the corpses and the contents of the kettles,' he wrote, 'it is evident that our wretched countrymen had been driven to the last resource – cannibalism – as a means of prolonging existence.' The suggestion that British explorers might have engaged in a practice from which the empire was liberating the inhabitants of lands it colonized was simply too shocking to be believed.

Charles Dickens, for example, found the accusation intolerable, and argued that it could not possibly be true. There was the question of the reliability of hearsay evidence in a foreign language to start with. There was the example of other Englishmen enduring extreme hunger without eating one another – Captain Bligh, for example, cast adrift by the mutineers on the *Bounty*. And could the corpses not have been disfigured by bears or wolves? But the most telling argument he advanced in his tuppenny magazine, *Household Words*, was that it was simply against the natural order of things. Without a shred of evidence he asserted that it was much more likely that the sailors had been attacked and killed by 'Esquimaux'. Experience showed that 'savages' were all very well, and perfectly deferential when the white man was strong. But the moment he appeared weak or vulnerable, 'the savage has changed and sprung upon him'. British explorers would never resort to cannibalism. But 'we believe', he wrote, 'every savage to be in his heart covetous, treacherous, and cruel; and we have yet to learn what knowledge the white man – lost, houseless, shipless, apparently forgotten by his race, plainly famine-stricken, weak, frozen, helpless, and dying – has of the gentleness of Esquimaux nature'. This was the antithesis of the idea of the 'noble savage', for nobility was the product of civilization. 'The better educated the man, the better disciplined the habits, the more reflective and religious the tone of thought, the more gigantically improbable the "last resource" [cannibalism] becomes.' The myth of the twenty-first century is of a Brotherhood of Man. The myth of the imperial age was of a sort of league table of humanity, with the Europeans permanently at the top.

And then along came Darwin. At first glance, a theory about the common origins of humanity might be expected to undermine a belief in European superiority. Instead, the imperial mentality found comfort in the revolutionary doctrine of evolution. The anxiety which racked the Church on discovering that, in Darwin's resonant sentence, 'Man still bears in his bodily frame the indelible stamp of his lowly origin' did not shake the conviction of superiority very much. Indeed, in *The Descent of Man*, Darwin appeared to offer an evolutionary justification for European colonialism. Starting from the premise that 'the western nations of Europe . . . now so immeasurably surpass their former savage progenitors, [that they] stand at the summit of civilization', he determined that 'the civilized races of man will almost certainly exterminate, and replace the savage races through the world'. Indeed, perhaps the most curious thing of all was the superiority he claimed in seeing descent from a 'heroic little monkey' or 'an old baboon' instead of from 'a savage who delights to torture his enemies, offers up bloody sacrifices, practises infanticide without remorse, treats his wives like slaves, knows no decency, and is haunted by the grossest superstitions'.

For every clergyman who denounced Darwin, a crank or polemicist embraced him. But *The Descent of Man* offered a philosophy which comforted the imperially minded. Within a decade or so, Darwin's conjecture had been reconciled with the practice of planting the flag in other parts of the world. In 1876, a writer in the *Melbourne Review* put it succinctly: 'Survival of the fittest means that might – wisely used – is right.' From this beginning he went on to assert that 'the inexorable law of natural selection' led to 'exterminating the inferior Australian and Maori races . . . The world is better for it.' Indeed, the whole world would be much improved if the same theory was applied everywhere, preserving the better specimens of humanity, instead of 'actually promoting the non-survival of the fittest, protecting the propagation of the imprudent, the diseased, the defective, and the criminal'. In a country initially settled as a penal colony this was pretty rich.

The question of the relationship between colonizer and colonized was most acute in Africa, which Europeans were busy appropriating for different foreign flags. Explorers like Richard Burton returned from their travels to tell the Royal Geographical Society of strange places where the women tilled the ground while the menfolk sat and span cotton; of cannibals and concubines; of chiefs who were ready to offer travellers the enjoyment of their wives, sisters and daughters; of a king who for amusement had chopped off the hands of an irritating wife and then commanded her to use her stumps to search his head for lice; of enemies enslaved and flogged; of children murdered. Burton understood the appetite for exotic stories, shrugged his shoulders and concluded that the only way to govern in Africa was by 'an iron-handed and lion-hearted despotism'. Africans were examined, anatomized, weighed and measured. The existence of human beings so visibly different from Europeans both worried and intrigued them. Anthropologists and scientists from the colonial powers set about answering the question 'What are they?'

The anti-slavery campaign had run on the slogan 'Am I Not a Man and Brother?', which might perhaps have been answer enough in itself. But the slogan had been intended to change the behaviour of the *perpetrators* – other Europeans, African tribes which sold their victims into slavery, and the Arabs who used religion to justify the practice. Any suggestion that Africans really *were* brothers and sisters would have raised all sorts of issues about the legitimacy of the whole imperial exercise, so the question of defining an African amounted to a definition of a European. Scientists and pseudo-scientists tried to tackle the issue. In 1863, for example, a speech-therapist and amateur anthropologist, James Hunt, presented a paper – *On the Negro's Place in Nature* – to promote his belief in polygenesis, the theory that different human races had had different origins. He dedicated his paper to Richard Burton, then serving as British consul at Fernando Po, a pestilential island off the west African coast ('the very abomination of desolation', Burton called it), because the 'outer barbarians' of the general public lacked the explorer's understanding of the continent. Hunt's theory ruled out any possibility of a brotherhood of man. He proposed instead a natural hierarchy, in which the white man was at the top: Africa had had the 'benefit' of Egyptian, Carthaginian and Roman colonization, but none had properly 'civilised' its inhabitants. 'Except some knowledge of metallurgy they possess no art . . . The reflective faculties hardly appear to be at all developed.' He added the footnote: 'It is said that when the Negro has been with other races, he has always been a slave. This is quite true.'

From physical examination he observed that, while their bodies were better suited to African weather than those of white men, black people were shorter, less stable, with 'inferior eyesight, cruder tastes and less developed sensibilities'. Yet at birth there was hardly any difference: 'young Negro children are nearly as intelligent as European children; but the older they grow the less intelligent they become. They exhibit when young, an animal liveliness for play and tricks far surpassing the European child.' Hunt then leaped to the conclusion that the 'incapacity' of Africans was the consequence of puberty – the African's brain simply stopped growing earlier than the brain of a European. As the skull settled and assumed recognizably African characteristics, the space available for the development of the brain shrank. 'This premature union of the bones of the skull may give a clue to much of the mental inferiority which is seen in the Negro race.' This did not put the African right at the bottom of the heap, for in slavery he had demonstrated a tremendous capacity for work, which made him not entirely beyond the possibility of redemption. But 'the analogies are far more numerous between the Negro and apes than between the European and apes . . . the Negro is inferior intellectually to the European . . . [and] can only be humanised and civilised by Europeans'.

When Hunt delivered his crackpot confection to a meeting of the British Association for the Advancement of Science, in Newcastle-upon-Tyne, 'my statement of the simple facts was received with such loud hisses that you would have thought the room had nearly been filled with a quantity of Eve's tempters instead of her amiable descendants'. What had especially incited the abuse was his defence of slavery. 'Our Bristol and Liverpool merchants', he said, had, 'perhaps, helped to benefit the race when they transplanted some of them to America'. He insisted he was not suggesting a restoration of the slave trade, which was plainly evil. But it was evil only because it was indiscriminate. What, he wanted to know, was wrong with giving Africa the opportunity to export 'her worthless or surplus population'? The catcalls and hisses demonstrate the depth of popular commitment to a more humane set of values. Hunt's pernicious nonsense struck at Britain's main moral cause in the world, did not gain widespread support and is interesting only for the light it throws on how thoughtful Britons struggled to find a way of comprehending the moral justification for the empire. Much more common was a belief within missionary organizations of a 'hierarchy of civilisation' which acknowledged that some foreign cultures – notably in countries like Japan – although different from Britain's, were nonetheless of 'the highest international rank'. Next on the ladder came comparatively sophisticated societies 'under Christian rule or influence', like India. The indigenous peoples of 'low civilisation' which had not yet been brought under European rule or influence were at the bottom of the tree.

Yet a genuine affection for Africa and Africans could be seen in the Church of Scotland missionary who built the extraordinary church in Blantyre, David Clement Scott. He preferred, he said, to think of

Christ taking upon himself 'the form of Africa [which] bears the sins of the world's rulers', and asked, 'How long are we as a nation going to lay our selfishness, our meanness, our falsehoods, our lusts, yea, and the whole burden of our sins upon this Lamb of God?' Often this concern for indigenous peoples expressed itself in a conviction that Africans were 'child-like'. The term is repugnant to modern ears, but it was not intentionally malicious, for many of the missionaries saw their role as protecting indigenous people. 'Watching that the interests of the native, in the days of his immaturity, are neither overlooked by the Empire authorities, nor overborne by white settlers or traders, without a protest being raised', was the way one of their number put it. Give or take a few words, it could sound like the campaigning talk of a modern pressure group working in the developing world.

CHAPTER SEVEN

'Producing capital meals with three bricks and a baking pot'
The Handbook for Girl Guides, or How Girls
Can Help Build up the Empire, 1912

In H. Rider Haggard's late-Victorian adventure yarn *She*, two Englishmen set off for darkest Africa to discover the origins of a legend. Intrepid, level-headed chaps in Norfolk jackets, they carry the conventional prejudices about primitive peoples, the dangers of polluting the blood by intermarriage between races, and so on. But, instead of the usual imperial spoils, the two men fall among a cave-dwelling tribe ruled over by 'She-who-must-be-obeyed', the queen Ayesha, one of the greatest femmes fatales ever invented. Although the novel was published – and an instant best-seller – in the year of Queen Victoria's golden jubilee, Ayesha is a different sort of monarch altogether. When the Englishmen first enter her kingdom, a kindly native explains how it works: 'In this country the women do what they please. We worship them, and give them their way, because without them the world could not go on; they are the source of life.' This is a bit of a tricky one for our flannelled heroes; the narrator replies, 'Ah,' adding that 'the matter [had] never struck me quite in that light before.'

Just in case the whole narrative becomes altogether too subversive, She-who-must-be-obeyed does not have the black skin of most Africans, being, by some freakish occurrence, a pale-skinned descendant of King Solomon – the 2,000 years she has spent living in a complex of caves has clearly not done much for her complexion. In the chapter at the heart of the book, 'Ayesha Unveils', our heroes get a closer look. 'She lifted her white and rounded arms – never had I seen such arms before – and slowly, very slowly, withdrew some fastening beneath her hair. Then all of a sudden the long, corpse-like wrappings fell from her to the ground, and my eyes travelled up her form.' The men are dumbstruck until they catch sight of her face.

> This beauty, with all its awful loveliness and purity, was *evil* . . . Though the face before me was that of a young woman of certainly not more than thirty years, in perfect health, and the first flush of ripened beauty, yet it had stamped upon it a look of unutterable experience, and of deep acquaintance with grief and passion . . . and it seemed to say: 'Behold me, lovely as no woman was or is, undying and half-divine; memory haunts me from age to age, and passion leads me by the hand – evil have I done . . . and sorrow shall I know till my redemption comes.'

It is enough to burst the buttons on a Victorian gentleman's waistcoat.

Before long, of course, the narrator succumbs. 'I am but a man, and she was more than a woman . . . then and there I fell on my knees before her, and told her in a sad mixture of languages that I worshipped her as never woman was worshipped, and that I would give my immortal soul to marry her.' Being an Englishman, of course, our hero soon snaps out of it, escapes the danger of sexual subjugation, and by the end of this tremendous adventure fantasy has returned to the sanity of Victoria's England, where, whatever else may be said, women knew their place.

Rider Haggard knew his market – *She* became one of the best-selling books of all time. He also knew the empire, having been dispatched to South Africa by a father who considered him 'only fit to be a greengrocer', and, at the age of twenty, raised the flag in Pretoria when Britain annexed the Transvaal. By the following year he was the youngest head of a government department in South Africa, running the Transvaal High Court: the empire could be very generous to those who seized the opportunity. Rider Haggard returned home with a deep appreciation of the very striking masculinity of Britain's imperial culture. Allan Quatermain, the big-game hunter who narrates another of his tales, *King Solomon's Mines*, reassures readers early on that 'I can safely say that there is not a petticoat in the entire history.' *King Solomon's Mines* is the grandfather of the Lost World genre of books about vanished kingdoms. But it also celebrated the fact that – with a very few exceptions like the archaeologist and colonial administrator Gertrude Bell – empire-building was a largely male thing.*

★

* They were marked out by their moustache habit, which became commonplace for European soldiers in the East India Company's Bombay Regiment in 1854, largely because Indian soldiers laughed at clean-shaven men. Soon the fashion had taken hold everywhere. Canny businessmen offered pomades, wax, scissors and curling tongs to make facial topiary appear even more impressive. Piers Brendon, author of one of the most readable of empire histories, even believes that the state of the moustache carries a message about the state of the empire. When Kitchener set out to retake Sudan he wore what was to become the most famous facial hair in the world (as seen on the First World War 'Your Country Needs You' recruiting poster). By contrast, Anthony Eden, the Prime Minister responsible for the bungled attempt to capture the Suez Canal in 1956, had a weedy apology for a moustache (see p. 264). Other stigmata of empire were not on public display, although another distinguished empire historian, Ronald Hyam, suggests that the growth of the moustache was complemented by the snipping off of the foreskin. How much the increasing popularity of male circumcision was to do with discouraging masturbation later in life and how much to do with health considerations in the tropics is a question unlikely ever to be resolved.

The departure of young men from Britain to try their luck in the expanding empire had two obvious social consequences. Firstly, it drained the pool of available marriage prospects for the young women left behind. And secondly, it raised the challenge of where the young men were to find an outlet for their own sexual and romantic needs. In the early days in India, they seem to have made their own arrangements, often on a commercial or semi-commercial basis. 'I now commenced a regular course of fucking with native women,' writes Edward Sellon in one of the rare accounts of sexual relations in the early days of the Raj. In his memoirs he paints a picture of available young Indian women who 'understood in perfection all the arts and wiles of love'. There is no reason to believe that Sellon, who had arrived as a young cadet of the East India Company in 1834, was being impeccably accurate: his entire career (including a work called *The Romance of Lust*) testifies more to commercial need than anything else. But nor is there any particular reason to disbelieve him, and none at all to assume that British soldiers in India were entirely celibate. Sellon reported that most important temples had troupes of dancing girls attached to them, whose job it was to sing and perform traditional 'Nautch' dances, and 'to prostitute themselves in the courts to all comers, and thus raise funds for the enrichment of the place of worship to which they belong'. He knew of cases where 'Nautch girls' had been paid 200 rupees for a single night's company, which was 'not very much to be wondered at, as they comprise some of the loveliest women in the world'. Elsewhere, he claimed to recall two distinct classes of prostitutes: one charging two rupees for her services, the other, an infinitely superior creature, five. The 'fivers' were 'the handsomest Mohammedan girls', and in his long experience of 'English, French, German and Polish women of all grades of society' he had never found one to compare with these 'salacious, succulent houris'. They did not drink, they were scrupulously clean, shaved their pudenda, dressed sumptuously, wore flowers in their hair, played musical instruments and sang sweetly. There was no suggestion from Sellon that women might have been driven to sell themselves by anything as odious as poverty or misfortune. They fulfilled the male fantasy of being happy hookers. India, he preached, was a place where more or less any sexual service was available, free of shame, if not free of charge.

It is certainly true that in their imperial possessions the British encountered cultures with very different – and much more open – attitudes to sex than they were used to at home. In India, for example, young Britons gawped in astonishment at the decorations on the walls of some Hindu temples, with their depictions of intercourse in all sorts of positions not normally encountered in the rectories of Hampshire.* After being posted to India in 1842 the great orientalist Richard Burton set about investigating the sexual possibilities with the indefatigable dedication which would later characterize his attempts to find the source of the Nile. He became convinced that women in tropical countries were more passionate than men, reported the belief that if a man gave a woman seven large cloves to eat on the seventeenth of the month she became insatiable, noted the prevalence of lesbianism in Muslim harems, developed a connoisseur's eye for Nautch girls, and recorded that British objections to the well-established custom of beheading unfaithful wives had merely created a glut of semi-professionals, so that 'if a young officer sent to the bazaar for a girl, half a dozen would troop to his quarters'.

Sexual relations were quite as exploitative, then, as the East India Company's other relations with India. But significant numbers of early British visitors made more permanent arrangements and took Indian wives and mistresses, who seem to have occupied a recognized position in society. Although later politicians and officials claimed to be scandalized when missionaries reported that miscegenation was occurring, it would have been more astonishing if men possessed of the energy to leave Britain and seek their fortune overseas were not also keen to satisfy more immediate physical and emotional needs – soldiers and adventurers have behaved in much the same way

* Sadly, the story of the supposed origin of the missionary position, as the only arrangement which British missionaries believed suitable for the beastly business, is probably untrue.

since long before Julius Caesar picked up his sword. There is ample
evidence of easy social relations in the early stages of the British presence in India. Johan Zoffany's 1780s Lucknow painting *Colonel
Mordaunt's Cock Match* shows the notoriously louche nawab of
Oudh★ enjoying himself among English officers. Colonel James
Skinner, founder of the Indian cavalry regiment Skinner's Horse,
was the son of a Scottish officer and his Rajput mistress and, although
it was denied by many of his family, eighty children claimed him as
their father. One of the great spectacles of early nineteenth-century
Delhi was said to be the sight of the East India Company Resident,
Sir David Ochterlony, taking the evening air by riding an elephant
around the walls of the Red Fort, followed by his thirteen Indian
wives, each mounted on her own elephant. The wills of employees in
the East India Company archive show that while Ochterlony may
have been more energetic than most, his multicultural marital
arrangements were not necessarily all that unusual. Charles Theo-
philus Metcalfe, who became acting governor general in the 1830s,
had three Anglo-Sikh children, one of whom, James Metcalfe, commanded an army unit which fought at the siege of Lucknow during
the Mutiny.

The records show that in the 1780s about one in three East India
Company men left all their worldly goods to an Indian woman. By
1800, the proportion had dropped to one in four, by 1810 to one in
five, by 1820 to one in seven, and by 1840 there are no Indian women
mentioned in any official Company wills. This is not, of course, to say
that sexual relations between Indians and British stopped. Richard
Burton's service in the subcontinent did not begin until the 1840s,
but, in an unerringly male way, he certainly noticed the benefits for
a British officer when he took a local lover:

★ The nawab was an Olympic-class voluptuary, whose English factotum described
him as 'a curious compound of extravagance, avarice, candour, cunning, levity,
cruelty, childishness, affability, brutish sensuality, good humour, vanity and imbe-
cility'. He took a lot of drugs, had elephant-drawn carriages inside which he could
give comfortable dinner parties for a dozen guests at a time, and maintained a
harem of 500 women. He was just the sort of pet ruler the British liked. Colonel
Mordaunt commanded his bodyguard.

She keeps house for him, never allowing him to save money, or if possible to waste it. She keeps the servants in order. She has an infallible recipe to prevent maternity, especially if her tenure of office depends on such compact. She looks after him in sickness, and is one of the best nurses, and, as it is not good for man to live alone, she makes him a manner of home.

The language is revealing: 'a manner of home' points up the temporary nature of the relationship – the real home is in Britain, and the declining number of Indian women mentioned in wills coincides with the growing preoccupation with a British moral mission in India. In practice, the 'recipe to prevent maternity' was anything but 'infallible'. The Anglo-Indian community which resulted came to occupy a convenient – if sometimes awkward – position as a sort of buffer between the Raj and the Indians. They spoke English as a first language, were usually Christian in belief, and often discharged the sort of role in officialdom (on lower pay) that white men might once have been expected to perform. By the time of independence there were reckoned to be 300,000 Anglo-Indians living in the subcontinent.*

In 1804, the East India Company grudgingly decreed that Anglo-Indian wives of British soldiers should be entitled to a living allowance, but that because they had been 'born in India and habituated to live chiefly on rice, the wants and wishes of the Half Caste are much more confined than those of a European woman'. As a consequence, they would be entitled to only one-twentieth of the allowance given to British wives. When their husbands returned home to Britain they were not to expect to accompany them, because when their menfolk later threw themselves upon poor relief, no parish could be reasonably expected to take responsibility for supporting foreign

---

* Without the Anglo-Indian community, it is fair to say, the railways, telephone exchanges and customs service of British India could not have functioned. Since independence they have found life harder, although their excellent command of colloquial English has ensured jobs in places like call centres. They have all sorts of unexpected talents. At an Anglo-Indian tea party in Chennai, one of the prominent members of the local community turned to me proudly and pointed out how well everyone danced. 'It's part of our heritage,' he said, 'natural rhythm. We got it from the British.'

wives – better they remain in India. Yet did they really belong in India, either? In 1791, the Company had tried to ban mixed-race men from senior positions, on the grounds that they would never command the respect due to whites. And the ambiguity of the social position of mixed-race children could trouble their fathers. Anglo-Indians were often considered exceptionally good-looking, but Sir David Ochterlony's letters record his worries about what might become of his Anglo-Indian daughters. Their 'dark blood' made them vulnerable to mockery from the white community. Yet could he really face the prospect of their adopting an Indian identity and possibly ending up in a Muslim prince's harem?

By 1820, the Company had decided it was better to try to forestall such worries altogether. A manual of that year warned new arrivals to be on their guard against the 'insinuating manners and fascinating beauty' of Eurasian girls, for fear of making 'a matrimonial connexion which he might all his life-time regret' as he languished in the social isolation into which a wife with a darker skin would plunge him. But, like almost all efforts at prohibition of pleasure, the decree was doomed to failure. The 'bibi', or mistress, was simply a fact of life. Even in 1859, Garnet Wolseley – one of the many Irishmen who, like the Scots, found the empire was the making of them – admitted in a letter that he had acquired an 'eastern princess' who performed 'all the purposes of a wife without giving any of the bother'. He sorted himself out by establishing a more permanent arrangement nine years later, marrying Louisa Erskine and becoming a devoted father to the garden designer Frances Wolseley. Would he – could he – have achieved his subsequent eminence as commander in chief of the army if he had kept his eastern princess? For it is noticeable that the greater the British control over India, the more their tolerance of these cross-cultural relationships shrank.

The uprising in 1857 – and the answering brutality of the British – left a very long legacy of bitterness and mistrust between the two cultures. From now on, the races would maintain some distance. The decision that henceforth India would be run not by the East India Company but by the British government meant greater involvement by elected politicians, and required administration on a much more formal basis. The development of fast steam ships, the opening of the Suez Canal in November 1869 and then the laying of telegraph cables made it possible for London not merely to state its will but to intervene to make sure it was carried out. This was to bring about a big change in how the British saw India, and, in turn, how they saw themselves.

The Company's opening up of India had delighted some Europeans. In the 1780s Sir William Jones declared Sanskrit 'more perfect than the Greek, more copious than the Latin, and more exquisitely refined than either', and enthused Europeans with the notion that India lived and breathed ancient civilization. At much the same time a young East India Company officer, Charles Stuart, was enjoying daily walks along the banks of the Ganges where he took purifying bathes. As he rose through the officer class Stuart's devotion to Hinduism deepened: he built a temple, ate according to Hindu ritual and published pamphlets telling European women they would be much better off – and more attractive – if they were to take up wearing the sari. 'Hindoo' Stuart was passionately opposed to the increasingly vocal demands being heard in Britain that missionaries be allowed to spread the gospel among the heathens of India. He did not prevail.★ As British power grew, so too did the unshakeable conviction that They Knew Best. What William Jones and 'Hindoo' Stuart had seen as beauty and mystery increasingly looked like a freak show, with – as one visitor described it – Hindu holy men 'standing for half a day on their heads, barking all the while for alms; some of their heads entirely covered with earth; some with their eyes filled with mud, and their mouths with straw; some lying in puddles of water; one man with

★ Like the great orientalist Sir William Jones, Stuart is buried among dozens of less culturally sympathetic colonists in South Park Street Cemetery in Calcutta. Jones's grave is marked by a stained stone obelisk thrusting its way up through the trees, the crossed cannon which often decorated the graves of soldiers replaced in his case by crossed spades, in recognition of his talents as an archaeologist. Major General Stuart lies in a (now rather badly restored) 'Hindu' tomb, in front of which a dog had just whelped when I visited. His greatest memorial, though, is his large assembly of Hindu art, which forms the core of the British Museum collection.

his foot tied to his neck, and another with a pot of fire on his belly; and a third enveloped in a net made of rope'.

The religious convictions which gripped Victorian Britain were altogether more understated. But it would be a mistake to underestimate the intensity of the religious enthusiasms – Methodism, evangelicalism, the Oxford Movement, schisms big and small – which swept the country in the nineteenth century. All, in different ways, contributed to a belief that it was the duty of those to whom truth had been revealed to communicate it to others. The East India Company had always recognized a limited role for the Christian Church, in supplying garrison chaplains or supervisors of military orphanages. But the Company had now been displaced by governments vulnerable to public opinion, and by the middle of the nineteenth century the missionary societies in Britain had hundreds of thousands of pounds to spend each year in saving souls. However much the different Christian denominations might squabble among themselves, all agreed on their ineffable superiority to the native religions of the colonies. Busybody missionaries became a fact of life.

Once communications between Britain and India had improved, there was less and less excuse for men stationed in the subcontinent to adapt to local customs, least of all sexual customs. Soon there was no need for soldiers, officials and traders to keep a mistress in the bibi house. They could live, instead, a tropical replica of life in England, an existence which did not so much embrace India as defy it. The laying of railway tracks meant that European wives in India could be packed off to the hill stations in hot weather or, once the Suez Canal had opened, could perhaps be sent home to England for sickness or childbirth. Even those men who had arrived in the country as bachelors had only to wait for the start of the longed-for Cold Season and the arrival of what later became known as the Fishing Fleet – young women from the home country out to net themselves a husband from among the single men serving in India. As one twentieth-century official recalled, the racial discrimination was quite blatant. 'In the hot weather you took out what was called the "B" class girl, usually Anglo-Indians, who were dears in every way and the greatest fun. But the moment the cold weather started they were taboo, because all the young girls from Roedean, Cheltenham and the great schools of Britain came out in the P&O liners and you were expected to toe the line.' Throughout the Cold Season – of which Christmas was the high point – the young men and women circled each other at parties, dances and sports events, sizing up who might make a decent marriage partner. The women who failed to find anyone suitable went back to England, nicknamed 'returned empties'.

The presence in India of what came to be known as 'memsahibs' (a corruption of 'ma'am' and 'sahib') changed everything. In the 1830s a magistrate in India had written home that he had 'observed that those who have lived with a native woman for any length of time never marry a European . . . so amusingly playful, so anxious to oblige and please, that a person after being accustomed to their society shrinks from the idea of encountering the whims or yielding to the fancies of an Englishwoman'. He would not have dared to write like that fifty years later: let the Englishwoman loose in India and she fought her corner. Later generations have endowed the memsahibs with an unappealing reputation, as superficial snobs and irredeemable racists who ended an era of happy coexistence. But, like any group of human beings, they must have been a varied bunch. There were plenty who never bothered to go beyond learning 'Kitchen Hindustani' in order to shout instructions at servants. But there were others who developed a genuine affection for the country, founded orphanages, taught in schools and sacrificed their own health to improve the health of Indians. Women confident enough to reject the role assigned to them by men could sometimes become forceful enemies of the very masculine business of imperialism. Like the Victorian socialist Annie Besant, they could find the colourful abundance of Indian spiritualism an intoxicating alternative: when she moved to India in 1893, Besant took to wearing Hindu mourning dress in grief at what the British had done to the country, and spent decades encouraging Indians to throw off colonial rule.

Subversive figures like these were, of course, hugely outnumbered by the conventional memsahibs, exerting what they considered a civilizing influence in the military cantonments, towns, cities and hill stations. How many younger officers wanted to cohabit with an

Indian woman when the colonel's wife so clearly disapproved? Indian sexual gymnastics were no match for raised British eyebrows.

The presence of hostesses meant different sorts of social gatherings – elaborate picnics and dinner parties, tennis and badminton tournaments, amateur theatricals and Sunday attendance at mock-Gothic churches with corrugated-iron roofs. The memsahibs endured the sweltering heat in stays and bonnets rather than saris and sandals. Though some of them did valuable work on their own account in schools, clinics and colleges, much of the time they must have been bored senseless. The men at least had a clear mission and in their spare time could retreat to the clubs they had founded, where they smoked cigars and drank too much. In these refuges, the maleness of colonization survived for generations. (Even in the 1920s when an incompetent rickshaw-driver delivered a woman visitor to the United Service Club in the hill station at Simla, a horrified porter barred her way by snatching a notice from the wall and holding it up between them. It read 'Dogs and other noxious animals are not allowed in the Club'.) The expatriate men and women lived together in communities of bungalows (the name comes from 'Bengal') behind self-important gates and gravel drives, with scratchy lawns in homage to Camberley and Godalming, filling their gardens with English flowers, fighting a never-ending war to keep the termites from eating the piano and placing wicker chairs on the verandah so they could meet Indian tradesmen without letting them intrude on the holy of holies within. In the world's biggest spice-garden they lived on over-boiled vegetables, tinned fruit and suet puddings.

The memsahibs have become the lightning-conductor for much that was wrong with imperial India. But they can hardly be blamed for all of it. In truth, they can hardly be blamed for it at all, unless they can also be taxed with engineering the religious revival which swept Victorian Britain, plotting the Mutiny, inventing the telegraph, building the Indian railways and then digging the Suez Canal which made their access to India so much easier. Once the British had decided that their overseas possessions were something more than a trading arrangement, separation of the races was inevitable. Among the expat community it became an ideological conviction that, to be treated as rulers, the British had to behave like rulers. 'Decent' behaviour in front of the natives mattered. It was not merely that the natives must see you doing the right thing, but that the rest of the white community must do so too: failure to strike the right attitude risked undermining the whole imperial edifice. To a free spirit, the social conventions – receiving visitors, tiffin, dressing for dinner every night – must have seemed as suffocating as the climate. Yet from the moment she stepped on to Indian soil, the young wife was taking part in an exhibition in a heated glass case.

The challenge of maintaining an English way of life in the tropics was enormous. Admittedly, women who in England might have had to manage with few or no domestic staff might have several servants in India. On the other hand, the conditions of life – notably the suffocating heat – added an unwanted challenge to the most mundane tasks. A soldier's wife who arrived in mid-nineteenth-century India was told by a fellow memsahib with experience of 'hot-weather housekeeping' that the challenge in cooking meat was 'to grasp the fleeting moment between toughness and putrefaction when the joint may possibly prove eatable'. As the century wore on, the memsahibs were helped by improvements in imperial food technology – tinning, bottling and preserving. But still, the sort of meal which might be conjured out of the available ingredients was not necessarily guaranteed to be a treat. It was memorably depicted by E. M. Forster's description of a Raj dinner party in *A Passage to India*: 'The menu was: Julienne soup full of bullety bottled peas, pseudo-cottage bread, fish full of branching bones, pretending to be plaice, more bottled peas with the cutlets, trifle, sardines on toast: the menu of Anglo-India ... the food of exiles, cooked by servants who did not understand it.'

Fortunately, guidance was available to the imperial hostess in the form of *The Complete Indian Housekeeper and Cook* (published in 1888), a sort of *Mrs Beeton* for young memsahibs, 'giving the duties of mistress and servants, the general management of the house and practical recipes for cooking in all its branches'. Largely written by Flora Annie Steel, the wife of a civil servant stationed in the Punjab, it contains brisk, practical advice on just about everything from cooking food to treating dog bites. There was nothing aristocratic about Mrs Steel (her father had been a political agent, brought low by the collapse of a colonial bank), but in India she was still a member of the ruling class and her wry weariness shines through on every page. It would be unfair to describe her as hostile to Indians, but she remained part of the Raj, and the manual's object was not to assist wives to become Indian but to help them create as closely as possible a replica of life in Britain. Her recipes run from the prosaic (braised cutlets) to the exotic (kidneys with champagne or Ferozepur cake). But the advice on how to run the kitchen might stand for the whole British presence in India: 'Dirt, illimitable, inconceivable dirt must be expected, until a generation of mistresses has rooted out the habits of immemorial years.' The newly arrived wife should learn the local language as soon as possible, if only to be able to order the staff better, because 'the Indian servant is a child in everything save age and should be treated as a child; that is to say, kindly, but with the greatest firmness'. There was, needless to say, no shortage of menials of one sort or other, from butlers, through cooks and *khitmutgars* who served the food and *musolchis* who did the washing up, to *bheesties* to look after supplies of water, an *ayah* to tend the children, a *syce* or groom for the horses, a *dirzie* to do the sewing and a *dhobi* for the laundry, not to mention the sweepers who emptied bedpans and the gardeners tending the sweet peas. They were to be controlled by rigorous routine, rewards and punishments, enforced by constant vigilance. The primary responsibility was to set an example, because an untidy mistress would soon find herself with untidy servants and a lax one with lazy servants. Succumbing to the idea that if you want a job doing properly you should do it yourself was disastrous. The manual asserted in italics: '*Never do work which an ordinarily good servant ought to be able to do. If the one you have will not or cannot do it, get another who can.*'

The possibility of creating some tropical approximation of the English Home Counties made life more tolerable for the expats. But the permanent presence of white women in India raised some troubling sexual anxieties for the men of the Raj. The British saw the potential for depravity all around them – men who wore inadequate clothing, dancing girls, erotic temple carvings. Even in the 1920s a former editor of the *Civil and Military Gazette* wrote a book about India in which the first chapter was entitled 'The Land of the Sex-Mad Millions'. The pure Englishwoman, symbol of English innocence, had to be zealously guarded. Inevitably, hanky-panky was much more likely to occur within the British community: a man who dispatched his wife to the comparative comfort of a hill station while he continued to work on the Plains during the hot season had to be utterly confident he could trust her. As the (female) author of *The Englishwoman in India* commented in 1909:

> the grass widow in the Hills has pitfalls . . . to contend with; and perhaps the two most insidious are amateur theatricals and the military man on leave. It is hardly too much to say that one or other of these dominant factors in Hill station life is accountable for half the domestic tragedies of India . . . for a woman who is young, comely, and gifted with a taste for acting, Simla is assuredly not the most innocuous place on God's earth.

As the verse about hill stations went:

> Jack's own Jill goes up the hill,
> To Murree or Chakrata;
> Jack remains, and dies in the plains,
> And Jill remarries soon after.

But as the hill-station graveyards testify, women and children were at enormous physical risk themselves. In 1875, the eminent gynae-cologist Edward Tilt described how British women in India were not only prey to every passing disease but were also likely to suffer chronic inflammation of their wombs. Most would suffer from 'deranged menstruation', inducing 'abdominal pains, nervousness, depression of spirits, and perhaps hysteria'. Women who endured this 'morbid womb' with its 'hideous progeny' would return to England unable to breed. Any women who gave birth in India risked all the hazards they would have faced at home, together with the added dangers of the climate, local diseases, inadequate nursing care and terrible sanitation. Those who survived and stayed too long in India merely postponed the fate of their line: the *Pioneer* warned in 1888 that European children settled permanently in India would 'die out about the 4th generation, degenerating steadily up to that point'. Many families would send their children back to Britain to avoid this fate and to be educated at one of the new empire-minded boarding schools popping up across the country at the time. And it was the practice of sending children home for their schooling that created probably the greatest emotional hardship for British women in the empire – many would not see their children for years on end and, when they did, they might barely recognize each other. This unique colonial arrangement was not only enormously painful for the mother but would go on to haunt a generation of British children who would grow up in England with the memory of absent parents. Rudyard Kipling, sent from India to Southsea, England, in 1871 at the age of six referred, in his autobiography, to his adoptive child-hood home as 'The House of Desolation'. The writer Alan Ross, born more than fifty years later, describes a similar experience, hav-ing been sent to England from Calcutta at the age of seven: 'When the time came, the prospect of seeing my parents again, and having to own emotional allegiance to people I could scarcely remember, became increasingly embarrassing. Before long it was my parents who appeared to be strangers.'

You can see why those women who were not naturally robust felt the need to act tough. And so the starchy manners, the close but not-quite-right replication of life at 'home', the slightly out-of-date mannerisms, the shabby gentility, delineated the imperial presence, and perhaps stopped the women from understandably falling apart. 'What would India be without England, and what would the British Empire be without Englishwomen?' commented an impressed Ger-man. Their arrival in numbers in India obliged the British to define who they were: if they were going to live in a self-sustaining com-munity, they had to be confident about what was and what was not 'British'. This was not, of course, something that was invented over-seas. Like the English plants in their bungalow gardens, it had been taken with them from home. Sometimes, like some of the plants, it went a little odd in the unusual climate. But it was still identifiably the same genus, and was nurtured for being at risk and slightly unlikely. Transplanted from nineteenth-century Britain – a country increasingly sure of its purpose and in the grip of a religious revival – it rooted itself in the red soils of the empire and clung on.

It was not a role for shrinking violets. But then, a woman's position in colonial India was not particularly easy. The heat, the humidity, monsoon rains and the swirling clouds of dust could destroy an English rose in the space of a year or two. The clothes she was expected to wear made matters worse. To the restrictions imposed by the role ascribed by the men of empire were added the daily chores of trying to keep clothes clean, stopping meat putrefying and seeing that there was enough water for a rudimentary bath at the end of the day, all of it in relentless heat, homesickness, often absent husbands, interminable railway journeys, the fear of tropical sickness striking a child (later often replaced by that numb, never cauterized wound, when they were sent off to boarding school at the age of seven), the temptations posed by single men and the menace of flirtatious other wives. And all to be endured in the foul smell that a capricious wind might waft around at any time from the thunderbox at the back of the bungalow.

India, the jewel in the imperial crown, was one thing. But in many other corners of the empire the entire edifice rested on the shoulders of one young man in a pair of shorts. As the idea of themselves as rulers of the world took ever firmer hold, the British were obliged to grapple with how these imperial subalterns were to live in the absence of European women. The French, for example, had come to a policy in which young men serving in west Africa were advised that they could both serve their own interests and help to Gallicize the continent by contracting 'temporary marriages' for the duration of their tour of duty. The British considered this typically French, and officers of the Sudanese Political Service, who prided themselves on being an elite, rather gloried in celibacy. But elsewhere a number of men out in the bush made their own arrangements. Across much of the rest of Africa and in the Far East, informal relationships between lonely young men and local women became commonplace. In Sarawak and Malaya the practice was either recognized or encouraged: the 'sleeping dictionary' being an established way of learning the local language. But when power was distributed so unequally, it was dangerous: how could a magistrate dispense justice fairly when he might be sharing his bed with a relative of one of the aggrieved parties? In typically British fashion, these things were not noticed, as long as no one drew attention to them.

But in 1908 the case of Hubert Silberrad, an assistant district commissioner in the Nyeri district of Kenya, blew the arrangement open. Silberrad had bought two Kenyan girls (for forty goats apiece) from a colleague who had been promoted. They were troublingly young – one of them, aged twelve, was extremely reluctant to be passed on, the other agreed to the arrangement in exchange for a monthly wage. When, three years later, Silberrad attempted to acquire a third mistress (of similar age) and one of his own policemen objected, Silberrad locked him up for the night, on grounds of insubordination. Two white neighbours, a Mr and Mrs Scoresby Routledge, came to express their outrage and then Mr Routledge rode four days through the rain to complain to the Governor in Nairobi. The Governor ordered a private investigation, which concluded that Silberrad had brought the administration into disrepute by 'poaching'. Silberrad lost a year's seniority and the Governor issued a circular to his officials, warning that, 'morals apart', such practices were 'in every way detrimental to the interests of good government'. The punishment testifies to the distinct priorities of colonial administrators. But what outraged the Routledges was less the rights of Kenyans than the well-being of the empire. Mr Routledge refused to let the matter rest and wrote a letter to *The Times* outlining the facts of the case and claiming that 'the interests of this country [are] suffering from the demoralization of native women by British officials'. This was precisely the sort of incident guaranteed to set off a bout of hand-wringing in Britain. A debate in parliament followed, which in turn obliged the Colonial Secretary, Lord Crewe (one of the most buttoned-up men ever to grace British public life – a cabinet colleague claimed to have a constituent who had lost her mind while listening to one of his speeches), to issue what became known as the 'Concubine Circular' in January 1909.

Formally, the document had no name, although the file for comments and replies was entitled 'Immoral Relations with Native Women'. Crewe recognized that, as far as some long-established members of the service were concerned, he was whistling in the wind, and the Circular was never even sent to various empire territories, such as the West Indies and the Seychelles where intermarriage between black and white was far from rare. Two versions were eventually produced – one warning old hands of the danger to the empire posed by scandal, and another addressed to junior men, threatening fire and brimstone. Taking native mistresses was 'injurious and dangerous' and 'disgrace and ruin' awaited those who made the mistake of entering into 'arrangements of concubinage with girls or women belonging to the native populations'. To make sure the parents of recruits were not scandalized, the document was issued to them only on arrival in the colony. Some of the colonial settlers found the celibacy now imposed upon officials a just reward for their exercise of an often resented authority. To the tune of 'The Church's One Foundation' they showed their sympathy by singing:

> Pity the poor Official
> Whene'er he gets a stand,
> He may not take a bibi
> He has to use his hand.
>
> And so he saves his money,
> His character – his job,
> And only has to answer for
> His conduct to his God.

It was a small price to pay for the glory of the empire.

So what were girls to be told about their contribution to the empire? In September of the year of Lord Crewe's circular, the organizers of the Boy Scout movement's first large rally were slightly nonplussed by the arrival of small groups of young people claiming to be Scouts, but who were definitely not boys. What was to be done with them? Scouting was about toughening up boys and equipping them for life on the frontier, and if girls were to be considered for the same role, it would never succeed in instilling manly values.

Like many empire-builders, Robert Baden-Powell knew more about the natives of Matabeleland than he did about his fellow countrymen who happened to be devoid of the Y sex chromosome: he was fifty-two and would not marry for another three years (to a woman thirty-two years his junior). So he consulted his sister, Agnes, and invited her to take on the leadership of an organization to enable girls to do their bit. By the outbreak of the First World War the Girl Guides (they took their name from the famous regiment of Gurkha guides in India) had 40,000 members. 'Guides! remember the future of our Empire lies in your hands,' the B-Ps thundered. 'It is in your power to make or spoil the British nation.' This was, however, to be accomplished in a very different manner from the role assigned to boys. Their imperial destiny was to become healthy girls, loyal wives and moral mothers. 'Britain has been made by her great men,' wrote Agnes Baden-Powell and her brother in *The Handbook for Girl Guides, or How Girls Can Help Build up the Empire*, 'and these great men were made great by their mothers.'

The girls were allowed to share some of the excitement of Scouting, learning how to find their way by the stars, how to clean their teeth with a stick, or 'How to Secure a Burglar with Eight Inches of Cord'.* They were taught the prevailing belief in the uplifting qualities of 'playing the game'. Mainly, though, it was the function of girls to learn how to help males to expand and consolidate the empire. 'It is men's work to defend the Empire in person, and to be prepared to fight for their country and their homes. But you must not forget that

---

* 'Make a slip-knot at each end of your cord. Tie his hands behind him by passing each loop over his little fingers. Place the burglar face downward, and bend his knees. Pass both feet under the string, and he will be unable to get away' (Baden-Powell and Baden-Powell, *The Handbook for Girl Guides*, pp. 291–2).

you can play a very important part in holding the Empire by becoming experts at ambulance work and nursing.' Settling in a colony could offer many 'delightful prospects', such as 'turning packing-cases into furniture' and 'producing capital meals with three bricks and a baking pot'. The thing to remember was that 'To a true-hearted girl who wishes to make a man happy, there is bliss in an African hut.'

CHAPTER EIGHT

'The more of the world we inhabit the better
it is for the human race'
Cecil Rhodes, 1877

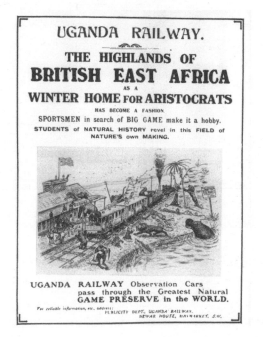

The hero of Rudyard Kipling's 1893 short story 'The Bridge-Builders'
is a no-nonsense Scottish engineer. Findlayson is building a railway
bridge across the mighty Ganges. Thousands upon thousands of
Indian labourers have toiled for three years constructing the stone
plinths and riveting together the British-made steel girders which
will cross the biggest river in the entire subcontinent. The Viceroy
himself is to be present at the opening of the causeway. As a reward
for his tireless efforts Findlayson dreams of being made a Companion
of the Star of India, the Victorian decoration invented to honour

congenial Indian princes and particularly significant British public servants.* Then one night the engineer receives a telegram from a British outpost further upstream. There is a huge flood rolling down from the Himalayas, which will strike the uncompleted bridge in hours. The work of empire risks destruction by a force of nature and an alarmed Findlayson orders the massive camp gong to be struck, waking the entire workforce. The site foreman, Peroo, 'a lascar† familiar with every port between Rockhampton and London', will organize the emergency flood defences in the little time available before the torrent strikes. Several hours later, with the rain pouring down on the two exhausted men, the roiling flood arrives. There is nothing more to be done, and Peroo takes an old tobacco tin from his waistband, opens it and offers the engineer a couple of brown pellets, to 'kill all weariness, besides the fever that follows the rain'. It is opium, and before he knows where he is, this upstanding Scot is delirious, dreaming of talking animals, many-limbed Indian gods and praying in sacred temples.

His bridge survives the flood, but that is entirely due to the quality of British engineering rather than to any Indian gods. Findlayson is rescued from his druggy reverie by an Indian prince with the sporty affectations and languid disdain of an English education. The episode with the opium is not mentioned again. British modernity has tamed ancient India.

Massive engineering works stamped the British presence upon the world, evidence not merely of technological achievement, but demonstrations of purpose. Inside a metal tube in the public library at the diamond town of Kimberley, for example, is the rolled-up map of Africa on which

---

* Becoming a Companion was to achieve the lowest of the three decorations within the order, for the British graded these things precisely, with the highest ranks reserved for the Viceroy and for Indians who had been fortunate enough to have princely parents yet pliant enough to let the British install an agent telling them how to run their state. A Companionship would be sufficient reward for a stolid engineer. There is no indication Findlayson imagines any honours going to labourers and craftsmen.

† An Indian sailor.

Cecil Rhodes drew a pencil line the entire length of the continent depicting the railway which he hoped would one day run the 5,000 miles from the Cape of Good Hope at the southern tip of Africa to Cairo and the Mediterranean. That line was never completed, but on 7 November 1885 the last spike was driven into another track that had been laid through the Rockies, over bogs and prairies, through floods and forest fires, snowfall and avalanche, and that effectively created the Dominion of Canada by tying in British Columbia to the rest of the country. Thirty years later, Western Australia was welded into the Commonwealth of Australia by a track that crossed endless desert and included 300 miles of dead-straight line.

Perhaps the most openly imperialist railway line of all was the link built in the 1890s between the Indian Ocean and Lake Victoria in east Africa. It is now a rackety, dirty, unreliable thing, a wholly inadequate memorial to the 2,498 workers who lost their lives building it. At different times this remarkable route carried a young Queen Elizabeth, Winston Churchill and Theodore Roosevelt. The latter in 1909 spent most of the time when he wasn't either eating or sleeping sitting on an observation platform at the front of the locomotive. 'This embodiment of the eager, masterful, materialistic civilization of today', he wrote, 'was pushed through a region in which nature, both as regards wild man and wild beast, does not differ materially from what it was in Europe in the late Pleistocene.' Now, as you rattle out of Nairobi you are advised to shut the window, because if you don't there's a good chance someone will lob a pile of human shit through it. The train passes through Kibera, the biggest shanty town in Africa, home to perhaps a million people, which formally doesn't exist yet whose cardboard, wood and corrugated-iron shacks probably house a third of the population of the capital – not that anyone ventures in to take an accurate census. But then the whole of Nairobi was an accident – it just happened to have the last bit of flat ground where colonial engineers could turn around a locomotive before the line they were building snaked its way up through the highlands towards Lake Victoria. The ugly mess of a city which grew up on the swampy ground has nothing much to commend it, even a century later.

At the time, the newspapers called this ambitious piece of engineering the Lunatic Line and even when it was finished the commissioner appointed by London to 'look after' east Africa admitted he had really no idea what its purpose was. The truth was that the motive for the line lay in the recently created German colony next door (now Rwanda, Burundi and the mainland part of Tanzania). The Uganda Railway, to give it its formal title (although almost its entire length lay within modern Kenya), was an imperial gesture, a giant metal spike nailing together British territory and providing a direct link between the Indian Ocean and the lake which was the source of the Nile. And the hardships they had to overcome to build it! Over a million railway sleepers had to be laid in relentless heat, yet it reached such an altitude that – on the Equator – it serviced what was said to be the coldest railway station in the British Empire. From here it plunged down into the Great Rift Valley on an incline so steep it was initially considered impossible for any railway line. Angry tribespeople fought to prevent the line crossing their land. In the single month of November 1896 a total of 27½ inches of rain fell, making work impossible. The following February, malaria swept through the camps. Dysentery struck repeatedly. Tropical heat and poor sanitation turned scratches into sores. Biting flies laid eggs which grew into maggots under the skin. Pneumonia struck down those with weak chests. There were even outbreaks of bubonic plague. An Indian army officer, Colonel J. H. Patterson, the engineer who had been given the task of overseeing work on the railway, dealt with the first of these outbreaks by putting a match to the camp.

This exceptional man also had to tackle the most dramatic hazard of all, during the building of a bridge at Tsavo. 'Our work was soon interrupted in a rude and startling manner,' he recalled later. 'Two most voracious and insatiable man-eating lions appeared upon the scene, and for nine months waged an intermittent warfare against the railway and all those connected with it.' Night after night the two lions stalked the camp, picking off a man here, another there, dragging them into the bush as the rest of the camp lay awake listening to the victims' screams. The labourers built thorn fences, set fires, stationed watchmen and soon began strapping their beds as high up in the surrounding trees as they dared. Next, they simply refused to continue working and demanded to leave, saying they had signed up 'to work for the government not to supply food for lions'. Colonel Patterson summoned the District Officer, who arrived after dark with an African sergeant, and as they walked to the colonel's camp one of the lions leaped upon them, its claws tearing through the DO's shirt and the skin on his back, before the creature dragged the sergeant away into the bushes. The men listened to the animal chomping its way through the sergeant's bones.

Attempts to poison the lions with the contaminated carcasses of dead transport animals failed. ('The wily man-eaters would not touch them, and much preferred live men to dead donkeys,' wrote the colonel later.) Patterson built a platform in one of the trees and settled down to wait for a shot at the lions, but when one of them appeared he realized to his horror that the animal was stalking *him*. Eventually, of course, high-velocity rifle defeated four-legged beast, at which point labourers poured out of the camp and threw themselves at his feet in gratitude. The colonel shot dead the second lion some time later, but only after narrowly escaping the same fate as the District Officer's sergeant and scores of others.* How many people had been taken by the lions is unknown – the only figure established with any precision was the total number of 'coolie' Indian labourers eaten by the lions, which was twenty-eight.

In the late 1890s, over 30,000 Indians had been brought to Africa on three-year contracts specifically to build the railway. British admiration for their railway-building skills was soon offset by anxieties about conditions in the camps in which they lived. There was, some of the white colonists claimed, a worryingly high proportion

---

* Patterson had the skins made into rugs, which he later sold to a museum in Chicago. Despite their being a little moth-eaten by then – and still punctured by bullet holes – the museum's taxidermist managed to recreate the lions, which were put on display in 1928. They are now the motif for T-shirts, mugs, posters and caps in the museum gift shop. Earnest forensic scientists who recently examined the skull of the first lion concluded that it had suffered from 'a severe abscess of the lower right canine that would have prevented it from killing large vigorous prey'. The railway workers were a sort of convenience food.

of thieves among them, who were introducing Africans to crime. The camps were alive with venereal disease and frequently sizzled with tension between Hindus and Muslims. They were crowded with 'prostitutes, small boys and other accessories to the bestial vices so commonly practised by Orientals'. To make matters worse, many of the coolies had passed themselves off to their recruiters in Punjab or Gujerat as having skills they turned out not to possess. Yet from this small army of Indian workers emerged not only one of the most impressive railways ever built, but also one of the most economically productive – and politically discriminated against – communities in Africa. Imperial British feelings towards these workers were always ambiguous. In the hierarchy of races that the British imagined to exist, the Indians sat higher than poor Africans. But the station-master *babu*, with his sonorous English, was considered a comical figure. (One of them was supposed to have sounded the alarm about another man-eating lion with the telegraph message: 'Pumping-engine employee wickedly assassinated by fractious carnivore. I unable pacify it. Situation perilous. Implore you alleviate my predicament.')

Yet the British could also see how one part of the empire might nourish another part and encouraged more Indians to migrate to the region: 'Indian trade, enterprise and emigration require a suitable outlet. East Africa is, and should be, from every point of view, the America of the Hindu,' said the British Special Commissioner in Uganda, Sir Harry Johnston, in 1901. During the First World War, Indian soldiers were deployed to combat the guerrilla war being fought from German East Africa, and at war's end prominent Asians argued that, since they had been just as active as the British settlers in developing Kenya, why should they not have similar rights to vote and to acquire land? The Colonial Office cooked up a characteristically inadequate compromise – limited representation on the legislative council, while, for the sake of their health, the highlands of the country were to be kept exclusively for white settlers. This tiered idea of citizenship more or less pacified the white settlers, and was grudgingly accepted by many Indians. But it did nothing at all for the indigenous African population, and, unsurprisingly, when independence came to Kenya in 1963 the Asians felt the force of their resentment. As the first President, Jomo Kenyatta, implemented a policy of 'Africanization' they were increasingly resented, treated as scapegoats and forced from their businesses. Many decided to take at face value the promise that those who held British passports were entitled to live in Britain. Between 1965 and 1967 over 20,000 Kenyan Asians arrived in Britain. A few years later, in 1972, Uganda's home-grown tyrant, Idi Amin, decided to exploit African resentment at the commercial success of the Indian community, and gave Ugandan Asians ninety days to leave the country. About 30,000 emigrated to Britain and began to rebuild their lives, in many cases from scratch. They took their work ethic with them, rejuvenating some decaying British businesses and often starting small, family-run corner shops, open for long hours every day of the week, which transformed the high streets of Britain in a way the empire-builders could never have anticipated.

In the summer of 1877 a young Englishman sat down at his desk in a small corrugated-iron shack in a mining town in South Africa and wrote his will. This was an odd enough thing for any twenty-four-year-old to do. Even odder was what he proposed to do with his worldly goods. In a four-page, handwritten letter, Cecil Rhodes left everything he had for the creation of a world government.

In an accompanying 'Confession of Faith' Rhodes explained how this would be done. A Secret Society would be formed, which would eventually 'render wars impossible and promote the best interests of humanity'. World peace is the dream of children or idealists and – as the failures of the United Nations and the proliferation of wars across the globe testify – has never been achieved. But Cecil Rhodes's plan had one practical mechanism. It would be a racial rule, to be achieved by exporting settlers from Britain across the world. Global govern-ment would then be exercised from a parliament in London, to which the settlers would send representatives. The scope of his ambition was breathtaking. The territories to be colonized included 'the entire continent of Africa, the Holy Land, the Valley of the Euphra-tes, the Islands of Cyprus and Candia [Crete], the whole of South America, the islands of the Pacific not heretofore possessed by Great

Britain, the whole of the Malay Archipelago, the seaboard of China and Japan', and, for good measure, 'the ultimate recovery of the United States of America as an integral part of the British Empire'.

The man who saw this colour-saturated vision of imperialism had been born the fifth son of the vicar of Bishop's Stortford in Hertford-shire, and his own life bore witness to the possibilities that empire offered those with the nerve to seize a chance. Rhodes's father had evidently no great expectations of him and packed the boy off as a gan-gling teenager to South Africa in 1871. Here he soon joined the torrent of chancers, roustabouts, remittance men and ne'er-do-wells pouring on to the dusty fields near the Orange River where a fifteen-year-old farmer's son had picked up a curious-looking stone one day and set off a diamond rush. Rhodes and his brother staked a claim on a little flat-topped hill soon to become what was reckoned to be the biggest hole in the ground ever dug by hand. A fellow digger describes a thin, fair-haired, blue-eyed young man seated on an upturned bucket, gazing down on the spectacle beneath him, as uncountable numbers of other young men (most of the really hard work was being done by the black labourers) tore into the ground and hoisted buckets to the surface on a spider's web of wires. The settlement which grew up around the hole, soon to be named Kimberley (after the Colonial Secretary) was a dusty, drab place of open drains, dead animals and drunks. For most of the prospectors the vision of sudden, immense wealth remained no more than a dream – it was said that the only people who made consistent money were the dealers who came into town with wagon-loads of water. But the earth did contain great quantities of diamonds – by the time the mine was worked out the Big Hole would yield nearly 3,000 kilograms of them. Rhodes had a natural talent for mining, acute commercial sense (for example, get-ting hold of a pump to empty the mine of water) and a good measure of luck. So the will that Rhodes drew up in South Africa was not quite the parcelling out of a few books and trinkets which might be expected from most twenty-four-year-olds.

The oddly schizophrenic life Cecil Rhodes led at this time – long university vacations in the single-minded frenzy of Kimberley and misty term-times in Oxford mingling with the men who would run the country – moulded his view of the world. In his first year in Kimberley, Rhodes had read Winwood Reade's *The Martyrdom of Man*, a sweeping analysis of how, by a process akin to evolution, mankind might be perfected. Rhodes later declared, 'That book has made me what I am.' Rhodes was struck by the power in the world of certain religions, especially 'the Romish Church', of which he observed that 'every enthusiast, call it if you like every madman, finds employment in it'. In place of religious mumbo-jumbo, Cecil Rhodes preferred racial mania. 'I contend', he wrote, 'that we are the finest race in the world and that the more of the world we inhabit the better it is for the human race.' When he returned to South Africa, Cecil Rhodes soon had the chance to put his convictions into action, and in so doing became the most sabre-toothed of all empire-builders. 'It is our duty to seize every opportunity of acquiring more terri-tory,' he had written, 'and we should keep this one idea steadily before our eyes that more territory simply means more of the Anglo-Saxon race, more of the best, the most human, most honourable race the world possesses.'

Rhodes was an unusual advertisement for this exemplary, honour-able breed. As ruthless in the political career he now sought as he was in his business dealings, he displayed that hypocritical talent for con-cealing self-interest behind high-mindedness that England's enemies so despise. He used his position in parliament to advance his own business interests and played so fast and loose in his dealings with African rulers that it is remarkable any of them ever trusted a white man again. By the late 1880s, an increasingly fleshy Rhodes was in control of most of the output of the Kimberley diamond mine, hav-ing bought out his rival, Barney Barnato, a one-time music-hall entertainer, boxer and bouncer who had schemed and cheated his way from birth in Whitechapel to immense wealth and some emi-nence in South Africa.* Rhodes's tactics in creating an effective monopoly were more grey than white, but it is unarguable that he

---

* Like Rhodes, Barnato did not make old bones. He died when he jumped over-board from the steamer carrying him back to England for Queen Victoria's diamond jubilee in 1897, a few weeks short of his forty-fifth birthday.

did in the end make out what was believed at the time to have been the largest cheque ever written, for 'Five Million, Three Hundred and Thirty Eight Thousand, Six Hundred and Fifty Pounds Only' – to take control of the company.* After more frenetic digging, the hole in the ground in Kimberley continued to grow, eventually reaching a depth of nearly 700 feet, with a circumference of almost a mile. Though the drains of Kimberley still stank, the diamond barons built themselves fancy mansions and the place had the wealth to become the first city in the southern hemisphere to install electric street lights. A fortunate 250 citizens of this fur-coat-and-no-knickers settlement were members of the squat two-storey Kimberley Club, at whose bar it was said that you could find more millionaires per square foot than anywhere else on earth. Here men who could have given the term nouveau riche a bad name attempted to ape the behaviour and prejudices of the exclusive gentlemen's clubs of St James's: Rhodes's offer to put Barney Barnato up for membership of this parvenu paradise is said to have been one of the inducements that persuaded the East End boy to sell out to him.

But empire was the thing. After Kimberley, Rhodes ensured his fortune by investing in the newly founded mines which began to extract gold from the massive deposit discovered in the Transvaal. He parlayed his wealth into political power, untroubled by too many worries on such questions as whether it was entirely proper for him to buy secret control of southern Africa's leading newspaper, the *Cape Argus*. The stones which had made him rich had a value entirely dependent upon the absurd enthusiasms of human fashion, but Rhodes claimed to see permanent, practical benefits for the world in bringing as much territory as possible under British rule. It was, inevitably, a highly selective vision which even he acknowledged came at a cost: land was a great deal more important to him than any nonsense about human rights. In 1887, for example, he told the House of Assembly in Cape Town that 'the native is to be treated as

---

* In 1888 Rhodes would merge Kimberley Central into a new company, De Beers Consolidated Mines Ltd, which he controlled and which is still the biggest diamond-mining company in the world.

a child and denied the franchise . . . We must adopt a system of despotism in our relations with the barbarians of South Africa.' It is as
redundant to wonder whether Rhodes was a racist as to question
whether he wore a moustache on his self-satisfied face, for the evidence is overwhelming. When he plotted his Cape-to-Cairo railway
or, as prime minister of the Cape, cast lustful imperial eyes on the
lands beyond the Limpopo and Zambezi rivers he was not thinking
of the welfare of anyone but 'the Anglo-Saxon race'.

Rhodes – whose African ambitions meant he acquired the inevitable nickname 'Colossus' – was an empire-builder on the scale of
Clive of India, and when he wanted to exploit the mineral rights
obtained from the Matabele king, Lobengula (in exchange for a
promise of money, a thousand rifles and a boat), the British government gave him a chartered company similar to the old East India
Company. Under the motto 'Justice, Commerce, Freedom', with a
couple of dozy dukes on the board, the British South Africa Company, with Rhodes at its helm, could do more or less as it pleased in
southern Africa, seizing land, making treaties, laying down the law
and running its own banking system and police force. Rhodes promised that the firm would people the territories it acquired with settlers
whose loyalty would be to queen and country. By the end of 1890, he
was the most powerful man from the southern Atlantic to the Indian
Ocean, running the company, Prime Minister of the Cape and chairman of the diamond business. The great tracts of land about to fall
under the sway of his company would become known as Rhodesia
(today Zambia and Zimbabwe), and he was not yet forty. The American writer Mark Twain was unable to decide whether Cecil Rhodes
was a lofty patriot or the devil incarnate, but observed that, either
way, 'When he stands on the Cape of Good Hope, his shadow falls to
the Zambesi.' True to form, the British Establishment laid aside worries about Rhodes, elected him to membership of the Athenaeum
Club and in February 1895 had him sworn of the Privy Council.

But then this Napoleonic figure stumbled. Rhodes's vision of an
Africa dominated by Anglo-Saxons was threatened not by the poorly
armed, comparatively unsophisticated tribes who had lived there
since before the days when the British wore woad, but by the Boers,

the descendants of Dutch settlers who in the middle of the seventeenth century had established a colony at the tip of southern Africa.
To escape the British they had for decades been migrating further and
further away from the coast. Rhodes now cooked up a plot to seize
by force the goldfields of the Boers' colony in the Transvaal. The
man he chose for this task was an old friend from Kimberley, Dr
Leander Starr Jameson, an unscrupulous, socially ambitious gambler.
One of the reasons for Dr Jameson's presence in southern Africa was
his belief that the drier climate would be good for his health. He
stayed because the living was comparatively easy and the wealth he
accumulated great. Just after Christmas 1895 the doctor launched his
raid into the Transvaal at the head of a force of badly equipped police
and assorted riff-raff volunteers. The idea had been that, when they
saw the British column, the Uitlanders – the largely British prospectors who had poured into the Transvaal to prospect for gold, and
who paid most of the taxes yet were denied the vote – would stage
their own rebellion against the Boers: the Jameson Raid was to be the
detonator that fired the explosion. But the rising never came, and
four days after he had thundered into the Boers' territory, Jameson
ingloriously surrendered to them. This ineptly planned and incompetently executed pantomime had several consequences, one of
which was to force Rhodes's resignation from the premiership of the
Cape Colony and another of which was to lay the ground for the
South African War between the Boers and the British, which cost
many thousands of the lives of his precious Anglo-Saxons.

It is estimated that between 1815 and 1912 some 21.5 million people
emigrated from the British Isles – there can hardly have been a family
that did not have a relative living somewhere overseas. The biggest
single group are believed to have been drawn to the United States,
but millions more settled in the empire, and in so doing created a
British diaspora. The imperial historian Ronald Hyam estimates that
by 1900 two-thirds of the English-speaking people lived outside
Europe. Most had been driven to leave by need: when Robert Louis
Stevenson sailed on an emigrant ship from Glasgow in the summer
of 1879 he described it as a 'shipful of failures, the broken men of

England', whom any casual observer might well have assumed were all 'absconding from the law'. But there were plenty of other motives, too. Some joined gold rushes, established farms or ran trading stations. Others went to serve the Crown, still more hoped to win one: another Kipling short story, 'The Man Who Would Be King', tells of a couple of one-time soldiers who establish themselves as monarchs in the remotest corner of Afghanistan. Needless to say, it all goes wrong, but anyone deterred could turn instead to the great fictional model for those with monarchical ambitions, Daniel Defoe's story of a man washed up on a tropical island, *Robinson Crusoe*. 'How like a King I look'd,' says Crusoe as he marvels at the island he controls; James Joyce thought him 'the true symbol of the British conquest'. (In mid-nineteenth-century Borneo, James Brooke established himself as an authentic 'white rajah'. The second rajah of Sarawak, for whom the *Oxford Dictionary of National Biography* summons a wheelbarrow-load of adjectives – 'brave, ruthless, decisive, pragmatic, austere, dignified, parsimonious, reserved, and self-sufficient' – ruled as 'both an English gentleman and an oriental despot'. The third rajah walked away from the kingdom in the 1940s.) For most of the remainder who left Britain, life in the empire promised freedom of one sort or another – from class, from creditors, from penury, from religious oppression. Living abroad offered a better life, at lower cost. For many there was something about the mere act of leaving the ordered society in which they had grown up which allowed them to breathe more freely. 'I have never felt entirely myself till I had put at least the Channel between my native country and me,' as Somerset Maugham put it.

How to manage this restlessness? Britain's overseas possessions did not make the Statue of Liberty's offer to 'your poor, your huddled masses yearning to breathe free', which appealed so much to the hungry Irish desperate to escape British rule. The British Empire was scattered across the globe, and different parts of it were deemed to have different attractions and different functions. West Africa, with its sweaty climate and sickly reputation, was a great deal less appealing than the bright, airy highlands of Kenya, for example, and throughout the early years of the twentieth century the leader of the Kenyan settler community, Hugh Cholmondeley, third Baron Delamere, fought to keep the place in the hands of a certain class of white person. Many in the Colonial Office were easily pushed into agreement. The attractions of the highlands to the well-bred Englishman were obvious enough. Land was cheap, the climate was kind, the streams were full of trout and the whisky was plentiful. As Lord Cranworth, who emigrated there in 1906, explained, there were two reasons to go to east Africa: (a) big-game shooting, and (b) shortage of cash. Sir Hesketh Bell, appointed high commissioner in neighbouring Uganda the previous year, noted that 'British East Africa is fortunate in starting with such a class of immigrants' and advocated a policy not very dissimilar to the plantations of Ireland:

> If British East Africa is really to become a 'white man's country' – which most of the settlers seem to think it should be – then it would be better to limit its territory, as far as possible, to those regions which are fit for European settlement. The outlying areas, which are manifestly only suitable for negro occupation, would more advantageously be placed within the boundaries of a territory that may ultimately be developed as a truly African State.*

It was high-handed stuff. In fairness, many of the whites in what became Kenya turned out to be pretty successful as farmers, becoming wealthy growing tea and coffee. But they then consolidated their position by creating a (whites-only) legislature which passed laws imposing hut taxes and banning others from growing coffee. Similar things were happening in Rhodesia, but to a rather different class of white settler. While Kenya was for the upper classes, Cecil Rhodes's creation offered to many of the servicemen demobilized at the end of the Second World War land and wealth they could never have found at home, with vast swathes of the best land reserved for them. To give a sense of what this meant, the Land Tenure Act of 1969, a

---

* By contrast, Bell considered that his own territory, Uganda, was 'emphatically a black man's country and European settlement is out of the question'.

statute which purported to offer a fairer division of the spoils between whites and blacks, meant that Rhodesia's 250,000 white people could now own *only* as much land as five million black citizens.

This promotion of white settlement in the twentieth century might have been comprehensible at the height of the empire, for it offered agricultural development and the creation of a cadre of imperial loyalists. But it was at odds with the proclaimed political purpose of twentieth-century empire: by the 1920s, the fashionable belief was in 'custodianship' of less developed lands. In 1923, the Colonial Secretary declared that 'primarily Kenya is an African territory, and His Majesty's Government think it necessary definitely to record their considered opinion that the interests of the African natives must be paramount, and that if, and when, those interests and the interests of the immigrant races should conflict, the former should prevail'. The writing was on the wall. When Kenya broke free of the empire in 1963, the white community learned the lesson that the white community in Zimbabwe – the site of Cecil Rhodes's grave – were to discover a few decades later, that efficiency in production cannot defy majority rule for ever.

This did not become a problem in those places where the indigenous population had been either entirely wiped out or reduced to such pitiful states that the settlers encouraged by Britain could do more or less as they pleased. Canada, Australia and New Zealand had been the destination of the majority of British migrants. None of these territories had been white before the arrival of colonists, of course, but they could all become attractive destinations to help solve a recurrent political anxiety in Britain. The industrial revolution had turned the country into the first state in modern history in which most of the population lived in smoky, overcrowded cities that seemed to breed sickly citizens. The open spaces of empire stood in bright and breezy contrast. In the 1830s, for example, a young man named Edward Gibbon Wakefield had devised a theory for exporting surplus population. Wakefield was no great figure of probity (at the time he was in prison for abducting an heiress) but his idea had superficial plausibility. British colonies could not develop, he argued, because they lacked labour, so he proposed that land there might be sold to those who wished to try their luck as farmers, and the money raised then used to transport workers from Britain. There were many holes in this plan, not the least of them being the need to define what was a reasonable price, to say nothing of who had title to sell anything in the first place. Wakefield promoted settlement schemes all over the place, from South Australia to Canada, but his most successful was in New Zealand, and in May 1839 he dispatched his brother and son to buy land at the other end of the earth. Their vessel arrived in New Zealand in the record time of ninety-six days, to be followed, a few months later, by the first group of migrants.

The circumstances under which the settler community came to dominate New Zealand still rankle with the islands' original inhabitants. It is certainly true that a dozen or so Maori chiefs had appealed to the British for protection – mainly from European traders and the rowdy crews of whaling ships. It is also true that the government was troubled by the possibility of a French settlement being established there. And there were calls from missionaries for British intervention. The government in London dispatched an emissary, William Hobson, a straightforward naval captain, with strict instructions from the Colonial Secretary that he was to play fair with the tribal chiefs: any land he bought in the name of the government, for example, was to be territory they could surrender 'without distress or serious inconvenience to themselves'. Hobson drew up what he thought was a document which safeguarded the interests of both parties and it was translated into the Maori language by a couple of missionaries. On 6 February 1840, at Waitangi, some forty Maori chiefs and a gathering of frock-coated Europeans signed the treaty. In the following weeks, messengers scurried about the country collecting the signatures of another 500 chiefs.

But what had they agreed to? Unfortunately, the Treaty of Waitangi was less than crystal clear, since the English and Maori versions turned out to be imprecise translations of each other. The Maoris appear to have believed that the treaty allowed Queen Victoria nominal government, in exchange for which the Maoris were to be offered protection and left to manage their own affairs. But there was no real Maori concept of sovereignty, for there was no single ruler of the whole country.★ Settlers poured on to the land: at the time of the treaty there were reckoned to be about 2,000 white people in New Zealand and an estimated 125,000 Maori. Within the next twenty years the number of settlers would rise to 100,000. By the 1890s a (white) historian was explaining the imperative that drove things: 'A fertile and healthy Archipelago larger than Great Britain' simply could not be left in the hands of 'a handful of savages – not more, I believe, than sixty-five thousand in all and rapidly dwindling in numbers'. One hundred years later, well over half the population was classified as European. Maoris made up fewer than eight in every hundred citizens.

A sort of settlement mania bubbled away. In 1870, even John Ruskin, the outstanding art critic of his day, delivered himself of the judgement that England faced the highest challenge ever presented to a nation:

> This is what she must either do, or perish: she must found colonies as fast and as far as she is able, formed of her most energetic and worthiest men – seizing every piece of fruitful waste ground she can set her foot on, and there teaching these her colonists that their chief virtue is to be fidelity to their country, and that their first aim is to be to advance the power of England by land and sea.

We have simply no idea how many indigenous peoples in the British Empire were killed either directly or indirectly by the settlers arriving from Britain to make real these dreams and schemes. No one bothered to keep a tally. But we can be certain that it was a very large number indeed. Those not killed by gun or sword perished by exposure to hitherto unknown diseases imported by explorers, soldiers and settlers.

Perhaps the most tragic of all was the fate of the original inhabitants of Tasmania, of whom the word 'genocide' can be accurately

★ Argument over this unfortunate treaty continues, while the site of the signing now offers itself as the perfect venue for weddings, as the place where 'two peoples forged a relationship that has grown into nationhood'. For an additional fee, you can arrive by boat, as Hobson did, and plant 'a seed of commitment' in the gardens of the British Residency. In 2010 eleven couples chose to take up the offer.

used. These short, shy, nomadic people were ethnically distinct from
the Aborigines of mainland Australia, from whom they are thought
to have been isolated for perhaps 8,000 years. Apart from animal
skins, they wore few clothes, smearing their bodies with red ochre
and wearing simple necklaces of shells or bones. No one knows how
many of them were living on the island when the Dutch explorer
Abel Tasman arrived there in 1642 – they built no towns and migrated
from place to place as the seasons changed. Theirs was an extremely
unsophisticated culture: they were said to have been unable to start a
fire, to have no specialized stone tools, to have been unable to cut
down a tree or to hollow out a canoe, and their language seemed to
Europeans to have no grammar. It is perfectly possible, of course,
that their lack of development – tantamount to a crime in the minds
of so many Europeans – was exaggerated, in order to justify their
persecution. But when Captain Cook landed on the island in 1777 he
had certainly found them unthreatening. What contact the native
Tasmanians had with outsiders – mainly groups of sealers on the
coast, who bought or abducted women – brought them nothing but
misfortune, with venereal disease causing many to become infertile,
and others dying from pneumonia, tuberculosis and influenza.

When the British decided to use the island as a penal colony in
1803 there were perhaps 8,000 of these unfortunate people left. They
now faced a trial of strength with citizens of the most technologically advanced nation on earth. In the convicts who had been
transported to Tasmania they met individuals already brutalized by a
penal system which had shipped them across the world and then
dumped them. The free settlers who followed were hardly more sensitive. Indigenous people were hunted down from horseback, caught
in steel traps, shot, speared, bludgeoned, poisoned and mutilated.
Not a single European was ever punished for the murder of Tasmanian Aborigines, although there is an account of a flogging ordered
because a settler had forced a woman to wear the head of her freshly
murdered husband on a string around her neck. The young Charles
Darwin, who visited Tasmania in 1836, thought the extirpation of the
Aborigines was 'unavoidable'. 'I do not know', he noted drily, 'of a
more striking instance of the comparative rate of increase of a civilised

over a savage race.' As many as could be found of the original Tasmanians were rounded up by Christian missionaries and shipped to Flinders Island, a dozen miles away, 'for their own safety'. Here they were given new names and introduced to the Bible and the meaning of money. Flinders Island has a strange Orcadian beauty, but the aborigines found its barren shores unutterably depressing, and while the evangelists preached, the Tasmanians perished. By 1847, fewer than fifty were alive and soon afterwards the project was abandoned, the natives shipped back to their island, to drink themselves to death under the gaze of visiting anthropologists.

In May 1876, the last full-blooded member of their community on the island, a woman named Truganini, died at the age of seventy-three. A tiny woman (she was said to be only 4 feet 3 inches tall) with a whiskery face, her mother had been murdered by Europeans. Her sister had been kidnapped by Europeans. Her stepmother had been abducted by Europeans. Her husband had been drowned by Europeans. She had been raped by Europeans. Sterile from sexually transmitted diseases, she became a settlers' prostitute. Unsurprisingly, photographs of her in old age do not show her smiling. In later years she had paired up with the last surviving male in her community, and had been desolate when white scientists had dissected his dead body to feed the learned societies' appetite for evidence of the differences between the races: her own last words were 'Don't let them cut me, but bury me behind the mountains.' She did not get her wish. Two years after burial in a prison grave she was disinterred, her body boiled, and her skeleton strung together for exhibition in the Tasmanian Museum, where she remained on display until 1947.

CHAPTER NINE

'Patriotism, conventionally defined as love of country, now turns
out rather obviously to stand for love of more country'
John M. Robertson, *Patriotism and Empire*, 1899

By the end of the nineteenth century no one in the country could
have been unaware that Britain commanded the biggest empire the
world had ever seen. City streets bore the names of imperial battlefields, and plants brought to Britain by imperial botanists bloomed in
suburban gardens. Most of the bread the British ate was made with
wheat imported from the empire. Caribbean sugar and Indian tea★

★ The Indian tea plantations, established to reduce the dependence on China, were
an imperial creation, as were tea and coffee plantations in Kenya and rubber

were on every high street. 'Tommy Atkins', the put-upon imperial soldier, was a stock character in the music hall, and the morning newspapers were his chorus. Writers like Rider Haggard, R. M. Ballantyne, G. A. Henty and plenty of bombastic imitators fed the imaginations of teenage boys with adventure tales like *King Solomon's Mines* or *With Wolfe in Canada: The Winning of a Continent*. It was twenty years since flush-faced drunks had first fallen out of pubs at closing time singing the bouncy chorus lines:

> We don't want to fight, but by Jingo if we do,
> We've got the ships, we've got the men, we've got the money too.

Why, in 1895 Joseph Chamberlain had even turned down an invitation to become home secretary in favour of running the colonies.

The grandest showing-off of empire came two years later, in the festivities to mark Queen Victoria's sixty years on the throne. The parade ten years earlier, celebrating the fiftieth anniversary of her reign, had had a smattering of exotic maharajahs in attendance, but the event was, essentially, a domestic affair, the plump little queen in her black dress receiving the applause of her people. As her reign progressed, the tide of red – the colour chosen by imperial cartographers to mark out British possessions – lapped across the world so quickly that maps had to be recoloured and reference books rewritten. By 1897 the ambitions of Germany were a cloud on the horizon, but there had really been no power to challenge Britain's pre-eminent status since the defeat of Napoleon at the battle of Waterloo in 1815. The army was twice the size it had been when Victoria ascended to the throne, the navy four times larger. Joseph Chamberlain – 'Joseph Africanus' as the press called him – proposed that the diamond-jubilee parade should show the world what was what.

Just before she set out to take part in the parade that bright June morning Victoria went to the telegraph room in Buckingham Palace and sent a message across the world. '[From my heart I] thank my beloved people. May God bless them,' she said. Love them – in an

---

plantations in Malaya. One of the consequences of imperial trade was to make London the prime international trading centre.

odd, distant, hierarchical sort of way – she probably did. For years courtiers had twittered at the inappropriateness of her closeness to Abdul Karim – 'the Munshi' – who had filled the void left by the death of her Scottish ghillie, John Brown. The empire had been none of her doing – she merely had the good fortune to accede to the throne at a time that enabled her to become the Mother of the 'Mother Country'. But she certainly loved the baubles of empire, badgering her favourite Prime Minister for the title 'Empress of India' in order, among other considerations, that her eldest daughter's marriage to the Crown Prince of Prussia should not mean that as an empress she would one day outrank her mother. In 1876, when Disraeli enabled her to sign herself 'Queen and Empress' (of a place she had never set eyes upon) he made an ageing widow very happy.

By the measure of history this period of British glory had been short lived, and the city through which the queen processed still seemed an almost accidental imperial capital. But the work of rebuilding that capital to make it look like the heart of an empire was far from complete (and, indeed, was never completed). Mid-century occupants of Downing Street had spent nearly three decades looking out at mountains of rubble as workers threw up the great edifices of the Foreign Office, Colonial Office and India Office: with their elaborate porticoes, sculptures and murals, these were buildings designed to impress upon everyone the extent of British power. But there were hardly enough avenues available to mount the magnificent parade which was planned: London had few of the boastful boulevards of Paris or Berlin. As ever in British public life, the desire to show off had been undermined by constant worry about the cost of it all. The great imperial army, for example, was run from a War Office in Pall Mall where the drains were so bad that it was widely assumed that when the Secretary of State, the Under-Secretary and the Assistant Under-Secretary all died within months of each other in 1861–2 the drains were at least partly responsible. In 1875, *The Times* reckoned that the risk of sickness or death in the building 'should rank in point of danger at about the same level as an Ashantee [west African] campaign'. But the department was not rehoused until 1906. Elsewhere, Trafalgar Square celebrated Nelson, and another mock-Roman column, in Waterloo Place, glorified the former commander in chief of the army, the Duke of York. Cleopatra's Needle towered over the Thames and equestrian statues of generals dotted the capital. But the spoils of empire in the British Museum were buried away among the little streets of Bloomsbury and the showily imperial Admiralty Arch was not built until long after Victoria's death (it was intended as a memorial). The greatest testament to the country's status was not a building at all but the recently opened Tower Bridge, which raised and then bowed itself for the ships which went out to the corners of empire, commercial functionality dressed up in mock-medieval flimflam.

Yet as a spectacle Victoria's parade did not disappoint. In addition to the shining swords and glittering cuirasses of the British cavalry, thousands of troops had been summoned from all over the world. The flag-waving crowds watched, alternately awestruck and curious, as one after another they came – Canadian hussars and Indian lancers, Cypriot police in fezzes, white-gaitered Jamaicans, enormous Australian cavalrymen and Hong Kong policemen in coolie hats, Maoris and Dayaks, rajahs and maharajahs. The *Daily Mail* reported the event as testifying to the 'Greatness of the British Race'. 'How many millions of years has the sun stood in heaven?' it wondered. 'But the sun never looked down until yesterday upon the embodiment of so much energy and power.' In front of bunting-strewn buildings and flag-draped lampposts, before open windows filled with onlookers, specially built spectator podiums and pavements crammed with hat-waving clerks and jolly girls, the cavalcade made its way towards St Paul's Cathedral, the so-called parish church of the empire. The *Daily Mail*'s star reporter certainly got the intended message:

> Up they came, more and more, new types, new realms at every couple of yards, an anthropological museum – a living gazetteer of the British Empire. With them came their English officers, whom they obey and follow like children. And you begin to understand, as never before, what the Empire amounts to. Not only that we possess all these remote outlandish places . . . but also that these people are working, not simply under us, but with us – that we send out a boy

here and a boy there, and a boy takes hold of the savages of the part he comes to, and teaches them to march and shoot as he tells them, to obey him and to believe in him and to die for him and the Queen.

And there in the midst of this purple pageant rode the old queen, sombre in black and grey, holding a long-handled parasol, smiling and bowing to the crowd. An occasional tear rolled down Victoria's cheek, for she was genuinely moved by the crowd's enthusiasm, writing in her journal, 'No one ever, I believe, has met with such an ovation as was given to me, passing through those six miles of streets . . . The cheering was quite deafening, and every face seemed to be filled with real joy.'* Outside St Paul's, Victoria being too doddery to climb the steps, God – or his representatives – came to her. As the queen sat in her carriage, the choir on the cathedral steps chanted the Lord's Prayer and the Bishop of London declaimed a special jubilee prayer. At the benediction, the matriarch of empire wept openly. As the *Daily Mail* put it, she had come to pay homage to the One Being More Majestic Than She.

There was the occasional slip-up in the festivities, of course – one of the more notorious being the disappearance of a massive diamond brought as a gift for Victoria by the nizam of Hyderabad – and there were those who found the whole spectacle distinctly unappealing: the first Independent Labour MP, Keir Hardie, pointed out that people would have been cheering just as lustily if they were celebrating the installation of a British president, while in Dublin a coffin draped in the skull-and-crossbones flag was carried towards the castle, the seat of British power in Ireland, to the beat of a muffled drum. But even the earnest socialist Beatrice Webb admitted to her diary that 'imperialism is in the air, all classes drunk with the sightseeing and hysterical loyalty'. The celebrations continued with choral concerts and fêtes, garden parties, Royal Navy vessels dressed overall (with all their flags flying), military reviews, the unveiling of statues, banquets, Sunday-school galas and a march-past of 4,000 public

---

* She is supposed to have taken some comfort from the words which came from behind her – 'Steady, old lady! Whoa, old girl!' until she realized it was the colonel of the 2nd Life Guards trying to control his overexcited mare.

schoolboys. Free food was given to the poor in the West Indies, convicts were set free in India – and in Britain there was the usual gallimaufry of tatty souvenirs (although the golden-jubilee bustle that played 'God Save the Queen' every time you sat down did not make a reappearance, perhaps because each time it sounded everyone around felt they had to stand up).

Running this vast enterprise was now Britain's main international preoccupation. But the empire seemed to require ever more land to make it function, a policy not of 'What I have, I hold' but of 'What I have requires me to have more.' Or, as one dissident tartly put it, 'patriotism, conventionally defined as love of country, now turns out rather obviously to stand for love of more country'. The thing had been intellectually incoherent from the start: there had never been a strategic plan to hold sway across the globe. What had developed in its place was the strange product of ruthless opportunism and earnest idealism, courage and smugness, confidence and anxiety. Was it because they knew that at one level the whole thing was really a confidence trick that the British behaved as they did, ready to meet the calculated rebuff or the off-hand slight with ruthless 'teach them a lesson' force? Because by the time Victoria celebrated her sixty years on the throne there had been no fewer than seventy wars, expeditionary campaigns or punitive raids fought in her name, everywhere from New Zealand to Canada. In the year of her jubilee parade alone, British troops sacked Benin in reprisal for the king's reluctance to be colonized, were fighting on the North-West Frontier and were advancing on the capital of Sudan to avenge the death of General Gordon. No one was to be allowed to take Victoria's empire lightly. In August of the previous year the Royal Navy had fought the shortest war in history, when the sultan of Zanzibar died and his twenty-nine-year-old nephew had the temerity to declare himself successor without first seeking the approval of the British Consul on the island. When the young man refused a British ultimatum to quit the palace, the three British warships in the harbour opened fire. It was two minutes past nine in the morning. By 9.40 it was all over. The British had fired around 500 shells and about 5,000 rounds from their machine guns and rifles. Five hundred Zanzibaris were dead or wounded, for one wounded British petty officer. As *Small Wars: Their Principles and Practice* had explained, the year before the jubilee, in campaigns against savages 'mere victory is not enough. The enemy must not only be beaten. He must be beaten thoroughly . . . What is wanted is a big casualty list . . . they must feel what battle against a disciplined army means.' Once the enemy started to run, they were to be pursued by cavalry, their villages burned and their crops destroyed. An example had to be made.

But while imperial troops put down dissent, anxiety stalked the consciences of some of those who thought about what it was all for. As long ago as the year of Victoria's accession, her Prime Minister, Lord Melbourne, had been troubled by the 'necessity by which a nation that once begins to colonize is led step by step over the whole globe'. But still the possessions piled up, until by the later decades of the century a belief had taken hold that it was, in the words of one great colonial administrator, Britain's 'manifest destiny' to rule an empire. This was not, he explained, for any reason as crude as 'earth hunger', but was in the interests of those who were lucky enough to find themselves living under British domination. If Britain was governed by Christian principles, it should be possible to 'foster some sort of cosmopolitan allegiance grounded on the respect always accorded to superior talents and unselfish conduct and on the gratitude derived from favours conferred and those to come'. The man who held these beliefs, Evelyn Baring, was to play the most significant role in one of Britain's most idiosyncratic possessions – even though it never formally became a part of the empire.

For strategists, imperial ambitions were offset by real practical anxieties. Keeping the empire safe meant, above all, safeguarding India, the grandest possession. That in turn required complete confidence in the security of the Middle East, and especially the safety of the Suez Canal, which had opened in 1869 and had cut the journey time to India from months to mere weeks. The anxiety which racked the minds of the guardians of empire was that Egypt lay within the Ottoman Empire, which had been in steady decline throughout the nineteenth century. There had been suggestions before that the safest way to protect British interests was to seize control of Egypt, talk which Viscount Palmerston had earlier disdainfully dismissed, telling a fellow aristocrat that Britain really did not want to control the country 'any more than any rational man with an estate in the north of England and a residence in the south would have wanted to possess the inns on the north road. All he could want would have been that the inns should be well kept, always accessible and furnishing him when he came with mutton chops and post-horses.' But the condition of the country which controlled access to so much of the vital waterway grew worse and worse, and the Egyptian Khedive – the viceroy appointed by the Turks – was a feeble fellow, who had already sold the British government his country's shares in the canal. Although the place was under Turkish rule, British business had piled into Egypt: the country was so well suited to the production of cotton that substantial fortunes could be made in a very short time (during the disruption caused by the American Civil War, exports increased ten-fold). The Egyptian state was too weak to take proper advantage of the business, and it was Europeans who developed the banking, irrigation and communication systems. Egypt was a tailor's dummy of a country.

With hindsight, what happened next might seem inevitable. Nationalist Egyptians nursing a great variety of grievances rose up against the foreign influence, under the leadership of Urabi Pasha, a colonel in the army. At first, the British Prime Minister, William Ewart Gladstone, supported the idea of 'Egypt for the Egyptians', which fitted with his scepticism about many of the claims made for empire, as he had demonstrated in voicing his sympathy for proposals for Home Rule for the Irish. He had no plan to invade Egypt. Yet that was what he ended up doing, taking Britain to war with the bizarre – if not quite articulated – aim of maintaining the authority of the Ottoman Empire. There was a noisy group of angry businessmen with money at stake, while the great majority of ships passing through the Suez Canal flew the British flag. When a bombardment of Alexandria in 1882 failed to cow the revolt, the British parliament voted money to send an army, under the command of General Sir Garnet Wolseley. Landing forces at either end of the canal, Wolseley made an audacious advance, culminating in an attack before dawn on the Egyptian forces at Tel el Kebir. In half an hour he had destroyed a force of more than 20,000, with the Highland Brigade, which led one wing of the attack, in no mood to take many prisoners. Two days later, the British flag was flying over Cairo and a feverishly grateful Gladstone was soon offering Wolseley a barony.

Egypt never formally became part of the empire. Indeed, the British kept insisting that they'd be leaving shortly: they repeated the claim no fewer than sixty-six times between 1882 and 1922. The problem was that it was never entirely clear when their conditions for withdrawal would be met, and if these conditions included a properly functioning democracy and educational system the British did not seem to be doing a great deal to bring them about. In theory, the country was still under an Ottoman viceroy with an Egyptian cabinet. But Evelyn Baring, the believer in 'manifest destiny', was transferred from India, with the very modest title of consul general. In reality no Egyptian minister could stay in office if he opposed Baring's proposals, earning the Consul General the inevitable nickname 'Over' Baring. He was soon ennobled as Lord Cromer and was known in Egypt simply as 'The Lord', the enormous residence built for him on the banks of the Nile being the 'bayt al lurd' or 'house of the lord'.* The British flag flew above the citadel Saladin had built against the Crusaders and colonial officials ran the public finances. The Egyptian army was disbanded and reconstituted under a British commander in chief. The Veiled Protectorate, as this system of government was known, functioned by having (not so) shadow British officials in all important government departments. British soldiers watched over the Nile. British brokers struck deals for Egyptian-grown cotton. British vessels crowded the harbour in Alexandria. And on the most famous river in civilization, Thomas Cook ran steamers carrying

---

* The building still provides the British ambassador to Egypt with a splendid residence, even if the price of Egyptian freedom was the construction of a highway between the elegant lawns and the Nile, and the State Department has erected one of the ugliest American embassies anywhere in the world next door. A portrait of Lord Cromer still hangs in the British ambassador's study and a pair of stone lions taken by Lord Kitchener from a former Khedival palace still guard the door.

visiting Europeans to see the ruins of another Egypt, of 5,000 years earlier.

As so often in the history of the empire, one thing led to another. For by taking control of Egypt the British had also assumed responsibility for Sudan, upstream on the Nile, and the biggest country in Africa, much of which had been under Egyptian authority for sixty years. Gladstone was about to learn that seizing Egypt was like putting your hand in a hole and discovering you've stuck your fingers inside a primed mousetrap.

There was nothing particularly enticing about this enormous expanse of not very much. Sudan's most important city was – and remains – Khartoum, at the point where the White Nile meets the Blue Nile, both of which are today spanned by bridges of varying degrees of ugly functionality. Both rivers are a dirty brown. The rutted streets are jammed with smoky, hooting vehicles, the government offices with dozy and decision-averse civil servants. In summer the temperature climbs to over 50 degrees Celsius. Alcohol is illegal and in 2009 the country's President earned the distinction of becoming the first serving head of state to have an arrest warrant issued against him by the International Criminal Court.

Here, in early January 1885, a guttering lantern in the window of what is now the Republican Palace revealed a European sitting at a table, writing. Closer inspection would have discovered a thin, restless man in his early fifties, of average height, with the reddened skin of years of military service in the sun. When he fixed you with his grey-blue eyes, it was, someone said, as if he looked straight into your soul. Charles Gordon had survived over 300 days of siege. Very shortly, he would become the empire's most dramatic martyr.

He was a very singular man. Although he was the ninth child of a general and his body had worn a British military uniform for nearly forty years, his head buzzed with metaphysical abstractions. He had no taste for money (in fact, he demanded his salary be reduced). He had no taste for women. He had no taste for comfort. His religious beliefs having convinced him of an afterlife, he also seems to have had an authentic death-wish. He had used a rather less testing time, in command of the Royal Engineers detachment in Mauritius, to work out the location of the Garden of Eden (he could demonstrate conclusively that it was on an island in the Seychelles). He had stalked alone into confrontations with killers on a previous mission in Sudan and shown a maverick wisdom in trying to defuse tension in Basutoland. In China he had led a rag-bag army which extinguished a rebellion. In South Africa he inspected his troops in a shabby frock coat and top hat. He had calculated the precise positions in the Holy Land of the crucifixion and burial of Christ. He was, in short, courageous, self-reliant and slightly loopy. 'Much as I like and respect him,' said a friend who found his mood-swings incomprehensible, 'I must say, *he is not all there.*'

This strange man had been on his way to take up an appointment in the king of the Belgians' appalling slave colony of the Congo when his ship stopped in Southampton. News of his presence in England reached the great newspaperman W. T. Stead, a journalistic genius lucky enough to live at a time when his own ambition ran in step with the growing expectations of the British people. Stead had the three essential requirements for a successful journalist: a knack for the vivid sentence, an unshakeable conviction that he was right, and an intuitive understanding of public feeling. He also had a healthy suspicion of established authority and a lively social conscience. (His greatest coup came in July 1885, with a series of still horrifying articles in which he exposed the existence of under-age brothels in London: newspaper vendors besieged the *Pall Mall Gazette* offices, clamouring for more copies, after which parliament raised the age of consent from thirteen to sixteen.) Stead recognized in the ascetic, visionary, independent-minded Gordon an imperial hero and took himself down to Southampton to conduct an interview. The problem of the moment was called the Mahdi, a man eleven years younger than Charles Gordon, claiming an even closer relationship with God. The Mahdi swore he was God's elect, 'the chosen one', who would lead the people of Sudan in a holy war to throw off the exploitative rule of the Egyptians and create a society of equals (apart from their slaves, of course). The problem for London was that, since the British ran Egypt, the Mahdi's uprising was also a revolt against the empire. In

November 1883, an army under the command of Colonel William Hicks ('Hicks Pasha') was dispatched to deal with the revolt. The force contained a handful of European officers and thousands of poorly trained and largely useless local recruits. When the Mahdists' green banners swept down on them they were wiped out. Delirious with belief in the Mahdi's genius, some of his followers now began to drink the water in which he had washed, convinced that it would cure their illnesses. This was the sort of enemy to delight any decent journalist, and Stead was one of the best. When he met Gordon, the Sudan crisis was the focus of his interview.

Stead was convinced he had found the man to assert British values against fundamentalist jihad.* Gordon was politic enough in conversation with the reporter to stress that he did not want to embarrass the British government. His only concern, he claimed, was the welfare of the local people, for whom he had developed a genuine affection during earlier service in the country in the 1870s. 'The Soudanese are very nice people,' he said, who 'deserve the sincere compassion and sympathy of all civilized men.' Yet they were being abandoned to 'their Turkish and Circassian oppressors', and 'they deserve a better fate'. Stead – who like many great journalists combined puritan zeal with low guile – immediately recognized a cause: delivering 'a better fate' was the central conviction of all those who believed in the destiny of the British Empire. The Mahdi promised the usual jihadi stuff about a paradise in which no one drank, smoked, danced, clapped their hands or spent too much time with the opposite sex. Gordon was the man to offer something different.

Gladstone's government was in no mood to send another force up the Nile. But the newly emergent mass media began to behave in a way which has since become tediously familiar. The *Pall Mall Gazette* bellowed that Gordon must be dispatched to Khartoum and soon the entire herd was mooing. In no time, there were crowds in the streets

---

* The Mahdi's great-grandson, a delightful, Oxford-educated former prime minister, rejects the description, preferring to see his ancestor as a sufi who denied the material world. Unfortunately, as we sat in his peaceful garden in Omdurman, I forgot to ask him quite how that worked with the Mahdi's reputed seventy wives.

chanting 'Gordon Must Go!' and the government caved in. But he was emphatically not being sent there to bag another colony: Gordon was to go to Khartoum, evacuate all those who wished to leave, and then report back. The Foreign Secretary himself came to Charing Cross station to see him off at the start of his journey, although Gladstone's secretary was wise enough to spot the risks of sending someone like Gordon to a place where he would be beyond any effective control. 'He seems to be a half cracked fatalist,' he reflected, 'and what can one expect from such a man?' 'Half cracked fatalist' was right. Gordon made his way up the Nile towards Khartoum in a buzz of thoughts, counter-thoughts, flashes of inspiration, second thoughts, third thoughts and fourth thoughts which he fired back to Evelyn Baring in Cairo by telegraph, sometimes at the rate of twenty or thirty a day – a pattern which was to continue until the (rapidly approaching) end of his life. Baring soon decided that the only way to deal with Gordon's dispatches was to let them pile up, and then to settle down in the evening and attempt to make out what was going on in his head. General Gordon reached Khartoum in the middle of February, declaring that he came without soldiers, but with God on his side, and entered the city promising to leave. Yet soon he was speaking not about evacuation, but about the fact that for Egypt to be secure, 'the Mahdi must be smashed up'.

In a matter of weeks, however, he was in no position to smash up anyone. He was stuck in Khartoum, surrounded by 30,000 jihadists. His earlier announcement that he would not be staying had had the predictable – if not predicted – effect of ensuring that there was no incentive for anyone to join him. What had begun as an evacuation had turned into a siege. There were occasional negotiations, in one of which the Mahdi's emissaries invited Gordon to surrender and become a Muslim. The rest of the time, it was a question simply of enduring. The Mahdi aimed to starve the town into surrender. Gordon – in careless disobedience of his orders – lived in hope of a relief column arriving.

But it was not only Gordon who was besieged. So too were Gladstone and his government, for Gordon continued to send his torrent of messages, some of which were published, and the public clamoured for the cabinet to dispatch a force to rescue a national hero. Gladstone hated the idea, but finally gave in when his Secretary for War, Lord Hartington, threatened to resign. General Wolseley was ordered to assemble a relief expedition. 'It's funny that a man whom it took one journalist to send should take our only general, two thousand camels, a thousand boats, and ten thousand men to bring back,' remarked a knowing diplomat. But it was already too late. The expedition took months to make its way towards Khartoum, while inside the town things went from difficult to dreadful. Gordon was virtually alone in his rooms in the palace, scanning the landscape beyond the town through his telescope, praying, reading his Bible and writing his journal on scraps of paper and telegraph forms. As ever, this impossible character was greatly aware of the impression he made – a merchant who visited Gordon later recalled begging him not to light candles in the windows, for fear of giving his presence away to the enemy. At this, the general became furious, lit candles all over the room, put a lantern on a table by one of the windows and sat at it. He turned to the merchant and said, 'When God was portioning out fear to all the people in the world, at last it came to my turn, and there was no fear left to give me. Go and tell all the people of Khartoum that Gordon fears nothing, for God has created him without fear.' In his journal, which he decorated with cartoon sketches, he notes that he shares his meals with a mouse, despises the indolence and slovenliness of his Egyptian soldiers and dreams of never having to return to Britain: he would rather live like a tribesman with the Mahdi than be obliged to go out to dinner in London every night. On 14 December 1884 he sent a message reading:

> NOW MARK THIS, if the Expeditionary Force, and I ask for no more than two hundred men, does not come in ten days, *the town may fall*; and I have done my best for the honour of my country. Good-bye
> C. G. Gordon
> You send me no information, though you have lots of money.
> C.G.G.

Characteristically, this was followed, two weeks later, by a message which said the precise opposite: 'Khartoum is all right. Could hold out for years. CG Gordon. 29.12.84'.

This was nonsense. As even the Mahdi knew from the deserters who crossed to his lines, by now almost every living thing that could be eaten – even rats – had been devoured. The waters of the Nile, which had provided a natural defence, were falling all the time. At around three in the morning of 26 January 1885 Khartoum was woken by the sound of tens of thousands of jihadists swarming into the town. It was all over very quickly and very savagely. Gordon's contempt for his Egyptian troops had been justified, and in their emaciated state they were unable to put up much of a fight anyway. The Mahdi's men were aflame with what they conceived to be holy passion and stormed on towards the palace. Gordon had positioned himself on the roof, picking off invaders as they approached. Finally, they swarmed so close that he could no longer point the gun down at them over the edge of the roof. If he had had any hope of saving his life earlier in the fight, by this stage he must have known that the end for which he had professed such enthusiasm was at hand. He returned to his room and put on his white uniform. Then, taking his revolver and sword, he went and stood at the top of the stairs to await the inevitable. It was shortly before sunrise.

There are several different versions of what happened next. Some accounts have Gordon going down fighting, but the preferred story was that he stood at the head of the steps and faced down his attackers for some seconds, until, with a cry of 'O cursed one, your time has come,' one of them gathered his wits, lunged forward and drove his spear into Gordon's body. Apart from having him in the wrong uniform, this was the scene depicted in George William Joy's picture of a stiff-upper-lipped Englishman glaring down contemptuously at the dozen attackers about to stab him to death. For once, the word 'iconic' is appropriate, for the image of the lone, outnumbered white man about to fall to a mass of alien weapons, one hand hanging by his side, the other across his breast, really became an icon of empire. It fitted the imperial belief of a lonely mission to an ungrateful world. The popularity of the painting was nothing to do with Sudan, which much of the British population would have been hard put to identify on a map. The place did not matter. What they cared about was an *idea* of what the empire was about, not money or power, but moral purpose, perfectly expressed through a half-cracked general.

The Mahdi had wanted to take Gordon alive, for his plan was to keep him in chains until he abandoned his faith and became a Muslim. But in the frenzy Gordon's head was hacked from his body, which was tossed down a well. The head – the blue eyes half closed, the hair now apparently white – was taken away in a cloth, shown to the Mahdi and then stuck in the branches of a tree, where every passing child could throw a stone at it. Inside Khartoum, there followed two days of looting, killing and rape. Women who survived were placed in cages, so that the Mahdi's senior officers could choose whom they wanted as concubines. The British relief column finally reached Khartoum, on 28 January 1885, on what would have been Gordon's fifty-second birthday. It was two days late. The British retreated down the Nile.

News of the catastrophe reached London in the first week of February. The poet and anti-imperialist Wilfrid Scawen Blunt had despised the whole venture, characterizing the rescue force as 'a mongrel scum, of thieves from Whitechapel and Seven Dials, commanded by young fellows . . . without beliefs, without traditions, without other principle', so he was one of the very few people not to see it as a disaster. He said he could 'not help singing all the way down in the train' from London to the countryside. For public opinion generally, the news struck like a torrential thunderstorm. By choosing to defend Khartoum, instead of merely evacuating those who wished to leave the city, Gordon had disobeyed his orders and he freely conceded in his diary that if he had been in charge, he would never have employed himself, 'for I am incorrigible'. As Baring remarked later, 'A man who habitually consults the Prophet Isaiah when he is in a difficulty is not apt to obey the orders of anyone.'

But Gordon's wilfulness and disobedience didn't matter – to the public he was a hero. And more than a hero, a martyr, whose death sanctified the imperial mission. For days crowds gathered at Downing Street in the hope of jeering Gladstone for having failed to send the rescue mission soon enough – the Grand Old Man, or GOM, as he had previously been known, became the MOG – Murderer of Gordon. Queen Victoria wrote a letter in her own hand to Gordon's sister. 'That the promises of support were not fulfilled – which I so frequently and so constantly pressed on those who asked him to go – is to me *grief inexpressible!* Indeed it has made me ill . . . I do so keenly feel, the *stain* left upon England, for your dear Brother's cruel, though heroic fate!' The composer Sir Edward Elgar planned to write a symphony about him. Robert Louis Stevenson wrote that 'England stands before the world dripping with blood and daubed with dishonour.' General Wolseley was said to have taught his dog to growl at the mention of Gladstone's name. Gordon's chief advocate in the press, Stead, depicted a saint who had broken off from his military duties during the siege 'to try to nurse a starving little black baby into life' and who had seen himself as no more than 'the passive instrument of a Higher Power'. The tribute he wrote for the *Pall Mall Gazette* even now reads as if tear-stained. 'In him were incarnate the characteristics of the heroes of our national story. The chivalry of Arthur of the Round Table, the indomitable valour and saintly life of the Great Alfred, and the religious convictions of Oliver the Protector.' It ended: 'If in the defence of England's honour it is necessary to go to Khartoum, it is not to avenge Gordon's death,' because the general had taken himself there only out of duty to God, to empire and to 'the poor Soudanese'. Britain owed it to its own higher calling to destroy the Islamists.

Charles Gordon should never have been allowed anywhere near Khartoum. There was sufficient scuttlebutt to suggest that he might have had a drink problem. He was certainly impulsive, emotional, religiously obsessed (he compared himself during the siege to Uriah the Hittite, the soldier abandoned in battle by King David, in order that he could steal his wife, Bathsheba), bad-tempered, unreliable, obstinate and self-absorbed. When the Consul General in Cairo reflected on the hero of Khartoum, he concluded that 'General Gordon does not appear to have possessed any of the qualities which would have fitted him to undertake the difficult task he had in hand.' Nonetheless, he was forced to conclude that 'no Christian martyr tied to the stake or thrown to the wild beasts of ancient Rome, ever faced death with more unconcern than General Gordon. His faith was sublime.' The Mahdi did not live to enjoy his triumph of self-determination for very much longer, dying after a short, violent illness only six months later, mourned by his supposed seventy wives. A mighty tomb was raised, its shining dome visible far out into the desert.* His rule, with its slavery, hand-loppings and floggings to death, passed to the Khalifa Abdullah, who soon felt secure enough to send a letter to Queen Victoria, warning her that her only chance of survival lay in converting to Islam, otherwise 'Thou shalt be crushed by the power of God and his might, or be afflicted by the death of many of thy people . . . by reason of thy Satanic presumption.' The queen did not reply.

In 1896 – the year before Victoria's diamond jubilee – the newly elected Conservative government in London decided to settle the issue of Sudan once and for all. Ministers were now worried that if they did not take the region, then the French might, and with it the headwaters of the Nile. There was the usual – and in this case certainly fatuous – worry about a risk to the Suez Canal. And there was the death of Gordon to avenge. Command of the expedition was given to the man whose pediment moustache and imperious gaze would later make him the poster boy of the British Empire, General Horatio Herbert Kitchener. Ruthless, scheming, vain, arrogant, vulgar, vaultingly ambitious and glacial in manner, as a younger officer Kitchener had taken part in the failed attempt to rescue Gordon. This time, with no need to stage a rescue, progress was steady and utterly determined. Kitchener's army advanced up the Nile laying railway tracks as it went. Up the railway line came more troops, guns and even armoured gunboats, which had been built in London, disassembled

---

* It was destroyed when the British later retook Khartoum, a 1929 guidebook claiming that the body had been removed and 'burned in the furnace of one of the steamers' on the Nile, with the ashes tossed into the river, because 'the building had become a symbol of rebellion and fanaticism, the goal of pilgrimages and the centre of fraudulent miracles'. The current dome appears to be coated in anodized aluminium and is not visible miles out into the desert for the simple reason that the desert has been built upon and the air is now heavy with pollution.

and then reassembled on the Nile under the eye of Gordon's nephew, Major 'Monkey' Gordon of the Royal Engineers.* The newly founded *Daily Mail* called Kitchener 'The Sudan Machine', a well-chosen phrase, as his army closed on Khartoum like some steam-driven leviathan.

By September 1898, Kitchener's army had reached Omdurman, across the river from Khartoum. Through his binoculars a young Winston Churchill, a self-assured cavalry officer-cum-war reporter with the 21st Lancers, could see the pale dome of the Mahdi's tomb rising above the mud walls of the town. In front of the walls was the astonishing sight of the waving banners of perhaps 50,000 men on horses and on foot, in a line about 4 miles across. Kitchener's force was half as big. But it contained forty-four guns and the small flotilla of gunboats, which poured shells into the town. Soon after dawn on 2 September the Khalifa's medievally equipped force advanced and was met by shells from Kitchener's artillery. Still, in a display of astonishing bravery, the force came on, and at a distance of 2,000 yards the British infantry prepared to volley-fire into them. Again, the Arabs advanced, in their holy uniform of long, patched smocks. Next the Maxim guns (which could pour out 600 rounds a minute) opened up, and then, at 800 yards, the Martini-Henry rifles of the Egyptian and Sudanese troops in Kitchener's column.

Churchill claimed that Kitchener encouraged his men 'to regard the enemy as vermin – unfit to live', and the blood-letting was so one-sided that at one point the general was compelled to call out, 'Cease fire! Cease fire! Oh what a dreadful waste of ammunition!' Even so British cavalry, including Winston Churchill, made a super-fluous mounted charge just for the hell of it. By 11.30 that morning Kitchener was able to comment that the enemy had been given 'a

---

* One of these gunboats remains in Khartoum, where for many years it served as the clubhouse of the Blue Nile Sailing Club until an exceptional flood washed it up on to the shore, where it still sits, its 12-pound gun painted a bright cerulean blue. A man who had made the place his home was not receiving visitors when I called. Since the departure of the British the Blue Nile Sailing Club looks to have fallen on hard times and now seems to be mainly a campsite for Europeans making the road journey through Africa from the Cape to Cairo.

good dusting'. There were almost 11,000 Sudanese dead on the ground, with an estimated 16,000 wounded. Out of a force of 26,000, the British had lost forty-eight officers and men, with 382 wounded. Kitchener rode into Khartoum as his troops looted the place. He ordered the Mahdi's tomb destroyed, claiming it would otherwise become a focus for resistance to the occupying army. The Mahdi's skull, the story went, he planned to keep for use as an inkstand or drinking cup. When the story later reached the ears of a disgusted Queen Victoria, she is said to have ordered its immediate return. It was dispatched inside a kerosene tin for burial. (Churchill was not convinced by the gesture: he thought the tin might have contained anything, maybe 'even ham sandwiches'.)

By then, Kitchener had long accomplished his purpose. On 4 September, four army chaplains conducted a service in front of the palace where Gordon had been hacked to death. A guard of British soldiers sang Gordon's favourite hymn, 'Abide with Me', and three cheers were raised for the queen and another three for the Khedive of Egypt, the cipher whose name justified the adventure. Gordon's death had been avenged and Kitchener returned to England the following year a hero. At the end of a parliamentary debate in which Lord Charles Beresford conceded that perhaps the 'disentombment' of the Mahdi 'might have been done in a very much better manner', Kitchener was voted a large gift of public money and all was right with the world once more.

The British like to see their military history as a succession of scrapes – the Armada or the Battle of Britain, for example – in which they are outnumbered and outgunned and survive by guts and ingenuity. It seems to demonstrate a higher moral purpose. But much of the story of their empire is testament not to moral but to technological superiority. Omdurman avenged the death of their martyr. But the Dervishes had spears, while the British had rifles and machine guns. As Hilaire Belloc put it in *The Modern Traveller*, published that year:

> Whatever happens, we have got
> The Maxim Gun, and they have not.

★

There was an imperial coda to this massacre. Five days after the Khalifa's forces were wiped out at Omdurman, a boat came drifting down the Nile bearing unmistakable evidence of having been shot up. The crew described how they had been on a foraging mission upriver, near the town of Fashoda, when they had come under fire from the riverbank. Who their attackers were they knew not, just that they were black soldiers under the command of white officers. As Winston Churchill told the story, curious British officers then dug into the wooden hull and extracted nickel-covered bullets of the kind used only by European forces. This was firm evidence that some other European power was encroaching on to what Kitchener had now established was British territory. But which one? Could it be a Belgian expedition which had set off from the Congo? Italians advancing their country's repeated claims to some of the spoils of Africa? Might they be French? The crew of the boat were asked what flag had been flying, but were unable to agree on the colours they had seen.

Gathering a couple of battalions of Sudanese troops, two companies of Cameron Highlanders, an artillery battery and four Maxim guns, Kitchener set off upriver with five of his gunboats. As he approached Fashoda on 18 September 1898, the identity of the intruders was settled, for he was greeted by soldiers carrying a letter from a Major Jean-Baptiste Marchand. It had the impertinence to welcome him, in the name of France. The British Empire in Africa was hung on a north–south axis, along the lines of Cecil Rhodes's dream of a railway line from the Cape to Cairo. French possessions in Africa were concentrated on the Atlantic coast of west Africa, although the French had recently taken control of the fly-blown but strategically important territory of Djibouti on the Horn of Africa. Paris dreamed of linking the two and Fashoda was the point where the British north–south line crossed the French east–west line. Marchand and his small group of officers had spent two years hacking their way across the continent on a march from west Africa. By comparison with the British force, the Frenchmen were in a poor state, exhausted, short of ammunition for their rifles and with no artillery at all. Kitchener congratulated the major on his endurance. Marchand pointed to his men and replied that the achievement was all theirs. At this point, Kitchener decided, 'I knew he was a gentleman.' Blithely ignoring the French flag which was flying above the fort, he then ordered that the British and Egyptian flags be raised, the national anthems played and salutes fired from the gunboats. Then, leaving a colonel, troops, four artillery pieces and a couple of Maxim guns behind him, he continued his progress upriver.

Kitchener sent news of the confrontation through to London by the telegraph which had been laid down the Nile from Khartoum to Cairo: this was an impasse which would have to be sorted by the British and French governments. For three months Marchand and his little band defiantly maintained a Gallic presence on a miserable island in the river. From their base on the other side of the island, the British appeared from time to time, offering newspapers brought upriver from Khartoum and beyond, which the French paid for in vegetables. From first-hand accounts, Churchill reported that 'a feeling of mutual respect sprang up between Colonel Jackson and Major Marchand'.

The restraint at Fashoda was not matched back in Britain and France, where mobs on either side of the Channel were infuriated by the outrageous 'expansionism' of the other country. A few perhaps agreed with Wilfrid Scawen Blunt's acid observation that the confrontation resembled nothing so much as a 'wrangle between two highwaymen over a captured purse', but anger was the dominant emotion. At one stage, it even looked as if it might come to war between the countries. For months, the foreign ministries wrangled. The British were intransigent. The French weighed their dreams of an African empire against the need for an ally against the dangers from an increasingly menacing Germany. At Fashoda, the months passed in a sweaty stand-off until finally came the orders from Paris. The French government had blinked. The soldiers who had toiled their way across Africa were ordered to haul down the tricolour, and then, with elaborate courtesy and after a decent breakfast, the French went on their way. The only expression of passion came when, having watched his flag lowered, a junior French officer ran to the flagpole, tore it down, shook his fists and tore his hair. In Churchill's words, it was 'a bitterness and vexation from which it is impossible to withhold sympathy, in view of what these men had suffered use-lessly'. Three months later, Britain and France formally agreed which were their respective spheres of influence, carving up most of the continent of Africa. Other European powers muttered and moaned, but had to put up with it. And Sudan, a million square miles of the continent, was now a weird entity, not technically a British colony, not Ottoman, but under notional joint Egyptian and British control. As Churchill put it, a diplomatic fourth dimension had been dis-covered. What the local people – whose future was being determined by largely indistinguishable groups of red-faced white men – made of it all we can only try to guess.

What lessons can we draw from the story of Egypt and Sudan? First, that not all the empire was accumulated by design: there seems little reason to doubt Gladstone when he said that he had no great desire to acquire either place. The problem was that, as his cabinet colleague William Edward Forster remarked of the Sudan crisis, Gladstone could 'persuade most people of most things, and above all he can per-suade himself of almost anything', a talent which has afflicted more recent moralists in Downing Street: the compulsion to 'do some-thing' is a distinct imperial inheritance and is still felt not just by prime ministers but by the British population and its press. There was then, of course, a large element of racial prejudice in this self-appointed responsibility which found expression in pure rage that other races were getting out of hand. When riots broke out in Alex-andria in the summer of 1882, killing several dozen Europeans, the Liberal Charles Dilke – a man who believed in the British as a sort of benevolent master race – noted in his diary that 'Our side in the Commons is very jingo about Egypt. They badly want to kill some-body. They don't know who.' That leitmotif of so much late nineteenth-century imperial policy – a desperation to protect India – was another element, just as it had been the reason for Disraeli's decision to buy shares in the new Suez Canal in the first place. Busi-nessmen who believed their money was at risk roared on demands for military action. The jingoism Dilke had observed in parliament was shared by much of public opinion and was whipped up by the press, which presented Charles Gordon as a sort of Messiah. Succumbing to that pressure put the Sudan mission in the hands of a zealot, who, like many empire-builders, presented the task he had been given as a moral mission. That was Gordon's particular madness, but the slow speed of communications meant that the success or failure of the imperial project was forever in the hands of individuals in distant lands, and the government of the home country just had to live with the consequences. On top of all of that was the need to make sure that the British kept other colonists out.

CHAPTER TEN

'Play up! Play up! And play the game!'
Henry Newbolt, 'Vitaï Lampada', 1892

What was to be done with a place like Sudan? Like everywhere else, once the conquest was finished there came the problem of administration. If you had any faith in the empire, this was a task which might stretch for centuries. And the bigger the empire became, the greater the number of people required to make it function. When the acquisition of territories was a by-product of free enterprise, it could be left to Jack the Lads of one variety or another. Better still, it could be done indirectly, through treaties with local chiefs and kings, who retained the dignities of power in exchange for surrendering the reality or paying a ransom. This was how it worked in much of India, where hundreds of rajahs and nawabs, maharajahs, nizams, walis and badshahs★ were accorded the courtesies of apparent sovereignty – replete with artillery salutes – but whose strings were pulled by British residents or agents. A similar system was adopted once Africa had been colonized, a 'dual mandate', in which local chiefs continued to rule their tribes while the British ran the army, organized taxes, managed the colony's foreign relations and plundered its natural resources. These arrangements had the obvious advantage for the British of requiring fewer officials while affording maximum profit and it is at least arguable that had some similar concessions been made in North America, then perhaps Britain might have hung on to its colonies there a little longer and said goodbye to them with more grace.

By the late nineteenth century the possession, retention and running of an empire was Britain's main international preoccupation, and it required a dedicated corps of individuals as its officers. At the grandest end of things – being the queen-empress's personification in India, for example – the representatives of the Crown were expected to be imposing figures. Lord Curzon, Viceroy at the turn of the century, had been haunted since his Oxford days by a verse beginning:

> My name is George Nathaniel Curzon.
> I am a most superior person,

which made him the right sort of chap for the job, and Viscount Mountbatten, the last Viceroy, was a genuine member of the British

---

★ The variety of titles reflected the subcontinent's multiple influences: Hindu, Muslim, Mongol, Ottoman, Persian and more. The names could be very confusing, as a baffled Edward Lear acknowledged, when he asked:

> Who, or why, or which, or what, Is the Akond of Swat?
> Is he tall or short, or dark or fair?
> Does he sit on a stool or a sofa or a chair,
> or squat,
> The Akond of Swat?

He needn't have worried so much: within a few years, the British had redesignated the ruler of Swat as a wali. The significant thing was that, however grand the title, all the apparent rulers of the states within British India were mere princes. There was only one queen, and she was an empress, and thousands of miles away.

royal family. All were supplied with the robes and carriages, decorations and retainers, to give them an appropriately viceregal appearance. But the vast majority of officials were mere executives, untroubled by questions of how long one country might exercise authority over another, or indeed why it had been acquired in the first place. Their job was to make it function. The job could have a particular charm for younger siblings of smart families who would not inherit titles and estates. 'Many there were', writes the empire historian Ronald Hyam, 'who discovered that pig-sticking in India or Kenya was more exciting than grouse-shooting in Scotland or Yorkshire, or that being a district officer responsible for millions was more satisfying than being a country magistrate in Berkshire.' But by the time the empire reached maturity, the calls for manpower were too great and the needs too complicated for them to be filled merely by aristocrats, either great or small. The growth of empire demanded a formal system of government, and an officer corps to make the queen's writ run. They were a very special breed.

They used to tell a story in the Sudan Political Service about Colonel Robert Savile ('Savile Pasha'), who spent seventeen years governing great swathes of the country in the early twentieth century. He was returning for home leave on a P&O liner when he met a stranger in one of the bars on board. The man told him he was travelling from India, whereupon the colonel asked him whether he had by any chance ever come across his brother, who was serving out there. 'What is he called?' asked the stranger, and then, when he heard the answer, exclaimed, 'By Jove, Savile, I *am* your brother!' It sounds like something out of *Monty Python*. In fact the story was told – and loved – by members of the SPS, who were lampooning themselves long before the post-imperial generation thought of doing so. But few occupations have suffered a greater fall in esteem than that of the colonial officer. A year before independence he is out in the middle of nowhere building a school, driving through a road or opening a dispensary. The next he is not merely redundant, but comical, a pompous clown in over-sized shorts whose only interests in life are the propagation of groundnuts, the state of the cricket team and the next bridge night at the club. It matters not that many former British possessions have retained much the same system of administration (even twenty-first-century India still has 'collectors', and below them other, instantly recognizable colonial-style officials). But, with the end of empire, those who had made the system function became like the lamplighters of gaslit London when the streets were electrified. Colonial officials belonged on a page of history which the British imagined they had turned, and need never revisit.

There is a scene in *The Jewel in the Crown*, Paul Scott's novel set in the dying days of the Raj, when Duleep Kumar decides that to better himself he should travel to England to train as a lawyer. He has noticed that – even though his family are wealthy landowners – 'the callowest white-skinnned boy doing his first year in the covenanted civil service could snub them by keeping them waiting on the verandah of the sacred little bungalow from whose punkah-cooled rooms was wafted an air of effortless superiority'. His father makes light of the supposed snub – what's a few minutes hanging around? Better to stay in India and become an even richer man. The young British official is a fool to refuse gifts from Indians (because he has been taught that they are bribes), when 'in forty years, he will be poor, living on his pension in his own cold climate'. Ah, the son replies, but during those forty years he will have wielded power. His father is incredulous. 'What is this power?' he asks. 'He will have settled a few land disputes, seen to the maintenance of public works, extended a road, built a drain, collected revenues on behalf of Government, fined a few thousand men, whipped a score and sent a couple of hundred to jail. But you will be a comparatively rich man. Your power will be material, visible to your eyes when you look at the land you own.'

The father's depiction of the life of the former colonial official is acute. At the end of their careers most did seem to retire to a life of genteel tedium in Cheltenham or somewhere, in which the highlight of the day was the *Times* crossword or the letters page of the *Daily Telegraph*. But, unless you believe that societies can function without roads and drains and law and order, the list of duties discharged by the imperial official is rather impressive. In one young man were encompassed all the duties performed in other societies by councillors, officials, magistrates, surveyors, engineers and tax collectors. To all intents and purposes, the local colonial official *was* the government. And, unlike many of the possible alternatives, it was a system pretty free of corruption. It is true that at the end of his career the DO could generally expect nothing more than to look out on the rain from a less than luxurious sitting room. But during his years of service overseas there was almost nothing to which he might not have been expected to apply his hand or brain. If you could stand the loneliness, it could be a rich life. In well-established colonies there might be a comfortable bungalow, a well-trained cook and an expat community with clubs, hill stations and social events at which you could meet friends and colleagues. But in northern Kenya it was not unknown for a district officer to travel for an entire day merely on the off-chance that there might be another DO visiting the little thatched building in the middle of thousands of square miles of desert that – in a characteristic joke – was called the Royal Wajir Yacht Club.

Where was the empire to find young people robust enough to live this sort of life? When he looked back on a lengthy career, Frederick Lugard,* Britain's pre-eminent proconsul in Africa, was in no doubt. The empire had been made and maintained by the products of the Victorian public schools. They 'produced an English gentleman with an almost passionate conception of fair play, of protection of the weak, and of "playing the game". They have taught him personal initiative and resource, and how to command and obey,' he said. In the twenty-first century this is the sort of talk which draws nothing but snorts – where's the 'fair play' in being colonized? But if you are to live under someone else's rule, better, surely, that it is represented by an individual out for something more than his own prosperity. The Victorian public schools did not exist solely to manufacture colonial officials and army officers, but the values they inculcated were particularly attuned to the needs of empire – resilience, reliability, obedience when instructed and initiative when the individual was left to his

* Bearer of an imperial moustache as impressive in its way as that of Lord Kitchener, Lugard had quit Britain soon after reading Rider Haggard's *The Witch's Head*, whose hero sets off for Africa after being crossed in love. Lugard had had the same experience, with a flighty divorcee.

own devices. Men who considered that their mission in life was to sit about thinking were no use at all, and might well turn out like that figure of moral turpitude, the scandalous poet Wilfrid Scawen Blunt, who responded to Kipling's guff about 'the white man's burden' –

> Send forth the best ye breed –
> Go bind your sons to exile
> To serve your captives' need

– with the observation that 'the white man's burden, Lord, is the burden of his cash'.★ Instead, the public schools were trying to turn out steady, reliable chaps whose minds would be free of the danger of seditious thoughts – or, indeed, too much thought of any kind. In the middle years of the nineteenth century, school after school was established across the country (and older foundations reinvented) to satisfy the demands of an expanding middle class. The ideal product of these institutions was 'a decent chap'. To achieve this paragon, there was much emphasis on learning classical Greek and Latin and how to play a straight bat in cricket.

Cricket mattered. At King's School in Worcester the memorial to those who died in the First World War took the form of a new pavilion, inscribed with the words 'In Memory of those who, having learnt in this place to play the game for their school, played it also for their country during the years 1914–1919'. The reference is to one of the most resonant of imperial poems, Henry Newbolt's 'Vitaï Lampada'. Newbolt was the son of a vicar and won a scholarship to Clifton College, where he rose to become head boy. The lines are worth quoting again:

> There's a breathless hush in the Close to-night –
> Ten to make and the match to win –
> A bumping pitch and a blinding light,

★ Blunt had supported Urabi Pasha's revolt and for a while persuaded Gladstone to leave Egypt to the Egyptians. When the revolt failed, his poem 'The Wind and the Whirlwind' predicted nemesis:

> Thou hast thy foot upon the weak. The weakest
> With his bruised head shall strike thee on the heel.

An hour to play, and the last man in.
And it's not for the sake of a ribboned coat,
Or the selfish hope of a season's fame,
But his captain's hand on his shoulder smote –
'Play up! Play up! And play the game!'

The sand of the desert is sodden red –
Red with the wreck of a square that broke;
The Gatling's jammed and the colonel dead,
And the regiment blind with dust and smoke.
The river of death has brimmed its banks,
And England's far, and Honour a name,
But the voice of a schoolboy rallies the ranks –
'Play up! Play up! And play the game!'

The poem has spent much of the century since its composition being
lampooned.★ Yet it would be hard to exaggerate the importance of
sport in the creation of an imperial spirit. It was coincidence that the
empire grew at the very time that, at home, the rules of so many sports –
soccer, rugby, cricket, tennis, golf, for example – were either invented
or codified and their first national championships created. But the cult
of sport was made for the cult of empire. It was more than the creation
of a healthy officer class. There was something in the conventions of a
game – loyalty to the team, obedience to the rules, unquestioning
respect for the authority of the referee – which spoke of the imperial
design.† Cricket, in particular, was *more* than a game: its customs were
believed to be civilizing in themselves. The empire may have been built
by mavericks. But it was held by those who played by the rules.

★ The second verse had been inspired by a battle fought in the doomed attempt to
rescue General Gordon. The engagement was described by Winston Churchill at
the time as the most savage action ever fought by British troops in the Sudan, during which the square formation in which the soldiers fought did indeed break. By
the time the First World War (in which the poet worked for the clandestine War
Propaganda Bureau) was over, even Newbolt himself was slightly sick of the poem,
calling it a 'Frankenstein's monster' he'd created.
† The beliefs inculcated at school could, said one not entirely sympathetic observer, be reduced to Ten Commandments running from Number One – 'There is

And there were numerous genuine testimonials to the moral benefits of sport, sometimes from unlikely sources. The Trinidadian writer and radical C. L. R. James, for example, felt the improving influence of the sport when he was sent to Queen's Royal College before the First World War. It was the most prestigious school on the island, where cricket featured prominently. 'Rapidly we learned to obey the umpire's decision without question, however irrational it was,' he recalled.

> We learned to play with the team, which meant subordinating your personal inclinations, and even interests, to the good of the whole. We kept a stiff upper lip in that we did not complain about ill fortune. We did not denounce failures, but 'Well tried' or 'Hard luck' came easily to our lips. We were generous to opponents and congratulated them on victories, even when we knew they did not deserve it. I knew what was done and what was not done.

Which was precisely what cricket was intended to teach.

It was not, of course, the only game taken around the world, for by the late nineteenth century the British had become sport-obsessed. When Lord Cromer arrived in Cairo to take up his post running Egypt, less than a year after the 1882 battle of Tel el Kebir, he discovered that 'every department of the Administration was in a state of the utmost confusion. Nevertheless a race-course had already been laid out and a grandstand erected.' By then, tracks had been created all over the world, from Africa to India, Hong Kong to New Zealand. Eustace Miles, the proprietor of a cranky health-food shop on the King's Road, Chelsea, was one of the greatest apostles for the imperial benefits of sport. He observed that when the British took some new place 'we do not merely rule people with the rule of iron, but we admit them to our own life; we do not treat them like slaves, but we say to them, for example, "Come and play Football", or "Have a try at Cricket". This is surely one way to their respect and also to their affection and loyalty. We bring them something which is

---

only one God, and the Captain of the XV is his prophet' – and ending in Number Ten – 'I must show no emotion and not kiss my mother in public.'

not only useful, but also pleasant.' And at the Gezira Sporting Club founded by the British in Cairo, they continue to take him at his word. You can still watch horse-racing and play golf, croquet, hockey, lawn tennis, table tennis, squash and cricket.

The image of the men who graduated from the playing fields of England to run the empire has never really recovered from *Sanders of the River*, the colonial officer created by that master of the potboiler, Edgar Wallace, who dispenses justice to 'child-like' west Africans while sitting cross-legged on a chair, an unlit cigar clamped in his mouth, a Browning pistol on his hip. 'I am Sandi,' he says, 'I am a man quick to kill and no respecter of kings or chiefs. I have ploughed little kings into the ground and the crops of my people have flourished on the bones of princes.'* Edgar Wallace may have considered this sort of dialogue made for an amusing narrative, but as a picture of the colonial official it was complete tosh. The diaries and letters of district officers tell a much more mundane story. It was frequently a life of stoical endurance, rudimentary comforts, terrible food, tedious bureaucracy and numbing loneliness, in pursuit of small initiatives – a bridge here, a bit of irrigation there – which might better the lives of the community in which the DO found himself.

And in addition to the frustrations of life in the bush, DOs had to cope with the clods in London. 'Documents no longer needed may be destroyed,' a Colonial Office directive is imagined to have ordered, 'provided copies are made in duplicate.' The Whitehall bureaucrats so often seemed simply not to have a clue about the realities of life overseas. 'Why, some of them seem to think that you can govern a West Indian colony with a fiddle and a ham-bone,' exploded the Governor of the Leeward Islands (and former Oxford rower), Sir Clement Courtenay Knollys. The early twentieth-century diaries of

---

* In a spectacular example of trickery or political misjudgement, in the 1935 film version of the book the black singer Paul Robeson was somehow induced to play the part of Bosambo, the quaint, big-headed, foolish African who makes the mistake of thinking he can outsmart the white official. When Robeson saw the final product, which was dedicated to 'the handful of white men whose everyday work is an unsung saga of courage and efficiency', he was understandably furious.

Sir Hesketh Bell bubble with ideas he had for cultivating citrus fruit
while governing in the West Indies (he'd been told that American
men considered grapefruit to be good for the liver and American
women thought it a contraceptive) or how to create an insurance
scheme to protect islanders from the financial effects of hurricanes.
These men might occasionally wonder whether the places to which
they had been sent were worth the effort. But they rarely questioned
the moral basis of their work: they believed they were 'doing good'.
In a world before the United Nations and aid agencies, this was
another side to colonialism.

Recruiters for the Sudanese Political Service – which considered
itself a cut above most colonial administrations – sought a very particular type of person. Within three years of Kitchener's capture of
Khartoum, small numbers of civilian officials began to arrive from
Britain and between 1901 and 1930 there were never more than twelve
men selected in a year. This was a tiny force in a vast expanse –
at any one time a mere 125 men, running a territory four times the
size of Texas, 150 times as big as Yorkshire. Since those chosen were
likely to have to deal with anything from a broken town drain to
the settling of vendettas by knife murder, the selectors were after
candidates who could demonstrate leadership, stamina and a steady
head. Most of those who made the grade were graduates of Oxford
or Cambridge, but the selection board had a definite preference
for reliability over cleverness: one applicant was rejected because
the selectors did not care for the fact that he had 'by accident' left
his copy of that morning's *Times* newspaper lying about *with the
entire crossword completed*. They preferred the sort of man likely to
have played sport for his university: Sudan was said to be 'The Land
of Blacks Ruled by Blues'. Those who satisfied the selectors were
sent off to learn Arabic, how to administer the law, a little anthro-
pology, some basic first aid and the rudiments of surveying and
drainage: in one young man were to be contained all the necessities
of civilization.

For the right sort of person, it wasn't a bad job. The service offered
three months' home leave every year, on the grounds that nine

months was quite long enough to expect anyone to endure the Sudanese climate, and for much of the year the young official might be alone out in the bush. There was the prospect of retirement at fifty, which meant the chance of a second career. But they were not expected to think about getting married any time soon. A very large proportion of those selected came from country families, presumably because their background meant they were accustomed to the open air and the squirearchy's traditional responsibilities towards the village community. A remarkably high proportion of those who qualified – one-third – were the sons of clergymen.

Much of the rest of the empire was officered by the Colonial Office. By comparison with the grand edifice housing the Foreign Office, with its frescos of Britannia imposing her will upon the world, the Colonial Service was a shabby establishment with temperamental lifts, odd-shaped rooms and smoky chimneys, the below-stairs quarters of the imperial drawing room, where armies of servants laboured to make pretension real. Colonial administration was not for everyone. A man desperate to make a fortune might be willing to brave an infernal climate, ghastly diseases, alien cultures and other sweaty discomforts in the service of the East India Company. But serving the Crown for a salary was a less attractive prospect. 'Beware and take care of the Bight of Benin,' ran a cautionary verse about the White Man's Grave of West Africa, 'For one who comes out, there are forty go in . . .' In the early days, colonies had to make do with what they could get. 'Bankrupts, divorcees, cashiered army officers – all were grist to the mill,' writes a colonial historian. They did not even need to be gentlemen. 'Mr Rowland called today,' ran one Colonial Office memo. 'He seemed an energetic keen little chap, though he is not beautiful to look at (rather like a cheese-maggot) and drops his H's. [But] he has made several trips to the Gold Coast and is not afraid of the climate.' They weren't all like that, however. Oddly, one of those who passed the selection process in 1904 was the future pillar of the Bloomsbury Group and enemy of imperialism Leonard Woolf, who left England for Ceylon accompanied by a miniature edition of Shakespeare, a four-volume set of Milton, ninety volumes of Voltaire and his fox-terrier, Charles. He then spent a thoroughly miserable seven years in one of the most enchanting places on earth.*

It could not continue indefinitely in quite such a haphazard style. After the First World War, with the empire bigger than it had ever been, the recruitment business was centralized and formalized. For decades, the task of choosing the core of the Colonial Service then became entrusted to an extraordinary man, Major (later Sir) Ralph Dolignon Furse, a thin, patrician character straight out of Central Casting. He had been wounded, and won a DSO and bar, in the First World War. He had collected a third-class degree in Greats at Oxford. He had played rugby and cricket for Balliol College. He had married the daughter of Henry 'Play up! Play up! And play the game' Newbolt. Now it was his responsibility to find men who would keep a straight bat in whichever corner of the empire they found themselves. Towards the end of his career in 1948 Furse still sometimes wore the brown tweed suit in which he had turned up for work in 1910. He had the stiffest of stiff upper lips: once, while staying in Canada, he had been offered a strange liqueur to drink. Furse drained the glass and went to bed, where he suffered a terrible night. Several weeks later his hostess discovered that the bottle had contained shampoo. She wrote to him to apologize, adding, 'We had often heard of the standard of English manners. Now we know.'

In seeking suitable candidates, Sir Ralph did nothing so obvious as to advertise for applicants. Instead, to ensure that no 'rubbish' (his word) came through the door, he operated a network of 'recruiting spies'. These were mainly Oxbridge dons who knew the sort of chap that Furse was looking for – after that, it was a mere matter of references and interview. Furse and his assistants sat together in a room next to that of the Secretary of State, large enough for them to interview several candidates simultaneously. His questions were unpredictable. ('Don't turn round – or look at your watch – there's a big clock on the wall behind you. How long has this interview

---

* George Orwell was another anti-imperialist who satisfied the India Office examiners, passing the test to become an empire policeman in Burma, after the usual spell at a crammer.

lasted?' 'Do you think you could tell a smoking-room story to an African elder?' 'How would you get to Lord's from here, assuming you can't afford a taxi and the match is nearly over? Anyhow, what match is on there today?') By the time of his retirement Furse was pretty well stone deaf and unable to hear their answers anyway, a disability which he felt in no way disqualified him from judgement. Sometimes, while apparently talking to one candidate, he was in fact evaluating another out of the corner of his eye. 'A man's face may not reveal that he is intensely nervous,' he wrote in his memoir *Aucuparius* (Aucuparius was a character in classical mythology whom he had once been told – wrongly – was a bird-catcher). 'But a twitching foot, or hands clenched under the table, will tell you this.' Furse's system was based upon hunch. Most important of all was the handshake – the slightest suggestion of limpness and you might as well kiss goodbye to your ambition.

This selection system continued throughout the period between the wars, with the successful candidate being able to look forward to a telegram containing a sentence such as 'YOU HAVE BEEN ALLOCATED UGANDA'. There was usually a proviso about passing the medical examination and getting a 'satisfactory' degree, but this was not generally especially taxing: Furse carried a torch for 'that admirable class of person whom the university examiners consider to be worthy only of third-class honours'. The selection process was intended to weed out the cad, the feeble, the too clever: what was wanted was steadiness, authority and biddability – you did not want a man somewhere out in the bush deciding to question why he was there. On the other hand, the good name of the empire might depend upon an ability to act independently. When one of the men Furse had chosen for the service reflected on his life, he concluded that 'a service of amateur humanists was . . . admirably suited to the administration of unsophisticated peoples'. A modicum of learning was necessary, of course. But much more important than first-class degrees were the sort of skills you might learn on the public-school playing fields. 'I was head of my house, I was deputy head of the school, captain of rugger, and company sergeant-major in the Officer Training Corps,' recalled one former district officer, 'so when eventually I found myself in the bush in Nigeria on my own I wasn't worried about it in the slightest way.' The selection process had worked. Though he would probably never have put it quite as baldly, Furse understood the crucial fact that running an empire was partly a big bluff. The sort of person he especially prized was a 'boy' he had sent to Nigeria. Within months of his arrival, the young man had been left in sole command of a district, when serious rioting broke out. Murders were committed, buildings were burned and the young District Officer had neither soldiers nor police to restore order. Suddenly, a rampaging mob appeared on his doorstep, led by a large woman. The official walked out alone to face the rioters, then suddenly threw his arms around the woman's waist, kissed her on both cheeks and invited her in for a talk. The unrest was over.

This sort of presence of mind could not really be taught. Indeed, since a single individual might be expected to discharge the duties of magistrate, administrator, public-works engineer, mediator, estate manager, occasional doctor and general father-figure (even if not a father himself), the formal instruction for the task was either limitless or extremely limited. With the empire so vast, it was often just irrelevant. A district officer sent to Northern Rhodesia (now Zambia) recalled that he 'spent three months in the old Imperial Institute learning about tropical products which did not grow in Northern Rhodesia; Mohammedan law, which did not run there; and the elements of government accounting, which were still too unreal to us to be absorbed'. At the end of the training, a novice official collected his kit from the approved outfitters and off he went on the steamer to Africa, clutching his phrase book, ready to brave scorching sun and biting insects, malaria and loneliness, and sometimes, in the middle of nowhere, meeting the man he was to replace – flaming drunk by nine in the morning because Furse's system had made a mistake.

Doorkeepers do not make policy and Sir Ralph Furse had stood like an especially superior doorkeeper to the Colonial Service. (He had become so well known that when he eventually retired there were fears that the supply of candidates would dry up: his successor – Furse's own brother-in-law, Henry Newbolt's son – had to beg the department to reannounce his appointment because no one had any idea who he was.) Latterly, Furse had expressed occasional anxieties about aspects of the imperial mission – 'What shall it profit the African if we save his soil and he loses his soul?' he wondered. But at the close of his career he concluded – as he had to do – that the empire had been A Good Thing. He recited an idiosyncratic list of achievements: 'The abolition of slavery; the suppression for the most part of cannibalism and tribal warfare; the long campaign against disease and want; the example of justice and fair play; the introduction of cricket and the rule of law; some slight shrinkage of the kingdom of fear ruled over by the dark gods – and so on down a long and not unimpressive record of beneficent service.' It was not Furse's function to question the moral judgement on which the whole thing rested.

At first sight, Robert Baden-Powell (his socially ambitious mother had invented the double-barrel) was the sort of steady, low-brow Englishman for whom the empire might have been created. As it was, B-P invented imperial service for millions who would never have made the grade as colonial officials, even in the Bight of Benin. What Ralph Furse did for the Colonial Service, B-P did for millions of others.

It is unlikely that Robert Baden-Powell would have passed the entrance test for the Colonial Service himself. At his public school he had not troubled the examiners much, but had turned out to be good at throwing himself around in goal on the football pitch. Failing to get into university, he joined the army, where, during service in Afghanistan, he witnessed the hanging of recalcitrant tribesmen with the casual indifference of an occasional visitor to a provincial theatre. He shot tigers, lions, hippos, buffalo, and produced a guide to Indian field-sports, *Pig Sticking and Hog Hunting*. And, just as he was sure of the superiority of his own countrymen, so he was certain of the woeful inadequacy of other races. 'An occasional lick from a whip is, to an unintelligent savage, but a small matter,' he wrote. When the Matabele people rebelled in 1896 against the 'white pioneers of civilization', Baden-Powell had been thrilled to be part of the military campaign against them – 'a tussle with the niggers' was like knocking back 'a couple of glasses of champagne'. B-P belonged to that

comparatively small group of empire-builders who not only believed
these things, but were successful evangelists for them. He was an
ardent self-publicist, whose broad ambitions for celebrity stood in
contrast to the narrowness of his mind. His *Adventures of a Spy* is full
of tips about keeping an eye out for 'foreign-looking gentlemen' in
London who will probably turn out to be dastardly secret agents.
It recounts his experiences tramping around enemy territory in the
eastern Mediterranean, posing as a butterfly collector, his notebook
full of sketches of forts, disguised within drawings of the wings and
bodies of moths. Biographers have been unable to find any evidence
to support many of his espionage claims, and to read his jaunty, self-
confident, irrepressibly upbeat books is to spend an uncomfortably
long time in the company of a juvenile ego-maniac. But, like Winston Churchill, B-P understood that the burgeoning mass media
could accomplish three things at once – make his name, make his fortune and spread the gospel of empire.

It was the 217-day siege of Mafeking during the Second Boer War
(1899–1902) which established B-P's reputation. The wars between
the two settler communities of South Africa were set off when the
longer-established descendants of Dutch settlers determined to
defend their autonomy against the expansionist ambitions of the
British Empire. Since the British had no shortage of men in uniform –
they would eventually have to send 500,000 soldiers to fight in South
Africa – and the Boers had no formal army at all, their inability to
assert British rule in the first conflict came as a terrible shock. The
siege at Mafeking in the second war vividly demonstrated their
difficulty. The British had become accustomed to getting their way
in colonial battles, a success they generally attributed to superior
training and moral values, but which was really much more to do
with the fact they usually had more sophisticated weapons. This
time, the Boers had gone on an arms-buying spree before the war
began and equipped themselves with modern rifles and even some
artillery. This was to be no one-sided 'tussle with the niggers', and
the Boer 'commandos' had one other great asset: as a light, irregular
force ready to live off the land, they could fight the most mobile and
effective guerrilla campaign the British had ever faced. The war

developed into a vicious and very squalid conflict, in which the conventions of 'civilized warfare' were repeatedly ignored.* The British would eventually win – how could they not, against a scrappy bunch of bandoliered farmers cantering around the veldt? – but only at the cost of tremendous damage to their reputation, when the world learned that the response to the Boer offensive had been to burn down their farms, poison their wells and intern women and children in 'concentration camps', where many died of sickness and hunger. The exposure of the appalling conditions in the camps was largely the work of Emily Hobhouse, another member of that small, heroically subversive band of women who insisted on sticking their noses into the work of imperial menfolk. One can date the beginnings of the terminal sickness which carried off the British Empire to the South African campaigns. The British won the Second Boer War too, but lost something much more important. Too many people knew that the texts of sermons on Britain's civilizing mission were hanging on the barbed wire of the South African veldt.

In 1899, Colonel Baden-Powell had been sent to rustle up new recruits for the second British war effort, and had not been much impressed by the calibre of men he found. 'They are bad riders and bad shots,' he reported – quite the opposite of the Boer irregulars. Any plan to use his recruits to harry the Boers was not going to work. Instead, in October 1899, B-P assembled a mountain of stores and settled down inside the town of Mafeking. Large claims were later made, not least by Baden-Powell himself, for the importance of the siege which soon became inevitable. It is true that the town sat on a railway line and that, despite its small population (about 1,700 whites and 5,000 black people), it had the appurtenances of a little sophistication – library, prison, hospital and so on. But one could as easily say that the siege which then developed became an immensely famous action for a mainly fatuous target (Kitchener is said to have

---

* 'Sooner or later we are bound to catch them,' Kitchener, commanding the overstretched British forces, wrote to two small boys who had sent him a letter, 'but they give a lot of trouble. The Boers are not like the Sudanese who stood up to a fair fight. They are always running away on their little ponies.'

claimed later that there were people in the War Office under the impression that the town – about as far from the sea as you can get in South Africa – was the nearest sea-port to Pretoria). In later life, B-P seemed increasingly unsure how many Boers had been besieging the town. He could not have known with any precision at the time, but as the years went by his estimate rose, from 8,000 in his report after the engagement, to 10,000 in his autobiography thirty years later, until by the time of a radio broadcast in 1937 he was claiming to have tied down 12,000 enemy. In fact, it seems that many of the Boer besiegers had left after a few weeks, but that, of course, did little to lessen the horror of the siege. B-P's defenders claim that in keeping his force inside the town, he diverted more of the Boer forces than he could ever have done by trying to chase them across the veldt with his incompetent militia: once an attractive target like Mafeking presented itself, plenty of Boers were occupied in trying to beat the place down into surrender. Nonetheless, as one of B-P's officers, Major de Montmorency, wrote in his diary, it was surely the oddest action ever taken by a cavalry officer to have 'burrowed into the ground at the very first shot being fired . . . and commenced to eat his horses'.

The true importance of the siege of Mafeking to the British was less what it was than what it represented. B-P was an inspirational siege commander and a clever tactician, deceiving the watching Boers by having his men appear to lay minefields or move around as if they were negotiating (non-existent) barbed-wire fences. He turned the railway workshops over to production of guns. He made a point of appearing unflappable, even as shells whistled over his head into the town – 'A second shell sang a little nearer and raised clouds of dust not two hundred yards away,' said a witness. 'The colonel closed the book which he had been reading, and, marking the place, rose quietly, whistling to himself, as is his habit, and as a third shell wrecked a couple of outstanding buildings, said "You had better come inside." ' When his jaunty dispatches, the most famous of which was boiled down by his signaller to 'All well. Four hours' bombardment. One dog killed,' appeared in the London newspapers B-P became a hero in the Nelson mould. His initials, claimed the drum-bangers at home, stood for 'British Pluck'.

Like many empire heroes, it sounds as if Baden-Powell might have been born for extreme adversity. The burden was not shared evenly, of course. Everyone went hungry, but the whites got much better rations than the black people, and in his subsequent accounts of the siege B-P hardly mentioned the Africans' big contribution to Mafeking's survival. But he was in his element and the embattled little community provided a stage – both metaphorical and literal – for his indefatigable cheeriness and vanity. B-P designed Mafeking banknotes and his head replaced that of the queen on postage stamps. The tedium of month after month under siege was eased by his encouragement of concerts, plays, cricket matches, gymkhanas and flower shows. At concerts he would appear on stage in fancy dress and sing in a silly voice. Were there occasions when his audiences wondered whether it might not be preferable to go over to the Boers than to sit through another of his hilarious monologues, practical jokes or imitations of birdsong?

Eventually, a relief column reached the town and Mafeking joined the list of 'scrapes' in which the British delight. When news of the relief of the town reached Britain, a new verb entered the English language. To 'maffick' meant to join the crowds of thousands who took to the streets in uproarious celebration, waving Union flags and carrying pictures of B-P in his broad-brimmed hat.

> Mother, may I go and maffick,
> Tear around and hinder traffic?

as Saki's couplet put it. Military parades swaggered in front of Queen Victoria. Portly mayors of industrial cities made thunderous speeches about the superiority of British values. Hotels printed their menus on khaki paper, adorned with photos of B-P on the cover. Fireworks were lit (the finale of the display in Twickenham was a blazing likeness of B-P). In Dover a mob wrecked the offices of a member of the local chamber of commerce, because they had decided he was 'pro-Boer'. Much drink was taken. In St Paul's Cathedral Canon Henry Scott Holland preached that, like Lucknow, the name Mafeking would thrill Englishmen's hearts for many a long year, proving their tenacity, pluck and refusal to know when they were beaten.

When Baden-Powell returned to England he did so as a hero, garlanded with praise even from the worst poet in Scottish literature,
William Topaz McGonagall:

> Oh! think of them living on brawn extracted from horse hides,
> While the inhuman Boers their sufferings deride,
> Knowing that the women's hearts with grief were torn
> As they looked on their children's faces that looked sad and forlorn.

> For 217 days the Boers tried to obtain Mafeking's surrender,
> But their strategy was futile owing to its noble defender,
> Colonel Baden-Powell, that hero of renown,
> Who, by his masterly generalship, saved the town.

It was with this background that B-P's most famous book, *Scouting for
Boys*, appeared in 1908, if not quite as a celebrity memoir, then certainly with a celebrity author. His customary tone – part martinet
and part breezy chorus-leader – pervades the whole text of a book
now estimated to have sold over 150 million copies. The opening lines
of the book make plain B-P's purpose. 'I suppose every boy wants to
help his country in some way or other.' He gave examples of the way
in which his corps of teenage boys in Mafeking had cheerfully cycled
through shot and shell delivering messages. The popularity of the
book tells you something about the tone of British society at the
time. But the really clever thing about it was that instead of merely
telling young people what they ought to do to help the empire,
Baden-Powell made Scouting a personal, homely adventure. For
sure, there were plenty of instructions about attitudes – ' "Country
first, self second" should be your motto,' for example. Yet what child
could resist the advice that every boy ought to know how to shoot,
to fish or 'to be very clever at passing news secretly from one place
to another, or signalling to each other'? There was plenty more: 'It
is very necessary for a Scout to be able to swim, for he never knows
when he may have to cross a river, to swim for his life, or to plunge
in to save someone from drowning.' B-P even managed to make
keeping your room tidy sound exciting: 'because he may yet be suddenly called upon to go off on an alarm, or something unexpected:

and if he does not know exactly where to lay his hand on his things he will be a long time in turning out, especially if called up in the middle of the night'.

The nightmare lurking at the back of Baden-Powell's mind was of a nation which no longer had the resources to defend either itself or its empire. Scouting was intended to do for poorer boys what the public schools aimed to achieve for the sons of the middle and upper classes. The urban slums in which army recruits grew up were having a catastrophic effect on their health: it was said that over half of the young men examined during the Boer War had failed relatively undemanding medical tests. In the aftermath of war, the government formed an Interdepartmental Committee on Physical Deterioration. B-P identified the problem at once. There were too many 'loafers' and 'slackers', hanging around on street corners with their hands in their pockets, smoking, drinking and watching sport instead of playing it. So *Scouting for Boys* had plenty of advice about well-being. 'Scouts breathe through the nose, not through the mouth,' runs one memorable admonition; 'in this way they don't get thirsty, they don't get out of breath so quickly; they don't suck into their insides all sorts of microbes or seeds of disease that are in the air; and they don't snore at night, and so give themselves away to an enemy.' In B-P's original manuscript there had been more intimate advice, on the subject of sex, a matter which troubled him deeply: masturbation was a definite symptom of slackness, causing weakness, headaches, shyness, palpitations of the heart 'and if he carries it on too far he very often goes out of his mind and becomes an idiot. A very large number of the lunatics in our asylums have made themselves mad by indulging in this vice although at one time they were sensible cheery boys like any one of you.' A Scout, by contrast, was 'clean in thought, word and deed'.

B-P had considered naming the youth organization which grew from these admonitions 'Young Knights of the Empire' (in one especially odd sentence, he even claimed the twelfth-century Crusader king Richard I – 'the Lion Heart' – as 'one of the first of the Scouts of the Empire'). It is certainly true that much of the Establishment saw Scouting as a way of maintaining the moral health of the nation.

Lord Rosebery (Prime Minister in 1894–5), for example, believed
that a country 'trained in the Boy Scout theory . . . would be the
greatest moral force the world has ever known'. The London *Evening
Standard* noted that 'The Boy Scout at 19 will be something very different from the cigarette-smoking street-corner loafer, who diversifies
his indolence by occasional bursts of hooliganism. He will be smart,
clean, alert, well-mannered.'

The endorsement of the ruling class of the time and the uniforms,
hierarchies and badges were sufficient to condemn the movement in
the growing ranks of critics of empire.* But Scouting became the
most successful youth organization of all time not because it was part
of a scheme for world domination but because it recognized the universal appetite for what seem to be adventures. By the second decade
of the twenty-first century it had 400,000 members in the UK with
28 million others scattered across 216 countries, some – like the 4 million in India and the 4.5 million in the United States – citizens of
former imperial possessions, but millions more – like the 17 million
in Indonesia – who belong to nations which were never part of the
empire. What's not to like about an organization whose members are
instructed to perpetrate a random good deed each day? ('Such small
things as these: sprinkle sand on a frozen road where horses are liable
to slip; remove orange or banana skins from the pavement, as they are
apt to throw people down . . .')

When Baden-Powell's health collapsed he took himself off to live
in Kenya, where the climate made it easier to sleep under the stars
with his mouth shut. Even as he became frailer, he remained, in many
ways, a child to the end, self-obsessed, enjoying nothing more than
knots, campfires, songs and jokes. His final message to the Scouts of
the world was written some time before his death and contains the

---

* Much of the criticism is unfair: Scouting was never, as some on the left claimed,
anything like the youth movements of fascist Europe. Indeed, it was banned in
communist Russia, fascist Italy and 1940s Japan, and in Nazi Germany they much
preferred the Hitler Youth. Rule 4 of Scout Law – 'A Scout is a friend to all, and a
brother to every other Scout, no matter to what country, class or creed the other
may belong' – might be a motto for the multicultural age (quoted in Collis, Hurll
and Hazlewood, *B.P.'s Scouts: An Official History of the Boy Scouts Association*, p. 36).

advice that 'happiness doesn't come from being rich, nor merely from being successful in your career, nor by self-indulgence . . . the real way to get happiness is by giving out happiness to other people. Try and leave the world a little better than you found it and when your turn comes to die, you can die happy in feeling that at any rate you have not wasted your time but have done your best.' He signed it: 'Your Friend, Robert Baden-Powell.'

CHAPTER ELEVEN

'A thousand years scarce serve to form a state;
An hour may lay it in the dust'
Lord Byron, *Childe Harold's Pilgrimage*, 1812

It was not Edward VII's fault that his mother kept him from the throne by living such an unconscionably long time. But it was certainly his fault that he chose to spend so much of that apprenticeship at the card table, on the shooting field or in bed with other men's wives. Just inside the front door at Sandringham were installed a set of sit-down scales, the kind that were used to weigh jockeys before a race: Edward wanted to make sure the guests at his shooting parties had eaten so well that they left heavier than they had been on arrival. From an empire point of view, his entire reign seems to have been spent in digestion.

His inheritance was enormous. But it was quite strange. In India the British ruled an entire subcontinent, but in China they were contained in a few treaty ports. They had given up territories like the Mosquito Coast of Nicaragua, but clung to the Falkland Islands in the south Atlantic. They held Egypt, but not Persia, Burma but not Siam. The flag flew over enormous swathes of Africa and on tiny Pacific islands foisted on them by overexcited missionaries. As some jingoistic bean-counter at the *St James's Gazette* delightedly pointed out when Edward succeeded his mother in 1901:

> His Majesty rules over one continent, a hundred peninsulas, five hundred promontories, a thousand lakes, two thousand rivers and ten thousand islands. Queen Victoria ascended the throne of an Empire embracing 8,329,000 square miles; she handed it down to King Edward with three million miles added to it . . . The Empire to which Victoria acceded in 1837 covered one-sixth of the land of the world; and that of King Edward covers nearly one-fourth.

For the coronation of Edward the Caresser, an Eton schoolmaster, A. C. Benson, produced words to accompany Elgar's stirring *Pomp and Circumstance* march. The resulting anthem, 'Land of Hope and Glory', was a hymn to empire, still sung at that festival of faded nationalism, the Last Night of the Proms. But it was out of joint with the times even when written, for in Edward's reign the bounds of empire were hardly set wider still. There were a few administrative changes – a preposterous condominium with France in the New Hebrides,* altered status for British Somaliland, and so on, but no great tracts of territory were added to the motley variety of places marked in red. Indeed, when Francis Younghusband marched into the Tibetan capital, Lhasa, in 1904, the government was so worried about imperial overstretch that it told him to march out again, with the consolation prize of a minor decoration and more time to explore his strange ideas about mysticism. It was as if, having collected

---

* There were two official languages and two police forces, but joint punitive expeditions when the natives got restless. The courts contained British and French judges, but to ensure fair play the presiding judge was appointed by the king of Spain.

together an empire, no one was any longer quite sure what it was for. As H. G. Wells pointed out in 1914, the empire had 'no economic, no military, no racial, no religious unity. Its only conceivable unity is a unity of language and purpose and outlook. If it is not held together by thought and spirit, it cannot be held together.'

It would be a few years until everyone realized this was a trick that would never be pulled off, but in the meantime the smell of empire was almost permanently on the nation's breath. If enthusiasm flagged, there was always the imperial foghorn sounding in the *Daily Mail*, with its noisy proprietor Alfred Harmsworth crying, 'Empire first and parish after.' Yet the louder the huzzas of the imperialists, the more resonant came the howls of dissent. For there was now an increasingly vocal body of opinion questioning the moral and polit-ical basis of the entire enterprise. It was forty years or more since the Regius Professor of Modern History at Oxford, Goldwin Smith, had declared that holding colonies wasn't even protecting the national economy: the future lay with free trade. (*The Times* dismissed his ideas as being on a par with unworldly 'projects for general disarma-ment or for equalizing the political rights of the sexes'.) Now, working people – the value of whose labour was undercut by colo-nial enterprise and who provided the cannon-fodder for imperial armies – had a vehicle for their own anxieties about what was being done in the country's name. To the recently formed Independent Labour party, which brought working men into the House of Com-mons, the 'civilizing mission' was nonsense: 'We can no more send our civilisation to central Africa than we can send our climate there,' as one group of members put it. The true purpose of empire was to put off the day of reckoning between capital and labour. *Clarion*, newspaper of cycling and singing socialism, declared that it was on the side of those patriots who proclaimed 'England for the English', and would like to hear more of the less commonly shouted slogan, 'Africa for the Africans'. Wilfrid Scawen Blunt marked 31 December 1900 by correctly prophesying that the newly dawning twentieth century would see the end of the British Empire.

Even the true believers in empire were anxious. Lord Curzon shuddered to himself when he foresaw a Britain teeming with the starving unemployed, to which foreign tourists would flock to gaze upon the wonders of a dead civilization. The Boer War had shown how the mightiest power on earth could be brought low by a bunch of farmers, and recruitment for the army had demonstrated the appalling physical state of many of the slum-dwellers who were supposed to defend the flag. The nation could no longer feed itself, and the Germans were expanding their naval fleet. The upper classes were infiltrated by arrivistes who cared more for money than for duty. Trades unions were on the rise and industrial productivity was dropping. The worm of uncertainty ate away even at fervent imperialists like Joseph Chamberlain,★ who complained to the 1902 Imperial Conference that 'the weary Titan staggers under the too vast orb of its fate . . . We have borne the burden for many years . . . We think it is time that our children should assist us to support it.' Even Rudyard Kipling had watched the vast diamond-jubilee review of the fleet at Spithead (over 150 ships including twenty-one battleships and fifty-six cruisers) and seen not present power but future powerlessness:

> Far-called our navies melt away –
> On dune and headland sinks the fire –
> Lo, all our pomp of yesterday
> Is one with Nineveh and Tyre!

★

As it happened, the first British naval engagement of the First World War involved none of the enormous fleet Kipling had seen assembled at Spithead. It came in British imperial Africa.

On 5 August 1914, Mr Webb, the District Commissioner in the little trading station at Karonga, on the north-western shore of Lake Nyasa, received a coded telegram. 'Tipsified Pumgirdles Germany

★ 'England without an empire! Can you conceive it?' he asked in his last speech. 'England in that case would not be the England that we love . . . It would be a fifth-rate nation, existing on the sufferance of its more powerful neighbours. We will not have it.'

Novel' it read. After quickly consulting his code book, he began
sending frantic messages to British residents in the area, warning
them that their country was now at war. It would be hard to imagine
a place more remote from the slaughter set off by a pistol shot in
Sarajevo than Karonga, a sweltering former Arab slaving station on
the shore of a Rift Valley lake in a British protectorate in east Africa.
The town's main use was as a base for the British trading company on
the lake, and the military force available to Mr Webb consisted of
four white men and a handful of African policemen. But the lake also
lapped against the colony of German East Africa, and if the Germans
could transport troops across the water, the empire was in danger.
The colonial Governor, Sir George 'Utility' Smith, was adamant: the
entire German naval presence on the lake had to be neutralized at
once. This was in fact a single gunboat, the *Hermann von Wissmann*.
It was to be 'sunk, burned or otherwise destroyed'. The vessel chosen
to accomplish this appointment with destiny was the British gunboat
the *Guendolen*, captained by Commander E. L. Rhoades, RNVR, a
short, red-haired, bearded man with a well-pickled liver and a vast
repertoire of filthy songs. His enthusiasm for well-lubricated evenings of dirty jokes was shared by his good friend Herr Berndt. Until
now, the fact that Herr Berndt was commander of the *Hermann von
Wissmann* had not been a problem, and the two men often arranged
for their training exercises to coincide: their evenings in the bar much
enlivened when one or the other had managed to get his gunboat to
stage a successful mock attack.

Rhoades's first problem on receiving the order to destroy his
friend's vessel was that no one knew how to fire the Hotchkiss gun
with which the *Guendolen* was equipped. Eventually, he found an
African Lakes Corporation salesman who had once learned the basics
of gunnery years before. Then, having located some obsolete three-
pound ammunition, Rhoades set out on 8 August to engage the
Wissmann. To the commander's delight he found his friend's gunboat
drawn up high and dry on the beach, undergoing repairs. He ordered
the salesman to open fire. A cascade of shells now began to rain down
upon the bush, as the rapidly recruited gunners attempted to

counteract the effects of defective ammunition, lack of practice and the swell on the lake. Finally, after fifteen minutes, one of the shells found its mark. The sailors on the *Guendolen* raised a cheer and then were intrigued to see a man on the shore in white shorts and singlet jump into a small boat and begin to row furiously towards them. As he came nearer they recognized the oarsman and could hear him shouting. As one of them recalled later, he approached the *Guendolen* screaming, 'Gott for damn, Rrrrhoades . . . Gott for damn: vos you dronk?' Rhoades allowed Captain Berndt to clamber aboard, poured him a glass of whisky and then informed him he was a prisoner of war.

It turned out that German officials in this part of Africa had a more developed sense of playing the game than the British, even when they discovered that their telegraph link across Nyasaland had been cut. Three days after the strike on the *Wissmann*, Webb's counterpart on the German shoreline sent him a message by runner:

> Thanks to your extreme kindness in preventing the forwarding of despatches into our Colony, I am not clear whether England is at war with Germany or not . . . If you therefore wish to attack our province, I must most courteously remark that we are prepared to greet you in a somewhat unfriendly fashion. The position decidedly needs clearing up and therefore I beg you most politely and urgently to let me have a clear answer.*

*

The war in Africa – such as it was – does not bulk large in the memory of the British, who, like most northern Europeans, see the First World War through a periscope poked over the trenches of Flanders, across a vast expanse of mud, barbed wire and mangled bodies. They

---

* Coincidentally, the first shot fired by British land forces in the war had been in west Africa, by a sergeant of the Gold Coast Regiment, who had been part of a patrol sent into the German protectorate of Togoland to try to silence a powerful German radio transmitter there. The Germans surrendered within three weeks.

see an armageddon in which industrialized killing destroyed tens of thousands in very small areas. But it was also an imperial war, triggered by an act of rebellion against the Austro-Hungarian Empire, envisaged by Germany as a way of destroying the British Empire, used by the French to augment their empire and delivering the last rites to the Ottoman Empire. 'Take me back to dear old Blighty,' sang the British soldiers wading through the mud, 'put me on the train to London town.' How many of them knew that 'Blighty' had come into the army from an Urdu word originally meaning 'foreign'?* Great numbers of the empire soldiers who fought for the British had never set eyes on Blighty and never would. The British had been very quick at deploying them, though: within three months of the shot which killed the Archduke Franz Ferdinand in Sarajevo in 1914 and set off the war, Indian troops were being disembarked in Marseilles, to be transported north in support of the British Expeditionary Force. Of the 8.5 million troops who served in the British forces of the First World War, about a third were not British at all. Canada sent over 600,000 men. In Australia, the leader of the opposition Labor party invited a massive crowd in the town of Colac, Victoria, to think about what he called 'the Mother Country' and declared, 'Australians will . . . help and defend her to our last man and our last shilling.' Over 400,000 of his countrymen joined the imperial forces. Calculated per head of population, however, the most remarkable contribution came from New Zealand – 129,000 men, representing over half of those eligible for service.

But the largest of all empire contributions came from India, whose total of 1.4 million was bigger than the sum of soldiers from Scotland, Wales and Ireland combined. British army movement orders listed the 51st Sikhs, the 28th Dogras or the 74th Punjabis alongside battalions made up of farm boys from Somerset or pals from industrial Manchester. Advertising posters at home drew the Indians in with promises – 'Easy Life! Lots of Respect! Very Little Danger!

---

* 'Getting a Blighty' came to mean getting a wound serious enough to have you returned home without endangering your life. Such wounds were desirable enough to be sometimes self-inflicted.

Good Pay!' – which inevitably turned out to fall very far short of reality. But Gandhi believed those who signed up had moral right on their side, too. 'We are, above all, British citizens of the Great British Empire,' he said, 'our duty is clear: to do our best to support the British, to fight with our life and property.' Sixty-four thousand of the Indians died, a further 67,000 were wounded.

German empire-envy was well known. The Kaiser had dreamed of destroying British power by igniting a holy war, for example, which would spread to the empire's huge numbers of Muslim subjects. 'Our consuls in Turkey, in India,' he scribbled in the margin of a diplomatic telegram, 'must fire the whole Mohammedan world to fierce rebellion against this hated, lying, conscienceless nation of shopkeepers, for if we are to bleed to death, England shall at least lose India.' This notion of a jihad which would expel the British from India had been a German fixation for years. The railway line being driven from Berlin to Baghdad was physical evidence of the German commitment to the Ottoman Empire, and offered the possibility of a German presence in the Gulf – and thereby a menace to imperial communications with India. In 1898 the Kaiser had visited the Ottoman possessions and declared himself a friend of Islam. There were even rumours in the Turkish press – which his officials did nothing to scotch – that he might become a Muslim himself. And in November 1914 the sultan of Turkey responded to his courtesy by duly declaring holy war on Britain and its allies.

In 1917, after years when gains on the Western Front were measured in yards, the British government decided it was time for a dramatic victory in another theatre of the war. The commander chosen for this mission, Edmund Allenby, had initially been an imperial reject: even after an education at Haileybury, the former training school for the East India Company – augmented by sessions with a crammer – he still failed the exams for the Indian Civil Service. Twice. A career in an unglamorous Irish cavalry regiment, which at least offered the prospect of decent fox-hunting, had been a tolerable second-best and imperial soldiering turned out to suit him well. He emerged from the Boer War – which he had spent leading his troops on forays across the bush hunting out Afrikaner guerrillas – a colonel.* Allenby certainly looked the part – well over six feet tall, active, physically fit, the hair lacking on the dome of his head more than made up for by his bristling moustache. As he rose up the chain of command, his natural sympathy for his men grew deeper and his temper shorter: the slightest thing could set him off, especially a failure to wear chinstraps properly. In June 1917, 'the Bull' was summoned to see the Prime Minister, David Lloyd George, to be given a new task. The War Cabinet, he was told, wanted General Allenby to take command of a demoralized Egyptian Expeditionary Force, strike north and drive the Turks out of the remnants of their empire in the Middle East.

It did not seem a particularly promising command. It was true that the British still held their number-one objective in the region, the Suez Canal, ensuring that they could continue to move troops from India and Australasia to the European theatre. With the help of their German allies the Turks had built a defensive line to block any British advance from the south, running from Gaza on the Mediterranean coast inland 30 miles to Beersheba. Allenby was to smash through it and seize Palestine. In contrast to the war in Flanders, where the sucking quality of the mud seemed to express the stagnation of the campaign, the Middle East assault was to be one of dash and movement. Its prize offered one of the most dramatic symbols of the entire conflict, Jerusalem.

The force Allenby was to command was truly imperial, containing soldiers from across the empire, at perhaps its most exotic in the Imperial Camel Corps, a regiment made up of British, Australian and New Zealand cavalrymen, supported by artillery from the Hong Kong and Singapore Mountain Battery, which was made up of Indians. When he arrived to take command, he found the troops

---

* That was the least of his titles: at one point in the war he commanded a squadron of Inniskilling Dragoon Guards which had occupied the little tin-roofed settlement at the Sheba gold mine. This made him, he said, king of Sheba, and his wife the queen of Sheba.

downcast, for the Turks looked immovable. The Bull immediately drew up a plan, ordered roads built, commandeered all the beer in Egypt for his men and then moved his headquarters to a wooden shed ten miles from the front line. Four months later, Allenby's exotically assorted forces struck, not towards Gaza, which the Turks were expecting, but at Beersheba. One after another the Turkish strong-holds fell, as Allenby poured troops through each gap he created. By early December 1917 he had captured 60,000 prisoners and taken hundreds of guns. His army stood at the walls of Jerusalem, where one morning a couple of squaddies out collecting water were accosted by the mayor of the city. He had come out looking for someone to whom he could surrender the keys of Jerusalem. A fawning biog-rapher appreciated the historical echoes. 'Israelite, Assyrian, Greek, Roman, Jew, Arab, Crusader, Turk had entered Jerusalem as con-querors before the British,' he wrote. 'None of these nations can have been represented by one more impressive or worthier of his race than was Allenby, physically or morally.'

To Lloyd George, who claimed to have been familiar with the kings of Israel long before he had known the names of the kings and queens of England, the capture of Jerusalem was more resonant than most victories. For the first time since 1914, celebratory bells pealed at Westminster Abbey. Yet victory and occupation of the city would have to be handled carefully, for the empire claimed to protect all reli-gious beliefs. Indeed, Allenby himself could hardly have been unaware of the sensitivity of the issue: there were 90,000 Indians – many of them Muslim – deployed in Egypt, Palestine and, later, Syria. A 'D-notice' – that distinctively British form of censorship – had already gone out to all newspapers advising that there was to be no suggestion of a religious element to the capture. But Jerusalem was Jerusalem, and the most theologically contentious city in the world had been in Muslim hands since the Middle Ages. An official camera crew was dispatched to witness the historic moment when a place sacred to three faiths was 'liberated'.

The thing to avoid was any hint that Allenby came as a 'crusader'. Specifically, there was to be no suggestion of the bombast which had

marked the Kaiser's visit to Jerusalem in 1898, when he had ridden
into the city accompanied by brass bands, standard bearers, squadrons
of enormous German hussars in burnished helmets, detachments of
Turkish lancers and the sultan's bodyguard in wide blue oriental
trousers, red waistcoats and green turbans. He had been followed by
a cavalcade of pashas who looked as though they ate nothing but
Turkish Delight three times a day. The Kaiser himself sat smugly on
his horse, his chest splattered with decorations and his shining helmet
decorated with what he took to be a silk keffiyeh. Allenby, by contrast, obeyed the stage directions he had been given, dismounting
from his horse and entering the city by the Jaffa Gate on foot in his
British army uniform. He was attended by the usual small gaggle of
staff officers, among them Major T. E. Lawrence, who had borrowed
a uniform for the occasion. The politicians also insisted that Allenby
be accompanied by representatives of France, Italy and the United
States, despite the fact that they had played no part in the fighting,
much of which had been conducted by Australian and New Zealand
troops. To forestall unpleasantness with other Christian denominations, the Anglican Bishop of Jerusalem was denied a role, even
though he had offered to dress as an army chaplain for the day. No
flags were hoisted. Allenby walked to the Citadel, where Pilate is
believed to have judged Jesus, and there proclaimed martial law,
asked people to continue going about their daily business and promised to protect all sacred sites. As the *Daily Mirror* explained to any of
its readers who might be worried that the British weren't making
quite enough of their victory, 'This is because British generals and
the British people hate boasting.' Unlike the arrogant Kaiser, Allenby
was in Jerusalem merely to see fair play. It was not so much a victory
as the shouldering of a high responsibility.

Just before Christmas, Lloyd George rose in the House of Commons and invited MPs to imagine how 1917 would look from the
vantage point of 2017. He believed, he said, that 'these events in Mesopotamia and Palestine will hold a much more conspicuous place in
the minds and in the memories of the people than many an event
which looms much larger for the moment in our sight'. He was

wrong. Most of today's British have long forgotten, even if in the Middle East they remember their history slightly better.*

Allenby stayed firmly on message, repeatedly stating in the years ahead that his campaign had not been a crusade, that many of his soldiers had been Muslims and that Jerusalem's significance lay in its strategic position. He was a talented soldier who had executed his campaign brilliantly. But the capture of Jerusalem seemed to many to prove that the British Empire had some divine benediction: it is very hard to believe that the taking of any other Middle Eastern city would have merited quite the peal of bells. But if we were to take up Lloyd George's invitation to see the thing from the twenty-first century, the engagement with the Holy Land was the point at which the reach of the empire finally exceeded its grasp.

Allenby pushed on. His most impressive victory came at the battle of Megiddo – Armageddon of the Book of Revelation.[†] Damascus and Aleppo fell to his forces. But it is the figure of T. E. Lawrence – 'Lawrence of Arabia' – charging about the desert in flowing white robes at the head of a force of Arab irregulars, who is remembered in preference to the Bull. Lawrence's escapades were militarily much less significant, but carried political plangency, promised propaganda dividends and – especially by contrast with the quagmire of the Western Front – had about them an aura of dashing romance. The 'Uncrowned King of Arabia' fulfilled the sort of role in the public imagination that David Livingstone and Charles Gordon had once occupied – the courageous, half-cracked maverick unshakeably loyal to the empire.

---

* In Port Said, Egyptians celebrate the spring holiday of Sham el-Nessim with a bonfire. Rather like Guy Fawkes Night in England, it involves the burning of a dummy, often dressed up as the villain of the day. The festival is called Harq Allenby – the burning of Allenby.

[†] When the inevitable honours came, he chose to be Viscount Allenby of Megiddo and Felixstowe, a perhaps unexpected pairing, but no odder than Baron Kitchener of Khartoum and Aspall, which married the capital of a million square miles of Africa to a Suffolk village with a population of fifty-two, or Horatio Nelson, who became Baron Nelson of the Nile and Burnham Thorpe (population 396).

But playing God in the Holy Land was a dangerous game, which the empire turned out to play badly. The British ruling class had a romantic affection for the desert Arabs* – their dignity, their hospitality, their ease in the unownable wilderness – and many sincerely wanted to advance the cause of unity and freedom from Turkish rule. But the British also had a war to fight. And on top of that there was the historical problem of the French, who had their own imperial ambitions in the region. It is very hard indeed to look at the public and private agreements made by the British and not to feel embarrassment, disappointment and anger. The fact that they were all made in the customary combination of serpentine syntax and sonorous moral certainty does not help.

To begin with, there were the promises made to the Arabs. Britain had been a trading presence in the area since the time of Queen Elizabeth I, and as the pre-eminent imperial power had special status. An Arab revolt against Turkish rule would open another front in the war. The task of securing their agreement to fight against the Turks was in the hands of the British High Commissioner in Cairo, Sir Henry McMahon, who might have known plenty about India (he had been born there, drawn borders there and been impresario for the royal visit there in 1911) but was out of his depth in Arabia. McMahon wrote to the leader of the Hashemite clan, the Sharif, or religious leader, of Mecca, Hussein bin Ali, suggesting that an uprising would herald the arrival of that eternal will o' the wisp, an Arab nation. Hussein claimed descent from the prophet Muhammad, and was not to be bought cheaply. In return for rising against the Ottoman Empire, he expected money, guns and the title 'King of the Arabs'.† The first two commodities presented no problem to the British, and to appease Hussein's vanity the British letters opened with eighty-two words of fawning honorifics, including describing this romantic yet ineffectual man as 'him of the Exalted Presence and the Lofty Rank' and 'the

---

* An affection which lasted long into post-imperial times: Arabists dominated the Foreign Office for years. Urban, mercantile Arabs were another proposition altogether.

† Such a role has yet to exist, although one of the Sharif's sons did become king of Jordan and another the king first of Syria, then of Iraq.

Lodestar of the Faithful and the cynosure of all devout Believers'. Had the 'King of the Arabs' bothered with the details of the offer being made by the British, he might have wondered precisely what some of the small print about the promised Arab state meant, for example the condition that 'the districts of Mersin and Alexandretta, and portions of Syria lying to the west of the districts of Damascus, Homs, Hama and Aleppo, cannot be said to be purely Arab, and must on that account be excepted'. But he did not hesitate.

And, anyway, the British were soon to make another, contradictory set of promises to their allies, the French. This deal was the work of Sir Mark Sykes. At the outbreak of the First World War, Sir Mark had raised almost an entire army battalion from the tenants and workers on his Yorkshire estates and separately offered the government his expertise on the Ottoman Empire. Both were readily accepted. Sykes was given the job of reconciling the competing ambitions of Britain and France for the spoils of war when, as was expected, the Ottoman Empire was dismembered. Fortunately, since the French eyed Lebanon and Syria, while the British were after Transjordan and the oilfields of Iraq, Sykes and his French counterpart, Georges Picot, had a deal within a week. The two governments proclaimed a commitment to 'recognise and protect an independent Arab state or a confederation of Arab states', but the map they drew had lines sweeping across the Middle East, dividing it into zones shaded red or blue in which either Britain or France would have 'control'. Only what remained was left to the Arabs.

On top of the understandings given to their French and Arab allies the British now made a third commitment. In November 1917 they told the Jews of their new-found enthusiasm for a homeland in Palestine. The Zionist project was not a British invention, of course. At the turn of the century Theodor Herzl, an Austro-Hungarian, had tried and failed to get the Turks to allow the creation of a Jewish home in Palestine. Chaim Weizmann, who was to die as president of the newly founded state of Israel, was Russian, but moved to Britain convinced that 'England will understand the Zionists better than anyone else.' This was partly because he had recognized the British people's prevailing conviction about their mission in the world and he pitched Zionism to them as a means of securing the empire, while promising that Jewish settlement in Palestine 'would develop the country, bring back civilization to it'. It was the sort of language the imperial British could understand. The influence of the Zionists upon the British ruling class had nothing much to do with their numbers inside the country: the 1911 census revealed there were no more than 120,000 Jews in Britain, most of them pretty recent refugees from persecution in Poland and Russia. But that meant that the British elite was not only well aware of the religious myths of Judaeo-Christianity, but well aware of anti-Semitism, too. And, unlike many of the indigenous Palestinians, for whom there was a generalized romantic attachment, the Zionists had assiduously cultivated friends in high places. Winston Churchill, for example, was one. In 1908 he had decided that the creation of a Jewish state in the Middle East would not only offer Jews freedom from the danger of persecution, but would act as a 'bridge between Europe and Africa, flanking the roads to the East', and so would 'be an immense advantage to the British Empire'.

Arthur Balfour, the British Foreign Secretary in whose name the declaration of support for a Jewish homeland was issued on 2 November 1917, was an unlikely father for the bloody tragedy of Palestine and is best known for the observation that 'nothing matters very much, and few things matter at all'. Unfortunately, his statement of British attitudes to Palestine mattered very much indeed. Like Sir Mark Sykes, who had made the deal with the French, Balfour had been born immensely wealthy, inheriting a Scottish estate and a pile in St James's which gave him the means to indulge his interest in philosophy without too many irritating distractions about having to keep the wolf from the door. Eton and Cambridge conferred the finical nicknames – 'Pretty Fanny', 'Clara', 'the scented popinjay' – which adorned his political career. If anything, he seemed to accentuate the foppishness to disguise a calculating and often ruthless character: a newspaper reporter watching him at the dispatch box in the House of Commons wrote that 'Mr Balfour's whole life seems to be a protest against being called upon to do anything but sniff a heavily perfumed handkerchief while he sprawls in poses of studied carelessness on the benches of the House of Commons.' He was handsome, rich and clever, and, as fortunate people sometimes are, emotionally inept – his friend, rival and successor as foreign secretary, Lord Curzon, once remarked that 'Were any of us to die suddenly, he would dine out that night with undisturbed complacency, and in the intervals of conversation or bridge, would be heard to murmur, "Poor old George."' In November 1917, the sixty-nine-year-old Balfour was past the pinnacle of his career (he had previously been leader of the Conservative party and Prime Minister) and was serving as foreign secretary in the wartime coalition government. He had already supported a scheme to build a Jewish homeland in colonial east Africa. The Balfour Declaration, which now shifted this commitment to Palestine, was worthy of the man whose name it bore, and has been accurately described by one eminent historian as 'about as intelligible as the Athanasian Creed'.

The attractions for the British in yet another opaque document were obvious enough. But the audacity of the pledge was staggering: they were offering land belonging to one people as a gift to another, and disregarding the fact that the whole area lay within a different empire altogether. The promise of a homeland ensured Jewish support for the war effort and, by clothing British imperialism in the garments of Zionism, would also appeal to the Americans. The British would be there to see fair play between Jews and Arabs. But the reason for the convoluted form of words in the letter sent to the Anglo-Jewish leader Lord Rothschild was that the British recognized the trouble it could cause:

> His Majesty's Government view with favour the establishment in Palestine of a national home for the Jewish people, and will use their best endeavours to facilitate the achievement of this object, it being clearly understood that nothing shall be done which may prejudice the civil and religious rights of existing non-Jewish communities in Palestine, or the rights and political status enjoyed by Jews in any other country.

At the time, Palestine was over 90 per cent Arab.

The tortuous form of words has the stamp of a committee all over it, and, moreover, a British committee – sophisticated, ponderous and, on contentious points, oblique. What *was* 'a national home'? What would the British actually *do* if the 'civil and religious rights of existing non-Jewish communities' were compromised or violated? The cabinet wasn't much bothered: the document which Jews claimed gave the state of Israel its founding legitimacy was just one of several agreements knocked out in the region. Cynical doesn't really seem to do justice to the British behaviour. 'I do not deny that this is an adventure,' Balfour declared later. 'Are we never to have adventures? Are we never to try new experiments?' As for the Arabs who were to be dispossessed, he hoped that 'they will not grudge that small notch – for it is no more geographically, whatever it may be historically – that small notch in what are now Arab territories being given to people who for all these hundreds of years have been separated from it . . . That is the first difficulty. That can be got over and will be got over by mutual goodwill.'

If only everyone would see that nothing matters very much.

Britain emerged from the First World War battered and broke. Yet even though it was poorer, its empire was even larger. The British had learned from earlier experiences of empire and created thrones in the Middle East, on which sat pliant Anglophiles with British advisers, high commissioners and residents. These generally well-upholstered and harmless figures sent their sons to English schools and had armies trained, equipped and often commanded by British officers. Expanses of desert and mountain across which tribes wandered with herds of sheep and goats were turned into states. 'I had a well-spent morning at the office making out the southern desert frontier of the Iraq,' wrote Gertrude Bell, the 'oriental secretary' at the British High Commission in Baghdad, to her father on 4 December 1921. So much of the shape of the unstable state the British created in Mesopotamia was said to have been made out with the help of a line drawn in the sand by the cloche-hatted archaeologist: the great explorer and Arabist H. St John Philby called her 'the maker of Iraq'. Further south in the Gulf, British officials pulled the strings of 'protected' states or took tribal chiefs and made them potentates. And in Palestine, largely occupied by

Arabs but promised to Jews, Britain accepted the authority of a 'mandate' on behalf of the League of Nations, which it felt no other nation on earth could take on. Near Nazareth, Jewish settlers had established an agricultural co-operative. They named it Balfouria, to honour the British Foreign Secretary who had endorsed Zionism.

High on a hill overlooking Jerusalem, within an octagonal ochre stone wall, the British built a headquarters for their High Commissioner. It was close enough for the Muslim calls to prayer and the tolling bells of the Christian churches inside the Old City to waft across in the dry air. From the elegant formal garden the High Commissioner could look at the gold dome of the mosque – built at the point from which Muhammad was said to have ascended to heaven – and wonder whether a force of policemen in sand-coloured shorts would be enough to keep a lid on things.* The site chosen for his headquarters was called the Hill of Evil Counsel.

The spoils of war may have broadened the empire. But the effects of war weakened it. It was true that the acquisition of most of what had been German East Africa almost made possible Cecil Rhodes's dream of a railway line from the Cape to Cairo on British territory, should anyone ever get around to building it. Lord Curzon, who had served in Lloyd George's War Cabinet, sighed that 'The British flag never flew over more powerful or united an empire than now.' Figures like Curzon expected that the experience of shared hardship might have deepened the unity of empire. Had not the government of India given £100 million towards the war effort and sent so many thousands of soldiers? Canada had supplied wheat and vast quantities of munitions. Why, even the people of Marakei Atoll in the Gilbert Islands had offered coconuts for the troops.

But in fact, for all the talk of a shared destiny, the First World War loosened many of the bonds thought to hold the empire together. Although they fought as part of an imperial army, the enormous price paid by Canada, South Africa, Australia and New Zealand had given each a sense of their own distinctiveness. For the Canadians,

---

* The buildings are now occupied by the United Nations, from where officials of a dozen nationalities gaze down impotently as the city is colonized by Israel.

immensely costly battles like the engagement at Vimy Ridge were a sacrifice that was both imperial *and* distinctively Canadian. The war memorial at Delville Wood commemorates equally intense fighting by the South African Brigade during the Somme campaign. The events bulked large in each nation's growing sense that it was more than an overseas outpost. But the best-known example of the way the war encouraged nationalism is the 1915 Gallipoli campaign – as mismanaged and fatuous an operation as any ever perpetrated by British military planners. Like Allenby's later campaign in the Holy Land, this had been born of a desperation to break the muddy stale-mate on the Western Front. The plan enthusiastically advocated by the ambitious forty-year-old Winston Churchill – then First Lord of the Admiralty – was to sail British and French warships from the Mediterranean through the Dardanelles and to confront the Turks in Constantinople, opening the way for an attack on Germany through the 'soft underbelly' of eastern Europe. The assault turned into a dis-aster, as vessel after vessel struck mines or was shelled from well-placed Turkish artillery on shore. The subsequent decision to land soldiers to try to secure the passage proved even more misguided. Unclear about the precise objectives of the assault, provided with inadequate troops, the operation was a bloody shambles. Even Churchill was unable to justify the catastrophic and pointless loss of life and was forced to resign his post.

In nationalistic myth, Australia and New Zealand were born in the courage and determination shown by ANZAC soldiers during the maelstrom to which chinless British generals had consigned them. Both nations mark the date of the landings, 25 April, with memorial rituals, in the spirit of the Australian bush poet 'Banjo' Paterson's 'We're All Australians Now', written in 1915:

> The mettle that a race can show
> Is proved with shot and steel,
> And now we know what nations know
> And feel what nations feel.

The impression of big-boned country boys consigned to their fate by toffee-nosed English generals is one that turned out to be especially well suited to the developing sense of Australian nationhood: was it not to escape that sort of class prejudice that their ancestors had left the old country? It is a very partial version of the truth (the British suffered many more casualties in the operation). But it was enough. The empire that emerged from the war was a much less top-down association. It was soon time to send for the now septuagenarian Arthur Balfour, who chaired a committee which agreed that the white Dominions of the empire could in future be as independent as they chose.

At the end of the war, the whole conceptual framework of empire looked shaky. Empire had become an official project and the awful loss of life had done nothing at all to enhance belief in the wisdom of government. (The great celebrant of empire, Rudyard Kipling, had lost his own son at the battle of Loos in September 1915: just turned eighteen when he was last seen staggering through the mud, half his face hanging off.) The emerging force in British politics, the Labour party, was more interested in improving living conditions at home than in the country's possessions abroad. And internationally, US President Woodrow Wilson's elaboration of the fourteen points on which the peace settlement would be based had included a specific promise that all colonial claims would be settled on an 'absolutely impartial' basis in which the needs of the colonized would have just as much weight as those of the imperial power.

Increasingly, the language of British imperialism changed. Talk was no longer of some national destiny but of a duty of 'trusteeship', a responsibility owed by Britain to its colonies. If carried through effectively, this approach had the potential, as one distinguished historian put it, 'to convert the anti-imperialists of one generation into the imperialists of the next'. The bible of this approach was a book with the very dull title of *The Dual Mandate in British Tropical Africa*, written by the former Governor General of Nigeria, Frederick Lugard.* A short, slightly haggard man with an enormous forehead,

---

* Lugard was a true imperial figure. When he died – childless, like a surprising number of empire-builders – his memorial plaque read, 'All I did was to try and lay my bricks straight.'

Lugard laid out a guiding principle that, instead of governing directly, Britain should rule its territories with and through local chiefs, promoting the interests of both indigenous people and colonial power. For a while, this new gloss on imperialism disarmed the growing number of sceptics, until they pointed out the chasm between theory and reality, and asked whether it might not be a better idea simply to concentrate upon helping local societies to develop, and giving them their freedom as soon as possible. But this was not a campaign which enjoyed mass popular support – just as the imperial movement began to succumb to indifference and self-absorption, so did anti-imperialism. As one British left-winger wryly pointed out, if you wanted to empty a political meeting hall, you talked of Indian independence.

Promises of custodianship were no longer going to be enough for nationalists anywhere, and it was in India that the most pressing question arose, with a growing feeling that the subcontinent's great contribution to the war effort deserved proper recognition by the Mother Country. It had been striking that some of the most nationalistically minded Indians had been among the fiercest advocates of military service. They had realized there could be political dividends to come, even if the British hadn't quite grasped the point. 'I venture to say that the war has put the clock of time fifty years forward,' said the Hindu nationalist Madan Mohan Malaviya in 1917. He was right, for the war had shown Indians not only that there was nothing particularly special about a European culture which settled its differences by machine-gunning men as they floundered around in the mud, but had also revealed the extent of Britain's dependence on India for the defence of its empire: by the closing stages of Allenby's campaign in Palestine, one-third of his cavalry and two-thirds of his infantry were drawn from the Indian army. Indians held King's Commissions in the army and had been told they were fighting for freedom against tyranny. Indian industries had grown to meet the war effort and Indians had filled jobs once performed by Europeans who had been sent to the front. The entire war had been presented as a valiant defence against the menacing power of the German, Austro-Hungarian and Ottoman alliance. Yet at its end Indians had had to watch as the victorious imperial powers blithely carved up the remnants of the enemy empires, while seeming to believe that India might remain a British possession for ever. (For diplomatic consumption, this approach was later dressed up by Lloyd George in the language of paternal protection: 'if Britain withdrew her strong hand, nothing would ensue except division, strife, conflict and anarchy'.) Before the war, the Indian National Congress had been a cause for the Indian chattering classes. Soon it had a figurehead (in the intensely charismatic Mohandas Gandhi, who had returned to India from South Africa in 1915), an organization and an ideology. Indian labour was increasingly joining the first trades unions, and Islamic opposition looking for a focus for its disgruntlement. 'The people are restless', said a deputy commissioner in 1918, 'and discontented and ripe for the revolution.' The British attempted to buy off the discontent by 'helping' India towards the patently inadequate goal of 'responsible government' within the British Empire. It was never going to be enough.

And then came Amritsar.

In 1919, the city, near the border with present-day Pakistan (then part of British India), had a population of under 200,000 people – Sikhs, Hindus and Muslims. On 13 April it was more crowded than usual because it was Baisakhi, the Sikh New Year, and the city contained the sacred site of the Golden Temple. Three days before the festival, rampaging mobs had murdered five Englishmen, set buildings on fire and left a female missionary for dead. According to official reports, the local Commissioner requested the army to 'send an officer who is not afraid to act'. This turned out to be Reginald Dyer, a grey-haired, blue-eyed general, whose brick-red complexion testified to a lifetime military career in the subcontinent. Dyer took the train to Amritsar, where he issued a proclamation banning public meetings and imposing a curfew: anyone disobeying the rules risked being shot. In the days before efficient mass media, informing the population of their new conditions of life was an obvious problem. Dyer, meanwhile, worried that his forces in Amritsar were being steadily cut off from the world, as the railway line outside the town was sabotaged. So, on the morning of the 13th, he formed a column of soldiers and marched them about the city, stopping at nineteen public places and road junctions, where his proclamation was read out in various languages, with printed copies also being distributed. The order banned gatherings of more than four men in one place at one time and warned that anyone seen on the streets after eight in the evening was liable to be shot.

But that afternoon news reached the general of a public meeting to be held at the Jallianwala Bagh, an enclosed patch of ground about 200 yards long, close to the Sikh Golden Temple. It was surrounded by low walls and the backs of houses, and the main entrance was only wide enough for people to enter two abreast. During the afternoon it steadily filled with men, women and children, although there are no indications they were in an aggressive or even especially agitated mood. Dyer's loyal widow later explained that in the general's eyes this 'unexpected gift of fortune, this unhoped for defiance' gave him 'such an opportunity as he could not have devised', for the gathering 'separated the guilty from the innocent [and] placed them where he would have wished them to be – within reach of his sword'.

Since the main entrance to the Jallianwala Bagh was too narrow to drive an armoured car through, General Dyer marched in twenty-five Gurkha and twenty-five Indian soldiers armed with rifles, along with another forty Gurkhas armed only with *khukuris* (the traditional curved steel knives); in addition he had five parties of fifty soldiers each placed outside the city walls. In his account of the event after-wards, Dyer said that he estimated the size of the crowd, which was being addressed by a man on a platform, at 'about 5000'. He was wor-ried, he said, that unless he acted immediately his smaller force could be overwhelmed. So, without any warning, he gave the order to open fire. There was immediate panic. In the pandemonium some people were picked off as they tried to climb the walls, others as they tried to shelter behind bodies on the ground. Yet more were trampled underfoot. The shooting lasted between ten and fifteen minutes, during which time the soldiers loosed off 1,650 rounds, and it stopped only when Dyer judged that they would soon not have enough ammunition left to protect themselves if they were to be attacked on the way back to barracks. By that time men, women and children lay dead and dying all over the place. (The official casualty estimate later was 379 killed and 1,200 wounded.) Then, without bothering to attend to the wounded, Dyer marched his men out.

As news of the cold-blooded killing in Amritsar spread, the pressure to hold an inquiry became irresistible. A Scottish judge, Lord Hunter, was summoned, and his committee of inquiry, including both Indian and British members, heard evidence from witnesses including General Dyer, and then, predictably, split on racial lines. Dyer's decisions fitted a pattern – as demonstrated perhaps most graphically by the behaviour of British authorities after the Indian Mutiny, in the Zulu wars and in Sudan – of using devastating force to impose their will. But in the Jallianwala Bagh Dyer had been facing defenceless civilians. In trying to justify his actions afterwards, the general used a particularly telling expression. He had not attempted to clear the Bagh peacefully because 'then they would all come back and laugh at me, and I considered I would be making myself a fool'. This explanation from an unrepentant imperialist is curiously similar to George Orwell's later reflection on his unhappy time as an empire policeman that 'every white man's life in the East was one long struggle not to be laughed at'. The true reason for the need to 'give them a lesson' and to produce 'a sufficient moral effect' was not strength but fear.

The Committee produced its conclusions that Dyer had misread an unlawful assembly as a rebellion. The British government seemed shocked and censured the general for 'acting out of a mistaken concept of duty'; he was denied promotion and then resigned from the army. The *Daily Mail* claimed that he had been sentenced without trial, the *Morning Post* ran a campaign which raised £26,000 from the public, while a letter to *The Times* from Belgravia pointed out that 'When a handful of whites are faced by hundreds of thousands of fanatical natives, one cannot apply one's John Stuart Mill.' There were debates in the House of Commons in which much humbug was spoken by people who might have known better. Herbert Asquith maintained that there had never been anything like it 'in the whole annals of Anglo-Indian history'. A retired brigadier talked of how the empire rested on prestige and 'once you destroy that British prestige, then the empire will collapse like a house of cards'. A retired colonel asserted that the Amritsar massacre was the gravest blot on British history 'since we burned Joan of Arc'. And Winston Churchill – veteran of the mass machine-gunning of Sudanese – declared that it was 'an episode which appears to me to be without precedent or parallel in the modern history of the British Empire . . . an extraordinary event, a monstrous event, an event which stands in singular and sinister isolation . . . We have to make it absolutely clear, some way or another, that this is not the British way of doing business.' That was nonsense. Amritsar had laid bare a brutal truth about empire and no amount of guff about Anglo-India could now save it on the subcontinent. As Gandhi put it, 'We do not want to punish Dyer. We have no desire for revenge. We want to change the system that produced Dyer.'

As it turned out, the system broke first in Ireland.

How to contain or channel the persistent demands of nationalist opinion in Ireland had been a constant descant in British imperial politics for centuries. There had never been much the British wanted in Ireland – no great seams of gold, spices or expanses of prairie awaiting farmers – nothing but strategic security. Without being confident that Ireland would not provide a back door into Britain, it was impossible to plan expansion abroad. Yet throughout the centuries of British rule the Irish simply refused to abandon their campaigns to be free. It had been recognized in nineteenth-century debates over Home Rule that what was needed was some mechanism which would balance Irish demands for freedom with imperial demands for security. Perhaps – as was increasingly to be suggested for India – Ireland might be accommodated within the empire by being given dominion status, like Canada or Australia. But the critical difference with those places was that the people of Ireland had their own history, culture, mythology, religion and traditions long before the English, Scottish and Welsh soldiers had arrived to claim the place for the Crown. From an imperial point of view the other places were settlements. Ireland was a *nation*.

Since 1800, Irish MPs had had seats at Westminster, so it was not, technically, a colony. Irish people emigrated across the empire in huge numbers. Irish soldiers fought in Britain's colonial wars, in ranks from private to general. Ascendancy Irish, like Frederick Temple Hamilton-Temple-Blackwood, picked up colonial baubles as readily as their English and Scottish counterparts: Blackwood became viceroy of India and a marquess. Yet the way Ireland was treated by the government in London indicated that it was anything but an integral part of the Kingdom, for it is inconceivable that politicians would have allowed a million people to perish in the Great Famine of the 1840s had they been living in industrial Yorkshire or rural East Anglia instead of Ireland. The depth of the political hypocrisy about Ireland was shown when Gladstone began to espouse the cause of Home Rule. Lord Randolph Churchill told him that the idea amounted to a plan to 'plunge his knife into the heart of the British Empire', which rather gave the game away. In Conservative circles, this was a widely held view, and when Gladstone died without achieving his ambition, the opportunity to find a peaceful settlement died with him. Of course, the vast military resources of the British Empire could (just about) keep a lid on things by deploying the usual mechanisms of official inquiries and overwhelming force, as they demonstrated when the 1916 Easter Rising was put down within seven days and its leaders executed by firing squad. But the consequence was merely to radicalize a much larger section of the population.

In 1919 Jan Smuts, who had served in the War Cabinet and was about to become prime minister of South Africa, claimed that 'the Irish wound' was spreading poison – if the country was not given its freedom (he favoured some sort of dominion status), the British Empire 'must cease to exist'. Smuts had spotted the corrosive potential of the Irish question, even if his convictions prevented him from seeing how things would eventually turn out. (Two years later he drafted a speech on Ireland for the king to deliver which contained the marvellous blather, 'My world-wide Empire is a system of human government which rests on certain principles and ideals of freedom and co-operation, which must find their application in Ireland no less than in the other parts.') The difficult negotiations between Irish nationalists and the British government ended in independence for most of the island in 1922. When the Irish delegation arrived at Dublin Castle, to take power, a British lord lieutenant remarked that they were seven minutes late arriving, to which Michael Collins, President of the provisional government, replied that they could have the seven minutes: the British were 700 years late leaving.

The fact that Ireland was geographically so close and had been an integral part of the British state for so long meant that not everyone appreciated how significant a split this was. But if a land proclaimed to be part of the very Mother Country could become independent, then what message was being sent to the rest of the empire? As one of the Irish nationalist leaders put it thirty years later, 'if today India, and Burma, and Egypt are free Nations, they owe it primarily to our example and our softening effectiveness'.

CHAPTER TWELVE

'I did not even know that the British Empire is dying'
George Orwell, 'Shooting an Elephant', 1936

No. 70   THE BURMESE PAVILION.
                    THE BRITISH EMPIRE EXHIBITION.

The twelfth Earl of Meath looked a bit like Father Christmas. He had a bald head, a red face and an enormous white beard, and by end of the First World War, Reginald Brabazon was over seventy. He had never forgotten how, on a winter's day at Eton, a schoolmaster had accused his fellow pupils of 'spinelessness' for attempting to brush snow off their bare knees. 'You young worms!' the teacher berated them. 'Your fathers are the rulers of England, and your forefathers have made England what she is now. Do you imagine that if they had minded a little snow that Canada would ever have been added to the Empire, or if they had minded heat we should ever possess India or tropical Africa?' As an adult, Meath determined to ensure that the entire nation never forgot the importance of indifference to snow on knees.

The earl turned out to be an idiosyncratic imperialist, his career in the

British diplomatic service being terminated – at his in-laws' insistence – when he was posted to the impossibly 'remote' mission at Athens. He devoted most of the rest of his life to empire-building in the cities and suburbs of Britain. Meath's great anxiety was whether the nation – especially the poorer parts – quite appreciated the importance of the empire. Did Britain any longer have the moral fibre necessary to rule the world? Since Britain did not believe in mass conscript armies, Meath founded a Lads' Drill Association to promote marching and weapons-training, spent seventeen years as commissioner for the Irish Boy Scouts, and served as president of the Duty and Discipline Movement, dedicated to fighting 'slackness, indifference and indiscipline'. As his lordship put it – and the list of supporters from cabinet ministers and colonial governors to generals and archbishops indicates that he was hardly considered eccentric – the empire was built on the principle that imperialists could dominate others because they allowed themselves to be dominated. 'Britons have ruled in the past because they were a virile race, brought up to obey, to suffer hardships cheerfully, and to struggle victoriously.'

This 'subordination of selfish or class interests to those of the State' was what Meath and his friends believed had made the empire. As one school text put it at the height of empire, 'Every time one of us is courteous and civil to a foreigner he is doing his part as a good citizen, for he is helping to make his country liked and respected abroad . . . remembering that *to rule oneself is the first step to being able to rule others.*' It followed that too much sensitivity and independence of mind were a decided liability. All sorts of disciplines might be useful in achieving this subordination of the self to the greater good, including, oddly, folk dancing, because, left to their own devices, the urban working class would just drink, smoke cigarettes and lounge around on street corners. Meath's anxiety was not at all unusual, for by the early twentieth century much of the British elite was worried that the country might be losing the capacity for ruling the world. In addition to the Boy Scouts and the Duty and Discipline Movement, there was already a National Service League offering camps every summer to prepare the youth of the cities to serve their country, the Boys' Brigade promoting 'Christian manliness', and the

Anglican Church Lads' Brigade promising 'free discipline, manly games, and wholesome society'. The Commanding Officer of the London Cadet Battalion, Colonel Beresford, echoed the message of the Boy Scouts, explaining that his organization provided for ordinary boys 'many of the advantages of that Public School training which has so great an effect on moulding the characters of the upper and middle classes'.

These out-of-school activities complemented the not-very-subtle messages being passed on in the classroom. Without the British Empire, said *Cassell's Illustrated History of England*, 'the greater portion of the world outside Europe would revert to the darkness and barbarism of the Middle Ages'. *A School History of England* – a collaboration between Rudyard Kipling and the comically reactionary Oxford historian C. R. L. Fletcher★ – informed the country's children that 'it was on trade the Empire was founded, and by trade it must be maintained. But remember, a great trade needs a great defence by a great fleet and a great army. One gets nothing for nothing in this world.' The book advised its young readers that they should 'be prepared to fight at any moment'. It remained in print until 1930.

But the Earl of Meath's greatest creation was Empire Day, celebrated across Britain on Victoria's birthday, 24 May, even though the queen had been dead for fifteen years by the time it received government endorsement. On Empire Day plays were staged about heroic empire-builders like Wolfe, Clive and Livingstone and pageants mounted in which a trident-carrying Britannia was usually the central figure among hordes of blacked-up 'Sikhs' or smiling 'piccaninnies'. Local worthies and retired colonial officials gave talks in schools. There was much singing of the National Anthem, saluting of the flag and eating of Empire Meals. Meath's message was that empire was the gift of 'an all-wise and all-knowing Providence', which had bestowed 'boundless resources' and an 'unrivalled freedom and liberty'. The

---

★ He refused, for example, to let women attend his lectures, and wrote in his *School History* that democracy was still on trial in England: it would be the duty of the king to dismiss any government which planned to reduce the size of the navy or to give freedom to the colonies.

challenge was merely to get the people of Britain to understand their good fortune.

The biggest attempt to sell the empire to the citizens of Britain came in 1924. If a Londoner wanted an exotic day out in the jungles or on the prairies, Wembley was the place to be. Here, spread across 200 acres at what was then the edge of the city, the entire empire was on show. Roads had been laid (and christened by Kipling) and uncountable tons of concrete poured, to throw up the biggest buildings of their kind in the world. The most famous of these constructions, the twin towers of the football stadium, remained standing to the turn of the next century, but the other buildings, designed to hold examples of what imperial rule could achieve, succumbed within a few years of the end of the exhibition to the sprawl of the London suburbs. So there is no longer a Palace of Engineering alongside Engineers' Way, and the beguiling expanse of water which gave its name to Lakeside Way was long ago drained to be built over by a dreary conference centre. In 1924 you might have sauntered down Pacific or Atlantic Slope, and had presented to you 'the almost illimitable possibilities of the Dominions, Colonies and Dependencies'. (The words are from the official guidebook for the British Empire Exhibition.)

If you boarded the narrow-gauge 'Never-stop railway' trundling around the site, you might, as the train slowed, step out at the Palace of Industry, where you could watch soap, bread, chocolate, carpets or linen being made, see tea being packed, pottery fired and steel cut with a flame. In a Pageant of Empire, to a specially composed theme by the ageing Edward Elgar, Wolfe's victory on the Plains of Abraham and the conquest of New Zealand were re-enacted and 'settlers' sank wells, apparently turning bare earth into orchards and vineyards. A dozen girls gave twice-daily fashion parades showing off fabrics made in Bradford. In the Palace of Beauty there were more live models, posing as some of the most striking women in history, from Helen of Troy to 'Miss 1924'. At the Australian pavilion you could – inevitably – watch sheep being sheared. The highlight of the Palace of Engineering (the largest concrete building in the world) was a collection of locomotives and carriages and a display of imperial railway routes across the empire. The Ministry of Agriculture had a machine which showed the effects of ploughing and harrowing. The Ministry of Health exhibited a model sewage plant. A Burmese display featured a pagoda in Mandalay. The west African pavilion had a model of a Nigerian walled city. And from Sarawak had come a 30-foot stuffed python, with the outline of the pig it had swallowed moments before death clearly visible inside.

The style of the exhibition says much about the monochrome pleasures 1920s officialdom imagined would satisfy the masses: in the way of 'improving' displays, it was rather less fun than it pretended. Twenty-seven million visitors were lured through the Empire Exhibition turnstiles, though it is unclear whether this figure includes the Indians, Singhalese, Malays, Burmese, West Indians, Hong Kong Chinese, west Africans and three Palestinians described by the Official Guide as 'races in residence', their function being to stand around looking colourfully native while demonstrating local crafts. But there are only so many demonstrations of well-sinking a person can take, and the organizers sighed with frustration as they watched the crowds inexorably drift away from the sewage farm to converge on the Giant Switchback, amusement park and dance hall. Highbrows, meanwhile, disdained the whole thing and formed the WGTW (Won't Go To Wembley) Society. And when Bertie Wooster found himself dragged off to the Empire Exhibition in 'The Rummy Affair of Old Biffy', the only congenial place he discovered was the comparatively modest pavilion of the West Indies, a place clearly 'in certain fundamentals of life streets ahead of our European civilisation'. For it contained a Planter's Bar, where 'as kindly a bloke as ever I wish to meet' mixed Green Swizzle cocktails. 'If ever I marry and have a son,' Wooster remarked, 'Green Swizzle Wooster is the name that will go down on the register, in memory of the day his father's life was saved at Wembley.'*

It is hard to believe that visiting the exhibition changed anyone's

---

* I had assumed the Swizzle to be a figment of P. G. Wodehouse's imagination, until I came across the memoirs of the colonial Governor Sir Hesketh Bell. When serving in Dominica in 1905 he was visited by the Duke of Montrose and a couple

life. Indeed, the plodding ambition of the thing had been made clear
in King George V's speech as he opened it that April. 'We believe', he
said, 'that this Exhibition will bring the peoples of the Empire to a
better knowledge of how to meet their reciprocal wants and aspira-
tions.' And, just as George had none of Victoria's sheen, so the 1924
show had none of the pizzazz of the 1851 Great Exhibition. That had
been about flaunting Britain's genius to the world and had seemed to
promise a future in which science might solve most of mankind's
problems. The Empire Exhibition was the Great and Good talking to
hoi polloi about something they weren't especially interested in. 'I
brought 'em 'ere to see the glories of the empire,' says the father in
Noël Coward's *This Happy Breed*, as he watches his children head for
the amusements at Wembley, 'and all they think about is going on
the dodgems.' The empire had lost whatever sheen it once had –
even the steady stream of emigrants setting off from British shores to
build Cecil Rhodes's dream of a worldwide Anglo-Nation had by
now fallen away to the point where there were more migrants arriving in the British Isles than there were people leaving. There was
nowhere much left to colonize, anyway, and the business of government had passed from colourful empire-builders to dull-minded
empire-inheritors, for whom, as H. G. Wells recognized, 'Empire has
happened to them and civilisation has happened to them as fresh let-
tuces come to tame rabbits. They do not understand how they got,
and they will not understand how to keep.' Sure enough, there was
soon an Empire Marketing Board, to try to secure the enterprise by
promoting the products of Britain's scattered possessions to British

---

of other toffs. 'I introduced them to the brand of West Indian cocktail usually
known as a "swizzle",' he writes. Bell describes his version (evidently it came in
several colours) as comprising half a wineglass of water and the same quantity of
gin, half a teaspoon each of lime juice and sugar, a teaspoon of Chartreuse and a
generous dash of Angostura bitters. He counted it one of the greatest blessings of
the West Indies that a local shrub provided entirely natural swizzle sticks. 'This
implement, swiftly rotated between the two hands, transforms the cocktail into an
icy, pale-pink foam which, when gliding down a thirsty throat on a hot day, seems
to give a gleam of Paradise.' (Bell, *Glimpses of a Governor's Life*, pp. 80–81.)

citizens,★ which was followed by a trading doctrine of 'Imperial Preference' whereby a country which had sermonized the world on the life-giving virtues of free trade introduced tariffs on goods from countries which had the misfortune not to belong to its empire.

The 1924 exhibition seemed rather purposeless, a shop-window display laid out by officialdom to try to grab the attention of largely indifferent passers-by. The Canadian exhibit caught things well. It was a life-size equestrian statue of the Prince of Wales carved in refrigerated butter. It was destined to melt just as soon as someone switched the power off.

The Empire Exhibition was not the first attempt to stage a spectacular event to try to make the British people enthusiastic about their empire. But it was almost the last. As Lord Meath and the others who worried about the moral fibre of the nation had understood, the mass of the people were just not particularly interested in the imperial project. Custodianship, partnership and preparation for self-government were much less exciting ideas for a British audience than discovery, conquest, adventure and profit. By the 1930s a torpor had settled. If the empire wasn't expanding, what was it doing? No one seemed quite sure. Its face in popular culture became the cartoon character Colonel Blimp, with his walrus moustache, bad temper and fiercely held, stupendously stupid opinions, based upon a flush-faced booby his creator, David Low, had overheard holding forth in a Turkish bath near Charing Cross. Even the way the so-called Mother Country played cricket spoke of a new mood in which the old imperial links meant less and less, with the 1932 England touring team shamelessly attempting to intimidate Australian batsmen with 'bodyline' bowling: the Australian reaction was so furious that the tour was very

---

★ One of its best-known initiatives was a recipe for an Empire Christmas Pudding, allegedly supplied by King George's chef. This mighty delicacy required, among other ingredients, 3 pounds of currants, sultanas and raisins from Australia and South Africa, sugar from the British West Indies or British Guiana, cloves from Zanzibar, further spices from India, brandy from Cyprus or Palestine and rum from Jamaica. Britain supplied the flour, breadcrumbs, suet and a pint of beer. The Irish Free State got a look-in as a possible source of the five eggs required.

nearly cancelled midway through.* How had what had recently seemed eternal verities withered so quickly?

The motive force of empire – the impulse to go out and plant the flag – had gone: the 'Scramble for Africa' was long over and the business of the British Empire was increasingly administrative. As that great anti-imperialist George Orwell had noticed, technology had changed everything. 'The middle-class families celebrated by Kipling, the prolific lowbrow families whose sons officered the army and navy and swarmed over all the waste places of the earth from the Yukon to the Irrawaddy', had been in decline for years, he wrote.

> The thing that had killed them was the telegraph. In a narrowing world, more and more governed from Whitehall, there was every year less room for individual initiative . . . Well-meaning, over-civilized men, in dark suits and black felt hats, with neatly rolled umbrellas crooked over the left forearm, were imposing their constipated view of life on Malaya and Nigeria, Mombasa and Mandalay. The one-time empire builders were reduced to the status of clerks, buried deeper and deeper under mounds of paper and red tape.

And it was not merely that the style of colonial administration had been transformed by the speed of communications. By the 1930s, if a Robert Clive had emerged from some Shropshire market town dreaming of wealth and opportunity, he would have been better advised to sit in Britain watching reports from the trading floors of London or Hong Kong than to go to the trouble of travelling anywhere.

As the twentieth century ground on, the imperial idea lost its apparent glamour and its friends. The empire had become Official Business and the First World War had dulled any reverence for governments, flags, anthems and talk of national destiny. The war had touched every family in the land, and the minority who took an interest in international matters hung their hopes on different ideas of

---

* When the England manager visited the Australian changing-room on the first day the tactic was deployed, the captain refused to speak to him, saying only, 'There are two teams out there; one is playing cricket, the other is not.' It was a very long way from a commitment to 'Play up! Play up! And play the game.'

internationalism, in co-operative organizations like the League of Nations. The milk-and-water ideas of a Commonwealth might have better suited the mood of the times, but for the fact that the empire plainly still existed. Increasingly, it was the anti-imperialists who were the romantic figures. In September 1931, when the leader of the Indian independence movement, Mohandas Gandhi, took himself to Lancashire to see the effects of the boycott he had led of British-made cotton goods, even the mill-workers who had lost their jobs because of his actions turned out to cheer him. Of course he was quite as wily as any other politician. But given a choice between the ascetic campaigner in homespun cotton dhoti and Lord Willingdon, the much ornamented British Viceroy at the time (who ordered Gandhi's arrest after his return to India), it was no contest.* Empire Day still continued to roll around every year and the assiduous head teacher could borrow films and slideshows and gather pupils around a radio to listen to improving broadcasts about what was being done in their name. The children's reward was a half-day holiday. The BBC dutifully loyally churned out talks about the empire (and every Christmas hired actors like Laurence Olivier and John Gielgud to present more programmes slavishly celebrating it).† But the noisier the loud-speakers of officialdom, the more reverberant the empty echo. In the summer of 1938 a stuttering King George VI opened another Empire Exhibition, this time at Bellahouston Park in Glasgow. Pavilions of engineering and industry appeared again, and imperial produce was proudly displayed. But the weather was worse than usual and an Empire Exhibition Trophy football competition and

---

* When a reporter asked him about his clothes, Gandhi replied: 'You people wear plus-fours. Mine are minus fours.' But was it really appropriate to answer a summons to Buckingham Palace in loincloth, sandals and shawl? 'The King', he said, 'had enough on for both of us.'

† It kept at it for years. At Christmas 1947, for example, the BBC was hailing the Labour government's foolish scheme to grow groundnuts (peanuts) in Tanganyika as 'solid ground for hope, hundreds of miles of jungle cleared by science and the bulldozer with a real promise of a better life for African and European'. The scheme turned out to be a fiasco and was abandoned a few years later, at vast cost to the taxpayer.

much promotion of west Scotland manufacturing signally failed to catch the imagination. The official show was also matched by a Workers' Exhibition in the inner city, which set out to undermine the entire imperial project. The Empire Exhibition might display the products of empire, said one of the organizers, but 'at the Workers' Exhibition you will see what it has cost in human blood and sweat and exploitation to turn out these products'. The empire was a capitalist racket designed to exploit workers across the world, and the only beneficiaries were to be found among the board members and shareholders of private enterprise.

The protest exhibition attracted only a fraction of the visitors drawn to the official show. But it attested to the growing current of opinion which was not merely indifferent to empire but actively hostile to it. Imperial expansion had been the product of an age before proper democracy. It could not survive universal suffrage and the development of class politics. Unless they were willing to resort to racism (and mostly they were not) political leaders on the left could not reconcile possession of an empire with claims to represent ordinary people: where was the difference between the rights of workers at home and the rights of workers abroad? Anyway, the parties they led and the people they represented were more concerned with improving living and working conditions at home than with duties abroad. Empire-building belonged to history: they were concerned with the future.

Attempts to re-engage the public with the imperial project through events like Empire Day lingered, but proved no rival for football, the seaside or a day at the races. The next big exhibition in the imperial capital, the 1951 Festival of Britain, would be a much more distinctly chauvinistic production, the country's present and former overseas possessions getting a look-in only through exciting exhibits like 'minerals from the Commonwealth'.★

★

★ The fate of Empire Day testifies to the lack of interest. It limped on after the war, the movement's publication shrivelling from lavish magazine to leaflet, until even Winston Churchill declined an invitation to write a message for it. In 1958 it was renamed Commonwealth Day, in which guise it still exists, marked by a service in Westminster Abbey each March.

It was the Second World War which really sank the empire. As in the First War, a conflict with strictly European origins drew in races from all over the globe – Australian pilots flew in the Battle of Britain, Canadian sailors braved the battle of the Atlantic, Indians and New Zealanders fought at El Alamein. There was even a flicker of revival of British interest in Empire Day, with the Empire Day Movement's president talking of a fight against the Powers of Darkness, in which 'the fate of the Empire, and with it that of civilisation, is at stake'. But it was painfully apparent that the British Empire alone could not defeat the Axis powers: the outcome of the war would be determined by what happened in Russia and what came from America.

In August 1941, Prime Minister Winston Churchill sailed across the Atlantic on the British battleship HMS *Prince of Wales* for a secret rendezvous in Placentia Bay, Newfoundland, with American warships carrying President Roosevelt. The United States had yet to enter the Second World War and it would have stuck in the throat of any properly conscientious American to form an alliance to protect the British Empire: the country owed its very existence to rejecting it. Yet Churchill and Roosevelt managed to agree a statement, an Atlantic Charter, which laid out eight war aims. The very first of these stated that neither country was seeking any territorial gain from the conflict. The veteran of the battle of Omdurman may not have had his fingers crossed when he agreed this. But he certainly had anxieties about the third principle to which the men signed up, which claimed that the two governments 'respect the right of all peoples to choose the form of Government under which they will live; and they wish to see sovereign rights and self-government restored to those who have been forcibly deprived of them'. As various colonial officials around the world now quickly told him, you could hardly get a more unequivocal rejection of the principle of empire. Churchill later blithely told the House of Commons that what he'd had in mind was merely self-determination for the peoples of Nazi-occupied Europe. 'I have not become the King's First Minister', as he famously declared on a later occasion, 'to preside over the liquidation of the British Empire.' Perhaps so. But the fact remained that one of the country's greatest enthusiasts for empire had put his signature to a war aim which undercut its very existence.

Then came the greatest imperial calamity of the war. Until Stamford Raffles saw its potential in the early nineteenth century, Singapore had been just another pestilential Asian island, all swamp and discomfort. By banning slavery, promoting education, declaring equality before the law and asserting freedom of trade Raffles transformed the place.* Singapore flourished and the population boomed. A statue of a thoughtful-looking Raffles, arms folded, gazing down on the astonishing success of his creation, was standing outside the Victoria Memorial Hall in the heart of Singapore when, in February 1942, Japanese soldiers inflicted on the British Empire its greatest humiliation of the twentieth century. The hall itself was already serving as a temporary hospital to treat the casualties of Japanese bombing raids. Yet until the last possible moment the European community in Singapore had continued the routines of expat ease, in the misguided conviction that they were protected by the vast amounts of money Britain had invested turning the island into what was claimed to be 'the Gibraltar of the East'. Twenty-one square miles of dockyards, barracks, warehouses and fuel stores were shielded from attack by an array of heavy guns. Manning this garrison, as *The Times* had described them, were 'sturdy British infantrymen, Scottish Highlanders, bronzed young giants from Australia, tall, bearded Sikhs, Moslem riflemen fresh from service on the North-West Frontier, tough little Gurkhas, Malays from the Malay Regiment . . . the core of British strength in the Far East'.

But, as every student of military history knows, the crisis-planners had made the critical mistake of assuming that any attack on the island would come from the sea – the artillery had been equipped with armour-piercing shells and sited to fire at any approaching warship. In fact, the Japanese swept down the Malay peninsula from the north. It wasn't as if the British had not been warned. A military assessment in October 1940 had concluded that if the Japanese were

---

* Many local practices were respected. 'The Battas are not bad people,' he once said of a local Malay tribe, 'notwithstanding they eat each other.'

to invade Malaya, 'the survival of Singapore for more than a short period is very improbable'. And now the speed and ferocity of the Japanese advance were astonishing. From their base in occupied Siam (Thailand) the Japanese raced down by any available means of transport, including great numbers of bicycles, stopping for almost nothing: enemy wounded were butchered, surrendering prisoners were shot.

How could the defensive planning have been so inept? Churchill claimed that 'the possibility of Singapore having no landward defences no more entered my mind than that of a battleship being launched without a bottom'. Was there also some residue of a nineteenth-century belief in an innate racial superiority alive in the British high command, who seemed to consider that while the Japs might be able to defeat a Chinese army (as they had done in the invasion of Manchuria in the 1930s) they were no match for Europeans? 'I trust you'll chase the little men off,' had been the response of the Governor of the island, Sir Shenton Thomas, when a general reported that the Japanese had landed in Malaya. But the Japanese were formidable soldiers, commanded by a bold and ruthless general, Tomoyuki Yamashita.* The British forces may have contained elements from all over the empire. But they were largely untested and they were not especially well led: General Percival's military headquarters was known among the men as 'Confusion Castle'. As the enemy forces neared, an order went out that all the alcohol on the island was to be poured away, to prevent it falling into enemy hands and triggering a drunken Japanese rampage. Some Australian soldiers were seen face down in the gutter, scooping up whatever whisky they could. Panicking civilians fought their way on to vessels leaving Singapore, sometimes pushing Asians aside as they did so.

Before the war, Churchill had acknowledged that the island was a 'stepping stone' to Australia and New Zealand and, at the last minute,

---

* At the end of the war, 'the Tiger of Malaya' surrendered, was convicted of war crimes and hanged. As the authors of the *Oxford Companion to Military History* remark, 'it is difficult to suppress the suspicion that his principal crime was to have so humiliated the white man that his Far Eastern empires became untenable'.

dispatched the battleship HMS *Prince of Wales* and the battle-cruiser HMS *Repulse*. They sailed for Singapore on a tide of sonorous phrases. 'Thus', Churchill proclaimed, 'we stretch out the long arm of brother-hood and motherhood to the Australian and New Zealand peoples.' Unfortunately, the two great ships also sailed as unprotected as they might have done before the development of air power. Both were sunk by Japanese bombers. This left the defence of the island in the hands of 90,000 or so empire troops, many of whom had never heard a shot fired in anger. In London, an impotent Prime Minister issued increasingly frantic orders – that the entire male population should be used to build earthwork defences, that 'Commanders, Staffs and principal officers [were] expected to perish at their posts', that 'every inch of ground [was] to be defended', that there was to be no question of surrender 'until after protracted fighting among the ruins'. All in vain. Despite their advantage in numbers, the British were incapable of staunching the Japanese advance. Troops were rushed first to one sector, then to another, but always the wrong one. Japanese aircraft rained bombs down on the city. British generals accused Australian soldiers of running away. The Australian com-mander, General Gordon Bennett, levelled the familiar accusation that British commanders were stuffed shirts, while he himself scur-ried off to Australia, where, he claimed later, he was needed in order to brief people on how to fight the Japanese.

In his sweltering bunker Percival now had to make a decision. Per-haps the empire troops could hold the island, for the Japanese forces must almost be at their last gasp and their supply lines stretched close to breaking point. On the other hand, Percival's forces were either untested or the survivors of the defeated army which had fallen back through Malaya: beaten men do not fight as well as those who have never tasted failure. Churchill had ordered them to fight to the end. But there were terrified civilians everywhere and the water was run-ning out. Percival and his generals decided there would be fewer casualties if they threw in the towel. Had they had any idea of how grotesquely the Japanese would behave towards prisoners, they might have decided to fight on. But Percival did not know, as he also failed fully to grasp how vulnerable the exhausted and extended Japanese forces were. Yamashita understood that his troops' fatigue demanded swift finality. It must be unconditional surrender by the British. The newsreel footage of the negotiations shows the bull-necked Japanese general leaning across the table towards a thin, distressed Percival, who asks for a day to consider his response. Knowing that with a day's reflection the British might decide that they can, after all, fight on, the offer is refused: it must be all or nothing now. Percival looks around at his brigadiers and translator. His eyes blink furiously. And then he agrees to the biggest surrender of British troops in history. He and his generals had funked, and at some deep, instinctive level the whole empire shuddered. There could be no way back to the pre-war assertion of a natural right to rule.

It is as well to remember that the Japanese invaded as part of a plan to establish an empire of their own, and the brutal occupation of Singapore illuminated how benign the pre-war rule of the British had been. Japanese soldiers murdered and raped at will. They killed doctors, nurses and patients in hospital. Singapore was renamed Syonan-to, adults were forced into labour camps, children indoctrinated. Prisoners of war were used as slaves and the civilian population went very hungry. The rules of the Geneva Convention were completely ignored and all civilians obliged to proclaim the supremacy of the new master race (they were, for example, made to bow to any Japanese soldier passing on the street). The experience was sufficiently traumatic that at war's end Singaporean nationalists determined to ensure that they never again lived under foreign rule of any kind.

As the defeated British fell back to Singapore from the Malayan peninsula they had attempted to dynamite the causeway linking the island with the mainland. Like much of the rest of the defence of Singapore, it was a botched job. But the explosion made a massive noise, heard by the staff and pupils of a school on the island. When the headmaster asked what had caused the bang, an eighteen-year-old schoolboy, Lee Kuan Yew, told him that it was the sound of 'the end of the British Empire'.* The fall of Singapore had shown the world

---

* Or so he later claimed he had remarked. He became the first prime minister of an independent Singapore. The country had been declared a republic but there were

that Britain no longer had the capacity to protect its territories abroad. It was conclusive evidence that there was nothing superior about the white man and nothing permanent about his presence in the colonies. If the country couldn't hold an island which had been acquired as a protective outpost, what could it defend? 'The British Empire in the Far East depended on prestige,' wrote an Australian diplomat. 'This prestige has been completely shattered.'

To his immense disappointment, the British people thanked Winston Churchill for his inspirational wartime leadership by voting him out of office in 1945. The priorities of the Labour government which replaced him were crystal-clear. 'The nation wants food, work and homes,' said its manifesto, and the problems of the rest of the world were distinctly secondary. The party believed, of course, in a United Nations, in peace and friendship and in 'a common bond with the working peoples of all countries'. As for the empire, the new Prime Minister, Clement Attlee, had made it absolutely clear he considered that the principles of the Atlantic Charter, about which Churchill had been so one-eyed, applied to everyone. ('We have always demanded that the freedom which we claim for ourselves should be extended to all men,' he had said in 1941. 'I look for an ever increasing measure of self-government in Africa.') The Labour manifesto promised 'responsible self-government' for India and 'planned progress of our Colonial Dependencies', whatever that was. The Conservative manifesto by contrast, repeated the term 'Mother Country', which even then must have been getting pretty threadbare.

The mood of the world had changed. Britain was exhausted and bankrupt, France in a similar state. The two new world powers, the United States and the Soviet Union, both professed themselves to be 'anti-imperialists', with varying degrees of plausibility. The United

---

some aspects of the monarchical system that never lost their charm for Lee: he kept the post for thirty years. His eldest son became prime minister in 2004, his younger son was a prominent general and wealthy businessman, and his daughter ran the National Neuroscience Institute.

Nations, created in 1945 as the successor to the League of Nations, declared itself an institution committed to equal rights and self-determination. For years, the initiative had been shifting from the builders of empire to its dismantlers. Among those who, in Orwell's delicious phrase, took 'their cookery from Paris and their opinions from Moscow', (western) imperialism was An Inherently Bad Thing. But ideology was rather beside the point. The critical necessity was a sense of purpose. The objective of the breakers-up of empire was obvious enough. But what were the imperialists about? If the purpose of empire was really only to look after places until they could look after themselves – as had been maintained for years – then everything was reduced to a question not of principle but of timing. It is remarkable how hard it is to find evidence of really serious disagreement between the mainstream British political parties in the 1950s and 1960s about what ought to happen to the colonies: the claims for independence were undeniable. Both the left and right had decided that there was simply nothing to set against demands for self-determination – increasingly, those who did not feel a twinge of discomfort at the possession of an empire were simply ignorant. A Colonial Office survey in 1951 found that 59 per cent of those questioned were unable to name a single British colony, although one man did come up with 'Lincolnshire'.

The most pressing question after the war had been what to do about India. This, the grandest imperial possession, also had one of the strongest claims to self-government, the most charismatic leaders and some of the most colourful and effective anti-imperialist campaigns, with a real capacity to cause international embarrassment. Nationalists had been committed to complete independence since the 1920s and nothing the British had tried, neither plans for some sort of federation nor mass arrests, had done anything to weaken their resolve. The Second World War did nothing to improve the popularity of the imperial British with nationalists, but then neither the 'Indian National Army' which fought alongside the Japanese nor Gandhi's peaceful 'Quit India' movement had seriously imperilled

British rule. Churchill, who had been passionately opposed to independence, had hoped that victory would make Indians feel more fondly towards Britain. It did not. His own indifference to a terrible famine which struck Bengal in 1942 and 1943 – he refused all entreaties to divert food supplies – had done nothing to help. And had they known how he spoke in private, nationalists would have felt even angrier. 'I hate Indians,' he exclaimed once. 'They are beastly people with a beastly religion' – 'the beastliest people in the world next to the Germans'. As so often, he exaggerated: the people he really hated were not Indians in general, but what he called the 'Hindu priesthood' in the Congress movement campaigning for their country to be freed from the empire. Churchill's almost religious devotion to empire meshed with a conviction that India was simply too diverse a country to function as an independent state. Minorities, such as the Muslims, would be oppressed, and in particular he worried about the effects of the country's poisonous caste system, in which tens of millions of Dalits, or 'Untouchables', were condemned from birth to a life of discrimination and abuse. In a speech in 1931 he wondered whether 'if Christ came again into this world, it would not be to the Untouchables of India that he would first go, to give them the tidings that not only are all men equal in the sight of God, but that for the weak and poor and downtrodden a double blessing is reserved'.

Churchill's conviction that so-called Untouchables would be appallingly treated in an independent India has been horribly borne out since the British quit the subcontinent: even in the twenty-first century, Dalits suffer grotesque human rights abuses every day. The apparently paradoxical claim that only foreign occupation could protect indigenous people had taken root soon after Churchill first arrived in India as a cavalry subaltern in October 1896. Sharing a comfortable bungalow with two other young officers, he spent the long, hot hours between morning exercises and evening polo in a frantic course of self-improvement in which, first of all, he tackled Edward Gibbon's *Decline and Fall of the Roman Empire*, with its warning of how empires die. By the following summer he had worked out his convictions about the future of the British Empire: white colonies like Canada and Australia might be treated as near-equals, India never. Although he left the subcontinent that year, never to return, his views hardly altered for most of his life. In 1922 he was dismissing 'the chatterboxes who are supposed to speak for India today', contrasting them with the hundreds of millions of other people in the subcontinent for whom the empire was supposed to care. He told readers of the *Daily Mail* in 1929 that Britain had rescued India from barbarism and tyranny and that, thanks to the British, 'War has been banished from India; her frontiers have been defended against invasion from the north; famine has been gripped and controlled . . . Justice has been given – equal between race and race, impartial between man and man. Science, healing or creative, has been harnessed to the service of this immense and, by themselves, helpless population.' His devotion to empire found expression as paternalism – he described the people of India as 'children'. Self-government was simply inconceivable to him.

When, in January 1935, the National Government in Britain produced the enormous Government of India Act, envisaging a federation not very different to the solution he claimed to favour, Churchill objected passionately, describing it as 'a monstrous monument of sham built by pygmies'. Throughout the Second World War (to which – to the immense fury of many nationalists – the people of India were immediately committed in September 1939, on the signature of the Viceroy), Churchill retained his adamant objection to home rule. The Viceroy attempted to dampen Indian anger by promising that, when the war was over, the whole question of Indian government would be revisited. But in reality Churchill had no desire to reassess anything. (In 1944 he even sent the Viceroy a peevish telegram asking him why Gandhi hadn't died yet.) Leo Amery, Churchill's India Secretary, was so struck by the passion of his leader's hostility that he wondered whether 'on the subject of India, he is really quite sane'.

But India was a lower priority than fighting Nazi Germany and, under pressure from Labour members of the wartime coalition, a promise was made that, once the war was over, India would be free to decide its own future. This, he was told, was the price of Indian support against the Japanese. To meet Churchill's concern about the rights of minorities, the British promised that whatever entity emerged it could not be a state whose authority was denied by substantial elements in Indian political life – a pledge taken by India's many millions of Muslims as a promise that they would not be forced into a 'Hindu Raj', which in turn paved the way for the world's first invented Islamic state, Pakistan.

With the British people's ejection of Churchill at war's end, everything changed. The mood for independence was as strong as ever. The British Labour party saw the possibility of a new relationship between the two countries and sent Lord Mountbatten to India as the last viceroy, with instructions to disengage as fast as possible. In the House of Commons Churchill was appalled, talking about Britain 'scuttling' away from responsibilities. He blustered that in planning to quit 'territory over which we possess unimpeachable sovereignty' the Labour government was 'ready to leave the 400 million Indians to fall into all the horrors of sanguinary civil war – civil war compared to which anything that could happen in Palestine would be microscopic; wars of elephants compared with wars of mice. Indeed we place the independence of India in hostile and feeble hands, heedless of the dark carnage and confusion which will follow.' As he put it later, to leave India was simply 'shameful'.

For Churchill the villains of the piece were not the Indian people, but their leaders. (In December 1946 he was still talking of the 'Hindu Raj'.) The political class were 'men of straw of whom in a few years no trace will remain'. And the proposal to divide the subcontinent into predominantly Hindu and Muslim states would mean destroying what he saw as the greatest British achievement – unifying an enormous expanse of often warring states. Years after the event, he was still talking of 'Britain's desertion of her duty in India' as 'the most serious political blunder . . . certain eventually to bring grief and sorrow to the entire Western World'. Nonetheless – and it was a testament to Churchill's stature – he did eventually give his party's assent to Mountbatten's plans for a free, if divided, India, with the two new entities remaining within the Commonwealth. His prophecies of bloodshed and suffering at the time of independence came true, as people trapped on the wrong side of borders suffered the effects of mob violence or died attempting to escape it. But Churchill considered what was on offer to be better than some of the other possible outcomes, like independence outside the Commonwealth, and he recognized he was on the wrong side of history. In June 1948, George VI formally renounced the title of king-emperor – a 'melancholy event', said Churchill, 'only typical of what is happening to our Empire and Commonwealth in so many parts of the world'. He didn't like it, but he understood the current of events: no emperor, because soon there would be no empire. Once India had gone, what argument was there for denying freedom to Britain's other colonies?

In the land for whose capture they had rung the bells of Westminster Abbey in 1917, things were going from bad to worse.

The League of Nations, whose Mandate the British were supposedly exercising, had long withered away under the burden of its own irrelevance. Yet British troops remained in Palestine, discharging one of the most thankless tasks on earth. For a start, the land had a great deal more significance for both Jews and Arabs than it did for Britons, whose presence was clearly temporary and whose main function soon seemed to be to get shot at by both sides. In 1945 Winston Churchill noted bleakly that he was 'not aware of the slightest advantage that had ever accrued to Great Britain from the painful and thankless task' they had given themselves in the Holy Land. And yet a permanent solution which would satisfy both sides seemed maddeningly unachievable. With the defeat of Nazi Germany, the full extent of Jewish suffering in Europe had become horribly apparent to the world, and the Zionists' cry of 'never again' was unanswerable. The United States declared its support for the creation of a Jewish homeland, and the promises made by the British to the Arabs crumbled as growing numbers of European refugees smuggled themselves towards Palestine. Many of those the British intercepted were interned on the colony of Cyprus. But the arrival off the coast of Palestine in July 1947 of the SS *Exodus*, an old packet steamer with over 4,500 Jews aboard, showed how hopeless the British task was. The boat was halted and its desperate passengers, many of whom had only recently been liberated by the allies from concentration camps, were sent back to Europe. The French, who had allowed the refugees to board the vessel in Marseilles, refused to allow them to land on their return (unless they did so voluntarily), and the British decided to disembark them forcibly in occupied Germany, where they were accommodated in Nissen-hutted camps for displaced persons inside the British zone. Returning the Jews to camps in Germany – camps of any kind – turned an attempt at fair-minded migration management into a public-relations catastrophe.

In Palestine itself, the thankless mission of the soldiers trying to keep the two communities apart grew ever worse. There were 100,000 British troops – infantry, mechanized troops, elite airborne units and artillery regiments – deployed, along with thousands of members of the Palestine Police Force. Yet every week brought more evidence of their inability to keep a lid on things.

The British found themselves attacked by mobs, blown up by landmines, machine-gunned, mortared and kidnapped. Grenades were thrown from passing cars, haversack bombs left in public buildings. In the most spectacular attack, Jewish terrorists smuggled bombs into the basement of the King David Hotel, part of which served as British headquarters in Jerusalem, and murdered ninety-one people. The British military had a choice – get a grip and enforce law and order, or quit the country. But Clement Attlee had been elected prime minister to create the New Jerusalem in Britain: there was no interest in the old one and no enthusiasm for a new colonial war so soon after the ruinously expensive victory over Germany. In the end, in perhaps the most shameful demonstration of the emptiness of their imperial pretensions, the British declared that since they could not get Arabs and Jews to agree, they would hand the problem to the new United Nations. They then walked away. As the Chief Justice of Palestine put it in a letter, 'it surely is a new technique in our imperial mission to walk out and leave the pot we placed on the fire to boil over'.

The Mandate in Palestine had been a thirty-year exercise in hubris, and the British got out quickly and (for them) relatively painlessly. When Sir Henry Gurney, the unflappable Chief Secretary to the

Mandate, was asked by a Jewish delegation what he planned to do with the keys to his office, he replied, 'I suppose I shall put them under the mat.' On the morning of 14 May 1948 the Union Jack was lowered and the Red Cross flag raised in its place. Gurney left the building, was escorted to an airstrip and flew via Malta to Britain. He was being driven into London as the clocks struck midnight and the whole sorry Mandate interlude was finished. By then the shooting had already begun in Jerusalem.

The comfort blanket under which the British snuggled was called the Commonwealth. This was a concept no one could really object to, for the simple reason that no one has ever been able to say precisely what it is. The word started being bandied about in the 1880s, as the British sought a new relationship with Australia. The young Queen Elizabeth had a stab at explaining what it was in her Christmas message of 1953 – nothing to do with empire, but 'an entirely new conception, built on the highest qualities of the spirit of man', in which Britain was just one of many members, and leading 'still backward nations' on to a glorious future. In a later speech the queen's advisers amplified this as 'a group of equals, a family of like-minded peoples whatever their differences of religion, political systems, circumstances and races, all eager to work together for the peace, freedom and prosperity of mankind'. Who could possibly object to that?

In 1956, it fell to Elizabeth's second Prime Minister, Anthony Eden – a clever, sensitive man – to learn the harshest lesson about how the days of empire were well and truly over. Despite the withdrawal from Palestine, Britain still appeared to have plenty of power in the Middle East, with outposts at either end of the Suez Canal, in Aden and Cyprus, and air-force bases in Iraq. It financed and officered the Jordanian army and in 1953 had collaborated with the CIA in orchestrating a coup to overthrow the popularly elected Prime Minister of Iran, Mohammad Mossadeq, when he nationalized the Anglo-Iranian Oil Company. But – as the British were about to discover – this appearance of dominance was illusory, not so much because of anything observable in any of these places, but because of a change in world opinion. When the military ruler of Egypt,

Colonel Gamal Abdel Nasser, seized control of the canal in July 1956 he brought Britain into a head-on collision with reality.

This was the crisis which gave the British Empire its fatal wound. In a world where the initiative belonged to the people dismantling empires, the actions of a strutting military nationalist (as he was characterized in Britain) ought not to have caused quite so much surprise. Three months earlier, the young king of Jordan – a country created by the British – had turned on the commander of the nation's army, the Arab Legion, Sir John Glubb ('Glubb Pasha'), and given him twenty-four hours to return home. The expulsion of a much decorated professional soldier by a young man only recently out of Sandhurst marked the point at which the practice of (not so) discreet string-pulling by British advisers ended. Glubb arrived back in Britain with £5 in his pocket.

And now this. In the British Prime Minister, Anthony Eden, Colonel Nasser had chosen his enemy well. The son of a wealthy but bad-tempered baronet, Eden was handsome, charming, cultured (he had a rather fine eye for painting) and elegantly dressed – he even gave his name to a type of hat. The immediate impression was of a man who would have been more at home in Edwardian England than the post-war, post-imperial world in which he found himself succeeding Churchill in Downing Street in 1955. Eden had been conceived in the year of Queen Victoria's diamond jubilee, had been deeply mentally scarred by the First World War – which had killed two brothers and from which he emerged as the youngest brigade major in the British army – and belonged to that tradition of politicians who entered public life because it seemed the thing to do (both Lord Grey, Whig Prime Minister at the time of the Great Reform Act, and Sir Edward Grey, the long-serving Liberal Foreign Secretary said to have remarked in August 1914 that 'The lamps are going out all over Europe,' were distant relatives). But Eden had succeeded Churchill as prime minister when the lamps were going out all over the empire and when imperial self-belief, if not yet quite snuffed out, was certainly guttering. Even Eden's apparently imperial moustache was nothing like the extravagant growths of a Burton, Kitchener or Lugard. (In 1938, the Earl of Crawford had described Eden as 'altogether a most uncomfortable dinner companion' because of his vanity, including a 'moustache curled inside out', which 'always galls me'. By the time of the confrontation with Nasser it was feeble thing, which his wife had to blacken with her mascara before a television appearance.)

When he reached Downing Street Anthony Eden had served three periods as foreign secretary and considered himself to be on the right side of history – 'It was I who ended the "so-called colonialism" in Egypt,' he exclaimed at one point in the confrontation which now developed, 'and look at what Britain has done all over the world in giving the colonies independence.' He had said repeatedly that Britain could not expect to behave in the latter half of the twentieth century as it had behaved in the nineteenth. The Egyptian nationalization of the Suez Canal was not an imperial question, but an international one: freedom of navigation was essential to freedom of trade. And as the waterway by which oil was shipped to Britain, the canal was clearly a vital national interest. The legal justification which the British government sought for its anger was less than clear-cut, since the Attlee administration had nationalized the coal, steel and railway industries in Britain after the war. But – deny it though he might – there was a sense of imperial anger at work in Britain: Egypt had, after all, spent decades as the Veiled Protectorate. Race played its part, too. 'Politicians don't know Orientals like we do,' grumbled a retired brigadier at a gathering of old soldiers, 'they don't know that the only way to deal with them is to kick their backsides.' The Prime Minister was already smarting from the slight to Britain's reputation caused by the expulsion of Glubb Pasha (although not sufficiently animated to ensure that the man received his general's pension). And, in characteristic voice, the press turned on the Prime Minister. *The Times* declared, 'The seizure is an act of international brigandage,' while the *Daily Mail* bellowed that 'The time for appeasement is over. We must cry "Halt!" to Nasser as we should have cried "Halt!" to Hitler. Before he sets the Middle East aflame, as Hitler did Europe.' Since Eden had been conspicuous in his opposition to the appeasement of the 1930s, this was an especially hurtful (and stupid) accusation. Having lost two brothers in the First World War, and a son in 1945, Eden also had a great deal less enthusiasm for killing people than many a newspaper editor. His problem was that he was altogether too thin-skinned to shrug off the newspaper name-calling, and sat around in Downing Street waiting for the first editions of the newspapers to arrive so that he could immerse himself in the latest torrent of abuse from Fleet Street. As with so many bullies, the vulnerability of their victim merely egged on his oppressors.

In the event, what finished off British delusions about the country's place in the world was not what happened in Cairo or London but attitudes in Washington. Perhaps the British government might have defied the United Nations, with its feeble decision-making mechanisms, which ensured that the Russians could block any action against Egypt. But to do so required the support of the United States, which was on the verge of a presidential election and therefore in its customary four-yearly state of paralysis. The American Secretary of State, John Foster Dulles, made it clear that the United States was pinning its colours firmly to the fence. 'The United States cannot be expected to identify itself 100 per cent either with the colonial powers or the powers uniquely concerned with the problem of getting independence as rapidly and as fully as possible,' he announced. 'The shift from colonialism to independence will be going on for another fifty years.' Eden thought Dulles had deliberately misrepresented the British case: the issue was not colonialism but securing international control of the canal and freedom of movement. He was too much of a gentleman to tell the world that if anyone wanted an example of a truly imperial transoceanic canal they might care to look at Panama, a country created by United States power and now cut in two by a waterway secured by US troops stationed along its banks.

What's more, the external appearance of this dapper figure in his well-cut suits was deceptive. He had serious health problems. A botched operation for gallstones had left him with a damaged bile duct, making him prone to recurrent infections, biliary obstruction, fevers and liver failure. In October 1956 he was hospitalized after his temperature had reached 106 degrees. Doctors had also prescribed the amphetamine Benzedrine, which is now known to cause insomnia, restlessness and mood swings. Increasing exhaustion and lassitude left him moody and short-tempered under pressure: British policy was in the hands of a man whose physical condition almost precluded measured judgement. At one point he spluttered about Nasser on an open telephone line to his junior minister at the Foreign Office: 'I want him murdered.'

The assassination did not happen. But the French government, which already loathed Nasser for his vocal support of Algerian nationalists fighting to escape French colonial rule, weighed in on Britain's side. The political influence of both these colonial powers had been eclipsed by the United States, which continued to warn that world opinion would not tolerate a military intervention to regain the canal. But British newspapers thundered on, the *Daily Herald* pronouncing on its front page that 'Britain and the other Powers must swiftly show Nasser that they are going to tolerate no more Hitlers! . . . There is no room for appeasement.' Did no one in government hear the echoes of the press campaign to send General Gordon up the Nile to confront the Mahdi?

It was the French who came up with the plot. They proposed that the Israelis launch a strike into Egypt, which would give Britain and France the excuse to intervene between warring forces, and so secure the Suez Canal. Because of the need for the utmost secrecy, almost everyone involved in planning what became an enormous national humiliation told lie after lie. The Israeli invasion went ahead at the end of October 1956, and, as agreed, British and French paratroopers were dropped around the waterway. It was the day before the American presidential election. As bad luck would have it, the Russians had chosen the same time to send their tanks into Hungary to suppress a popular uprising. Could Washington condemn that invasion without also condemning the Anglo-French operation against Egypt? Those infallible panic-indicators, the currency markets, immediately began selling sterling, whose value plummeted: the Bank of England could not arrest the fall without the help of the Americans, who refused to act until there was a ceasefire. Eden, who was now taking pills to send him to sleep and others to keep him awake, faced a choice between losing face and seeing the national currency and economy implode. It was clear that the entire operation had to be abandoned.

At one point, British forces were landing and being withdrawn at the very same time. A broken Eden collapsed, telling his French counterpart, 'I'm finished. I can't hold on. The whole world reviles me . . . I can't even rely on all Conservatives. The Archbishop of Canterbury, the Church, the oilmen, everyone is against me . . . I can't dig the Crown's grave.' On 19 November, Eden's doctors told him he had to have a complete rest, and the writer Ian Fleming and his wife Ann offered the Edens the use of Goldeneye, their villa in Jamaica, as a place to recuperate. The day after the Edens' departure, the United Nations General Assembly passed a resolution by 63 votes to 5 demanding that the foreign forces be withdrawn from Egypt.

Eden's doctors judged that his health benefited from his holiday. But his absence created the strange situation where not only was he disconnected from the party's – and the nation's – nervous system, but cabinet colleagues began to feel it was better all round that he was away from London. 'Your return is likely to be regarded as a sign of panic,' warned Lord Salisbury in a cable to Jamaica on 4 December – it was better that Eden should stay away to 'complete your cure'. Ten days later the Prime Minister returned to England and appeared before a contemptuous House of Commons, to repeat the lie that there had been no plans to attack Egypt, and no collaboration with Israel. He swore that if he had 'the same very disagreeable decisions to take again', he would repeat them. There followed a miserable Christmas, and in early January 1957 Eden held a long cabinet meeting discussing anything but the Suez debacle, at the end of which he turned to the senior civil servant present and asked if there was anything more to consider. 'For a moment he was looking directly at me,' the official said later, 'and I saw in his eyes a man pursued by every demon. I have never seen a look like it in any man's eyes, and I hope I never do again.' A few days later it was all over. Anthony Eden told senior cabinet colleagues he had decided that his position was untenable. 'The doctors have told me that I cannot last long if I remain in office,' he said. He was willing to risk his life by continuing as prime minister, he said, but would not do so. That evening he went to Buckingham Palace to submit his resignation to the queen. As prime minister in late-Victorian Britain, perhaps Eden could have got away with a caper like the Suez intervention: might could make right. But the world was smaller now, and Britain's position within it smaller still. The Suez debacle was at least as great an imperial humiliation as the fall of Singapore. The symbols – the elegant yet sick Prime Minister, the increasingly valueless currency – were more eloquent than any speeches about the country's ambitions in the world. Britain's behaviour looked not merely high-handed but inept – it had lied about its intentions and then lacked the means to carry the day: a Full House of failure. The toothlessness of the British lion had been demonstrated to the world, as had the redundancy of imperial thought in the new world order: soon the United Nations would declare that all peoples had the right to self-determination. In an increasingly visible world there could be no more high-handed imperial adventures unless, like the Russians in Hungary, you were powerful enough not to give a damn.

It was all going so fast. An empire accumulated over centuries had vanished within a couple of decades. For the most part, independence came peacefully. But in a handful of places the British fought nasty little campaigns in which the challenge was essentially the same as that faced in the Boer War, in Ireland and in Palestine – how to fight an army which did not fight like an army: organizations which found shelter among the civilian population could rarely be brought to open battle and always retained the initiative. In 1951, Sir Henry Gurney – the man who had left his keys under the mat in the King David Hotel – was serving as high commissioner in Malaya, when he was shot dead in his official Rolls-Royce by guerrillas fighting to end British rule. In the nineteenth century a similar outrage would have brought down massive retaliation, disclosed to the public long after the event in jingoistic newspaper headlines. Thousands more people, including the last Viceroy of imperial India – assassinated by the IRA in 1979 – would lose their lives as the British tried frantically to discover an alternative identity and political strategy for the much more transparent post-war world.

Perhaps the most controversial of the British campaigns was in Kenya, against the Mau Mau, a clandestine organization whose power was bolstered by weird black-magic initiation rituals. Mau Mau was vicious and ruthless, with victims – some white, but the vast majority of them black – treated abominably. In one especially notorious incident, members of the organization set fire to the huts of villagers at Lari in central Kenya, then butchered them as they tried to escape: accounts described mothers being forced to watch as their children were killed and their blood drunk. Over one hundred Europeans were murdered. The reaction of the white settlers to the uprising was a mixture of hysteria and ruthlessness – they, after all, were the ones with the guns – and even though they had few friends among the government in London, it was soon clear that something had to be done. General Sir George Erskine, a career soldier who had acquired something of a reputation for lack of aggression during the Second World War, was dispatched to take command. He was no fan of the white settlers in Kenya, a country he is reputed to have called 'the Mecca of the middle class . . . a sunny place for shady people'. But he used the long British experience of fighting guerrilla campaigns – which dated as far back as the Boer War – to good effect, using intensive intelligence-gathering, elaborate propaganda operations and creative pseudo-gangs to infiltrate the Mau Mau.

In April 1954 Erskine launched Operation Anvil, in which, first, the whole of the capital, Nairobi, was searched, most of the population questioned and 24,000 people detained in camps. His forces then moved systematically through the countryside, detaining tens of thousands more suspects who were sent to camps. The tactics were effective, but at great cost: hundreds of prison-villages were created, and in some of them conditions were dreadful. Some of the interrogation methods were as brutal as anything endured by British prisoners during the Second World War. In the camp at Hola, where those considered especially hard-core members were detained, there occurred a scandalous case when eleven prisoners were beaten to death, as the camp authorities attempted to force them to work. Initial attempts to hush up the incident collapsed after an inquest revealed the true causes of death. In the early days of empire, news of the events might never have reached London. But now, not only did Whitehall officials know what was being done in the name of the

Mother Country, but politicians could express views on the subject. The House of Commons discussed the report into what had happened at the camp late one July night. The attack was led by the feisty Labour MP Barbara Castle, who accused the government of a 'nauseating parade of complacency' in its attempts to explain away what had happened. Then, at 1.15 in the morning, the Conservative Enoch Powell – once such a passionate believer in empire – rose. Powell was sickened by what he had heard. Mrs Castle had let the government – his own government – off lightly. In a speech which electrified an unusually crowded House, he went to the heart of why empire could not survive in the post-war world. 'All government, all influence of man upon man, rests upon opinion,' he told the MPs. It was simply impossible to have one set of standards for your behaviour at home and another for your behaviour in the colonies. 'What we can do in Africa, where we still govern and where we no longer govern, depends upon the opinion which is entertained of the way in which this country acts and the way in which Englishmen act. We cannot, we dare not, in Africa of all places, fall below our own highest standards in the acceptance of responsibility.' He sat down, overcome with emotion.

In its setting and its impact Powell's identification of the moral problem at the heart of modern-day imperialism echoed the criticisms Edmund Burke had made of the way that the East India Company behaved in the subcontinent. But his comments were delivered in an utterly changed world – a more intimate place, where news travelled fast and where Britain had a much diminished role. Indifference, the default setting for mid-twentieth-century feelings about empire, was not a foundation on which to attempt to maintain an imperium. It was not that anti-imperialism ever became a vastly popular political cause* – just that there was something in the air. To those who thought about it, the practice of imperialism seemed indefensible, and to those who didn't think the question was 'Who

* When a Labour party figure was asked why there weren't meetings being organized to protest at the conflict in 1950s Cyprus he gave the response 'Have you ever tried protesting to an empty hall?'

needs the bother?' The only significant colonial territories where the idea of independence was problematical were those – like South Africa or Rhodesia – with an entrenched white population. For the rest, independence was something whose time had come: no one who wished to get anywhere in politics could claim to believe in anything other than international equal rights, however vaguely expressed. When the patrician old Prime Minister Harold Macmillan, who had once been Colonial Under-Secretary, warned the South African parliament in February 1960 that 'the wind of change is blowing through this continent', he acknowledged as much. In Nigeria, later on the same tour, Macmillan asked the retiring Governor General, 'Are these people fit for self-government?' and received the reply 'No, of course not.' That would require another twenty or twenty-five years, said the official. 'What do you recommend me to do?' asked Macmillan. 'I recommend you give it to them at once,' said the Governor General. The alternative was that all the most talented people in the country would become rebels, and the British would spend the next two decades fighting to try to stave off what was inevitable, while incurring the opprobrium of the world. Nigeria left the empire a few months later, Sierra Leone and Tanganyika the next year, Uganda in 1962.

There was usually some member of the royal family present at the little ceremonies on dusty parade grounds when the flag was run down, acknowledgement of the regal dimension of empire. The rest of the crowd – officials in old-fashioned costumes and feathered hats, representatives of the new ruling class in national dress – listened as a military band marched in and played the anthems of the old and new countries. Flags old and new were saluted, glasses raised and toasts made. And then, summoning the remnants of their dignity, the British scuttled off home, farewells said to a creature of another age. By the turn of the twenty-first century, the massive enterprise which at the start of the twentieth century had straddled the globe was long gone – the speed with which the British jettisoned their empire takes some grasping. They let things go pretty fast (in the case of Palestine and India many would say much too fast). True, in 1982 the British fought to maintain their rule in the Falklands – a scattering of desolate islands at the other side of the earth – but that was a costly, risky enterprise against a military dictatorship, not an attempt to deny self-determination. In 1997, they quit their hugely successful colony in Hong Kong with hardly a murmur: while a war 8,000 miles away in the south Atlantic was a gamble, a confrontation with the Chinese army was a foregone conclusion. The expiry of the lease on part of Hong Kong seemed an appropriate metaphor for world dominance exercised by a small island in the north Atlantic. The dissolution of empire was as much the product of what was militarily feasible as its acquisition had been.

CHAPTER THIRTEEN

'We look on past ages with condescension, as a mere preparation
for us . . . but what if we are a mere after-glow of them?'
J. G. Farrell, *The Siege of Krishnapur*, 1973

On a sunny afternoon in Kolkata (or Calcutta as it was to the British)
hundreds of people – lovers, parents, children, shambling old folk
and squawling babies – mill around the gardens of a vast, improbable
pile of a building. At the gates, tuk-tuk drivers hustle for fares, hawk-
ers try to sell strips of sun-faded postcards and horribly skinny,
deformed beggars stick out their upturned palms. The building
behind them is a startling, 200-foot-high confection of white marble,
gleaming in the sunshine, part Renaissance Florence, part Fatehpur
Sikri. Like India's most famous building, the Taj Mahal, it marks an
act of devotion to a woman: the Viceroy, Lord Curzon, had planned
the Victoria Monument as the world's grandest memorial to the
queen whose reign saw the empire spread across the globe. He got his
wish. But it was always a white elephant: in the twenty years between
plans and completion, the British had transferred the imperial capital

to New Delhi. Within a further thirty years, they would quit the country altogether. On the nearby expanse of the Maidan, the immense park created by the British after their victory at the battle of Plassey, where once British troops drilled in the dewy early morning, there is a much more lively memorial. Thirty or forty impromptu games of cricket are taking place, generally with home-made bats, sometimes with home-made balls. The remarkable thing about all these crowds, cricketers or sightseers, is how few of them have any idea what the marble monument commemorates. Many seem hardly to have heard of Victoria. In the context of thousands of years of Indian history it is understandable: the British Empire was an interlude, growing over a few centuries and gone within a few decades.

Many empire-builders were left behind in India, and across town, behind the high walls of what was once the Great Cemetery, moss-covered urns and obelisks, columns and cupolas record their presence, killed in shipwrecks, drowned while crossing the river and a surprising number dead from lightning strikes. Most deadly of all to early settlers was 'Jack Morbus' – cholera. It was said you could have lunch with someone one day and be invited to their funeral by suppertime the next – the burials took place at night, in the light of flaming torches. Europeans thought themselves doing well to live through two monsoon seasons, and, when at last the cooler weather of winter arrived, the survivors would gather together to celebrate their achievement in simply being alive. A pyramid in the cemetery marks the grave of Elizabeth Jane Barwell, the great beauty of late eighteenth-century Calcutta, who threw a ball into hilarity by confidentially telling each of her young British suitors beforehand what colour dress she would be wearing: a dozen young men are said to have attended, all in an identical shade of pea-green. Another tomb contains the remains of four infant children from a single family, not one of whom lived to the age of two. Crows squawk in the mango trees. A child's home-made kite – a sheet of rice-paper on the thinnest of wooden frames – hangs from a wall, the pye-dogs scuttle from their shade when you approach and sulk at a distance. Few visitors call.

All that is now left of the British Empire to which India belonged are fourteen territories, political curiosities scattered across the oceans of the world, known perhaps to stamp collectors or corporate lawyers seeking a tax haven. They are mainly islands and bring no discernible benefit to Britain, which seems to regard them as a form of charity work, dispatching a governor ready to turn out at formal events in a plumed hat (as long as the local people will pay for such a thing) and happy to let the Girl Guides camp in the gardens of the Residence. Should an enemy menace or a hurricane strike, the old imperial power promises to send (and does send) warships and aid. Given a world map, most British citizens could not even stick a pin within a thousand miles of most of them (the Pitcairn, Henderson, Ducie and Oeno islands, anyone?). Many of them are inaccessible (it is a twelve-day journey by smelly fishing boat from Cape Town to Edinburgh of the Seven Seas, almost the only settlement on Tristan da Cunha – population 263 – and there's a good chance the sea may not allow you to disembark when you get there). But Edinburgh of the Seven Seas is a true metropolis by comparison with the Pacific island of Pitcairn, which has a total headcount of only fifty, descendants of mutineers on the *Bounty* and electors in the world's smallest democracy. The only thing these places have in common is the judgement they have made that they cannot make a go of things on their own. Occasionally, some Napoleon of Nowhere blusters about independence, but even on Bermuda, which has the largest population of these imperial relics, there is no great appetite for freedom. The empire on which the sun never set is reduced to a total overseas population of 200,000. On the other hand, between them these places do provide over 90 per cent of the biodiversity which Britain lays claim to.

There are further reminders of empire in the Union Jack which flutters in the corners of the flags of countries like Fiji, New Zealand and Tuvalu. Millions of people of British descent in Australia, Canada, New Zealand and South Africa (and thousands of settlers in places like Kenya and Zimbabwe) are a living legacy. Schools, solid government buildings, ornate railway stations, out-of-place cottages and tin-roofed neo-Gothic churches testify to the former presence of sun-burned foreigners in improbable places. War graves are scrupulously maintained.

But the physical memorials to earnest African missionaries, pickled Malayan planters and cricket-playing doctors on Pacific islands crack and tumble. The empire lives on less in stone and masonry than in the conventions of international trade and law and in the language of diplomacy, science and travel. It is evident in the mace which sits in parliaments across Africa; in the kilted Chinese who mark New Year's Eve in Hong Kong by playing the bagpipes; in the dusty monkey-skin hats of King's African Rifles veterans on Remembrance Sunday in Kenya; in the 'tuck shops' at Pakistani filling stations; in the very stones of Jerusalem (for it was the colonial Governor, Ronald Storrs, who decreed that all new building must be finished in local stone, which is why the city retains its magical golden colour); in games of croquet enjoyed by wealthy Cairenes at the Gezira Sporting Club; in racecourses in New South Wales and rugby grounds in Samoa; in the polite applause at the Delhi Gymkhana Club and the drill manual for the officer training academy in Baghdad – to say nothing of the borders of that troubled land, drawn in the sand with a lady archaeologist's umbrella.

And the empire has turned out to have a remarkable talent for causing trouble from beyond the grave. Britain has yet to elect a prime minister who doesn't take on a vaguely imperial tone of voice: none can resist the temptation to lecture other governments. Tony Blair took office promising to reinvent Britain and ended up sending its forces into action in six different conflicts. One British Prime Minister says it is time to stop apologizing for empire (Gordon Brown, 2005), the next (David Cameron, 2011) talks of tensions between India and Pakistan over Kashmir and says 'as with so many of the world's problems, we are responsible for the issue in the first place'. This is the authentic voice of post-war education, proud self-chastisement, a weird blend of Mr Pooter and Uriah Heap. Forgotten is the fact that India was partitioned to prevent the friction which the founder of Pakistan, Muhammad Ali Jinnah, said would otherwise blight the lives of Muslims: does Churchill's conversion to the cause of creating the world's first modern Muslim state also make Britain accomplice to the resurgence of political Islam?

These are complicated questions with which so many of the

British prefer not to grapple. Ignorance is profound, with much of the population aware, perhaps, that IPA beers were originally India Pale Ale, brewed in England for consumption in the subcontinent, but unaware of the reason why the British were there in the first place. Even British schoolchildren are not obliged to study the story of what their ancestors created. Perhaps in the dark recesses of a golf-club bar some harrumphing voice mutters about how much better the world seemed to turn when a great-uncle in baggy shorts ran a patch of Africa the size of Lancashire. But, by and large, no one has much to say about empire. Judgement has been passed and the case is closed. This, surely, is one of the peculiarities of our age. Just as the high-pomp imperialists assumed that the sun would never set on the empire, so the post-imperial age wallows unreflectingly in the assumption that the prejudices of its own generation will last for ever. Even Kipling could see through the pomp of his time.

At Ootacamund, in the Nilgiri mountains of southern India, the Indian owners of one of the bungalows built by the British offer a 'Raj Experience' – B&B, with English food presented on clumsy English furniture. The rack-and-pinion railway still climbs improbably up from the sweltering plains to the cool of the town they called 'the queen of hill stations'. A church, botanical gardens and golf course, half a dozen well-regarded schools with names like St Jude's and Laidlaw Memorial, all offer evidence of the colonial inheritance. The rich red soil of the terraced fields in the blue hills around the town is thick with 'English vegetables' – carrots, cabbages and cauliflowers. But 'Snooty Ooty' is now officially known by its Tamil name of Udhagamaṇḍalam, and many of its bungalows slowly succumb to the pleasant damp of the hills, the English flowers planted by the settlers long run to seed. The maharajah's summer palace struggles on as a hotel, its vast, galleried ballroom now little used, although if you ask nicely the manager will find you a cue for the snooker table up there. (The game was perfected one rainy afternoon, beneath the buffalo heads hanging high on the walls of the Ootacamund Club.) But most visitors prefer modern hotels, and the new businesses – manufacturing and pharmaceuticals – are what matter to the town now.

Most of the customers for the Raj Experience weekend in Ooty are British. There are other places, too, where they can also play at being harmless imperialists – among the stuffed-animal trophies at the Hill Club in Sri Lanka's hill station Nuwara Eliya, on the terrace at the mock-Tudor Norfolk Hotel in Nairobi, or by ordering a sickly Singapore Sling in the Long Bar at Raffles Hotel. Those who play this game know that that is all they are doing, in much the same way that visitors to stately homes in England gawp and wonder what it must have been like to live the life they see on display, and then hurry off to the comfort of the centrally heated suburbs. It is the British Empire as theme park, and the tourists no more believe in it than they believe in telekinesis or a flat earth: the Raj is gone, and gone for good. In that it resembles just about every empire which has presumed its permanence, whether Greek or Roman, Babylonian or Phoenician, Spanish, French or Portuguese. The Thousand Year Reich exists only in the minds of lunatics.

Living among foreign cultures to whom they generally (although not always) believed themselves superior obliged the British to consider who they were and to impose upon themselves a style of life in which some things were done and others were most definitely not done. But is there any real connection between the tourists enjoying their bland cheese sandwiches (white bread, crusts removed) in the spice garden of the world and the men and women who ruled so much of the planet? In 1850, the British Foreign Secretary, Lord Palmerston, could dispatch a squadron of Royal Navy warships to blockade the main port of Greece because the government there had refused to meet the exaggerated claims for compensation demanded by a Portuguese Jew, 'Don' David Pacifico, for damage done to his property by a mob. Palmerston proclaimed that, since Pacifico had been born in Gibraltar, he was entitled to the protection of the forces of the Crown, then the mightiest military power on earth. The Greek government paid up. Today, when the tourists return to Britain from the Raj Experience, they will find they are not even entitled to special treatment at the frontier of their own country, and must stand in line at UK Border Control, alongside men and women from over two dozen other states, no more special than any other citizen of the European Union, be they Latvian, French or German. Or even Greek.

The real Raj experience ended in 1947, and the empire came home to Britain long ago. When today's tourists return to England they will pass with hardly a glance the Indian restaurant on their high street, unaware that it was the search for spices to enliven the dreary English cuisine that took merchant venturers to the subcontinent in the first place or that the first Indian restaurant, Veeraswamy's, was opened by the man who had been official caterer for the Indian pavilion at the 1924 Empire Exhibition. Birmingham, once the manufactory of cheap tin trays for the empire, is now known for a distinctive style of balti ('bucket') cooking. Haworth, home of the authors of *Jane Eyre* and *Wuthering Heights*, even offers 'traditional Indian cuisine in the heart of Brontë country', a vision which would once have been comprehensible only to the talented sisters' laudanum-addled brother.*

In 1959, my parents took the family on our first foreign holiday. It was a sign, I suppose, that Prime Minister Harold Macmillan was right when he claimed that 'most of our people have never had it so good'. My parents had discovered remarkably cheap tickets on a passenger ship to Vigo in northern Spain. We spent a couple of happy weeks at a fishing village on the Atlantic coast, and then reboarded the vessel in Vigo harbour. The return journey to Southampton was utterly different from the voyage out. It turned out that the ship had been making a modern version of the old 'triangular trade'. I have no idea what she had carried from Spain across the Atlantic. But by the time the vessel had returned to Vigo for the final leg to England the holds and lower decks were packed with the descendants of slaves. Growing up in rural England I had never seen a black person before: the impression made by this crush of humanity, who had fashioned makeshift bedrooms in the fug of the holds, was astonishing. As time

* Laudanum was a diluted form of opium, manufactured in India. Increasingly, many upmarket Indian restaurants try to mimic the style of the Raj – all ceiling fans and sepia photographs. The kitchens of some of the grander establishments have appropriated the abbreviations of empire. A 'DC' is a dish cleaner and an 'OC' an onion cutter.

passed, I grew bolder and began to spend more time down in the
bowels of the ship, where wide-eyed black men fired eager questions
about Britain. Was it cold? Did it rain all the time? Were there lots of
jobs? Had I met the queen?

The last question was the only one I could answer definitively: I
had not. But the most baffling question was 'Is it true that the whites
beat the blacks with bicycle chains?' I was nine years old and had no
idea what my questioner – a smiling, avuncular figure with, he said,
a son about my age – was talking about and assumed it was something to do with cycle racing, of which I knew nothing, rather than
the weapon of choice for racist gangs. So I answered as nonchalantly
as I could, 'Sometimes, I think.' What impact this must have had on
the group of men travelling thousands of miles in hope of a better life
is still the stuff of an occasional bad dream.

His question must have been set off by the reports of the previous
year's rioting in Notting Hill and Nottingham, when gangs of young
white racists had rampaged through immigrant areas, attacking anyone
with a black skin. Macmillan made many of the appropriate noises,
condemning the riots and asserting the right of all British subjects to
walk the streets, regardless of their skin colour. But the disturbances
had shown how very empty were the claims which had been made by
kings, queens and colonial governors that the empire was some sort of
far-flung family. Within a couple of years Macmillan's government
was proposing radical steps to tackle not the readiness of young white
men to take up chains and knives, but the fact that so many people of a
different colour were arriving in Britain.

The flow of immigrants had been made possible by one of the final
gestures of imperial grandiloquence. The 1948 British Nationality
Act had promised free entry to the so-called Mother Country for all
Commonwealth and colonial subjects, evidence of the growing
belief that an association created by force might be turned into something more congenial. When 492 passengers and a dozen or so
stowaways debouched from the *Empire Windrush* at Tilbury in June
1948 they came from Caribbean islands where children bore the first
names of English heroes like Nelson and Milton and from schools
where many had learned to sing 'There'll always be an England' and

'Land of Hope and Glory'. One of them was a calypso singer, Aldwyn Roberts, who performed under the stage-name of 'Lord Kitchener'.

During the 1950s they were followed by many thousands more and the first black communities had soon been established in the big cities. But, as the race riots demonstrated, the immigration encouraged by government was triggering social tension: minds narrowed as the empire shrank. The immigrants' perfectly reasonable retort 'We're here because you were there' made plain the double-standards, and when the 1961 total of migrants exceeded 130,000 – a much larger number than had been anticipated – the government buckled. The charming idea of equality between the hundreds of millions of inhabitants of a fast-disintegrating empire was abandoned. Macmillan's Home Secretary blustered that the effect of the 1948 law had been to entitle one-quarter of the entire world population to enter Britain. (Did anyone ask quite how this had escaped the attention of the all-knowing officials in Whitehall, when the extent of British rule had been the boast of empire for the best part of a century?) A new 1962 Commonwealth Immigrants Act would now create a clear distinction between 'authentic' Britons and those whose skin was a different colour, its unambiguous intention being to stop new arrivals and to encourage those already here to go back whence they had come.

Like just about every other piece of immigration legislation dreamed up since, the law failed to curb mass immigration. Current United Nations forecasts project a UK population of over 70 million by 2050: when the 1962 Act was passed, it stood at about 53 million. The presence of significant numbers of people from one-time imperial communities has completely changed parts of Britain. The empire is not behind the British, it is living within them, for it has changed their very genetic make-up.

But the British have not found their one-time imperial identity at all easy to deal with. When the end of empire came, the easiest response for the British was to laugh at it. *Beyond the Fringe*, *Private Eye* and – with *That Was the Week That Was* – even the one-time imperial megaphone, the BBC, were delighted to oblige. Many of the leading perpetrators of the 1960s satire boom had been at schools intended to produce people to run the empire – Peter Cook claimed to have considered following his father into colonial officialdom in Nigeria, until he discovered that 'Britain had run out of colonies.'

In one sketch Cook interviewed Jonathan Miller as the Duke of Edinburgh, returning from attending Kenyan independence celebrations:

PRINCE PHILIP: I was there in a symbolic capacity.

INTERVIEWER: What were you symbolising?

PRINCE PHILIP: Capitulation. Mind you, of course, I was very well received. Mr Kenyatta [first leader of post-colonial Kenya] himself came to the airport to greet me and shook me very warmly by the throat as I got off the plane.

INTERVIEWER: Of course, Mr Kenyatta was at one time imprisoned by the British, wasn't he?

PRINCE PHILIP: Yes, well, that was when we thought he was a Mau-Mau terrorist. Now, of course, we realise he was a freedom fighter.

The satirists were lashing out at a world for which they had been told they had been educated, but which demonstrably no longer existed. They had breached a dyke, and pretty soon you could make any joke you liked about empire. Too many awkward questions otherwise.

It was coincidence that the withdrawal from empire marched in step with the increasing influence of the mass media. Could the concept of imperial rule have survived the scrutiny of the mass-media age? It seems unlikely. It was essentially a project which belonged to the ruling class, and the central ideological pretence of the electronic media is their claim to empower the masses. For sure, the empire glorified chancers, from pirates of the Caribbean to Henry Wickham, the 'father' of the colonial rubber trade: those who did well became rich and were garlanded with medals and knighthoods. But the tone of empire – the importance of the Crown, the significance accorded to local princes and tribal chiefs, the imperial honours system, the hierarchies of command and the very language of power – fixed it in a time before true democracy. It had been driven by a mixture of motives – greed and need, plan and accident, racial prejudice and missionary hope, strategic ambition and cynical calculation. But, however and whyever it grew, its subversive flaw was that, while the British boasted of their own long-held independence, the empire was built upon denying that very thing to others. As Lord Salisbury, the Conservative Prime Minister, Foreign Secretary and Secretary of State for India, once remarked, 'if our ancestors had cared for the rights of other people, the British empire would not have been made'. In that sentence he encapsulated the moral problem at the heart of imperial history. It promised freedom by denying it, and claimed to promote good government by rejecting self-determination. When in its later years it attempted to refine its purpose as a mere exercise in trusteeship, the British Empire acknowledged the seeds of its own irrelevance.

In the growing indifference of the early twentieth-century British to their empire, one senses how they had seen through the whole thing. At the end of the Second World War – a war fought 'for freedom' – they were given the opportunity to express a view on the empire and decided that they were simply not interested in continuing with it, thank you. In 1968, when Harold Wilson's Foreign Secretary told the US Secretary of State that Britain could no longer afford to maintain a military presence east of the Suez Canal, the American was appalled. He could not, he said, believe that the British people had decided that 'free aspirins and false teeth were more important than Britain's role in the world'. But that was exactly what they had decided.

And yet the creation, protection, extension and use of their empire had been the preoccupation of the British for generations. The question of what duty we owed to those we colonized was one of the determining issues in forging modern politics. In some ways, the whole imperial experience shaped the British as much as it shaped the places to which they took their flag, determining not merely how they looked at the world but how they saw themselves, helping to define the Englishman and woman, setting the tone of the educational system, restructuring the armed forces, broadening (and narrowing) the horizons of their statesmen, consolidating the monarchy and creating a worldwide diaspora. It is true, but not particularly

helpful, to remark that if it had not been the British doing the colo-
nizing, it would almost certainly have been somebody else: it remains
a fact of life that the strong abuse the weak. Some of the British
behaviour was appalling and some of it was admirable, but if you had
to live under a foreign government, it was better than many of the
other possibilities. The British Empire had begun with a series of
pounces. Then it marched. Next it swaggered. Finally, after wandering aimlessly for a while, it slunk away.

The British have spent the years since then alternately embarrassed
and ashamed. The Germans seem to have managed to forge a new
purpose for themselves, even though in recent history they have twice
visited Armageddon on much of the world. An alternative route for
Britain might have been for the country to throw in its lot with much
of the rest of western Europe, in the organization which has now
mutated into the European Union. After centuries of unhappy relations with continental Europe it would have required an astonishing
conversion. But the timing was all wrong, anyway. When Winston
Churchill first called for 'a kind of United States of Europe' in 1946,
Britain had not even quit India. When the foundations of the Union
were laid in 1951, the country still ruled much of Africa. By the time
that Harold Macmillan applied to join the Community, President de
Gaulle repaid British wartime sanctuary by excluding Britain: the
excuse he gave in his memoirs was that he was haunted by the 1898
Fashoda incident (when he had been all of eight years old).

Had Britain joined the European enterprise then, it might have
developed into something more respectable than it has become. But
to do so would have required the recognition that the British were
little different to the neighbours. Instead the British have been cush-
ioned from reality by the fact that, as the country has become a
decreasingly significant figure in the world, its people have been able
to live more and more comfortable lives. It clearly cannot last. Did
the British allow their economic enfeeblement because, for so long,
their empire gave them so many comforting illusions about their
place in the world? Instead of recognizing that national wealth is
born of work and enterprise, they basked in some stupid sense that
they were born to rule – it is not so far from a sense that the world

owed them a living. As their colonies slipped away, they had nothing with which to replace a vanishing sense of national purpose. And their openness to the rest of the world made the carcass of the Industrial Revolution easy pickings for others. They had entered the twentieth century in command of world trade. They began the twenty-first century struggling to compete and producing very little they could realistically call their own. Their car industry had more or less vanished, they had sold their electricity industry to anyone who would buy it, and even the water mains and sewers laid down by Victorian visionaries were now minor items on balance sheets produced in office blocks in the Ruhr. Even the great imperial sport of cricket, once governed by the Marylebone Cricket Club (MCC), is today run by a committee in Dubai.

The empire was Britain's main international preoccupation for a very long time. But instead of trying to grapple with the implications of the story of empire, the British seem to have decided just to ignore it. It is perhaps possible that this collective amnesia has nothing whatever to do with the country's lamentable failure to find a comfortable role for itself in the world. But it seems unlikely. The most corrosive part of this amnesia is a sense that because the nation is not what it was, it can never be anything again. If only the British would bring a measure of clarity to what was done in their country's name, they might find it easier to play a more useful and effective role in the world.

Acknowledgements

I have been very fortunate indeed in the people who have helped me. Jillian Taylor is the best researcher a writer could wish for – conscientious, imaginative and astonishingly industrious: I no sooner asked a question than had it answered, wherever she happened to be in the world at that moment. The book was commissioned by Tom Weldon, but on his departure to metadata wonderland it was Mary Mount who steered the thing from manuscript to book, without ever seeming to get agitated when things were not as she was expecting. The appearance of the book is entirely her work. Peter James, king of copy-editors, did his usual impeccable job.

Staff at the Bodleian Library of Commonwealth and African Studies at Rhodes House, the National Archives, British Library Newspapers at Colindale, the Imperial War Museum (Collections) and the London Library were all tremendously helpful. That magnificent place the British Library at St Pancras deserves special mention, as an example of a largely unsung, quietly efficient institution where it is a delight to work. In various one-time imperial territories, members of the Foreign Office were generous with their thoughts and hospitality – Dominic and Louise Asquith in Cairo, Howard and Gill Drake in Kingston and Richard and Arabella Stagg in Delhi in particular.

The television series which will follow this book was a bold commission by Jay Hunt, then Controller of BBC One, and was later supported by her successor, Danny Cohen. It was overseen by Basil Comely and was researched by the queen of television researchers, Jane Mayes, whose enormous suitcase of ancient maps, books and diarrhoea pills followed us around the world, with the exception of the Middle East, where Suniti Somaiya looked after us. Cameraman Mike Garner and sound recordist Dave Williams put up with incessant travel and inconvenience with immense good humour, even though endless hours in endless airports were never quite long enough to get us all to understand the simple challenge of a child's card game called Newmarket. Like replacement subalterns in 1916, four directors – John Hay, Roger Parsons, Robin Dashwood and David Vincent – led our forays in different continents. We were helped in India by Shernaz Italia, Neelima Goel, Abhra Bhattacharya and Iqbal Kidwai; in Israel by Noam Shalev; in Kenya by Andrew Nightingale; in Malawi by Chris Badger; in Hong Kong by Mark Roberts; in Jamaica by Susan Henzell; in Egypt by Ramy Romany; in Sudan by George and Makis Pagoulatos; in South Africa by Rick Matthews and in Canada by Pat Mestern. The series was worried over, chiselled and polished by series producer Julian Birkett and edited with great flair by Andrea 'Swoopy' Carnevali.

So many other people helped at one time or another that it seems unfair to mention only a few, but among them are Nicholas Utechin of the Sherlock Holmes Society; Melanie Jones, Education Manager of the Historical Association; Daniel Scott-Davies, at the Scout Association; Neil Griffiths, with the Royal British Legion Scotland; Lucy McCann, at the Bodleian Library of Commonwealth and African Studies at Rhodes House; Malcolm Barres-Baker, of the Brent Archives; Ian Bushnell, Chief Librarian for the Office of National Statistics; Rosemary Taylor, of the Office of National Statistics; Adrian Watkins, of the Church Missionary Society; Parwez Samuel Kaul, Principal of the Tyndale-Biscoe and Mallinson Schools in Kashmir; West Lothian Councillor Willie Dunn; Emma Davidson, of the Royal Society; Frank Kelly and Clare Kitcat at Christ's College, Cambridge; Ros Jemmett at Ardross Castle; the Wembley local history society; Gordon's School in Woking; Thomas Woodcock, Garter Principal King of Arms; Anna Beveridge at Marks and Spencer; Ranjit and Namita Mathrani of Veeraswamy; and Frank Savage, Matt Thoume, Helen Nellthorpe and Professor Patrick Salmon at the Foreign Office. I am very grateful to that legend in the world of indexing, Douglas Matthews, for his work in producing the final pages of the book. Ronald Hyam, doyen of imperial historians, was kind enough to read the manuscript for factual accuracy: any remaining howlers are mine alone, and he can't be blamed for bias or blind spots.

Notes

Introduction

6 'We shape our': Winston Churchill, speaking to the House of Commons, 28 October 1943), quoted in Churchill, *Never Give In!*, p. 358.

6 Arthur Hocart spent: Hocart, *Kingship*.

6 'My country is': Quoted in Hyam, *Understanding the British Empire*, p. 22. The king in question was Moshoeshoe.

9 'We are the finest': 'Confession of Faith, 1877', Oxford, Bodleian Library of Commonwealth and African Studies at Rhodes House, MSS Afr. t. 1.

10 'What is he': Hughes, *Tom Brown's School Days*, p. 80.

11 'a typical public-school': Henty, *With Roberts to Pretoria*, p. 6.

12 'We even think': Wood, *The Modern Playmate*, p. 75.

13 'who was our': Astley, *Fifty Years of my Life in the World of Sport at Home and Abroad*, vol. 1, p. 213.

13 'I think we': James, *Warrior Race*, p. 434.

Chapter One

16 'This town is': Talty, *Empire of Blue Water*, pp. 139–40.

16 'The Spaniards wondered': Sir Thomas Modyford in *Calendar of State Papers, Colonial: North America and the West Indies, 1574–1739*, quoted in Cundall, *Historic Jamaica*, p. 51.

16 'in the Spaniard's': The phrase comes from E. Hickeringill, *Jamaica Viewed* and is quoted in Nuala Zahedieh, 'The Wickedest City in the World: Port Royal, Commercial Hub of the Seventeenth-Century Caribbean', in Shepherd, ed., *Working Slavery, Pricing Freedom*, p. 7.

17 'I know many': Quoted in Whitfield, *Sir Francis Drake*, p. 149.

19 'to do and perform': Morgan's commission and instructions, BL, Add. MS 11268, fols. 68–72, quoted in *Dictionary of National Biography* entry, Nuala Zahedieh.

20 'the greatest mart': *Dictionary of National Biography* entry, Nuala Zahedieh; quotation from Morgan's relation, BL, Add. MS 11268, fol. 78.

21 'the buccaneers' daring': F. Gonzalez Suarez, *Historia General de Republica del Ecuador*, quoted in Rodger, *The Command of the Ocean*, p. 92.

22 'I don't wonder': Wright, ed., *Lady Nugent's Journal of her Residence in Jamaica from 1801 to 1805*, p. 57.

23 'the foundation of': An African Merchant, *A Treatise upon the Trade from Great Britain to Africa, humbly recommended to the Attention of Government*, quoted in Hague, *William Wilberforce*, p. 119.

24 '[a slave named]': Diary of Thomas Thistlewood, Friday, 30 July 1756, Lincolnshire County Archives.

25 'even the parsons': J. Latimer, *Annals of Bristol in the Eighteenth Century*, quoted in Williams, *Capitalism and Slavery*, pp. 60–61.

26 'I have not': G. Williams, *History of the Liverpool Privateers, with an Account of the Liverpool Slave Trade*, p. 594, quoted in Williams, *Capitalism and Slavery*, p. 63.

26 'the mainspring of': Malachi Postlethwayt quoted in J. F. Ross, 'The Phases of British Commercial Policy in the Eighteenth Century', *Economica* (1925), p. 143: see in Williams, *Capitalism and Slavery*, p. 51.

26 popular drama: For example, George Colman the Younger's *Inkle and Yarico*, which was set in the West Indies, was the second most popular play of the last quarter of the eighteenth century, after *The School for Scandal*: Troost, 'The Rise of the Comic Opera'.

27 'selling, bartering and': Quoted in Hague, *William Wilberforce*, p. 118.

28 'what is all this': Quoted in Walvin, *Black Ivory*, p. 17.

29 'We seem . . . to have': Seeley, *The Expansion of England*, p. 12.

30 'to possesse yᵉ welth': Quinn, ed., *The Voyages and Colonising Enterprises of Sir Humphrey Gilbert*, vol. 1, p. 160.

30 'such needie people': *Ibid*.

31 'remote heathen and': *Dictionary of National Biography* entry, Rory Rapple.

31 'We are as near': R. Hakluyt, *The principall navigations, voiages and discoveries of the English nation*, quoted in *Dictionary of National Biography* entry, Rory Rapple.

32 A Welsh member: See Bindoff, 'The Stuarts and their Style', p. 196.

33 'England was never': Letter quoted by Quinn, 'Sir Thomas Smith (1513–1577) and the Beginnings of English Colonial Theory', p. 552.

34 'excessive expence; both': *Ibid.*

34 'I cannot see': *Ibid.*

34 'cursed, hated, and': Sidney, *A Viceroy's Vindication?*, p. 81.

35 'planting of colonies': Ellis, *Life of William Penn*, p. 35.

35 Colonial settlement promised: Canny, 'To Establish a Common Wealthe: Captain John Smith as New World Colonist', p. 221.

36 'all you expect': Smith, *Captain John Smith*, p. 261.

37 'for the transplanting': William Clarke, *The Clarke Papers*, quoted in Latimer, *Buccaneers of the Caribbean*, p. 101.

37 'The seat of Empire': Edmund Waller, 'A Panegyric to my Lord Protector', quoted in Armitage, 'The Cromwellian Protectorate and the Languages of Empire', p. 532.

37 the title of emperor: 'Oliverus Maximus, Insularum Britannicarum Imperator Augustus', according to the rumour. *The diary of Ralph Josselin 1616–1684* and *Calendar of Clarendon State Papers*, vol. II: *1649–1654*, both quoted in Armitage, 'The Cromwellian Protectorate and the Languages of Empire', p. 532

Chapter Two

40 'for to the northward': W. Guthrie, *A New Geographical, Historical, and Commercial Grammar and Present State of the Several Kingdoms of the World*, quoted in Marshall, 'Empire and Opportunity in Britain, 1763–75: The Prothero Lecture 6 July 1994', p. 112.

42 'If Russia declares': Quoted in Kaplan, *Russian Overseas Commerce with Great Britain during the Reign of Catherine II*, p. 130.

42 'as he would': Nathaniel William Wraxall, *Historical Memoires of my own Time*, quoted in Jasanoff, *Liberty's Exiles*, p. 55.

42 'There is not a ray': William Cobbett, *Parliamentary History of England*, vol. XXII, quoted in Simms, *Three Victories and a Defeat*, p. 663.

42 'Everything human . . . has': *Newcastle Chronicle*, 19 August 1786, quoted in Simms, *Three Victories and a Defeat*, p. 665.

43 'Tho' we have not': John Andrews, *An Essay on Republican Principles, and on the Inconveniences of a Commonwealth in a Large Country and Nation,* quoted in Gould, *The Persistence of Empire,* p. 209.

44 'together with all': Quoted in Keneally, *Australians,* p. 31.

44 'in the name': Cook, *The Journals of Captain James Cook on his Voyages of Discovery,* vol. I: *The Voyage of the Endeavour, 1768–1771,* pp. 387–8.

47 'To check the petulance': Quoted in Beaglehole, *The Life of Captain James Cook,* p. 150.

47 'obligd to Plow': Quoted in Fara, *Sex, Botany and Empire,* p. 104.

48 'redound greatly to': Secret Instructions to Captain Cook, 30 June 1768, printed in Beaglehole, *The Life of Captain James Cook,* p. 148.

48 'the countrey . . . resembled': Joseph Banks, *Endeavour Journal* 2 (Sydney, 1962), quoted in Fara, *Sex, Botany and Empire,* p. 90.

50 'the door of the seas': Quoted in Fry, *The Scottish Empire,* p. 27.

52 'for all the East': Quoted in MacKenzie, 'Essay and Reflection: On Scotland and the Empire', p. 715.

52 'cornchest . . . where we': Quoted in *ibid.,* p. 721.

52 'as long as he': Quoted in *ibid.,* p. 718.

53 'We want more Scots': Quoted in *ibid.,* p. 725.

Chapter Three

54 'is stronger, fighting': Quoted in Simms, *Three Victories and a Defeat,* p. 515.

58 'What is England': Quoted in James, *Raj,* pp. 47–8.

59 'greater resemblance to': Anderson, *A Narrative of the British Embassy to China in the Years 1792, 1793 and 1794,* p. 102.

61 'and even were': Hanes and Sanello, *The Opium Wars,* p. 19.

61 'tyranny of a': Quoted in Barrow, *Some Account of Public Life and a Selection from the Unpublished Writings of the Earl of Macartney,* vol. II, p. 441.

61 ate the fleas: Anderson, *A Narrative of the British Embassy to China in the Years 1792, 1793 and 1794,* p. 123.

61 'there is not': Barrow, *Travels in China,* p. 333.

61 'the lordly grocers': [Anonymous], 'Observations on the Trade with China, London 1822', p. 458.

62 'not a necessity': Hanes and Sanello, *The Opium Wars*, p. 20.

63 'the safest and most': Both quoted in Hyam, *Britain's Imperial Century*, p. 28.

64 'a war more unjust': Hanes and Sanello, *The Opium Wars*, p. 79.

65 'Multitudes of our': *Ibid.*, p. 153.

65 'which could never': *The Times*, 3 December 1842.

66 'We have as much': Quoted in Kiernan, *British Diplomacy in China*, p. 251.

66 'not an amiable': Hochschild, *Bury the Chains*, p. 85.

67 'to the next insurrection': Boswell, *The Life of Samuel Johnson*, vol. IV, p. 54.

67 'it was time': Clarkson, *The History of the Rise, Progress, and Accomplishment of the Abolition of the African Slave-Trade by the British Parliament*, vol. 1, p. 210.

67 'There was no town': Quoted in Hochschild, *Bury the Chains*, p. 193.

67 'either fanatics or': Quoted in Fryer, *Staying Power*, p. 101.

67 'the blood-sweetened beverage': 'Poems Concerning the Slave Trade', Sonnet III, Southey, *The Poetical Works of Robert Southey*, vol. I, p. 66.

67 'as guilty of': *The Star*, Monday, 26 December 1791, quoted in Murphy, *Cox's Fragmenta*, p. 36.

68 'The people of': Romilly, *The Speeches of Sir Samuel Romilly in the House of Commons*, vol. I, p. 9.

68 'how much more': *Ibid.*, pp. 30–31.

Chapter Four

70 'a British subject': Hansard, 3rd series, vol. 112, col. 44, 25 June 1850.

71 'There is so much': Rosamund Lawrence, quoted in MacMillan, *Women of the Raj*, pp. 18–19.

72 'Let this be': Letter from Sir Thomas Roe to the East India Company, 24 November 1616, in Foster, ed., *The Embassy of Sir Thomas*, quoted in Judd, *The Lion and the Tiger*, p. 15.

72 'the unparalleled jewel': Letter to Sir Stephen Evance, John Dolben and Robert Pitt, printed in Historical Manuscripts Commission, *The Manuscripts of J.B. Fortescue, preserved at Dropmore*, vol. I, p. 32.

75 Nothing in history: Macaulay, 'Lord Clive', in *Critical and Historical Essays*, vol. III, p. 100.

75 'twenty-three ghastly figures': *Ibid.*

75 'the lounging place': *Calcutta Old and New*, quoted in Mukherjee, 'Myth of Empire – The story about the Black Hole of Calcutta refuses to die'.

76 'proclaimed to the heavens': Rabindranath Tagore, 'On the monument to the victims of the Black Hole massacre', quoted in Macfarlane, *The Black Hole, or the Makings of a Legend*, p. 207.

77 'both in their garb': Quoted in Harvey, *Clive*, p. 92.

77 'five hundred [enemy]': Quoted in *ibid.*, p. 219.

77 'disguised in a': Jasanoff, *Edge of Empire*, p. 30.

78 'In the field': Macaulay, *Macaulay's Essays on Clive and Hastings*, p. 77.

79 'the living were': Hunter, *The Annals of Rural Bengal*, vol. I, p. 26.

79 'We have had': Quoted in Harvey, *Clive*, p. 357.

79 'an opulent city': Speech made to a select committee of the House of Commons, March 1773, quoted in Macaulay, 'Lord Clive', reprinted in Macaulay, *Prose and Poetry*, p. 368.

80 'Lord Clive is himself': Paine, *The Political and Miscellaneous Works of Thomas Paine*, vol. II, p. 38.

81 'I have saved': Quoted in Gardner, *The East India Company*, p. 123.

81 'Were we to be': Burke, *The Writings and Speeches of Edmund Burke*, vol. V, pp. 402–3.

82 'there were gathered': Thomas Babington Macaulay, 'Warren Hastings', reprinted in Macaulay, *Prose and Poetry*, p. 455.

82 'brought before you': Edmund Burke, quoted in Dirks, *The Scandal of Empire*, p. 89.

83 'The wives of': Quoted in *ibid.*, pp. 110–11.

83 'the most culpable': Bryan, *The World's Famous Orations*, vol. VI, p. 50, n. 1.

83 'the condemnation we': 'At the Trial of William Hastings', 1788, printed in Sheridan, *The Dramatic Works of Richard Brinsley Sheridan*, p. 119.

84 'our fellow subjects': Quoted in Dirks, *The Scandal of Empire*, p. 302.

85 'a detestable expedient': Hansard, 1st series, vol. 26, col. 856, 22 June 1813.

85 'Our religion is': *Ibid.*, cols. 864–5.

85 'infused into oriental': Quoted in Rosselli, *Lord William Bentinck*, p. 19.

86 'It is your custom': Lieven, *Pakistan*, p. 359.

89 'I was a good': Quoted in Wagner, *The Great Fear of 1857*, p. 120.

90 'Surely we are': Letter to Sir Henry Lawrence, 24 June 1857, printed in Edwardes and Merivale, *Life of Sir Henry Lawrence*, p. 596.

90 'Here a round': Quoted in Rees, *A Personal Narrative of the Siege at Lucknow*, p. 357.

90 'The old – battered': Amy Horne, quoted in Ward, *Our Bones are Scattered*, p. 315.

92 'the Epic of': Chaudhuri, *English Historical Writings on the Indian Mutiny*, p. 104.

92 'Not Rome, not': Russell, *My Diary in India*, vol. I, p. 257.

92 'would surprise visitors': Kincaid, *British Social Life in India*, p. 116.

93 'It is impossible': Harris, *A Lady's Diary of the Siege of Lucknow, Written for the Perusal of Friends at Home*, various extracts, pp. 1–86.

95 'The scene was': Hibbert, *The Great Mutiny*, p. 341.

95 'Let us propose': *Ibid.*, p. 293.

96 'every tree and': Quoted in Morris, *Heaven's Command*, p. 244.

96 'I wish I were': Charles Dickens to Angela Burdett-Coutts, letter reprinted in Dickens, *The Letters of Charles Dickens*, vol. VIII, p. 459.

96 'Our endeavour to': Quoted in *Dictionary of National Biography* entry.

97 'by the time': Quoted in Dalrymple, *The Last Mughal*, p. 2.

Chapter Five

99 'no coyness, no': Quoted in Hibbert, *Africa Explored*, p. 36.

99 considered him a 'brute': Quoted in Reid, *Traveller Extraordinary*, p. 296.

99 'not a distinct': Quoted in Boswell, *The Life of Samuel Johnson*, vol. III, p. 209.

101 'As the prime': Part of a minute on Burton, written by Lord Salisbury to his Foreign Office officials in the Consular Department, quoted in Godsall, *The Tangled Web*, p. xxv.

102 'like a prize-fighter': The comment was made by Frank Harris. See Harris, *Contemporary Portraits*, p. 180.

102 'look of unspeakable': Quoted in Moorehead, *The White Nile*, p. 20.

102 'he was not': Burton, *The Lake Regions of Central Africa*, vol. I, pp. xiv–xv.

105 'We had scarcely': *Ibid.*, vol. II, p. 204.

105 'After a few': *Ibid.*, p. 209.

105 'used to snub': Quoted in Moorehead, *The White Nile*, p. 38.

106 'they ought to': Quoted in *ibid.*, p. 57.

106 'It was a sight': Speke, *Journal of the Discovery of the Sources of the Nile*, pp. 466–7.

107 'Speke appeared the': 'Explorations in Africa', *New York Times*, 2 July 1866.

107 'By God, he's': Quoted in Moorehead, *The White Nile*, p. 75.

108 'the only complete': Quoted in MacKenzie, *Popular Imperialism and the Military*, p. 16.

108 'I am not': Quoted in Riffenburgh, *The Myth of the Explorer*, p. 39.

110 'For God's sake': Robert Falcon Scott journal, Thursday 29 March, 1912, quoted in Scott, *Scott's Last Expedition*, p. 432.

111 'In his mind's eye': *The Zoological Gardens, Regent's Park – A Handbook for Visitors*, quoted in Jones, 'The Sight of Creatures Strange to our Clime: London Zoo and the Consumption of the Exotic', p. 7.

112 'The long lines': *Illustrated London News*, 8 June 1850, quoted in Jones, 'The Sight of Creatures Strange to our Clime: London Zoo and the Consumption of the Exotic', p. 14.

Chapter Six

114 'introductions by a': Smith, *Through Unknown African Continents*, pp. 363–4.

114 'It is religion': Smith, 'Christian Missions, Especially in the British Empire', p. 542.

114 12,000 British missionaries: Missionary societies spent £2 million per year: see Dr Robert Carr, 'The Evangelical Empire: Christianity's Contribution to Victorian Colonial Expansion', www.britishempire.co.uk.

114 'Confound all these': Quoted in Pakenham, *Out in the Noonday Sun*, p. 102.

114 'They spread the': Oliver, *Sir Harry Johnston and the Scramble for Africa*, p. 182.

114 'First the missionary': Quoted in Pakenham, *Out in the Noonday Sun*, p. 94.

116 'by victories of': Ogilvie, *Our Empire's Debt to Missions*, p. 5.

116 'when excited, a': George Seaver, *David Livingstone: His Life and Letters*, quoted in *Dictionary of National Biography* entry.

117 'Dr L is out': *Ibid*.

117 'I am terribly': 'David Livingstone's last letters deciphered', *Guardian*, 20 July 2010.

118 'his death has': *British Quarterly Review* 61 (1875) p. 397.

118 'the flag which': E. Grose Hodge, *Record*, 6 May 1910, quoted in D. W. Bebbington, 'Atonement, Sin and Empire, 1880–1914', in Porter, ed., *The Imperial Horizons of British Protestant Missions*, p. 19.

118 'the clergy are': Montgomery, *Foreign Missions*, pp. 1–2.

119 'pathetic . . . to see': Griff Jones, *Britain and Nyasaland*, quoted in Pakenham, *Out in the Noonday Sun*, p. 104.

119 'I am better': John Hine MSS, 7–9 October 1910, quoted in Pakenham, *Out in the Noonday Sun*, pp. 109–10.

120 'I can think': Quoted in Perham, *Lugard*, p. 104.

120 'To give peace': Churchill, *The River War*, vol. I, pp. 18–19.

121 'From the mutilated': Quoted in 'The Lost Arctic Voyagers', *Household Words*, 2 December 1854.

122 'the savage has': *Ibid*.

122 'The better educated': *Ibid*.

122 'heroic little monkey': Darwin, *The Descent of Man*, vol. II, pp. 796–7.

123 'Survival of the': Rusden, 'Labour and Capital', pp. 67–83.

123 'an iron-handed and': F. J. McLynn, *Burton: Snow upon the Desert*, quoted in Brendon, *The Decline and Fall of the British Empire*, p. 154.

124 'the very abomination': Burton, *Wanderings in West Africa from Liverpool to Fernando Po*, vol. II, p. 295.

124 'Except some knowledge': Hunt, *On the Negro's Place in Nature*, p. 27.

124 'This premature union': *Ibid*., p. 8.

125 'the analogies are': *Ibid*., pp. 51–2.

125 'my statement of': *Ibid*., Dedication.

125 'Our Bristol and': *Ibid*., p. 53.

125 'hierarchy of civilisation': Report by Commission VII on missions and governments to the Edinburgh conference in 1910, quoted in Brian Stanley, 'Church, State and the Hierarchy of Civilisation', in Porter, ed., *The Imperial Horizons of British Protestant Missions*, p. 65.

126 'the form of Africa': David Clement Scott, *Life and Work in British Central Africa*, quoted in Andrew C. Ross, 'Christian Missions and the Mid-Nineteenth-Century Change in Attitudes to Race: The African Experience', in Porter, ed., *The Imperial Horizons of British Protestant Missions*, p. 85.

126 'Watching that the': Ogilvie, *Our Empire's Debt to Missions*, p. 217.

Chapter Seven

128 'the matter [had]': Haggard, *She*, p. 118.

128 'This beauty, with': *Ibid.*, pp. 158–9.

128 'I am but': *Ibid.*, p. 193.

129 'I can safely': Haggard, *King Solomon's Mines*, p. 10.

130 'I now commenced': Quoted in James, *The Rise and Fall of the British Empire*, p. 222.

130 'to prostitute themselves': Sellon, *Annotations on the Sacred Writings of the Hindüs*, pp. 55–6.

130 'not very much': *Ibid.*

130 'the handsomest Mohammedan': Sellon, *The Ups and Downs of Life*, pp. 52–3.

131 'if a young': Quoted in Leigh, ed., *The Erotic Traveller*, p. 24.

132 Colonel James Skinner: Hyam, *Empire and Sexuality*, p. 115.

132 The records show: William Dalrymple, 'White mischief', *Guardian*, 9 December 2002.

133 'She keeps house': Burton, *The Life of Captain Sir Richard F. Burton*, vol. I, p. 135.

133 'born in India': Quoted in James, *Raj*, p. 218.

134 'insinuating manners and': Quoted in *ibid.*, p. 219.

134 'eastern princess': Garnet Wolseley to Richard Wolseley, 7 August 1859, Wolseley Private Papers, Hove, 163/1, quoted in Kochanski, *Sir Garnet Wolseley*, p. 24.

135 'more perfect than': Shore, *Memoirs of the Life, Writings and Correspondence of Sir William Jones*, vol. II, p. 170.

135 'standing for half': Quoted in James, *Raj*, p. 225.

136 'In the hot': Quoted in Allen, *Plain Tales from the British Empire*, p. 155.

137 'observed that those': S. Sneade Browne, *Home Letters written from India, 1828–41*, quoted in Hyam, *Empire and Sexuality*, p. 117.

138 'Dogs and other': Sharp, *Goodbye India*, p. 138.

139 'hot-weather housekeeping': Quoted in Barr, *The Memsahibs*, p. 99.

139 'The menu was': Forster, *A Passage to India*, p. 43.

140 'Dirt, illimitable, inconceivable': Steel and Gardiner, *The Complete Indian Housekeeper and Cook*, p. 86.

140 'the Indian servant': *Ibid.*, p. 12.

140 *'Never do work'*: *Ibid.*, p. 15.

141 the grass widow: Diver, *The Englishwoman in India*, p. 24.

141 'deranged menstruation': Quoted in Ardis and Lewis, eds., *Women's Experience of Modernity*, p. 146.

142 'die out about': Quoted in MacMillan, *Women of the Raj*, p. 99.

142 'The House of Desolation': Ricketts, *Rudyard Kipling*, p. 15.

142 'When the time': Ross, *Blindfold Games*, p. 69.

142 'What would India': Count von Königsmark, 'Die Engländer in Indien', quoted in Diver, *The Englishwoman in India*, Preface.

144 'the interests of': *The Times*, 3 December 1908. See also Hyam, *Understanding the British Empire*, pp. 417–39.

145 'injurious and dangerous': Quoted in Hyam, 'Concubinage and the Colonial Service: The Crewe Circular (1909)', p. 182.

145 'Pity the poor': Quoted in Nicholls, *Red Strangers*, pp. 72–3.

146 'Guides! remember the': Baden-Powell and Baden-Powell, *The Handbook for Girl Guides*, p. 413.

146 'Britain has been': *Ibid.*, p. 45.

146 They were taught: For example, the headmistress of Wycombe Abbey, who wrote that 'I think I do not speak too strongly when I say that games [for girls], *i.e.*, active games in the open air, are essential to a healthy existence, and that most of the qualities, if not all, that conduce to the supremacy of our country in so many quarters of the globe, are fostered, if not solely developed, by the means of games': Jane Frances Dove, quoted in Beale, Soulsby and Dove, *Work and Play in Girls' Schools*, p. 398.

146 'It is men's': Baden-Powell and Baden-Powell, *The Handbook for Girl Guides* , p. 414.

147 'delightful prospects': *Ibid.*

147 'To a true-hearted': *Ibid.*, p. 235.

Chapter Eight

149 'a lascar familiar': 'The Bridge-Builders', in Kipling, *Collected Stories*, p. 442.

149 'kill all weariness': *Ibid.*, p. 454.

150 'This embodiment of': Roosevelt, *African Game Trails*, p. 2.

151 'Our work was': Patterson, *The Man-Eaters of Tsavo and Other East African Adventures*, p. 20.

152 'The wily man-eaters': *Ibid.*, pp. 105–6.

153 'prostitutes, small boys': Jackson, quoted in Miller, *The Lunatic Express*, p. 387.

153 'Pumping-engine employee': Quoted in Hardy, *The Iron Snake*, p. 266.

153 'Indian trade, enterprise': *Ibid.*, p. 479.

154 'the entire continent': 'Confession of Faith', Oxford, Bodleian Library of Commonwealth and African Studies at Rhodes House, MSS Afr. t.1.

156 'That book has': Flint, *Cecil Rhodes*, p. 24.

156 'I contend': *Ibid.*

156 'It is our duty': *Ibid.*

157 'the native is': Verschoyle, *Cecil Rhodes*, pp. 159, 163.

158 'When he stands': Twain, *Following the Equator*, p. 708.

159 The imperial historian: Hyam, *Britain's Imperial Century*, p. 25.

159 'shipful of failures': 'The Amateur Emigrant', in Stevenson, *The Works of Robert Louis Stevenson*, ch. XVIII, pp. 10, 14.

160 'How like a King': Defoe, *Robinson Crusoe*, p. 236.

160 'the true symbol': James Joyce, *Daniel Defoe*, quoted in Hulme, *Colonial Encounters*, p. 216.

160 'brave, ruthless, decisive': R. H. W. Reece, 'Brooke, Sir Charles Anthoni Johnson (1829–1917)', *Dictionary of National Biography*.

160 'I have never': Quoted in Maugham, *Collected Stories*, p. xxii.

161 'If British East': Bell, *Glimpses of a Governor's Life*, pp. 106–7.

162 'primarily Kenya is': Quoted in Hyam, *Understanding the British Empire*, pp. 225–6.

164 'A fertile and': William Pember Reeve, *Long White Cloud*, quoted in Brendon, *The Decline and Fall of the British Empire*, p. 91.

164 'This is what she': Ruskin, *Lectures on Art*, pp. 29–30.

165 'I do not know': Most editions of *The Voyage of the Beagle* do not include this line (Darwin himself made changes to succeeding editions). The line was included in the 1839 *Journal of Researches into the Geology and Natural History of the various countries visited by H.M.S. Beagle, under the command of Captain FitzRoy, R.N., from 1832–1836*. The full passage appears in Nicholas and Nicholas, *Charles Darwin in Australia*, p. 97.

Chapter Nine

168 '[From my heart': Strachey, *Queen Victoria*, p. 419.

169 'should rank in': *The Times*, 19 August 1875, quoted in Port, *Imperial London*, p. 28.

170 'How many millions': Quoted in *ibid.*, p. 31.

170 'Up they came': G. W. Steevens, *Daily Mail*, 23 June 1897, quoted in Judd, *Empire*, p. 134.

171 'No one ever': Hibbert, *Queen Victoria*, p. 457.

171 'imperialism is in': Quoted in Judd, *Empire*, p. 133, and Hammertown and Cannadine, 'Conflict and Consensus on a Ceremonial Occasion: The Diamond Jubilee in Cambridge in 1897', p. 112.

172 'patriotism, conventionally defined': Robertson, *Patriotism and Empire*, p. 138.

173 'mere victory is': Callwell, *Small Wars*, p. 151. Callwell's book went through three editions by 1910.

173 'necessity by which': Melbourne to Howick, 16 December 1837, quoted in Darwin, 'Imperialism and the Victorians: The Dynamics of Territorial Expansion', p. 624.

173 'foster some sort': Earl of Cromer, 'The government of subject races', *Political and Literary Essays*, quoted in J. G. Darwin, 'Baring, Evelyn, first earl of Cromer', in *Dictionary of National Biography*.

174 'any more than': Quoted in Cromer, *Modern Egypt*, vol. I, p. 92, n. 1.

177 'Much as I like': Letter from Robert Hart (Inspector General of Chinese Maritime Customs) to J. D. Campell (his agent in London), 11 August 1880, printed in Fairbank, Bruner and Matheson, eds., *The I.G. in Peking*, p. 332.

178 'The Soudanese are': *Pall Mall Gazette*, 9 January 1884.

179 'He seems to': Quoted by Richard Davenport-Hines in *Dictionary of National Biography* entry.

180 'It's funny that': *Ibid.*

180 'When God was': Quoted in Moorehead, *The White Nile*, p. 263.

180 In his journal: Quoted in *ibid.*, p. 245.

180 'NOW MARK THIS': Quoted in *ibid.*, p. 258.

180 'Khartoum is all': Quoted in *ibid.*, p. 261.

182 'a mongrel scum': Quoted in Longford, *A Pilgrimage of Passion*, p. 214.

182 'not help singing': Quoted in *ibid.*, p. 215.

182 'for I am': Gordon, *Khartoum Journal*, pp. 56–7.

182 'A man who': Cromer, *Modern Egypt*, vol. I, p. 448.

183 'That the promises': Quoted in Moorehead, *The White Nile*, pp. 270–71.

183 Sir Edward Elgar: He abandoned the idea, but much of the music found its way into his oratorio *The Dream of Gerontius*, a setting to music of Newman's poem, which was a favourite of Gordon's.

183 'England stands before': Stevenson, *Selected Letters of Robert Louis Stevenson*, p. 276.

183 'to try to nurse': W. T. Stead, in *The Century: A Popular Quarterly*, vol. 28 (August 1884), p. 561.

183 'In him were': *Pall Mall Gazette*, 11 February 1885.

183 'General Gordon does': Cromer, *Modern Egypt*, vol. II, p. 11.

184 'Thou shalt be': Quoted in Moorehead, *The White Nile*, p. 287.

185 'to regard the': Churchill, *The River War*, vol. II, p. 196.

185 'a good dusting': Quoted in D'Este, *Warlord*, p. 105.

186 'even ham sandwiches': Brendon, *Winston Churchill*, p. 28.

186 'disentombment' of the Mahdi: Hansard, 4th series, vol. 72, col. 359, 5 June 1899.

188 'wrangle between two': Blunt, *My Diaries*, vol. I, p. 367.

188 'a bitterness and': Churchill, *The River War*, vol. II, p. 212.

189 'persuade most people': Forster, 13 May 1884, House of Commons, quoted in Shannon, *Gladstone*, p. 332.

189 'Our side in': Quoted in Hopkins, 'The Victorians and Africa: A Reconsideration of the Occupation of Egypt, 1882', p. 384.

Chapter Ten

193 'Many there were': Hyam, *Britain's Imperial Century*, p. 7.

193 'What is he': The story is told in Henderson, *Set under Authority*, p. 14, and obviously needs to be taken with a large pinch of salt.

194 'in forty years': Scott, *The Jewel in the Crown*, pp. 223–4.

195 'produced an English': Lugard, *The Dual Mandate in Tropical Africa*, p. 132.

196 'the white man's burden, Lord': Blunt, *The Poetical Works of Wilfrid Scawen Blunt*, vol. II, p. 285.

196 'In Memory of': Kernot, *British Public Schools War Memorials*, p. 30.

198 'Rapidly we learned': James, *Beyond a Boundary*, pp. 25, 26.

198 'every department of': Cromer, *Political and Literary Essays, 3rd Series*, pp. 13–14.

198 'we do not merely': Miles, 'Sport and Athletics, and the British Empire', pp. 491, 499.

199 'I am Sandi': Quoted in Anthony Kirk-Greene, 'Imperial Administration and the Athletic Imperative: The Case of the District Officer in Africa', in Baker and Mangan, eds., *Sport in Africa*, pp. 87–8.

199 'Documents no longer': Quoted in Morris, *Pax Britannica*, p. 189.

199 'Why, some of': Quoted in Bell, *Glimpses of a Governor's Life*, p. 79.

200 a tiny force: Kirk-Greene, 'The Sudan Political Service: A Profile in the Sociology of Imperialism', p. 21.

200 'by accident': Kirk-Greene, *Britain's Imperial Administrators*, p. 180.

201 from country families: Or 'from the families of members of the imperial civil service or professional classes who had their roots and traditions in the English countryside', writes Robert Collins, who analysed the recruitment figures in 'The Sudan Political Service: A Portrait of the "Imperialists"'.

201 'Beware and take': Quoted in Walvin, *Black Ivory*, p. 26.

201 'Bankrupts, divorcees, cashiered': Pakenham, *Out in the Noonday Sun*, p. 48.

201 'Mr Rowland called': Robert V. Kubicek, *The Administration of Imperialism*, quoted in *ibid.*, p. 48.

202 'We had often': Furse, *Aucuparius*, p. 189.

202 'Don't turn round': *Ibid.*, p. 148. This last wasn't necessarily a trick question. When another candidate was asked what he planned to do that afternoon and replied that he was planning to go to Lord's, he was met with the disarming 'Splendid. I'll just get my hat and come along with you.' (W. A. Dodd, manuscript contribution to Oxford Development Records Project, 'The Development of Education in Tanzania' (1982), Bodleian Library of Commonwealth and African Studies at Rhodes House, Oxford, MSS Afr. s. 1755, quoted in Baker and Mangan, eds., *Sport in Africa*, p. 94.

203 'A man's face': Furse, *Aucuparius*, p. 67.

203 the handshake: *Ibid.*, pp. 230–31.

203 'YOU HAVE BEEN': This was the title of Alan Forward's recollections of his time there as a district officer, although he did not receive his telegram until 1954.

203 'that admirable class': Furse, *Aucuparius*, p. 9.

203 'a service of': Bradley, *Once a District Officer*, p. 29.

203 'I was head': Allen, *Plain Tales from the British Empire*, p. 313.

204 'spent three months': *Ibid.*, p. 28.

205 'What shall it': Furse, *Aucuparius*, p. 145.

205 'The abolition of': *Ibid.*, p. 309.

205 'An occasional lick': Brendon, *Eminent Edwardians*, p. 220.

205 'a tussle with': *Ibid.*, p. 223.

207 'They are bad': Jeal, *Baden-Powell*, p. 220.

208 'burrowed into the': Maj. H. de Montmorency diary, quoted in Jeal, *Baden-Powell*, p. 222.

208 'A second shell': Quoted in *ibid.*, p. 247.

210 'I suppose every': Quoted in *ibid.*, p. 391.

210 ' "Country first, self': Baden-Powell, *Scouting for Boys*, p. 28.

210 'to be very clever': *Ibid.*, pp. 173–4.

210 'It is very necessary': *Ibid.*, p. 156.

210 'because he may': *Ibid.*, p. 142.

211 'Scouts breathe through': *Ibid.*, pp. 25–6.

211 'and if he': Jeal, *Baden-Powell*, p. 107.

211 'one of the first': Baden-Powell, *Scouting for Boys*, p. 215.

212 'trained in the': Brendon, *Eminent Edwardians*, p. 243.

212 'The Boy Scout': *Evening Standard*, 24 January 1911.

212 'Such small things': Baden-Powell, *Scouting for Boys*, p. 221.

213 'happiness doesn't come': http://scout.org/en/about_scouting/facts_figures/baden_powell/b_p_gallery/b_p_s_last_message.

Chapter Eleven

215 'His Majesty rules': *St James's Gazette*, undated press cutting, presumably January 1901, quoted in Adams, *Edwardian Heritage*, p. 18.

216 'no economic, no': 'Will the Empire Live', in Wells, *An Englishman Looks at the World*, pp. 37–40.

216 'Empire first and': Kaul, *Reporting the Raj*, p. 73.

216 'projects for general': *The Times*, 4 February 1862, quoted in Schuyler, 'The Climax of Anti-Imperialism in England', pp. 540–41.

216 'We can no': *Imperialism: Its Meanings and its Tendencies*, published by the city branch of the ILP, May 1900, quoted in Porter, *Critics of Empire*, p. 136.

216 'England for the': *Clarion*, 4 March 1893, quoted in Claeys, *Imperial Sceptics*, p. 173.

216 Wilfrid Scawen Blunt: Blunt, *My Diaries*, vol. I, pp. 375–6.

216 Lord Curzon shuddered: Lord Curzon, 'The True Imperialism', *Nineteenth Century* 63 (1908), quoted in Bernard Porter, 'The Edwardians and their Empire', in Read, ed., *Edwardian England*, p. 136.

217 'the weary Titan': Quoted in Amery, *The Life of Joseph Chamberlain*, vol. IV, p. 421.

217 'Far-called our navies': Rudyard Kipling, 'Recessional', *The Times*, 17 July 1897, reprinted in Kipling, *Poems, Ballads and Other Verses*, p. 55.

218 'sunk, burned or': Quoted in Ransford, *Livingston's Lake*, p. 238.

219 'Gott for damn': *Ibid.*, p. 241.

219 'Thanks to your': From the Imperial War Museum Archives, quoted in Paice, *World War I*, p. 20.

221 'We are, above': Quoted in Ferguson, *Empire*, pp. 305–6.

221 'Our consuls in': Marginal note by the Kaiser on a telegram from the German Ambassador in St Petersburg, quoted in Manjapra, 'The Illusions of Encounter: Muslim "Minds" and Hindu Revolutionaries in First World War Germany and After', p. 364.

223 'Israelite, Assyrian, Greek': Wavell, *Allenby*, p. 230.

224 'This is because': *Daily Mirror*, 11 December 1917, quoted in Bar-Yosef, *The Holy Land in English Culture*, p. 264.

224 'these events in': Hansard, 5th Series, vol. 100, cols. 2212, 2211, 20 December 1917, quoted in Bar-Yosef, *The Holy Land in English Culture*, p. 292.

226 'him of the': Mansfield, *The Arabs*, p. 165.

227 'England will understand': Rose, *Chaim Weizmann*, p. 137.

228 'would develop the': *Ibid.*, p. 144.

228 'bridge between Europe': Quoted in Ronald Hyam, 'Churchill and the British Empire', in Blake and Louis, eds., *Churchill*, p. 171.

228 'Mr Balfour's whole': Quoted in Brendon, *Eminent Victorians*, p. 89.

229 'Were any of': Quoted in *ibid.*, p. 79.

229 'about as intelligible': Quoted in *ibid.*, p. xv.

229 'His Majesty's Government': Quoted in Karsh and Karsh, eds., *Empires of the Sand*, p. 254.

230 'I do not': 'A Defence of the Mandate. Speech delivered by the Earl of Balfour, as the Lord President of the Council, on June 21st, 1922, in the House of Lords on a motion introduced by Lord Islington, proposing that Great Britain should not accept the Mandate for Palestine', in Balfour, *Speeches on Zionism*, pp. 59–64.

230 'they will not': 'Speech delivered at a public demonstration held by the English Zionist Federation under the Chairmanship of Lord Rothschild, on July 12th, 1920, at the Royal Albert Hall, for the purpose of celebrating the conferment of the Mandate for Palestine upon Great Britain and the incorporation of the Balfour Declaration in the Treaty of Peace with Turkey', in Balfour, *Speeches on Zionism*, pp. 23–5.

230 'I had a well-spent': Bell, *The Letters of Gertrude Bell*, vol. II, p. 149.

230 'the maker of Iraq': Philby, 'Gertrude Bell', p. 804.

231 'The British flag': Quoted in James, *The Rise and Fall of the British Empire*, p. 355.

233 'to convert the': Robinson, 'The Moral Disarmament of African Empire, 1919–1947', p. 88.

234 'I venture to': Speech by Madan Mohan Malaviya in the Imperial Legislative Council, 23 March 1917, in Malaviya, *Speeches and Writings of Pandit Madan Mohan Malaviya*, p. 129.

235 'if Britain withdrew': Lloyd George to the House of Commons, 2 August 1922, quoted in Rumbold, *Watershed in India*, p. 314.

235 'The people are': Morris, *Farewell the Trumpets*, p. 278.

235 'send an officer': Quoted in Collett, *The Butcher of Amritsar*, p. 240.

236 'unexpected gift of': Quoted in *ibid.*, p. 255.

237 'then they would': Quoted in *ibid.*, p. 336.

237 'every white man's': 'Shooting an Elephant', in Orwell, *The Orwell Reader: Fiction, Essays and Reportage*, p. 7.

237 'When a handful': Carlyon Bellairs, letter to *The Times*, 8 July 1920.

238 'an episode which': Sayer, 'British Reaction to the Amritsar Massacre, 1919–1920', p. 131.

238 'We do not': Quoted in *ibid.*, p. 133.

239 'plunge his knife': Quoted in Brendon, *The Decline and Fall of the British Empire*, p. 295.

239 'the Irish wound': Quoted in Keith Jeffery, 'Introduction', in Jeffery, ed., *'An Irish Empire?'*, pp. 6–7.

239 'My world-wide Empire': Quoted in *ibid.*, p. 7.

240 'if today India': O'Hegarty, *A History of Ireland under the Union*, p. 774.

Chapter Twelve

241 'You young worms!': Brabazon, *Memories of the Nineteenth Century*, p. 19.

242 'slackness, indifference and': *The Duty and Discipline Movement and the War*, leaflet (London, 1917).

242 'Britons have ruled': Meath, 'Duty and Discipline in the Training of Children', p. 9.

242 'subordination of selfish': Lord Meath, letter to *The Times*, 24 May 1921.

242 'Every time one': Arnold-Forster, *The Citizen Reader*, pp. 22–3. Arnold-Forster was a grandson of the great headmaster of Rugby, Thomas Arnold, and a future secretary of state for war.

243 'free discipline, manly': 'General Objects', Church Lads' Brigade, *Fifth Annual Report, 1896–1897*, quoted in Springhall, *Youth, Empire and Society*, p. 123.

243 'many of the': W. F. Airs and J. S. Streeter, eds., *Sixty Years a Cadet, 1889–1949: A Short History of the 1st London Cadet Battalion*, quoted in Springhall, *Youth, Empire and Society*, p. 77.

243 'the greater portion': *Cassell's Illustrated History of England*, vol. IX, pp. 195–6.

243 'it was on': Fletcher and Kipling, *A School History of England*, p. 186.

243 'an all-wise and': Lord Meath, address to the Empire Day Movement, 24 May 1904, quoted in MacKenzie, *Propaganda and Empire*, p. 232.

245 'in certain fundamentals': Wodehouse, 'The Rummy Affair of Old Biffy', p. 161.

246 'We believe', he said: Quoted in Wilson, *After the Victorians*, p. 273.

246 'Empire has happened': 'Will the Empire Live?', in Wells, *An Englishman Looks at the World*, p. 41.

248 'The middle-class families': Orwell, *The Lion and the Unicorn*, p. 36.

250 'at the Workers'': *Forward*, 13 August 1938, quoted in Britton, ' "Come and See the Empire by the All Red Route!": Anti-Imperialism and Exhibitions in Interwar Britain', p. 78.

251 'the fate of': Quoted in MacKenzie, *Propaganda and Empire*, p. 234.

251 'respect the right': Louis, *Imperialism at Bay*, pp. 123–4.

251 'I have not': Churchill, 'The End of the Beginning' speech, Mansion House, 10 November 1942, quoted in Sandbrook, *Never Had It So Good*, p. 281.

252 'sturdy British infantrymen': *The Times*, 8 December 1941.

253 'the survival of': Quoted in James, *The Rise and Fall of the British Empire*, p. 491.

253 'the possibility of': Churchill, *The Second World War*, vol. IV: *The Hinge of Fate*, p. 43.

253 'I trust you'll': Morris, *Farewell the Trumpets*, p. 452.

254 'Thus', Churchill proclaimed: Quoted in *ibid.*, p. 451.

254 'until after protracted': Quoted in Gilbert *Churchill: A Life*, p. 716.

255 'the end of': Quoted in Brendon, *The Decline and Fall of the British Empire*, p. 422.

256 'The British Empire': Quoted in Judd, *Empire*, p. 310.

256 'We have always': Attlee, quoted in the *Daily Herald*, 16 August 1941.

256 The Labour manifesto: Dale, ed., *Labour Party General Election Manifestos*, pp. 52, 59, 72.

257 'their cookery from Paris': Orwell, *The Lion and the Unicorn*, p. 63.

258 'I hate Indians': John Barnes and David Nicholson, eds., *The Empire at Bay: The Leo Amery Diaries, 1929–1945*, quoted in Louis, 'Churchill and the Liquidation of the British Empire'.

258 'if Christ came': Churchill, 'Our Duty in India', speech, 18 March 1931, printed in the *Spectator*, 6 June 1931, p. 533.

259 'the chatterboxes who': Callahan, *Churchill*, p. 28.

259 'War has been': *Daily Mail*, 16 November 1929, quoted in Herman, *Gandhi & Churchill*, p. 323.

259 'a monstrous monument': Mansergh, *The Commonwealth Experience*, p. 267n.

259 a peevish telegram: Wavell, *Wavell: The Viceroy's Journal*, p. 78.

259 'on the subject': Barnes and Nicholson, eds., *The Empire at Bay*, pp. 988, 993.

260 'territory over which': Hansard, 5th series, vol. 426, cols. 1256–7, 1 August 1946, quoted in Louis, 'Churchill and the Liquidation of the British Empire'.

260 'men of straw': Quoted in Louis, 'Churchill and the Liquidation of the British Empire'.

260 'Britain's desertion of': Quoted in Sarvepalli Gopal, 'Churchill and India', in Blake and Louis, eds., *Churchill*, pp. 470–71.

261 'melancholy event': Quoted in Herman, *Gandhi & Churchill*, p. 591.

261 'not aware of': Churchill note of 6 July 1945, quoted in Sherman, *Mandate Days*, p. 171.

262 'it surely is': W. G. Fitzgerald to Sir Harold MacMichael, 8 November 1947, quoted in Sherman, *Mandate Days*, p. 210.

263 'I suppose I': Quoted in Sherman, *Mandate Days*, p. 241.

263 'an entirely new': Quoted in Stewart, 'The British Reaction to the Conquest of Everest', p. 29.

263 'a group of': Speech in Ghana, 1961, quoted in James, *The Rise and Fall of the British Empire*, p. 557.

264 'The lamps are': Grey, *Twenty-Five Years*, vol. II, p. 20.

265 'altogether a most': Lindsay, *The Crawford Papers*, p. 590.

265 'It was I': Quoted in McDonald, *A Man of The Times*, p. 149.

265 'Politicians don't know': *New Statesman*, 15 December 1956, quoted in James, *The Rise and Fall of the British Empire*, p. 580.

265 'The seizure is': *The Times* and the *Daily Mail*, 28 July 1956, quoted in Pearson, *Sir Anthony Eden and the Suez Crisis*, p. 29.

266 'The United States': Dulles press conference, quoted in *ibid.*, p . 115.

267 'I want him murdered': Quoted in Kyle, *Suez*, p. 99.

267 'Britain and the': *Daily Herald*, 28 July 1956; quoted in Parmentier, 'The British Press in the Suez Crisis', p. 437, n. 12.

268 'I'm finished. I': Quoted in Brendon, *The Decline and Fall of the British Empire*, p. 496.

268 'Your return is': Quoted in Rhodes James, *Anthony Eden*, pp. 588–9.

268 'the same very': Quoted in *ibid.*, p. 592.

268 'For a moment': Quoted in *ibid.*, p. 594.

268 'The doctors have': Quoted in *ibid.*, p. 597.

270 'the Mecca of': Quoted in Berman, *Control and Crisis in Colonial Kenya*, pp. 372–3.

271 'All government, all': Quoted in Brendon, *The Decline and Fall of the British Empire*, p. 564.

272 'Are these people': Quoted in Horne, *Macmillan*, vol. II: *1957–86*, p. 190.

Chapter Thirteen

277 'as with so': *Daily Telegraph*, 5 April 2011.

282 at schools intended: Indeed, Richard Ingrams, Paul Foot, Willie Rushton and Christopher Booker of *Private Eye* had all been at Shrewsbury School together.

283 In one sketch: Quoted in Ward, *British Culture and the End of Empire*, pp. 104–5.

284 'if our ancestors': Quoted in Ferguson, *Empire*, p. 239.

284 'free aspirins and': Quoted in Ashton and Louis, eds., *East of Suez and the Commonwealth*, p. xlii.

Bibliography

Primary Sources

Bodleian Library of Commonwealth and African Studies at Rhodes House, Oxford, MSS Afr. s. 1755

Bodleian Library of Commonwealth and African Studies at Rhodes House, Oxford, MSS Afr. t. 1

Bodleian Library of Commonwealth and African Studies at Rhodes House, Oxford, MSS Brit. Emp. s. 415

Kingston, National Library of Jamaica, MS 105

Lincolnshire County Archives, Diary of Thomas Thistlewood

Newspapers

The Century: A Popular Quarterly

Daily Mail

Pall Mall Gazette

The Telegraph (Calcutta)

The Times

General Reference

Oxford Dictionary of National Biography

Oxford English Dictionary

Parliamentary Debates (Hansard)

Printed Sources

Abbott, George, 'A Re-Examination of the 1929 Colonial Development Act', *Economic History Review* 24 (1971)

Abernethy, David B., *The Dynamics of Global Dominance: European Overseas Empires 1415–1980* (New Haven, 2001)

Ackroyd, Peter, *London: The Biography* (New York, 2001)

Adams, William Scovell, *Edwardian Heritage: A Study in British History, 1901–1906* (London, 1949)

Addison, Kenneth N., *We Hold These Truths to be Self-Evident: An Interdisciplinary Analysis of the Roots of Racism and Slavery in America* (Lanham, Maryland, 2009)

Allen, Charles, *The Buddha and the Sahibs: The Men Who Discovered India's Lost Religion* (London, 2003)

——, *Plain Tales from the British Empire* (London, 2008)

Amery, Julian and J. L. Garvin, *The Life of Joseph Chamberlain*, 6 vols. (London, 1932–69)

Anderson, Aeneas, *A Narrative of the British Embassy to China in the Years 1792, 1793 and 1794* (London, 1795)

Anderson, Catherine E., 'A Zulu King in Victorian London: Race, Royalty and Imperialist Aesthetics in Late Nineteenth-Century Britain', *Visual Resources* 24 (2008)

Anderson, David, *Histories of the Hanged: Britain's Dirty War in Kenya and the End of Empire* (London, 2005)

Andrews, Kenneth R., *Trade, Plunder and Settlement: Maritime Enterprise and the Genesis of the British Empire, 1480–1630* (Cambridge, 1984)

[Anonymous], 'Observations on the Trade with China, London 1822', *Edinburgh Review* 39 (1824)

Ardis, Anne L. and Leslie Ann Lewis, eds., *Women's Experience of Modernity, 1875–1945* (Baltimore and London, 2003)

Armitage, David, 'The Cromwellian Protectorate and the Languages of Empire', *Historical Journal* 35 (1992)

Arnold, David, ed., *Imperial Medicine and Indigenous Societies* (Manchester, 1988)

Arnold-Forster, H. O., *The Citizen Reader*, 5th edn (London, 1886)

Ashton, S. R. and Wm. R. Louis, eds., *East of Suez and the Commonwealth 1964–1971* (London, 2004)

Astley, Sir John Dugdale, *Fifty Years of my Life in the World of Sport at Home and Abroad*, 2 vols. (London, 1894)

Attlee, Clement, *Empire into Commonwealth* (London, 1961)

August, T., 'The West Indies Play Wembley', *New West Indian Guide* 66 (1992)

Austen, Jane, *Emma* (London, 1996; orig. pub. 1815)

——, *Mansfield Park*, ed. Ian Littlewood (Ware, Hertfordshire, 2000; orig. pub. 1814)

Bacon, Francis, *The Essays of Francis Bacon*, ed. Clark Sutherland Northup (New York, 1908)

——, *The Works of Francis Bacon, Baron of Verulam, Viscount St Alban, and Lord High Chancellor of England*, 10 vols. (London, 1870)

Baden-Powell, Agnes and Robert Baden-Powell, *The Handbook for Girl Guides or How Girls Can Help Build the Empire* (London, 1912)

Baden-Powell, Robert, *The Adventures of a Spy* (London, 1924)

——, *Scouting for Boys: A Handbook for Instruction in Good Citizenship*, ed. Elleke Boehmer (Oxford, 2004; orig. pub. 1908)

——, *Young Knights of the Empire: Their Code and Further Scout Yarns* (London, 1916)

Baker, William J. and J. A. Mangan, *Sport in Africa: Essays in Social History* (London, 1987)

Balfour, Arthur, *Speeches on Zionism*, ed. Israel Cohen (London, 1928)

Banks, Joseph, *The Endeavour Journal of Joseph Banks, 1768–1771*, ed. J. C. Beaglehole, 2 vols. (Sydney, 1962)

——, *The Letters of Joseph Banks: A Selection, 1768–1820*, ed. Neil Chambers (London, 2000)

Bar-Yosef, Eitan, *The Holy Land in English Culture, 1799–1917* (Oxford, 2005)

Barnes, John and David Nicholson, eds., *The Empire at Bay: The Leo Amery Diaries*, 2 vols. (London, 1988)

Barnett, Correlli, *The Collapse of British Power* (London, 1972)

Barr, Pat, *The Memsahibs: The Women of Victorian India* (London, 1976)

Barrett, Michèle and Duncan Barrett, *Star Trek: The Human Frontier* (Cambridge, 2001)

Barringer, Tim and Tom Flynn, *Colonialism and the Object: Empire, Material Culture, and the Museum* (London, 1998)

Barrow, (Sir) John, *Some Account of Public Life and a Selection from the Unpublished Writings of the Earl of Macartney*, ed. John Burrow, 2 vols. (London, 1807)

——, *Travels in China* (London, 1806)

Barstow, Phyllida, *The English Country House Party* (Wellingborough, 1989)

Basu, Shrabani, *Curry: The Story of the Nation's Favourite Dish* (Stroud, 2003)

——, *Victoria and Abdul: The True Story of the Queen's Closest Confidant* (Stroud, 2010)

Bayley, Lady Emily, *The Golden Calm: An English Lady's Life in Moghul Delhi*, ed. M. M. Kaye (Exeter, 1980)

Beaglehole, J. C., *The Exploration of the Pacific* (London, 1966)

——, *The Life of Captain James Cook* (Stanford, 1974)

Beale, Dorothy, Lucy H. M. Soulsby and Jane Frances Dove, *Work and Play in Girls' Schools. By Three Headmistresses* (London, 1898)

Bean, C. E. W., *Official History of Australia in the War of 1914–18*, 15 vols. (Sydney, 1921–43)

Belich, James, *Replenishing the Earth: The Settler Revolution and the Rise of the Anglo-World, 1783–1939* (Oxford, 2009)

Bell, Gertrude, *The Letters of Gertrude Bell*, 2 vols. (London, 1927)

Bell, Hesketh, *Glimpses of a Governor's Life, from Diaries, Letters and Memoranda* (London, 1946)

Bell, Morag, Robin Butlin and Michael Heffernan, *Geography and Imperialism, 1820–1940* (Manchester, 1995)

Bentley-Cranch, Dana, *Edward VII: Image of an Era, 1841–1910* (London, 1992)

Besant, Annie, *India: Bond or Free? A World Problem* (London, 1926)

Berman, Bruce, *Control and Crisis in Colonial Kenya: The Dialectic of Domination* (London, 1990)

Bhatia, Umej, *Forgetting Osama Bin Munqidh, Remembering Osama Bin Laden: The Crusades in Modern Muslim Memory* (Singapore, 2008)

Bindoff, S. T., 'The Stuarts and their Style', *English Historical Review* LX (1945)

Bladen, F. M., *Historical Records of New South Wales*, 8 vols. (Sydney, 1892–1901)

Blake, Robert and Wm. Roger Louis, eds., *Churchill: A Major New Assessment of his Life in Peace and War* (New York and London, 1993)

Bliss, Robert M., *Revolution and Empire: English Politics and the American Colonies in the Seventeenth Century* (Manchester, 1990)

Blunt, Wilfrid Scawen, *My Diaries: Being a Personal Narrative of Events, 1888–1914*, 2 vols. (London, 1919–20)

——, *The Poetical Works of Wilfrid Scawen Blunt*, 2 vols. (London, 1914)

Bond, Brian, 'Recruiting the Victorian Army, 1870–92', *Victorian Studies* 5 (1962)

——, ed., *Victorian Military Campaigns* (London, 1967)

Boswell, James, *The Life of Samuel Johnson*, ed. John Wilson Croker, 5 vols. (London, 1831; orig. pub. 1791)

Brabazon, Reginald, Earl of Meath, *Memories of the Nineteenth Century* (London, 1923)

——, *Memories of the Twentieth Century* (London, 1924)

Bradley, Kenneth, *Once a District Officer* (London, 1966)

Brandt, Anthony, *The Man Who Ate his Boots: Sir John Franklin and the Tragic History of the Northwest Passage* (London, 2011)

Brantlinger, Patrick and William B. Thesing, eds., *A Companion to the Victorian Novel* (Oxford, 2002)

Brendon, Piers, *The Decline and Fall of the British Empire 1781–1997* (London, 2007)

——, *Eminent Edwardians* (London, 2003)

——, 'A Moral Audit of the British Empire', *History Today* 57 (2007)

——, *Winston Churchill: A Biography* (New York, 1984)

Brett, Judith, *Australian Liberals and the Moral Middle Class: From Alfred Deakin to John Howard* (Cambridge, 2003)

Bridges, R. C., 'The R.G.S. and the African Exploration Fund 1876–80', *Geographical Journal* 129 (1963)

Brinkley, Douglas and David R. Facey-Crowther, eds., *The Atlantic Charter* (New York, 1994)

Britton, Sarah, ' "Come and See the Empire by the All Red Route!": Anti-Imperialism and Exhibitions in Interwar Britain', *History Workshop Journal* 69 (2010)

Brodie, Fawn McKay, *The Devil Drives: A Life of Sir Richard Burton* (New York and London, 1984)

Brodrick, William, Earl of Middleton, *Records and Reactions, 1856–1939* (London, 1939)

Brown, Judith, 'Britain, India and the War of 1914–18', in *India and World War I*, ed. Dewitt C. Ellinwood and S. D. Pradhan (New Delhi, 1978)

—— and Wm. Roger Louis, eds., *The Oxford History of the British Empire*, vol. IV: *The Twentieth Century* (Oxford and New York, 1999)

Bruce, William Napier, *Life of General Sir Charles Napier* (London, 1885)

Bryan, William Jennings, *The World's Famous Orations*, 10 vols. (New York and London, 1906)

Bryant, G. J., 'Scots in India in the Eighteenth Century', *Scottish Historical Review* 64 (1985)

Buchan, John, *Greenmantle* (London, 1916)

Buckland, Frank, 'The Hippopotamus and her Baby', *Popular Science* (1873)

Buettner, Elizabeth, *Empire Families: Britons and Late Imperial India* (Oxford, 2004)

——, 'Going for an Indian': South Asian Restaurants and the Limits of Multiculturalism in Britain', *Journal of Modern History* 80 (2008)

Bullock, Alan and Maurice Shock, eds., *The Liberal Tradition: From Fox to Keynes* (Oxford, 1967)

Burbank, Jane and Frederick Cooper, *Empire in World History: Power and the Politics of Difference* (Oxford, 2010)

Burke, Edmund, *Reflections on the Revolution in France: and on the proceedings in certain societies in London relative to that event. In a letter intended to have been sent to a gentleman in Paris* (London, 1790)

——, *The Writings and Speeches of Edmund Burke*, ed. Paul Langford, 9 vols. (Oxford, 1981–2000)

Burnard, Trevor, *Mastery, Tyranny, and Desire: Thomas Thistlewood and his Slaves in the Anglo-Jamaican World* (Chapel Hill and London, 2004)

Burnett, Francis Hodgson, *The Secret Garden* (Middlesex, 2007; first pub. 1911)

Burton, Isabel, *The Life of Captain Sir Richard F. Burton*, 2 vols. (London, 1893)

Burton, Richard, *Falconry in the Valley of the Indus* (Oxford, 1997; orig. pub. 1852)

——, *The Lake Regions of Central Africa*, 2 vols. (New York, 1961; orig. pub. 1860)

——, *Wanderings in West Africa from Liverpool to Fernando Po*, 2 vols. (London, 1863)

—— and James M'Queen, *The Nile Basin*, 2 vols. (London, 1864)

Cain, P. J. and A. G. Hopkins, *British Imperialism: Innovation and Expansion, 1688–1914* (London and New York, 1993)

Callahan, Raymond, *Churchill: Retreat from Empire* (Wilmington, Delaware, 1984)

Callwell, Charles E., *Small Wars: A Tactical Textbook for Imperial Soldiers* (London, 1990; orig. pub. 1896 as *Small Wars: Their Principles and Practice*)

Cannadine, David, *Ornamentalism: How the British Saw their Empire* (Oxford, 2001)

Canny, Nicholas, 'The Ideology of English Colonization: From Ireland to America', *William and Mary Quarterly* 30 (1973)

——, ed., *The Oxford History of the British Empire*, vol. I: *The Origins of Empire, British Overseas Enterprise to the Close of the Seventeenth Century* (Oxford and New York, 1998)

——, 'To Establish a Common Wealthe: Captain John Smith as New World Colonist', *Virginia Magazine of History and Biography* 96 (1988)

Carlos, Ann M. and Stephen Nicholas, ' "Giants of an Earlier Capitalism": The Chartered Trading Companies as Modern Multinationals', *Business History Review* 62 (1988)

——, 'Theory and History: Seventeenth-Century Joint-Stock Chartered Trading Companies', *Journal of Economic History* 56 (1996)

Cassell, John, John Frederick Smith and William Howitt, *Cassell's Illustrated History of England*, 9 vols. (London, 1906)

Chamberlain, Joseph, *Mr Chamberlain's Speeches*, ed. Charles W. Boyd, 2 vols. (London, 1914)

Chatterton, Edward Keble, *Britain's Record: What She Has Done for the World* (London, 1911)

Chaudhuri, K., *The English East India Company: The Study of an Early Joint Stock Company, 1600–1640* (London, 1965)

Chaudhuri, Sashi Bhusan, *English Historical Writings on the Indian Mutiny* (Calcutta, 1979)

Chen, Jeng-Guo S., 'Gendering India: Effeminacy and the Scottish Enlightenment's Debates over Virtue and Luxury', *Eighteenth Century* 51 (2010)

Chesterton, G. K., *The New Jerusalem* (London 1920)

Chitty, Susan, *Playing the Game: A Biography of Sir Henry Newbolt* (London, 1997)

Churchill, Winston, *Blood, Toil, Tears and Sweat: Winston Churchill's Famous Speeches*, ed. David Cannadine (London, 1990)

——, *My African Journey* (London, 1908)

——, *My Early Life: A Roving Commission* (New York, 1930)

——, *Never Give In! The Best of Winston Churchill's Speeches* (London, 2003)

——, *The River War*, 2 vols. (London, 1899)

——, *The Second World War*, 6 vols. (London, 1948–54)

Claeys, Gregory, *Imperial Sceptics: British Critics of Empire, 1850–1920* (Cambridge, 2010)

Clark, Adrian, 'Pomegranates, Opium and Poppycock', *Northern Scotland* 2 (2011)

Clark, J. C. D., 'Protestantism, Nationalism, and National Identity 1660–1832', *Historical Journal* 43 (2000)

Clarkson, Thomas, *The History of the Rise, Progress, and Accomplishment of the Abolition of the African Slave-Trade by the British Parliament*, 2 vols. (London, 1808)

Collett, Nigel, *The Butcher of Amritsar: General Reginald Dyer* (London, 2005)

Colley, Linda, *Britons: Forging the Nation, 1707–1837* (London, 1992)

——, *Captives: Britain, Empire and the World, 1600–1850* (London, 2002)

Collingridge, Vanessa, *Captain Cook: The Life, Death and Legacy of History's Greatest Explorer* (London, 2002)

Collins, E. J. T., 'Food Adulteration and Food Safety in Britain in the 19th and early 20th Centuries', *Food Policy* 18 (1993)

Collins, Robert, 'The Sudan Political Service: A Portrait of the "Imperialists"', *African Affairs* 71 (1972)

Collis, Henry, Fred Hurll and Rex Hazlewood, *B.P.'s Scouts: An Official History of the Boy Scouts Association* (London, 1961)

Conekin, Becky, *The Autobiography of a Nation: The 1951 Festival of Britain* (Manchester, 2003)

Conniff, Michael L. and Thomas J. Davis, *Africans in the Americas: A History of the Black Diaspora* (New York, 1994)

Conrad, Joseph, 'Geography and Some Explorers', *National Geographic Magazine* 45 (1924)

Constantine, Stephen, Maurice Kirby and Mary Rose, eds., *The First World War in British History* (London, 1995)

Conway, Stephen, *The British Isles and the War of American Independence* (Oxford, 2000)

Cook, E. T. and A. Wedderburn, eds., *The Library Edition of the Works of John Ruskin*, 39 vols. (London, 1903–12)

Cook, James, *The Journals of Captain James Cook*, ed. J. C. Beaglehole, 4 vols. (Cambridge, 1955–74)

Corbett, Julian S., *England in the Seven Years' War*, 2 vols. (London, 1907)

Crane, David, *Scott of the Antarctic: A Life of Courage and Tragedy in the Extreme South* (London, 2005)

Cresswell, Nicholas, *The Journal of Nicholas Cresswell, 1774–1777* (New York, 1924)

Crocker, Walter Russell, *On Governing Colonies: Being an Outline of the Real Issues and a Comparison of the British, French and Belgian Approach to Them* (London, 1947)

Cromer, Evelyn Baring, Earl of, *Modern Egypt*, 2 vols. (London, 1908)

——, *Political and Literary Essays, 3rd series* (London, 1916)

Cross, Colin, *The Fall of the British Empire, 1918–1968* (London, 1968)

Cumberland, Richard, *The West Indian: A Comedy* (London, 1771)

Cundall, Frank, *The Governors of Jamaica in the Seventeenth Century* (London, 1936)

——, *Historic Jamaica* (London, 1915)

Cunningham, Hugh, 'Jingoism in 1877–78', *Victorian Studies* 14 (1971)

——, *The Volunteer Force, A Social and Political History, 1859–1908* (London, 1975)

Cunningham, Peter, *Hand-Book of London* (London, 1850)

Curtis, Wayne, *And a Bottle of Rum: A History of the New World in Ten Cocktails* (New York, 2006)

Dale, Iain, ed., *Labour Party General Election Manifestos, 1900–1997* (London, 2000)

Dalrymple, William, *The Last Mughal: The Fall of a Dynasty: Delhi, 1857* (London, 2006)

Dalton, Cornelius Neale, *The Life of Thomas Pitt* (Cambridge, 1915)

Dalziel, Nigel, *The Penguin Historical Atlas of the British Empire* (London, 2006)

Darwin, Charles, *The Descent of Man*, 2 vols. (New York, 1902; orig. pub. 1871)

——, *On the Origin of Species*, ed. Gillian Beer (Oxford, 2008; orig. pub. 1859)

——, *Voyages of the Adventure and Beagle* (London, 1860)

Darwin, John, *The Empire Project* (Cambridge, 2009)

——, 'The Fear of Falling: British Politics and Imperial Decline since 1900', *Transactions of the Royal Historical Society* 36 (1986)

——, 'Imperialism and the Victorians: The Dynamics of Territorial Expansion', *English Historical Review* 112 (1997)

——, 'Imperialism in Decline? Tendencies in British Imperial Policy between the Wars', *Historical Journal* 23 (1980)

David, Saul, *Victoria's Wars: The Rise of Empire* (London, 2006)

Davies, Kenneth Gordon, *The Royal African Company* (London, 1957)

Defoe, Daniel, *Robinson Crusoe*, ed. Michael Shinagel (London, 1994)

——, *Roxana: or, the Fortunate Mistress*, ed. John Mullan (Oxford, 1996)

——, *A Tour through the Whole Island of Great Britain,* ed. Pat Rogers (London, 1971; orig. pub. 1724–7)

D'Este, Carlos, *Warlord: A Life of Churchill at War, 1874–1945* (London, 2009)

Devine, T. M., *Scotland's Empire 1600–1815* (London, 2003)

Dickens, Charles, *The British Academy Pilgrim Edition of the Letters of Charles Dickens*, ed. Madeline House, Graham Storey and Kathleen Tillotson, 12 vols. (Oxford, 1965–2002)

——, 'The Lost Arctic Voyagers', *Household Words* (1854)

Dickinson, H. T., ed., *Britain and the American Revolution* (London, 1998)

Dirks, Nicholas, *The Scandal of Empire: India and the Creation of Imperial Britain* (London, 2006)

Diver, Kathleen Helen Maud, *The Englishwoman in India* (Edinburgh and London, 1909)

Dooley, Howard, 'Great Britain's "Last Battle" in the Middle East: Notes on Cabinet Planning during the Suez Crisis of 1956', *International History Review* 11 (1989)

Dorril, Stephen, *MI6: Inside the Covert World of Her Majesty's Secret Intelligence Service* (New York, 2002)

Doyle, Arthur Conan, *The New Annotated Sherlock Holmes*, ed. Leslie Klinger (New York, 2006)

——, *The Penguin Complete Sherlock Holmes* (London, 2009)

——, *The Sign of Four* (London, 1982; orig. pub. 1890)

Draper, Nick, ' "Possessing Slaves": Ownership, Compensation and Metropolitan Society in Britain at the Time of Emancipation 1834–40', *History Workshop Journal* 64 (2007)

Drescher, Seymour, 'Whose Abolition? Popular Pressure and the Ending of the British Slave Trade', *Past & Present* 143 (1994)

Driver, Felix, *Geography Militant: Cultures of Exploration and Empire* (Oxford, 2001)

—— and David Gilbert, 'Capital and Empire: Geographies of Imperial London', *GeoJournal* 51 (2000)

—— and David Gilbert, 'Heart of Empire? Landscape, Space and Performance in Imperial London', *Society and Space* 16 (1998)

Duara, Prasenjit, ed., *Decolonization: Perspectives from Now and Then* (London, 2004)

Duberman, Martin, *Paul Robeson: A Biography* (New York, 1988)

Dunae, Patrick, 'Boy's Literature and the Idea of Empire, 1870–1914', *Victorian Studies* 24 (1980)

Duncan, Sara Jeannette, 'A Mother in India', in *The Pool in the Desert* (Teddington, 2007; first pub. 1903)

Dutta, Krishna, *Calcutta: A Cultural and Literary History* (Oxford, 2003)

Eade, Philip, *Sylvia: Queen of the Headhunters* (London, 2008)

Earle, Peter, *The Sack of Panama: Sir Henry Morgan's Adventures on the Spanish Main* (New York, 1982)

Edwardes, Sir Herbert Benjamin and Herman Merivale, *Life of Sir Henry Lawrence* (London, 1873)

Edwards, E., *The Life of Sir Walter Ralegh*, 2 vols. (London, 1868)

Eldridge, C. C., ed., *British Imperialism in the Nineteenth Century* (London, 1984)

Ellinwood, Dewitt C. and S. D. Pradhan, *India and World War I* (New Delhi, 1978)

Elliott, John Huxtable, *Empires of the Atlantic World: Britain and Spain in North America 1492–1830* (New Haven and London, 2006)

Ellis, George E., *Life of William Penn* (New York, 1904)

Esquemeling, A. O., *Bucaniers of America* (London, 1684)

Fairbank, John King, Katherine Frost Bruner and Elizabeth MacLeod Matheson, eds., *The I. G. in Peking: Letters of Robert Hart, Chinese Maritime Customs, 1868–1907*, 2 vols. (Cambridge, Massachusetts, 1975)

Fara, Patricia, *Sex, Botany and Empire* (Cambridge, 2003)

Farwell, Bryan, *The Great War in Africa, 1914–1918* (London, 1987)

Ferguson, Niall, *Empire: How Britain Made the Modern World* (London, 2004)

Fieldhouse, David, *The Colonial Empires* (London, 1966)

Fishlock, Trevor, *Conquerors of Time: Exploration and Invention in the Age of Daring* (London, 2004)

Fletcher, C. R. L. and Rudyard Kipling, *A School History of England* (Oxford, 1911)

Flint, John, *Cecil Rhodes* (London, 1976)

Forster, E. M., *A Passage to India* (London, 1985; first pub. 1924)

Frey, Charles, '*The Tempest* and the New World', *Shakespeare Quarterly* 30 (1979)

Frost, Alan, *Convicts and Empire: A Naval Question 1776–1811* (Oxford, 1980)

Fry, Michael, *The Scottish Empire* (Edinburgh, 2001)

Fryer, Peter, *Staying Power: The History of Black People in Britain* (London, 1984)

Fuchs, Barbara, 'Faithless Empires: Pirates, Renegadoes, and the English Nation', *English Literary History* 67 (2000)

Fulford, Tim and Peter Kitson, eds., *Romanticism and Colonialism: Writing and Empire, 1780–1830* (Cambridge, 1998)

Furse, Ralph Dolignon, *Aucuparius: Recollections of a Recruiting Officer* (London, 1962)

Fyfe, Hamilton, 'General Sir Edmund Allenby', *War Correspondent*, 12 October 1918

Galbraith, John S., *The Hudson's Bay Company as an Imperial Factor 1821–1869* (Berkeley, 1957)

Gardner, Brian, *The East India Company: A History* (London, 1971)

Geppert, Alexander C. T., 'True Copies: Time and Space Travels at British Imperial Exhibitions, 1880–1930', in Hartmut Berghoff, ed., *The Making of Modern Tourism: The Cultural History of the British Experience 1600–2000* (New York, 2001)

Ghosh, D. N., 'Representation of Slavery in English Literature', *Economic and Political Weekly* 36 (2001)

Ghosh, Durba, *Sex and the Family in Colonial India: The Making of Empire* (Cambridge, 2006)

Gilbert, George, *Captain Cook's Final Voyage: The Journal of Midshipman George Gilbert*, ed. Christine Holmes (Horsham, 1982)

Gilbert, Humphrey, *A Discourse of a Discouerie for a New Passage to Cataia* (London, 1576)

——, *Queene Elizabethes Achademy*, Early English Text Society (London, 1869)

Gilbert, Martin, *Churchill: A Life* (London, 1991)

——, *Churchill and the Jews: A Lifelong Friendship* (London, 2007)

——, *Winston S. Churchill*, vol. VII: *Road to Victory, 1941–45* (London, 1986)

Gill, Anton, *Ruling Passions: Sex, Race and Empire* (London, 1995)

Gillingham, Paul, 'The Macartney Embassy to China, 1792–94', *History Today* 43 (1993)

Gilmour, David, *The Long Recessional: The Imperial Life of Rudyard Kipling* (London, 2002)

Gilroy, Paul, *After Empire: Melancholia or Convivial Culture?* (London, 2004)

Girouard, Mark, *The Return to Camelot: Chivalry and English Gentlemen* (New Haven and London, 1981)

Gissel, Line, 'From Links of Iron to Slender Rope: Essays in the Empire and Commonwealth Essay Competition', *Round Table* 96 (2007)

Godsall, Jon R., *The Tangled Web: A Life of Sir Richard Burton* (Leicester, 2008)

Godwin-Austen, Lieut.-Colonel H. H., John Knox Laughton and Douglas W. Freshfield, eds., *Hints to Travellers, Scientific and General* (London, 1883)

Goodman, Jennifer R., *Chivalry and Exploration, 1298–1630* (Woodbridge, 1998)

Gordon, Charles, *General Gordon's Khartoum Journal*, ed. Lord Elton (New York, 1961)

——, *The Journals of Major-General C. G. Gordon, C.B., at Khartoum* (London, 1885)

Gosling, W. G., *The Life of Sir Humphrey Gilbert: England's First Empire Builder* (London, 1911)

Gould, Eliga, 'American Independence and Britain's Counter-Revolution', *Past & Present* 154 (1997)

——, *The Persistence of Empire: British Political Culture in the Age of the American Revolution* (Chapel Hill and London, 2000)

Grant, Charles, *Observations on the State of Society among the Asiatic Subjects of Great Britain, particularly with respect to morals; and the means of improving it (1792)* (London, 1797)

Gray, Herbert Branston, *The Public Schools and the Empire* (London, 1913)

Greenhalgh, Paul, *Ephemeral Vistas: The Expositions Universelles, Great Exhibitions and World's Fairs, 1851–1939* (Manchester, 1988)

Grey of Fallodon, Viscount, *Twenty-Five Years, 1892–1916*, 2 vols. (New York, 1925)

Grob-Fitzgibbon, Benjamin, *Imperial Endgame: Britain's Dirty Wars and the End of Empire* (London, 2011)

Gupta, Brijen K., 'The Black Hole Incident', *Journal of Asian Studies* 19 (1959)

Haggard, H. Rider, *King Solomon's Mines* (New York, 2004; orig. pub. 1885)

——, *She* (London, 2001; orig. pub. 1887)

Hague, William, *William Wilberforce: The Life of the Great Anti-Slave Trade Campaigner* (London, 2007)

Hakluyt, Richard, *Voyages and Discoveries: The Principal Navigations, Voyages, Traffiques and Discoveries of the English Nation*, ed. Edward Jack Payne (Oxford, 1907)

Hammertown, Elizabeth and David Cannadine, 'Conflict and Consensus on a Ceremonial Occasion: The Diamond Jubilee in Cambridge in 1897', *Historical Journal* 24 (1981)

Hancock, David, *A Different Nature: The Paradoxical World of Zoos and their Uncertain Future* (London, 2001)

Hanes, W. Travis and Frank Sanello, *The Opium Wars: The Addiction of One Empire and the Corruption of Another* (London, 2002)

Hannay, David, *The Great Chartered Companies* (London, 1926)

Hansen, Peter, 'Confetti of Empire: The Conquest of Everest in Nepal, India, Britain and New Zealand', *Comparative Studies in Society and History* 42 (2000)

Hardy, Ronald, *The Iron Snake* (London, 1965)

Harlow, Barbara and Mia Carter, *Imperialism and Orientalism: A Documentary Sourcebook* (Oxford and Malden, Massachusetts, 1999)

Harris, Frank, *Contemporary Portraits* (New York, 1920)

Harris, Mrs James, *A Lady's Diary of the Siege of Lucknow, Written for the Perusal of Friends at Home* (New Delhi, 2002; orig. pub. 1858)

Hart, Peter, *Gallipoli* (London, 2011)

Harvey, Robert, *Clive: The Life and Death of a British Emperor* (London, 1998)

Harwood, Kate, 'Some Hertfordshire Nabobs', in Anne Rowe, ed., *Hertfordshire Garden History: A Miscellany* (Hatfield, 2007)

Hayes, Derek, *Historical Atlas of Canada* (Vancouver, 2002)

Hayes, Edward, *Sir Humphrey Gilbert's Voyage to Newfoundland* (New York, 1910; orig. pub. *c.* 1583)

Hayward, Anthony, *Julie Christie* (London, 2002)

Heathorn, Stephen J., *For Home Country and Race: Constructing Gender, Class and Englishness in the Elementary School, 1880–1914* (Toronto and London, 1999)

Henderson, K. D. D., *Set under Authority: Being a Portrait of the life of the British District Officer in the Sudan under the Anglo-Egyptian Condominium, 1898–1955* (Castle Cary, 1987)

Henry, Bruce Ward, 'John Dee, Humphrey Llwyd and the Name "British Empire"', *Huntington Library Quarterly* 35 (1972)

Henty, G. A., *With Roberts to Pretoria* (New York, 1901)

Herman, Arthur, *Gandhi & Churchill: The Epic Rivalry that Destroyed an Empire and Forged our Age* (New York, 2008)

Heussler, Robert, *Yesterday's Rulers: The Making of the British Colonial Service* (London, 1963)

Hibbert, Christopher, *Africa Explored: Europeans in the Dark Continent, 1769–1889* (London, 1982)

——, *The Great Mutiny: India 1857* (London, 1978)

——, *Queen Victoria: A Personal History* (London, 2000)

Hillcourt, W. and O. Baden-Powell, *Baden-Powell: The Two Lives of a Hero* (London, 1964)

Hilton, Boyd, *A Mad, Bad and Dangerous People? England 1783–1846* (Oxford, 2006)

Historical Manuscripts Commission, *The Manuscripts of J. B. Fortescue, preserved at Dropmore*, 10 vols. (London, 1892–1927)

Hobsbawm, Eric, *Industry and Empire* (London, 1968)

Hobson, J. A., *The Psychology of Jingoism* (London, 1901)

Hocart, A. M., *Kingship* (London, 1927)

Hochschild, Adam, *Bury the Chains: The British Struggle to Abolish Slavery* (London, 2005)

——, *To End All Wars: How the First World War Divided Britain* (London, 2011)

Holmes, Margaret, *Royal Representations: Queen Victoria and British Culture, 1837–1876* (Chicago, 1998)

Hoock, Holger, *Empires of the Imagination: Politics, War and the Arts in the British World, 1750–1850* (London, 2010)

Hopkins, A. G., 'The Victorians and Africa: A Reconsideration of the Occupation of Egypt, 1882', *Journal of African History* 27 (1986)

Horne, Alistair, *Macmillan*, 2 vols. (London, 1989)

Horne, Charles, ed., *Source Records of the Great War*, 7 vols. (London, 1923)

Howe, Stephen, *Anticolonialism in British Politics: The Left and the End of Empire, 1918–1964* (Oxford, 1993)

Howell, Georgina, *Daughter of the Desert: The Remarkable Life of Gertrude Bell* (London, 2006)

Hughes, Matthew, 'General Allenby and the Palestine Campaign, 1917–18', *Journal of Strategic Studies* 19 (1996)

Hughes, Robert, *The Fatal Shore* (London, 1987)

Hughes, Thomas, *Tom Brown's School Days* (Cambridge, 1857)

Hulme, Peter, *Colonial Encounters: Europe and the Native Caribbean, 1492–1797* (London, 1986)

Hume, Ivor Noël, *The Virginia Adventure: Roanoke to James Towne – An Archaeological and Historical Odyssey* (London, 1997)

Hunt, James, *On the Negro's Place in Nature: a paper read before the London Anthropological Society (1863)* (New York, 1864)

Hunter, W. W., *The Annals of Rural Bengal*, 3 vols. (London and Edinburgh, 1868–72)

Huntford, Roland, *Scott and Amundsen* (London, 1979)

Huxley, Elspeth, *White Man's Country: Lord Delamere and the Making of Kenya*, 2 vols. (London, 1935)

Hyam, Ronald, *Britain's Declining Empire: The Road to Decolonisation, 1918–1968* (Cambridge, 2006)

——, *Britain's Imperial Century, 1815–1914* (Basingstoke, 2003)

——, 'Concubinage and the Colonial Service: The Crewe Circular (1909)', *Journal of Imperial and Commonwealth Studies* 14 (1986)

——, *Empire and Sexuality: The British Experience* (Manchester, 1990)

——, *Understanding the British Empire* (Cambridge, 2010)

Hynes, Samuel, *The Edwardian Turn of Mind* (London, 1968)

Inchbald, Geoffrey, *Imperial Camel Corps* (London, 1970)

Ito, Takashi, 'Between Ideals, Realities, and Popular Perceptions: An Analysis of the Multifaceted Nature of London Zoo, 1828–1848', *Society & Animals* 14 (2006)

James, C. L. R., *Beyond a Boundary* (Durham, North Carolina, 1993; orig. pub. 1963)

James, Lawrence, *Imperial Warrior: The Life and Times of Field-Marshal Viscount Allenby, 1861–1936* (London, 1993)

——, *Raj: The Making and Unmaking of British India* (London, 1997)

——, *The Rise and Fall of the British Empire* (London, 1994)

——, *Warrior Race: A History of the British at War* (London, 2001)

Jasanoff, Maya, *Edge of Empire: Conquest and Collecting in the East 1750–1850* (London, 2006)

——, *Liberty's Exiles: The Loss of America and the Remaking of the British Empire* (London, 2011)

Jeal, Tim, *Baden-Powell* (London, 1989)

——, *Baden-Powell: Founder of the Boy Scouts* (New Haven, 2001)

Jeffery, Keith, ed., *'An Irish Empire?': Aspects of Ireland and the British Empire* (Manchester, 1996)

Jenkinson, A. J., *What Do Boys and Girls Read?* (London, 1940)

Jones, Robert W., 'The Sight of Creatures Strange to our Clime: London Zoo and the Consumption of the Exotic', *Journal of Victorian Culture* 2 (1997)

Judd, Denis, *Empire: The British Imperial Experience from 1765 to the Present* (London, 1996)

——, *The Lion and the Tiger: The Rise and Fall of the British Raj, 1600–1947* (Oxford, 2004)

——, *The Victorian Empire, 1837–1901* (London, 1970)

Kaplan, Herbert H., *Russian Overseas Commerce with Great Britain during the Reign of Catherine II* (Philadelphia, 1995)

Karsh, Efraim, *The Arab–Israeli Conflict: The Palestine War 1948* (Oxford, 2002)

—— and Inari Karsh, *Empires of the Sand: The Struggle for Mastery in the Middle East, 1789–1923* (Cambridge, Massachusetts, and London, 1999)

Katz, Shmuel, *Lone Wolf: A Biography of Vladimir (Ze'ev) Jabotinsky*, 2 vols. (New York, 1996)

Kaul, Chandrika, *Reporting the Raj: The British Press and India, c. 1880–1922* (Manchester, 2003)

Kaye, M. M., *The Sun in the Morning* (London, 1990)

Kee, Robert, *The Green Flag: A History of Irish Nationalism* (London, 1972)

Keep, Christopher and Don Randall, 'Addiction, Empire, and Narrative in Arthur Conan Doyle's "The Sign of the Four" ', *Novel: A Forum on Fiction* 32 (1999)

Keneally, Thomas, *Australians: Origins to Eureka* (Crows Nest, New South Wales, 2009)

Kennedy, Dane, *The Magic Mountains: Hill Stations and the British Raj* (Berkeley and Los Angeles, 1996)

Kenny, Kevin, ed., *Ireland and the British Empire* (Oxford, 2004)

Kernot, C. F., *British Public Schools War Memorials* (London, 1927)

Kiernan, E. V. G., *British Diplomacy in China, 1880–1885* (Cambridge, 1939)

Kimche, Jon, *The Unromantics: The Great Powers and the Balfour Declaration* (London, 1968)

Kincaid, Dennis, *British Social Life in India, 1608–1937* (London, 1938)

King, Greg, *Twilight of Splendor: The Court of Queen Victoria during her Diamond Jubilee* (Hoboken, New Jersey, 2007)

Kipling, Rudyard, *Collected Stories* (London, 1994)

——, *The Naulahka: A Story of West and East* (London, 1892)

——, *Poems, Ballads and Other Verses* (New York, 1899)

Kirk-Greene, A. H. M., *Britain's Imperial Administrators, 1858–1966* (Basingstoke, 1999)

——, 'Public Administration and the Colonial Administrator', *Public Administration and Development* 19 (1999)

——, 'The Sudan Political Service: A Profile in the Sociology of Imperialism', *International Journal of African Historical Studies* 15 (1982)

Kitchen, James E., ' "Khaki Crusaders": Crusading Rhetoric and the British Imperial Soldier during the Egypt and Palestine Campaigns, 1916–18', *First World War Studies* 1 (2010)

Kitchen, Martin, 'The Empire, 1900–1939', in Chris Wrigley, ed., *A Companion to Early Twentieth-Century Britain* (Oxford, 2002)

Knight, Charles, ed., *London*, 6 vols. (London, 1841–4)

Knight, Donald and Alan Sabey, *The Lion Roars at Wembley* (1984)

Knox, Robert, *The Races of Men: A Fragment* (London, 1850)

Kochanski, Halik, *Sir Garnet Wolseley, Victorian Hero* (London, 1999)

Koenigsberger, Kurt, *The Novel and the Menagerie: Totality, Englishness, and Empire* (Columbus, Ohio, 2007)

Kubicek, Robert V., *The Administration of Imperialism: Joseph Chamberlain at the Colonial Office* (Durham, North Carolina, 1969)

Kyle, Keith, *Suez: Britain's End of Empire in the Middle East* (London, 2011)

Latimer, John, *Buccaneers of the Caribbean: How Piracy Forged an Empire* (London, 2009)

Leadbeater, Tim, *Britain and India, 1845–1947* (London, 2008)

Lecky, W. E. H., *A History of European Morals from Augustus to Charlemagne*, 2 vols. (London, 1877)

Leigh, Edward, ed., *The Erotic Traveller: An Astonishing Exploration of Bizarre Sex Rites and Customs by the Great Adventurer Sir Richard Burton* (New York, 1967)

Lenman, Bruce and Philip Lawson, 'Robert Clive, the Black Jagir and British Politics', *Historical Journal* 26 (1983)

Leslie, Charles, *A New and Exact Account of Jamaica* (Edinburgh, 1740)

Levenberg, Haim, *Military Preparations of the Arab Community in Palestine: 1945–1948* (London, 1993)

Levine, Philippa, ' "A Multitude of Unchaste Women": Prostitution in the British Empire', *Journal of Women's History* 15 (2004)

Levinson, Alfred A., 'Diamond Sources and their Discovery', in George Harlow, ed., *The Nature of Diamonds* (Cambridge, 1998)

Lieven, Anatol, *Pakistan: A Hard Country* (London, 2011)

Lindsay, David, Earl of Crawford, *The Crawford Papers: The Journals of David Lindsay, Twenty-Seventh Earl of Crawford and Tenth Earl of Balcarres (1871–1940), during the Years 1892 to 1940*, ed. John Vincent (Manchester, 1984)

Livingstone, David, *Missionary Travels and Researches in South Africa* (London, 1857)

Lloyd, Trevor, *Empire: The History of the British Empire* (London, 2001)

Longford, Elizabeth, *A Pilgrimage of Passion: The Life of Wilfrid Scawen Blunt* (London, 1979)

Looker, Mark, ' "God Save the Queen": Victoria's Jubilees and the Religious Press', *Victorian Periodicals Review* 21 (1988)

Louis, Wm. Roger, 'Churchill and the Liquidation of the British Empire', Crosby Kemper Lecture (29 March 1998)

——, *Ends of British Imperialism: The Scramble for Empire, Suez and Decolonisation* (London, 2006)

——, *Imperialism at Bay: The United States and the Decolonization of the British Empire* (Oxford, 1978)

——, *Ultimate Adventures with Britannia* (London, 2009)

—— and Ronald Robinson, 'The Imperialism of Decolonisation', *Journal of Imperial and Commonwealth History* 22 (1994)

Lucas, Sir Charles, *The Empire at War*, 5 vols. (London, 1921–6)

Lugard, Sir Frederick, *The Dual Mandate in Tropical Africa* (London, 1922)

Macaulay, Thomas Babington, *Critical and Historical Essays*, 3 vols. (London, 1850)

——, *Macaulay's Essays on Clive and Hastings*, ed. Charles Robert Gaston (Boston, 1910)

——, *Prose and Poetry*, ed. G. M. Young (London, 1952)

McCulloch, Gary, 'Empires and Education: The British Empire', in R. Cowen and A. M. Kazamias, eds., *The International Handbook for Comparative Education* (London and New York, 2009)

McDonald, Iverach, *A Man of The Times: Talks and Travels in a Disrupted World* (London, 1976)

McEwan, Cheryl, *Gender, Geography and Empire: Victorian Women Travellers in West Africa* (Aldershot, 2000)

Macfarlane, Iris, *The Black Hole, or the Makings of a Legend* (London, 1975)

McKenna, Mark and Stuart Ward, ' "It was Really Moving, Mate": The Gallipoli Pilgrimage and Sentimental Nationalism in Australia', *Australian Historical Studies* 129 (2007)

MacKenzie, John M., 'Empire and National Identities: The Case of Scotland', *Transactions of the Royal Historical Society* 8 (1998)

——, 'Essay and Reflection: On Scotland and the Empire', *International History Review* 15 (1993)

——, ed., *Imperialism and Popular Culture* (Manchester, 1986)

——, *Popular Imperialism and the Military, 1850–1950* (Manchester, 1992)

——, *Propaganda and Empire: The Manipulation of British Public Opinion, 1880–1960* (Manchester, 1984)

MacMillan, Margaret, *Peacemakers: The Paris Conference of 1919 and its Attempt to End the War* (London, 2001)

——, *Women of the Raj: The Mothers, Wives and Daughters of the British Empire in India* (New York and London, 2007)

McVeagh, John, *Tradefull Merchants: The Portrayal of the Capitalist in Literature* (London, 1981)

Malaviya, Madan Mohan, *Speeches and Writings of Pandit Madan Mohan Malaviya* (Madras, 1919)

Malcolm, Sir John, *The Life of Robert, Lord Clive*, 3 vols. (London, 1836)

Manchester, William, *The Last Lion: Winston Spencer Churchill: Alone, 1932–40* (New York, 1988)

Mangan, J. A., *Athleticism in the Victorian and Edwardian Public School* (Cambridge, 1981)

——, ed., *'Benefits Bestowed'? Education and British Imperialism* (Manchester, 1988)

——, 'Eton in India: The Imperial Diffusion of a Victorian Educational Ethic', *History of Education* 7 (1978)

——, ed., *Making Imperial Mentalities: Socialisation and British Imperialism* (Manchester, 1990)

——, ed., *Tribal Identities: Nationalism, Europe and Sport* (London, 1996)

—— and James Walvin, *Manliness and Morality: Middle-Class Masculinity in Britain and America, 1800–1940* (Manchester, 1987)

Manjapra, Kris, 'The Illusions of Encounter: Muslim "Minds" and Hindu Revolutionaries in First World War Germany and After', *Journal of Global History* 1 (2006)

Mansergh, Nicholas, *The Commonwealth Experience* (London, 1969)

Mansfield, Peter, *The Arabs* (London, 1978)

Marr, Andrew, *The Making of Modern Britain: From Queen Victoria to V.E. Day* (London, 2009)

Marsh, Peter, ed., *The Conscience of the Victorian State* (Syracuse, 1979)

Marshall, H. E., *Our Empire Story: Stories of India and the Greater Colonies* (London, 1908)

Marshall, P. J., *Bengal: The British Bridgehead: Eastern India 1740–1828* (Cambridge, 1987)

——, 'Britain and the World in the Eighteenth Century: III, Britain and India', *Transactions of the Royal Historical Society* 10 (2000)

——, ed., *The Cambridge Illustrated History of the British Empire* (Cambridge, 1996)

——, 'Empire and Opportunity in Britain, 1763–75: The Prothero Lecture 6 July 1994', *Transactions of the Royal Historical Society* 5 (1995)

——, *'A Free though Conquering People': Eighteenth-Century Britain and its Empire* (Aldershot, 2003)

——, ed., *The Oxford History of the British Empire*, vol. II: *The Eighteenth Century* (Oxford and New York, 1998)

——, 'The Personal Fortune of Warren Hastings', *Economic History Review* 17 (1964)

——, 'Reappraisal: The Rise of British Power in Eighteenth-Century India', *Journal of South Asian Studies* 19 (1996)

Maugham, W. Somerset, *Collected Stories* (London, 2004)

Mazower, Mark, *No Enchanted Palace: The End of Empire and the Ideological Origins of the United Nations* (Princeton and Oxford, 2009)

Meath, Lord, 'Duty and Discipline in the Training of Children', Essay No. 6 in *Essays on Duty and Discipline* (London, 1911)

Mellini, Peter, 'Colonel Blimp's England', *History Today* 34 (1984)

Meredith, Martin, *Diamonds, Gold and War: The British, the Boers and the Making of South Africa* (London, 2007)

Metcalf, Barbara and Thomas Metcalf, *A Concise History of India* (Cambridge, 2002)

Micklethwait, John and Adrian Wooldridge, *The Company: A Short History of a Revolutionary Idea* (New York, 2003)

Middleton, Dorothy, 'Guide to the Publications of the Royal Geographical Society, 1830–1892', *Geographical Journal* 144 (1978)

Miles, Eustace, 'Sport and Athletics, and the British Empire', in William Sheowring, ed., *The British Empire Series*, 5 vols. (London, 1899–1902)

Mill, James, *History of British India*, 6 vols. (London, 1817)

Miller, Charles, *The Lunatic Express: An Entertainment in Imperialism* (London, 2002)

Miller, Stephen, *Volunteers on the Veld: Britain's Citizen-Soldiers and the South African War, 1899–1902* (Oklahoma, 1964)

Milton, John, *The Doctrine and Discipline of Divorce* (London, 1820; orig. pub. 1645)

Mitchell, B. R., *British Historical Statistics* (Cambridge, 1988)

Montgomery, H. H., *Foreign Missions* (London, 1902)

Moorehead, Alan, *The Fatal Impact: The Invasion of the South Pacific, 1767–1840* (London, 1966)

——, *The White Nile* (New York, 2000)

Morgan, Susan, *Bombay Anna: The Real Story and Remarkable Adventures of the 'King and I' Governess* (Berkeley and London, 2002)

Morley, Catherine, *John Ruskin: Late Work 1870–1890. The Museum and Guild of St. George: An Educational Experiment* (New York and London, 1984)

Morris, Ellen K., 'Symbols of Empire: Architectural Style and the Government Offices Competition', *Journal of Architectural Education* 32 (1978)

Morris, James, *Farewell the Trumpets: An Imperial Retreat* (London, 1992; orig. pub. 1979)

——, *Heaven's Command: An Imperial Progress* (London, 1992; orig. pub. 1973)

——, *Pax Britannica: The Climax of an Empire* (New York, 1980)

Morris, Jan and Robert Fermor-Hesketh, *Architecture of the British Empire* (London, 1986)

—— and Simon Winchester, *Stones of Empire: The Buildings of the Raj* (Oxford, 2005)

Mount, Harry, *A Lust for Windowsills* (London, 2011)

Moxham, Roy, *The Great Hedge of India* (London, 2001)

Muir, Ramsay, *A History of Liverpool* (London, 1907)

Mukerjee, Madhusree, *Churchill's Secret War: The British Empire and the Forgotten Indian Famine of World War II* (New York, 2010)

Mukherjee, Mithi, 'Press, Justice, War, and the Imperium: India and Britain in Edmund Burke's Prosecutorial Speeches in the Impeachment Trial of Warren Hastings', *Law and History Review* 23 (2005)

Mukherjee, Rudrangshu, 'Myth of Empire – The Story about the Black Hole of Calcutta Refuses to Die', *The Telegraph* (Calcutta), 25 June 2006

Murphy, Simon, ed., *Cox's Fragmenta: An Historical Miscellany* (Stroud, 2010)

Nechtman, Tillman W., *Nabobs: Empire and Identity in Eighteenth-Century Britain* (Cambridge, 2010)

Neilly, J. Emerson, *Besieged with B.-P.: A Full and Complete Record of the Siege* (London, 1900)

Newell, Jonathan Q. C., 'Learning the Hard Way: Allenby in Egypt and Palestine, 1917–19', *Journal of Strategic Studies* 14 (1991)

Newsinger, John, *The Blood Never Dried: A People's History of the British Empire* (London, 2006)

Nicholas, F. W. and J. M. Nicholas, *Charles Darwin in Australia* (Cambridge, 2002)

Nicholls, Christine Stephanie, *Red Strangers: The White Tribe of Kenya* (London, 2005)

Niranjana, Tejaswini, 'Translation, Colonialism and Rise of English', *Economic and Political Weekly* 25 (1990)

Nugent, Maria, *Captain Cook was Here* (Cambridge, 2009)

O'Brien, Patrick, 'The Costs and Benefits of British Imperialism, 1846–1914', *Past & Present* 120 (1988)

O'Brien, Phillips Payson, 'The Titan Refreshed: Imperial Overstretch and the British Navy before the First World War', *Past & Present* 172 (2001)

Ogilvie, J. N., *Our Empire's Debt to Missions: The Duff Missionary Lecture, 1923* (London, 1924)

O'Gorman, Francis, *Late Ruskin: New Contexts* (Aldershot, 2001)

O'Hegarty, Patrick S., *A History of Ireland under the Union, 1801–1922* (London, 1952)

Oldfield, J. R., *Popular Politics and British Anti-Slavery: The Mobilisation of Public Opinion against the Slave Trade, 1787–1807* (Manchester, 1995)

Oliver, Roland, *Sir Harry Johnston and the Scramble for Africa* (London, 1957)

Orwell, George, *Burmese Days: A Novel* (London, 1935)

——, *Coming up for Air* (London, 2000; orig. pub. 1939)

——, *The Lion and the Unicorn: Socialism and the English Genius* (London, 1941)

——, *The Orwell Reader: Fiction, Essays and Reportage* (New York, 1961)

——, *The Road to Wigan Pier* (London, 1937)

Padmore, George, *The Gold Coast Revolution: The Struggle of an African People from Slavery to Freedom* (London, 1953)

Pagden, Anthony, *Peoples and Empires: Europeans and the Rest of the World, from Antiquity to the Present* (London, 2001)

Paice, Edward, *World War I: The African Front* (New York, 2010)

Paine, Thomas, *The Political and Miscellaneous Works of Thomas Paine*, 2 vols. (London, 1819)

Pakenham, Thomas, *The Boer War* (London, 1979)

——, *The Scramble for Africa* (London, 1991)

Pakenham, Valerie, *Out in the Noonday Sun: Edwardians in the Tropics* (London, 1985)

Palling, Bruce, *India: A Literary Companion* (London, 1992)

Palmer, Alan, *Dictionary of the British Empire and Commonwealth* (London, 1996)

Parkinson, Sydney, *A Journal of a Voyage to the South Seas, in his Majesty's Ship Endeavour* (London, 1773)

Parmentier, Guillaume, 'The British Press in the Suez Crisis', *Historical Journal* 23 (1980)

Parsons, Timothy H., *The British Imperial Century, 1815–1914* (Lanham, Maryland, 1999)

Patterson, Lieut.-Col. J. H., *The Man-Eaters of Tsavo and Other East African Adventures* (London, 1907)

Pearson, Jonathan, *Sir Anthony Eden and the Suez Crisis: Reluctant Gamble* (Basingstoke, 2003)

Perham, Marjorie, *Lugard: The Years of Adventure, 1858–1898* (London, 1956)

Peterhaus, Julian C. Kerbis and Thomas Patrick Gnoske, 'The Science of "Man-eating" among Lions (*Panthera leo*) with a Reconstruction of the Natural History of the "Man-eaters of Tsavo"', *Journal of East African Natural History* 90 (2001)

Peyrefitte, Alain, *The Immobile Empire*, trans. Jon Rothschild (New York, 1992)

Philby, H. St. J. B., 'Gertrude Bell', *Journal of the Royal Asiatic Society of Great Britain and Ireland* 4 (1926)

Phillips, Jim, 'A Successor to the Moguls: The Nawab of the Carnatic and the East India Company, 1763–1785', *International History Review* 7 (1985)

Plume, Christopher, ' "Strange and Wonderful": Encountering the Elephant in Britain, 1675–1830', *Journal for Eighteenth-Century Studies* 33 (2010)

Pocock, J. G. A., ed., *Three British Revolutions: 1641, 1688, 1776* (Princeton, 1980)

Pope, Peter E., *Fish into Wine: The Newfoundland Plantation in the Seventeenth Century* (Chapel Hill, 2004)

Port, M. H., 'Government and the Metropolitan Image: Ministers, Parliament, and the Concept of a Capital City, 1840–1915', *Art History* 22 (1999)

——, *Imperial London: Civil Government Building in London, 1851–1915* (New Haven and London, 1995)

Porter, Andrew, 'The Balance Sheet of Empire, 1850–1914', *Historical Journal* 31 (1988)

——, ed., *The Imperial Horizons of British Protestant Missions, 1880–1914* (Cambridge, 2003)

——, ed., *The Oxford History of the British Empire*, vol. III: *The Nineteenth Century* (Oxford, 1999)

Porter, A. N. and R. F. Holland, eds., *Money, Finance and Empire 1790–1960* (London, 1985)

Porter, Bernard, *The Absent-Minded Imperialists* (Oxford, 2004)

——, *Critics of Empire: British Radicals and the Imperial Challenge* (London, 1968)

——, 'Elgar and Empire', *Journal of Imperial and Commonwealth History* 29 (2001)

Potter, Lois, 'Pirates and "Turning Turk" in Renaissance Drama', in Jean-Pierre Maquerlot and Michèle Willems, eds., *Travel and Drama in Shakespeare's Time* (Cambridge, 1996)

Procida, Mary A., *Married to the Empire: Gender, Politics and Imperialism in India, 1883–1947* (Manchester, 2002)

Quinn, David Beers, 'Sir Thomas Smith (1513–1577) and the Beginnings of English Colonial Theory', *Proceedings of the American Philosophical Society* 89 (1945)

Quinn, D. B., ed., *The Voyages and Colonising Enterprises of Sir Humphrey Gilbert*, 2 vols. (London, 1940)

Ransford, Oliver, *Livingston's Lake: The Drama of Nyasa* (London, 1966)

Read, Donald, ed., *Edwardian England, 1901–1915* (London, 1982)

Reddie, Richard S., *Abolition! The Struggle to Abolish Slavery in the British Colonies* (Oxford, 2007)

Rees, L. E. Ruutz, *A Personal Narrative of the Siege at Lucknow* (London, 1858)

Rees, Siân, *The Floating Brothel: The Extraordinary True Story of an 18th-Century Ship and its Cargo of Female Convicts* (London, 2001)

Reich, Jerome, 'The Slave Trade at the Congress of Vienna: A Study in English Public Opinion', *Journal of Negro History* 53 (1968)

Reid, J. M., *Traveller Extraordinary: The Life of James Bruce of Kinnaird* (London, 1968)

Rhodes James, Robert, *Anthony Eden* (London, 1986)

Richards, Jeffrey, ed., *Imperialism and Juvenile Literature* (Manchester, 1989)

——, *Imperialism and Music: Britain, 1876–1953* (Manchester, 2002)

Richards, Thomas, 'The Image of Victoria in the Year of Jubilee', *Victorian Studies* 31 (1987)

Ricketts, Harry, *Rudyard Kipling: A Life* (New York, 2001)

Ridley, Jane, *The Architect and his Wife: A Life of Edwin Lutyens* (London, 2002)

Riffenburgh, Beau, *The Myth of the Explorer* (Oxford, 1994)

Ritz, E., 'The History of Salt – Aspects of Interest to the Nephrologist', *Nephrol Dial Transplant* (1996)

Robertson, James, 'Re-writing the English Conquest of Jamaica in the Late Seventeenth Century', *English Literary History* (2002)

Robertson, John M., *Patriotism and Empire* (London, 1899)

Robinson, R. E., 'The Moral Disarmament of African Empire, 1919–1947', *Journal of Imperial and Commonwealth History* VII (1979)

Rodger, N. A. M., *The Command of the Ocean: A Naval History of Britain, 1649–1815* (London, 2004)

——, *The Safeguard of the Sea: A Naval History of Britain, 660–1649* (London, 1997)

Romilly, Samuel, *The Speeches of Sir Samuel Romilly in the House of Commons*, 2 vols. (London, 1820)

Roosevelt, Theodore, *African Game Trails* (London, 1910)

Root, Nina, 'Victorian England's Hippomania', *Natural History* 102 (1993)

Rose, Norman, *Chaim Weizmann: A Biography* (London, 1986)

Ross, Alan, *Blindfold Games* (London, 1986)

Rosselli, John, *Lord William Bentinck: The Making of a Liberal Imperialist, 1774–1839* (London, 1974)

Rotberg, Robert, *The Founder: Cecil Rhodes and the Pursuit of Power* (Oxford, 1988)

Rubinstein, W. D., *Twentieth-Century Britain: A Political History* (Basingstoke, 2003)

Rumbold, Sir Algernon, *Watershed in India, 1914–1922* (London, 1979)

Rusden, Henry K., 'Labour and Capital', *Melbourne Review* 1 (January 1876)

Ruskin, John, *Lectures on Art: Delivered before the University of Oxford in Hilary Term, 1870* (Oxford, 1870)

Russell, William Howard, *My Diary in India: The Year 1858–9*, 2 vols. (London, 1860)

Rydell, Robert W., *World of Fairs* (Chicago and London, 1993)

Said, Edward, *Culture and Imperialism* (London, 1993)

——, *Orientalism* (London, 2003)

St Aubyn, Giles, *Queen Victoria: A Portrait* (London, 1991)

Salmond, Anne, *Two Worlds: First Meetings between Maori and Europeans 1642–1772* (Auckland and London, 1991)

Sandbrook, Dominic, *Never Had It So Good: A History of Britain from Suez to the Beatles* (London, 2005)

Sanders, William and Thomas Ackland, *A Digest of the Results of the Census of England and Wales in 1901* (London, 1903)

Sanderson, G. M., 'Gunfire on Nyasa', *Nyasaland Journal* X (1957)

Sayer, Derek, 'British Reaction to the Amritsar Massacre, 1919–1920', *Past & Present* 131 (1991)

Scates, Bruce, *Return to Gallipoli: Walking the Battlefields of the Great War* (Cambridge, 2006)

Schneer, Jonathan, *London 1900: The Imperial Metropolis* (New Haven and London, 1999)

Schuyler, R. L., 'The Climax of Anti-Imperialism in England', *Political Science Quarterly* 36 (1921)

Scott, Paul, *The Jewel in the Crown (The Raj Quartet)* (London, 2005)

Scott, Robert Falcon, *Scott's Last Expedition: The Journals* (New York, 1996)

Searle, G. R., *A New England? Peace and War, 1886–1918* (Oxford, 2005)

Seeley, J. R., *The Expansion of England*, ed. J. Gross (London, 1971)

Segev, Tom, *One Palestine, Complete: Jews and Arabs under the British Mandate* (London, 2000)

Sellon, Edward, *Annotations on the Sacred Writings of the Hindüs, being an epitome of some of the most remarkable and leading tenets in the faith of that people* (London, 1865)

——, *The New Epicurean or The Delights of Sex facetiously and philosophically considered in Graphic Letters Addressed to Young Ladies of Quality* (London, 1865)

——, *The Ups and Downs of Life* (Miami Beach, 1987; orig. pub. 1867)

Shannon, Richard, *Gladstone: Heroic Minister, 1865–1898* (London, 1999)

Sharp, Henry, *Goodbye India* (London, 1946)

Sharpe, Jenny, 'Figures of Colonial Resistance', *Modern Fiction Studies* 35 (1989)

Shaw, George Bernard, *John Bull's Other Island* (London, 1909)

Shepherd, Verene, ed., *Working Slavery, Pricing Freedom: Essays in Honour of Barry W. Higman* (Oxford, 2002)

Sheridan, Richard Brinsley, *The Dramatic Works of Richard Brinsley Sheridan, with a short account of his life by George G. Sigmond* (London, 1876)

Sherman, A. J., *Mandate Days: British Lives in Palestine, 1918–1948* (London, 1997)

Shore, John, Baron Teignmouth, *Memoirs of the Life, Writings and Correspondence of Sir William Jones*, 2 vols. (London, 1835)

Sidney, Henry, *A Viceroy's Vindication? Sir Henry Sidney's Memoir of Service in Ireland, 1556–78*, ed. Ciaran Brady (Cork, 2002)

Simms, Brendan, *Three Victories and a Defeat: The Rise and Fall of the First British Empire* (London, 2008)

Smith, A. Donaldson, *Through Unknown African Continents: The First Expedition from Somaliland to Lake Lamu* (London, 1897)

Smith, Adam, *An Inquiry into the Nature and Causes of the Wealth of Nations* (London, 1776)

Smith, George, 'Christian Missions, Especially in the British Empire', in William Sheowring, ed., *The British Empire Series*, 5 vols. (London, 1899–1902)

Smith, John, *Captain John Smith: A Select Edition of his Writings*, ed. Karen Ordahl Kupperman (Chapel Hill, 1988)

——, *Generall Historie of Virginia, New-England and the Summer Iles* (London, 1624)

——, *Works*, ed. Edward Arber, 2 vols. (London, 1884)

Smith, Jordan, ' "More Rude and Anticque than 'ere was Sodom": Piracy and the Tavern Community in Port Royal, Jamaica, 1680–1692', unpub. Curran Prize Essay (2010)

Smith, Michelle, 'Be(ing) Prepared: Girl Guides, Colonial Life, and National Strength', *Limina* 12 (2006)

Southey, Robert, *The Poetical Works of Robert Southey*, 10 vols. (Boston, 1878)

Speke, John Hanning, *Journal of the Discovery of the Sources of the Nile* (Edinburgh and London, 1863)

Speke, W. A., 'Eighteenth-Century Attitudes towards Business', in Arthur Pollard, ed., *The Representation of Business in English Literature* (London, 2000)

Spenser, Edmund, *A View of the Present State of Ireland* (1596), ed. W. L. Renwick (Oxford, 1970)

Springhall, John, 'Lord Meath, Youth, and Empire', *Journal of Contemporary History* 5 (1970)

——, *Youth, Empire and Society: British Youth Movements 1883–1940* (London, 1977)

Spufford, Francis, *I May Be Some Time: Ice and the English Imagination* (London, 1996)

Stanley, Henry Morton, *How I Found Livingstone* (London, 1872)

Stead, W. T., 'Chinese Gordon', *The Century: A Popular Quarterly*, 28 (August 1884)

Steel, Flora and G. Gardiner, *The Complete Indian Housekeeper and Cook*, ed. Ralph Crane and Anna Johnston (Oxford, 2010; orig. pub. 1888)

Sterne, Laurence, *The Life and Opinions of Tristram Shandy, Gentleman* (Oxford, 1983; orig. pub. 1759)

Stevenson, R. L., *Selected Letters of Robert Louis Stevenson*, ed. Ernest Mehew (New Haven and London, 1997)

——, *The Works of Robert Louis Stevenson* (London, 1924)

Stewart, Gordon, 'The British Reaction to the Conquest of Everest', *Journal of Sport History* 7 (1980)

——, 'Tenzing's Two Wrist-Watches: The Conquest of Everest and Late Imperial Culture in Britain, 1921–53', *Past & Present* 149 (1995)

Stockwell, Sarah, ed., *The British Empire: Themes and Perspectives* (Oxford, 2008)

Stoddart, Brian, 'Sport, Cultural Imperialism, and Colonial Response in the British Empire', *Comparative Studies in Society and History* 30 (1988)

Stoddart, D. R., 'The RGS and the "New Geography": Changing Aims and Changing Roles in Nineteenth-Century Science', *Geographical Journal* 146 (1980)

Storey, Graham and Kathleen Tillotson, eds., *The British Academy, The Pilgrim Edition: The Letters of Charles Dickens*, 8 vols. (Oxford, 1995)

Storrs, Ronald, *Orientations* (London, 1945)

Strachan, Hew, *The First World War*, vol. I: *To Arms* (Oxford, 2001)

Strachey, John, *The End of Empire* (London, 1959)

Strachey, Lytton, *Queen Victoria* (London, 1921)

Sullivan, Robert, *Macaulay: The Tragedy of Power* (Cambridge, Massachusetts, 2009)

Surridge, Keith, 'All you soldiers are what we call pro-Boer': The Military Critique of the South African War, 1899–1902', *Historical Association* (1997)

Talty, Stephan, *Empire of Blue Water: Captain Morgan's Great Pirate Army, the Epic Battle for the Americas, and the Catastrophe that Ended the Outlaws' Bloody Reign* (New York, 2007)

Theron, Bridget, 'King Cetshwayo in Victorian England: A Cameo of Imperial Interaction', *South African Historical Journal* 56 (2006)

Thompson, Andrew, *The Empire Strikes Back: The Impact of Imperialism on Britain from the Mid-Nineteenth Century* (London, 2005)

Thompson, Dorothy, *Queen Victoria: Gender and Power* (London, 1990)

Thomson, Joseph, *To the Central African Lakes and Back*, 2 vols. (London, 1881)

Thornton, A. P., *The Imperial Ideal and its Enemies: A Study in British Power* (London, 1959)

Tidrick, Kathryn, *Empire and the English Character: The Illusion of Authority* (London, 1990)

Tilt, Edward, *Health in India for British Women* (London, 1875)

Trench, Charles Chenevix, *Charley Gordon: An Eminent Victorian Reassessed* (London, 1978)

Trevelyan, Christopher, 'The 2/151st Indian Infantry "Frontier Force"', *Durbar: Journal of the Indian Military Historical Society* 21 (2004)

Trollope, Joanna, *Britannia's Daughters: Women of the British Empire* (London, 1983)

Troost, Linda, 'The Rise of the Comic Opera, 1762–1800' (1985 dissertation, University of Pennsylvania)

Troyna, Barry and Jenny Williams, *Racism, Education and the State: The Racialisation of Education Policy* (London, 1986)

Tunzelman, Alex von, *Indian Summer: The Secret History of the End of an Empire* (London, 2007)

Turley, David, *The Culture of English Antislavery, 1780–1860* (London, 1991)

Turley, Sophie K., 'Conservation and Tourism in the Traditional London Zoo', *Journal of Tourism Studies* 10 (1999)

Twain, Mark, *Following the Equator: A Journey around the World* (Hartford, Connecticut, 1897)

Tyndale, George, 'Urdu Brightens Up Yorkshire Streets', *Yorkshire Post*, 22 January 1976

Tyndale-Biscoe, C. E., *Character Building in Kashmir* (London, 1920)

——, *Coaching in Kashmir* (London, 1896)

——, *Tyndale-Biscoe of Kashmir: An Autobiography* (London, 1951)

Verschoyle, F., *Cecil Rhodes: His Political Life and Speeches, 1881–1900* (London, 1900)

Wagner, Kim A., *The Great Fear of 1857: Rumours, Conspiracies and the Making of the Indian Uprising* (Oxford, 2010)

Wahrman Dror, 'The English Problem of Identity in the American Revolution', *American Historical Review* 106 (2001)

Walvin, James, *Black Ivory: Slavery in the British Empire* (London, 2001)

——, *Britain's Slave Empire* (London, 2000)

——, *Slavery to Freedom: Britain's Slave Trade and Abolition* (London, 2007)

War Office, *Statistics of the Military Effort of the British Empire during the Great War, 1914–1920* (London, 1922)

Ward, A. R. and A. R. Waller, *The Cambridge History of English and American Literature*, 18 vols. (Cambridge, 1907–21)

Ward, Andrew, *Our Bones are Scattered: The Cawnpore Massacres and the Indian Mutiny of 1857* (New York, 1996)

Ward, Stuart, *British Culture and the End of Empire* (Manchester, 2001)

Wavell, A. P., *Allenby: A Study in Greatness* (London, 1940)

Wavell, Archibald, Earl Wavell, *Wavell: The Viceroy's Journal*, ed. Penderel Moon (London, 1973)

Webster, Wendy, *Englishness and Empire 1939–1965* (Oxford, 2007)

Wells, H. G., *An Englishman Looks at the World* (London, 1914)

Westgaph, Laurence, 'Built on Slavery', *Context* 108 (2009)

White, Nicholas, *Decolonisation: The British Experience since 1945* (Harlow, 1999)

Whitfield, Peter, *Sir Francis Drake* (London, 2004)

Williams, Eric, *Capitalism and Slavery* (Chapel Hill, 1944)

Wilson, A. N., *After the Victorians: The Decline of Britain in the World* (London, 2005)

Wilson, Ellen Gibson, *Thomas Clarkson: A Biography* (London, 1989)

Wilson, H. W., *With the Flag to Pretoria: A History of the Boer War, 1899–1900* (London, 1900–1902)

Winchester, Simon, *Outposts: Journeys to the Surviving Relics of the British Empire* (London, 2003)

Winder, Robert, *Bloody Foreigners: The Story of Immigration to Britain* (London, 2004)

Winks, Robin W., ed., *The Oxford History of the British Empire*, vol. V: *Historiography* (Oxford and New York, 1999)

Winter, J. M., 'Britain's "Lost Generation" of the First World War', *Population Studies* 31 (1977)

Withey, Lynne, *Voyages of Discovery: Captain Cook and the Exploration of the Pacific* (Berkeley and London, 1989)

Wodehouse, P. G., 'The Rummy Affair of Old Biffy', in *Carry on, Jeeves* (London, 2008; orig. pub. 1925)

Wolffe, John, *God and Greater Britain: Religion and National Life in Britain and Ireland, 1843–1945* (London, 1994)

Wood, John George, *The Modern Playmate: A Book of Games, Sports and Diversions for Boys of All Ages* (London, 1875)

Wood, William, *A Survey of Trade in Four Parts* (London, 1718)

Wright, Philip, ed., *Lady Nugent's Journal of her Residence in Jamaica from 1801 to 1805* (Barbados, 2002)

Young, Donald, ed., *The Search for the Source of the Nile* (London, 1999)

Younghusband, Sir Francis, 'India', in (Sir) Charles Lucas, ed., *The Empire at War*, 5 vols. (London, 1921–6)

Index